Current English

Current English

석종환 편저

경상대학교출판부

서 문

오늘날 우리는 정보의 홍수 속에 살고 있다. 특히 최첨단 과학문명 시대에 정보는 경쟁력인 동시에 생존의 필수조건이 되고 있다. 우리는 수많은 정보를 인터넷이라는 매개체를 통해 시시각각으로 접할 수 있는데 이러한 정보에 접근하기 위해서는 영어가 필수적일 것이다. 현재 영어가 차지하고 있는 정치적, 경제적, 사회적, 문화적 영향력을 고려할 때, 영어능력은 곧 사회의 주류로 나아갈 수 있는 첫 걸음이라 할 수 있을 것이다. 따라서 영어를 학습하는 것은 대학에서 아주 중요한 일이다.

이러한 맥락에서 본 교재는 빠르게 변화하는 세계 속에서 국내뿐만 아니라 국제적인 관점에서 정치, 경제, 사회, 문화, 과학 등을 다루는 기사에서 발췌한 글 읽기를 통해 영어능력을 향상시키는 것을 목표로 편집된 것이다. 따라서 기사와 관련된 사회적 배경과 흐름을 파악할 수 있도록 상세한 주석을 제시할 뿐만 아니라 영어의 문법, 문장구조의 분석과 어휘에 대한 해설을 통해 영문을 해독할 수 있는 능력을 높일 수 있도록 하였다. 가장 최근의 국내외 흐름을 그대로 반영하는 다양한 분야에 대한 시사적인 글 읽기는 학생들의 세계와 자신에 대한 이해의 폭을 넓힐 수 있을 것이고, 다양하고 복잡한 현대사회에 적응하고 대응하는 능력을 기를 수 있도록 해 줄 것이다.

본 교재는 2013년에 일어난 국내외 주요 사건이나 이슈들을 다루고 있다. 시사적인 글들은 시간이 지나면 그 가치가 떨어지는 한계가 있지만 사건이나 이슈들의 내용뿐만 아니라 시사적인 용어나 표현을 숙지하는 것이 시사영어 학습의 주요 목표이기 때문에 나름대로 그 의의가 있다 할 것이다. 본 교재를 통해 시사영어에 대한 관심과 흥미가 높아지게 되고 지속적으로 시사영어에 접근함으로써 영어학습의 즐거움을 만끽할 뿐만 아니라 정보의 시대에 부응하는데 도움이 되었으면 하는 것이 편저자의 바람이다.

수없이 접하는 영어 관련 서적에 또 하나를 추가함으로써 독자들의 선택에 혼란을 더하지 않을까 하는 우려가 있지만 영어 학습에 도움이 될 수 있는 더 우수한 교재가 나올 수 있는 자극제가 되었으면 하는 기대를 하면서 출판을 허락해 준 대학출판부 관계자에게 깊은 감사를 드린다.

2014년 8월

편저자 석종환

Contents

01.

New era of hope

President Park Geun-hye[1)] began her five-year term Monday after taking the oath of office in her *inauguration ceremony[1] at the *National Assembly plaza[2]. She returned to Cheong Wa Dae, the presidential house that she left in tears more than 33 years ago after her father, former President Park Chung-hee, was assassinated by his *spy agency chief[3].

In her inaugural speech, she pledged to live up to the will of the people by "achieving *economic rejuvenation[4], the happiness of the people and the *flourishing of our culture[5]." Specifically, she said the new administration will usher in a new era of hope whereby "the happiness of each citizen becomes the *bedrock[6] of our nation's strength which in turn is shared by and benefits all Koreans."

It is appropriate for Park to declare a "creative economy[2)]"

1 inauguration ceremony
취임식

2 National Assembly plaza
국회광장

3 spy agency chief
중앙정보부장
(현 국가정보원장)

4 economic rejuvenation
경제부흥

5 flourishing of culture
문화융성

6 bedrock
근저(basis), 기반

1) **President Park Geun-hye** (1952~) (대한민국 18대 대통령) 2013년 2월 25일 취임, 5대~9대 대통령(1963-1979) 박정희의 2녀 1남 중 장녀.

7 economic revitalization 경제 활성화

8 IT(information technology) industry 정보통신 기술 산업

9 Ministry of Science and Technology 과학기술부

10 transition team 인수위원회

as a driver for *economic revitalization[7], given that the country's economic growth based on traditional manufacturing has limitations. She made it clear that science and technology, and the *IT industry[8] lie at the heart of a creative economy, heightening hopes that the new mammoth *science ministry[9] will contribute a great deal to creating more jobs.

Hopefully, her pledge to embark on the making of a "Second Miracle on the Han River[3)]" will be delivered without a hitch, particularly considering that the people's expectations for Park, the daughter of a dictator who laid a solid foundation for the nation's economic progress at the expense of democracy, remain high.

It's also encouraging that the nation's first female President renewed her resolve to "economic democratization," a major departure from her silence on the potentially explosive issue last week when the *transition team[10] unveiled Park's policy

2) **creative economy** (창조경제) 창조경제란 말은 영국의 경영전략가인 존 호킨스(John Howkins)가 2001년 펴낸 책 The Creative Economy에서 처음 사용됐다. 그는 '창조경제란 새로운 아이디어, 즉 창의력으로 제조업, 서비스업 및 유통업, 엔터테인먼트산업 등에 활력을 불어넣는 것'이라고 설명하고 있다. 2013년 2월 25일 박근혜대통령이 취임사에서 창조경제를 강조함으로써 다시 한번 관심을 끌고 있다. 박대통령은 "창조경제는 과학기술과 산업이 융합하고, 문화와 산업이 융합하고, 산업 간의 벽을 허문 경계선에 창조의 꽃을 피우는 것"이라며 "경제부흥을 이루기 위해 창조경제와 경제민주화를 추진해 가겠다"고 강조했다(네이버 지식백과, 한경 경제용어사전).

3) **The Miracle on the Han River** (한강의 기적) is a term used to refer to South Korea's postwar export-fueled economic growth, including rapid industrialization, technological achievement, education boom, large rise in living standards, rapid urbanization, skyscraper boom, modernization, successful hosting of the 1988 Summer Olympics and co-hosting of the 2002 FIFA World Cup. This growth was accompanied by a democratization and globalization that transformed the country from the destruction of the Korean War to a wealthy and developed country with a globally influential economy and prominent multinational conglomerates such as Samsung, LG, and Hyundai-Kia(Wikipedia).

*road map[11]. Park pledged to put a high priority on restoring the middle class, supporting small- and medium-sized companies and preventing chaebol from abusing their power.

Park rightfully urged North Korea to abandon its nuclear ambitions without delay and embark on a path to peace and shared development. She was also right to leave the possibility open for the two Koreas to seek harmony through a "*trust-building process on the Korean Peninsula[12]."

As leader of Asia's fourth-largest economy, Park faces tough challenges. In addition to mounting demand for welfare, she is tasked with achieving *grand reconciliation and national unity[13] by embracing the 48 percent who didn't vote for her in the December presidential election. To do this, she needs to *promote communication[14], listen carefully to her opponents as well as the voices of the general public and willingly reflect their opinions in *state affairs[15] with an open mind.

But what we see and hear is the opposite. On Sunday, Park pressed ahead with the appointment of Yoon Chang-jung as presidential spokesman despite *rampant[16] criticism about the former *far-right political commentator[17]. Park is destined to fail unless she changes her secretive and uncommunicative leadership style.

koreatimes.co.kr February 26, 2013

11 road map
(일 · 계획 등에 일목요연하게 정리한) 지침

12 trust-building process on the Korean Peninsula
한반도 신뢰 프로세스

13 grand reconciliation and national unity
대화해와 국민통합

14 promote communication
소통을 촉진시키다

15 state affairs
국정

16 rampant
걷잡을 수 없는, 만연하는

17 far-right political commentator
극우 정치평론가

WORDS and STRUCTURES

taking the oath of office 취임선서를 하다

Barack Obama officially began his second term as the 44th U.S. president after taking the oath of office in front of Chief Justice John Roberts in a private ceremony at the White House on Sunday, January 20.

버락 오바마는 1월 20일 일요일 백악관의 비공개 행사에서 존 로버트 연방대법원장 앞에서 취임선서를 한 후 미국의 44대 대통령으로서 그의 두 번째 임기를 공식적으로 시작했다.

She returned to Cheong Wa Dae, the presidential house ***that*** she left in tears more than 33 years ago.

= She returned to Cheong Wa Dae, the presidential house **+*(and)*** she left ***it***(the presidential house) in tears more than 33 years ago.

그녀는 청와대로 되돌아갔는데, 청와대는 그녀가 33년보다 더 이전에 눈물 속에서 떠났던 대통령 관저이다.

Cheong Wa Dae, the presidential house

= Cheong Wa Dae, (***and it is***) the presidential house(대통령 관저)

(,는 동격의 역할을 함)

that은 관계대명사

usher in 안내하다, 예고하다, 알리다

usher in an era of peace

평화시대의 도래를 알리다

whereby (격식) (관계부사) (그것에 의하여) ~하는 바의(by which); 그리고 그것으로 인하여

an arrangement whereby that company will buy more imports

그 회사가 더 많은 수입품을 산다고 하는 협정

The new administration will usher in a new era of hope ***whereby*** "the happiness of each citizen becomes the bedrock of our nation's strength ***which*** in turn is shared by and benefits all Koreans"

and by it(the new era of hope), the happiness of each citizen becomes the bedrock of our nation's strength

and it(the bedrock of our nation's strength) in turn is shared by all Koreans

and it(the bedrock of our nation's strength) benefits all Koreans
새 정부는 새로운 희망의 시대를 예고할 것인데, 그 희망의 시대에서 모든 시민의 행복이 우리 국력의 토대가 되고, 결국 우리 국력의 토대는 모든 한국인에 의해 공유되고 모든 한국인들에게 이익이 될 것이다.

give that ~을 고려하면

This is quite a project, given that the city is also hosting the 2014 World Cup
이 도시가 2014 월드컵을 유치하고 있는 점을 감안하면 이것은 대단한 프로젝트가 아닐 수 없다.

She made it clear that science and technology, and the IT industry lie at the heart of a creative economy, ***heightening*** hopes that the new mammoth science ministry will contribute a great deal to creating more jobs.
= She made it clear that science and technology, and the IT industry lie at the heart of a creative economy, ***and it heightens*** hopes that the new mammoth science ministry will contribute a great deal to creating more jobs.
그녀는 과학과 기술, 그리고 IT산업이 창조경제의 중심에 있다는 것을 분명히 했는데, 그것은 새 거대 과학기술부가 더 많은 일자리를 창출하는데 많이 기여할 것이라는 희망을 높여준다.

embark

1. (배 · 비행기에) 오르다, 승선하다, 탑승하다(on)
   embark for America 미국을 향해 출항하다
   I embarked at Busan 부산에서 승선했다

2. embark on(upon) A (문어) (A(사업 등)에) 진출하다, 착수(종사)하다
   embark on[upon] a new career (adventure) 새로운 생활 (모험)을 시작하다
   embark upon motherhood 어머니가 되다
   embark on an enterprise in show business 흥행계에 진출하다

without a hitch 문제없이

What can you do to make sure they go off without a hitch?
뭘 해야 순조롭게 진행될 수 있을까요?

deliver 이행하다

Not all promises are delivered in such epic proportions, but even the smallest ones deserve fulfillment.
모든 약속이 그렇게 영웅적으로 이행되지는 않으나, 가장 작은 약속도 마땅히 지켜져야 된다.

at the expense of 희생으로 하여, 대가로

He did it at the expense of his health. 그는 건강을 희생하고 그것을 했다.

urge 촉구하다, 요구하다

1. 촉구하다

Sasae urged South Korea to suspend all projects near Dokdo.
사사에 차관은 독도 주변의 모든 프로젝트를 중단하도록 촉구했다.

2. 요구하다

They urged the president to make an apology and start concentrating on a welfare-focused policy.
그들은 대통령의 사과와 복지기반정책에 주력해 주기를 요구했다.

mounting (한정적)점차 증가하는

the nation's mounting foreign debt 국가의 늘어나는 외채

reconciliation 화해, 중재, 조정

a spirit of reconciliation 화해의 정신
effect a reconciliation 화해를 하다
There was no hope of a reconciliation between the two families.
두 가족 사이에는 화해의 희망이 전혀 없었다.

press ahead 추진하다

The government will press ahead with its plan to set up a research center for Goguryeo history under the Prime Minister's Office.
정부는 국무총리산하 고구려사 연구센터 설립을 추진할 계획이다.

destined 운명의, ~할, 틀림없는

She was destined to failure.
그 여자는 실패하게 되어 있었다.

unless 만일 ~아니라면

unless she changes her secretive and uncommunicative leadership style
= ***if*** she does ***not*** change her secretive and uncommunicative leadership style
만일 그녀가 그녀의 비밀스럽고 소통하지 않는 지도스타일을 바꾸지 않는다면

Memo

02.

Pursuit of happiness

Upon being sworn in as the 18th president of the Republic of Korea this morning, Park Geun-hye will embark on the pursuit of happiness for the Korean people. She plans to enhance their happiness by spending more on welfare. She believes it is worthwhile to pursue happiness for the Korean people as a whole as elusive and costly as the goal may be.

Few would dispute the pursuit of happiness is a misplaced objective for Park's five-year *presidency[1]. Korea has been surging forward for economic advancement since her late father, President Park Chung-hee, launched his first five-year economic development plan[1)] in the early 1960s.

Korea was one of the poorest countries in the world when her father, an *Army general[2], took power in a *military coup[3] in 1961. His immediate task was to feed the starving people. As Korea has now become the 15th largest *economy[4] in the world, it can definitely afford to spend more on welfare, if not as much as the new president intends.

1 presidency
대통령 직(임기)

2 Army general
육군 장성

3 military coup
군사 쿠테타

4 economy
(경제 주체로서의) 국가

5 per capita income
1인당 소득

Happiness does not go hand in hand with national wealth, as indicated by Gallup[2)]'s recent survey of people in 148 countries in the world. The survey ranked Korea, a country with *per capita income[5] surpassing the $20,000 level, surprisingly low — 97th, together with Greece, Mongolia, Kazakhstan and the Czech Republic.

True, measuring the level of happiness a country's people

1) **five-year economic development plan** (경제개발 5개년 계획) 5 · 16 이후 1962년의 제 1차 5개년계획을 시발점으로 하여 1991년까지 6차의 5개년계획이 시행되었다. 1992년부터 1996년까지 계획된 제 7차 경제개발 5개년계획은 1993년 대통령의 취임 시 5년 단임의 대통령 임기와 맞지 않아 「신경제 5개년 계획」으로 수정되면서 이전 계획과의 단절이 생기게 된다.
한국의 경제개발 5개년계획은 다음과 같은 일반적 성격을 가지고 있다. 첫째, 그것은 물량적 차원에서의 성장우선계획이었다. 그것은 광공업을 성장주도 산업으로 하여 전략부문과 사회간접자본의 집중적 개발에 중점을 둔 불균형 성장모형이었다. 둘째, 그것은 자원동원과 배분의 중점을 공업화에 둔 공업화계획이었다. 셋째, 그것은 공업화에 필요한 투자재원의 조달을 경제협력을 통한 적극적인 외자도입에 의존한 계획이었다.
1962~1991까지 6차에 걸친 계획을 통하여 한국경제는 연평균 17.6%의 GNP성장률을 달성하였다. 1인당 GNP도 1961년의 83달러에서 1992년에는 6,749달러로 80배 이상 증가하였다. 또한 산업구조가 1차 산업 중심에서 중화학공업 중심으로 발전하였다.
이 기간에 수출은 연평균 약 27.4%로 급속히 증가하여 1960년에는 32.8백만 달러에 불과하던 수출실적이 1995년에는 125,058.0백만 달러에 달했다. 수출상품구조도 경제개발이 진전됨에 따라 1차 상품 중심에서 공산품 중심으로, 경공업 중심에서 중공업 중심으로 바뀌었다. 수입의 경우 수출증가율보다는 완만하였지만, 역시 연평균 약 18.7%로 증가하여 1960년에 343.5백만 달러였던 것이 1995년에는 135,118.9백만 달러에 달하였다.
제 7차 계획을 수정하고 수립된 신경제 5개년계획은 이전의 경제개발계획들과는 달리 제도와 의식개혁을 통해 국민의 참여를 이끌어낸 후, 성장잠재력을 확충하고 국제시장기반을 확충하며 국민생활여건의 개선을 뒷받침하고자 한 것이다. 7차 계획과는 고통분담 등 경제 활성화를 위한 국민의 동참과 희생을 요구한다는 점, 경제정의의 실현을 목표로 경제개혁과제를 제시하고 있는 점, 행정규제완화를 강조한다는 점 등에서 차이가 있다(네이버 지식백과, 경제학사전).

2) **Gallup**, Inc., is an American research-based, global performance-management consulting company. Founded by George Gallup in 1935, the company became famous for its public opinion polls, which were conducted in the United States and other countries. Gallup works with major businesses and organizations around the world.
In 1988, four years after George Gallup died, Selection Research (SRI) purchased the company from its heirs. SRI wanted the Gallup name to use on its polls, which gave them more credibility and higher response rates. Today the poll is used to gain visibility. Some of Gallup's key practice areas are employee engagement, customer engagement, talent management, and well-being.
Gallup has nearly 40 offices in more than 20 countries. World headquarters are in Washington, D.C. Operational headquarters are in Omaha, Nebraska. Gallup's current Chairman and CEO is Jim Clifton.
There are about 2,000 employees in the privately held company, working in four divisions: Gallup Poll, Gallup Consulting, Gallup University, and Gallup Press(Wikipedia).

feel is an elusive task. Questions may be raised about the validity of the survey, which asked 1,000 people in each country if they were well-rested, had been treated with respect, smiled or laughed a lot, learned or did something interesting and had feelings of enjoyment the previous day.

Still, it can be surmised, based on the survey, that Korean people feel less happy than the average person in the world, though they belong to the Organization for Economic Cooperation and Development[3)], the Paris-based club of well-to-do nations. This undoubtedly speaks volumes about what the nation needs to do for its people.

Against this backdrop, Park has *committed herself to[6] shifting the "paradigm of *administering state affairs[7]" and placing the happiness of the people on top of her *political agenda items[8] since she was selected as the *presidential nominee[9] of the ruling Saenuri Party last year. The key to her project is 135 trillion won in additional spending on welfare over the next five years.

Now the question is how to *finance the welfare plan[10]. She says a substantial amount of money will come from additional revenue that will be raised when her administration reduces the nation's gray economy[4)], *plugs tax loopholes[11] and retires many of the *tax credits[12] and other *tax favors[13]. But the

6 committed herself to
공약(약속)하다

7 administering state affairs
국정을 운영하는

8 political agenda items
정치적 과제(의제) 목록

9 presidential nominee
대통령 후보(지명자)

10 finance the welfare plan
복지계획의 재원을 마련하다

11 plugs tax loopholes
세금탈루를 막다

12 tax credit
세액 공제, 세금 공제

13 tax favors
세제특혜, 면세

3) **Organization for Economic Cooperation and Development** (경제협력개발기구) 1961년 발족, 프랑스 파리에 사무국을 두고 있음; 약어 OECD.

14 collect more taxes
더 많은 세금을 거두다

15 tax revenues
세입금

16 mortgage payments
주택담보대출 상환금

17 household debt
가계부채

amount would be woefully small. Among the alternatives will be to *collect more taxes[14] and delay her election promises that are not deemed urgent.

Another obstacle is slowing growth, which will cut back on *tax revenues[15]. Moody's Investors Service[5)] has recently lowered Korea's 2013 growth outlook to 3 percent, which would mean a 2 trillion won shortfall in tax revenues.

Spending more on welfare, however, will not guarantee greater happiness for Korean households, whose debt the Bank of Korea says is approaching the 1,000 trillion won level. Who would laugh a lot, do something interesting and have feelings of enjoyment when they are under the threat of being forced out of their homes because they cannot make good on their *mortgage payments[16]? The astronomical amount of *household debt[17] is a ticking time bomb for the nation.

In addition to speeding up economic recovery and defusing the time bomb, her administration will also have to breathe

4) **grey(gray) economy** (회색경제) 공식 통계에 계정되지 않은 경제 활동 A Grey Market, or parallel market is the trade of a commodity through distribution channels which, while legal, are unofficial, unauthorized, or unintended by the original manufacturer. The most common type of grey market is the sale of imported goods (brought by small import companies or individuals not authorized by the manufacturer) which would otherwise be more expensive in the country to which they are being imported. An example is drugs being imported into nearby wealthier nations where the drug manufacturer charges a higher price for a similar or equivalent product.
The term grey economy, however, refers to workers being paid under the table(은밀히), without paying income taxes or contributing to such public services. It is sometimes referred to as the underground economy or "hidden economy."(Wikipedia).

5) **Moody's Investors Service** (미)(무디스(사)) 미국의 금융 정보 서비스 및 신용 평가 회사.

new life into the moribund *property market[18] and create jobs for young people in particular.

Another diversion from the pursuit of happiness is the precarious security to which South Korea is exposed, as North Korea is pushing ahead with a plan to arm itself with nuclear weapons and *intercontinental ballistic missiles[19]. Park, who wanted to build peace by launching what she called the "Korean Peninsula process" of trust building, will now have to determine how she will respond to the increasing security threats from the North.

Given the worsening economic conditions and the *security threat[20] from the North Korean communists, odds are stacked against Park's pursuit of happiness for the South Korean people. Still, she could gain insight from her father, who, *against all odds[21], pulled the nation out of extreme poverty and helped turn it into a global industrial powerhouse.

koreaherald.com February 25, 2013

18 property market
부동산 시장

19 intercontinental ballistic missiles
대륙간 탄도미사일

20 security threat
안보위협

21 against all odds
강한 저항을 무릅쓰고, 역경을 딛고

WORDS and STRUCTURES

upon + -ing ~하자마자

Upon hearing news of the pope's resignation, U.S. President Barack Obama said in a statement,"On behalf of Americans everywhere, Michelle and I wish to extend our appreciation and prayers to His Holiness Pope Benedict XVI.
교황의 사임소식을 듣고 버락 오바마 미국대통령은 성명을 통해, "전 미국인들을 대신하여 미셸과 본인은 교황 베네딕토 16세 성하(聖下)를 위해 감사와 기도를 드리고 싶다고 말했다.

swear in 선서 받고 취임시키다(하다)(swear – swore – sworn)

She will be sworn in, saying, 'I do solemnly swear before the people that I will faithfully execute the duties of the President by observing the Constitution, defending the State, pursuing the peaceful unification of the homeland, promoting the freedom and welfare of the people, and endeavoring to develop national culture.'
박 당선인은 취임식에서, '나는 헌법을 준수하고 국가를 보위하며 조국의 평화적 통일과 국민의 자유와 복리 증진 및 민족문화의 창달에 노력하여 대통령직을 성실히 수행할 것을 국민들 앞에 엄숙히 선서 합니다'라고 선서하게 된다.

On February 25, Korea will ***swear*** in Park Geun-hye as the country's first female president.
2월 25일, 한국은 한국의 첫 여성대통령으로서 박근혜를 선서 받고 취임시킬 것이다.
→ Park Geun-hye will ***be sworn*** in as the country's first female president by (Korea).

as elusive and costly as the goal may be

= ***though*** the goal ***may be*** elusive and costly 비록 그 목표는 비용이 들고 달성하기는 어려울지라도

As favorable as it may appear at first glance, wind energy requires turbines to be built in remote areas or at sea.
풍력에너지는 언뜻 보기에는 좋아 보일 수 있는데, 풍력에너지를 사용하기 위해서는 먼 지역이나 바다에 터빈을 건설할 필요가 있다.

elusive 1. (사물 · 사람이) 손에 잡히지 않는, 눈에 띄지 않는
2. (뜻 · 성격 등이) 파악하기 어려운, 알기 어려운
3. (성과 등이) 달성하기 힘든

few / a few

However, few have received proper treatment for the serious problem.
하지만 이러한 심각한 문제에 대해 적절한 치료를 받은 사람은 거의 없었다.

Northern Alberta is mostly covered by forest and few people live there.
북부 알버타는 대부분 숲으로 덮여있고 거의 사람이 살지 않는다.

Only a few Korean students said they are very happy.
소수의 한국 학생들만이 행복함을 느낀다고 답했다.

surge forward 뻗어가다

As the kayak that had surged forward with the wave began to slow down, the cries also subsided.
쭉쭉 뻗어가던 카약이 속도를 줄이기 시작하면서 환호성도 잦아들었다.

can afford to + V ~할 수 있다

Now she can afford to buy a four-bedroom house for her family.
이제 그녀는 그녀의 가족을 위해 침실 4개짜리 집을 구입할 수 있다.

if not

= ***even if*** it can***not*** do as much as the new president intends to spend on welfare
비록 새 대통령이 복지에 쓸려고 하는 것만큼 많이 쓸 수는 없다하더라도

rank 분류하다, 평가하다

We ranked his abilities very high. 우리는 그의 재능을 아주 높이 평가했다.

measuring the level of happiness a country's people feel is an elusive task
한 나라의 국민이 느끼는 행복의 수준을 측정하는 것은 파악하기 어려운 일이다.
= measuring the level of happiness ***(which)*** a country's people feel
= measuring the level of happiness ***+(and)*** a country's people feel ***it***(the level of happiness)

The poll asked about 1,000 people in each of 148 countries if they were well-rested, had been treated with respect, laughed a lot, learned or did something interesting, and felt feelings of enjoyment.
이 조사는 148 개국에서 각각 약 1,000명의 사람들에게 잘 쉬었는지, 사람들이 존경심으로 대우받았는지, 많이 웃었는지, 재미있는 것을 배우거나 했는지, 즐거움을 느꼈는지를 물었다.

surmise+(목) / surmise+that절 ~을(~이라고) 추측(짐작)하다

From the looks on their faces, I surmised that they had had an argument.
그들의 얼굴 표정을 보고 나는 그들이 말다툼을 했다고 추측했다.

well-to-do 부유한

The well-to-do consumers have a tendency to believe that higher prices mean better quality.
부유한 고객들은 고가(高價)가 좋은 품질을 의미한다고 믿는 경향이 있다.

speak(tell, express) volumes (증거 등이) 명백하다, 웅변적으로 보여주고 있다

Her actions spoke volumes of her hopes to meet him.
그녀의 행동은 그를 만나려는 희망을 여실히 보여줬다.

against backdrop ~을 배경으로

Against this backdrop, the Prime Minister's Office recently announced energy-saving measures.
이런 배경에서 국무총리실은 최근에 에너지를 절약하는 방안들을 발표했다.

It will still cost a ***substantial*** amount of money.
그것은 여전히 상당한(엄청난) 양의 돈이 들 것이다.

raise 모으다, 조달하다

They raised money to help people in need through this event.
그들은 이 행사를 통해서 어려운 사람들을 돕기 위해 돈을 모았다.

Meanwhile, IBK is also looking to raise at least $1 billion in bonds.
한편 기업은행도 올해 채권발행을 통해 최소한 10억 달러를 조달할 계획이다.

retire 폐기하다

Treasury stock may be eventually retired or reissued.
금고 주는 결국 폐기되거나 재발행 될 수 있다.

deem + (목적어) + (to be) … ~을 (…이라고) 생각하다, 여기다

We have now deemed the area safe. 우리는 그 지역을 이제 안전하다고 여겼다.
= The area has now been deemed safe
I deem him (to be) a fool. 나는 그를 바보라고 생각한다.

delay her election promises ***that*** are not deemed urgent
= delay her election promises ***+(and) they***(election promises) are not deemed urgent
긴급하지 않다고 여겨지는 그녀의 선거공약들을 미루다.

cutting back on 줄이다

South Koreans are cutting back on their spending habits as the nation's economy drops.
한국의 경제가 침체되면서 한국인들은 소비습관을(씀씀이를) 줄이고 있다.

shortfall 부족액

The shortfall is predicted to fall to around $10 billion by the year-end.
이 부족액은 연말까지 약 100억 달러로 떨어질 것으로 예상된다.

make good on 이행하다

In addition, the Kim Jong-il regime ought to make good on its denuclearization agreement.
게다가 김정일 정권은 비핵화합의를 이행해야 한다.

mortgage [mɔ́:rgidʒ] 주택 담보 대출, 모기지, 융자

That's my mortgage payment.
그게 제 집 값 갚을 돈이다.

ticking bomb 시한폭탄

Time to take steps to defuse ticking bomb.
시한폭탄은 지금 해제해야만 한다.

moribund 빈사상태의

The government unveiled yesterday a long-awaited package of measures that is aimed to prop up the moribund venture industry and revitalize the tech-heavy Kosdaq market.
정부는 어제 빈사상태에 빠진 벤처산업을 부양하고 기술주 중심의 코스닥시장 활성화를 위해 오랫동안 기다려왔던 대책들을 내놓았다.

diversion (목적 · 방향 · 주의 등을) 다른 데로 돌리기, 전환

For the government, the war was a welcome diversion from the country's economic problems.
정부로서는 그 전쟁이 국가의 경제문제들에서 사람들의 주의를 돌리게 해주는 반가운 사건이었다.

precarious 불확실한, 위험한, 위태로운

Taiwan faces arguably the most precarious security environment in the world.
대만이 세계에서 가장 위태로운 안보환경에 직면한 것은 거의 틀림없는 사실이다.

be exposed to 노출되어 있다

'The longer a person is exposed to poverty at childhood, the worse the achievement levels become,' researchers said.
'한 개인이 어린 시절에 가난에 더 오래 노출되면 될수록, (학업)성취도는 더 나빠진다'고 연구원들은 말했다.

arm itself with 스스로 무장하다

The problem is that the South will find it nearly impossible to arm itself with nuclear weapons.
문제는 남한이 자체핵무장 하는 것이 거의 불가능에 가깝다는 것이다

push ahead(forward) (군대 · 탐험대 등이) (~을 향해) (곤란을 무릅쓰고) 급히 나아가다, (계획 등을) 추진하다(with)

Evidently, the president had been clandestinely pushing forward with the project ever since the start of his Presidential term.
분명한건, 그 대통령은 대통령임기 시작부터 그 사업을 비밀리에 추진해 왔었다.

given 감안하면

It may be difficult at first for her administration to implement all sustainable economic policies smoothly, given her low approval rating hovering below 44 percent.
박대통령이 44%에 못 미치는 낮은 지지를 받고 있는 상황을 감안하면 박근혜 행정부가 모든 지속가능한 경제정책을 원만하게 실행하는 것은 처음에는 어려울 수도 있다.

odds 승산, 가능성

The odds were against us. 형세는 우리에게 불리하다.

stack the cards 불리한 상황에 놓이게 하다

The odds are stacked against you at the casino and you should expect to lose more often than you win.
카지노에서 당신은 이길 승산이 불리하기 때문에 따기보다는 저 자주 잃을 것이라 기대하는 것이 좋다.

To ***gain insight*** into human behavior, people should look into themselves first.
인간의 행동에 대한 통찰력을 가지려면, 먼저 자기 자신부터 들여다 보아야한다.

powerhouse 강력한 그룹(조직, 나라), (스포츠) 최강팀

Surely, the nation emerged as a powerhouse in winter sports due to the number of medals it managed to earn.
물론, 한국은 이번 올림픽에서 많은 메달을 따내면서 동계스포츠의 강국으로 급부상했다.

03.

Shared Wounds in Korea

The inauguration of South Korea's first female president, Park Geun-hye, on Monday is a trip down memory lane for most South Koreans — especially those in their 50s and 60s, whose support at the polls[1)] ensured her election victory last December.

For this "5060 generation," as Koreans call it, Ms. Park has always been an emotional touchstone. She was the nation's first daughter when her father, the dictator Park Chung-hee[2)], ruled from 1961 until he was assassinated in 1979. For the last five of those years, she was also South Korea's first lady — replacing her mother[3)], who was killed in 1974 in a botched attack on Mr. Park by a North Korean *sympathizer[1].

Now she is returning to her childhood home, South Korea's *Blue House[2]. I was a young child in South Korea in 1979, and

1 sympathizer 동조자

2 Blue House 청와대

1) **polls** 한국의 제18대 대통령을 선출하기 위한 선거로 2012년 12월 19일에 실시됨.

2) **Park Chung-hee** 1979년 10월 26일 대통령 박정희는 중앙정보부장이었던 김재규에 의해 암살됨.

3) **her mother** 박근혜의 어머니(1974년 8월 15일 광복절 기념식장에서 저격범 문세광에 의해 피살됨).

3 in public
사람이 있는데서, 공개적으로

4 antidote
해독제, (나쁜 영향 등에 대한) 방어(교정) 수단

an antidote for a recession
경기후퇴에 대한 해결책

5 something
~대(代), ~사람(서로 다른 세대에 속하는 사회 · 경제적 연령 집단)

6 eerily
무시무시하게, 무서워하여, 불가사의하게

7 campaign
선거운동, 유세

I vividly recall the day Mr. Park was assassinated. My parents, in whispers, warned me not to breathe a word outside about it. Speaking about the government *in public[3] could get you arrested. So I went to school, weighed down with my secret until I saw students crying. It turned out that they knew too, and soon just about everyone in school was in tears.

People did not explain their anguish — whether it was sorrow or fright. But Park Chung-hee was the only leader we children had known, and I remember someone whispering that with him gone, North Korea would attack us.

Interestingly, that level of fear was not so different from what I witnessed last year in Pyongyang, North Korea, where I was researching a book. When their leader Kim Jong-il died, young North Koreans fell into despair. Their faces went dark, as though the sky had fallen, or as if they had lost a parent. The government rushed out an *antidote[4]: broadcasts of their new 20-*something[5] leader, Kim Jong-un, who resembled his grandfather Kim Il-sung so much that it seemed the genes had skipped a generation from the *Great Leader[4)] to his grandson.

Similarly, Park Geun-hye looks *eerily[6] reminiscent of her mother, whom South Korean history books have cast as the nation's ultimate first lady — a martyr. During the *campaign[7], Ms. Park borrowed a page from that script by reminding voters that she herself, having never married or had children,

4) **Great Leader** 김정은의 아버지 김정일을 가리킴.

had nobody to mother except the people.

Consider her roles: daughter, first lady, mother. Emotional symbols to lean on in a nation that the World Economic Forum[5)] ranks 108th out of 135 in *gender equality[8]. This woman, widely lauded as her country's first female president, is no symbol of latent feminism[6)] but of something far more traditional - a girl who grew up before the nation's eyes, only to lose both parents violently, and then become the mother for whom they had carried a torch since her own mother's

8 gender equality
양성평등

5) **World Economic Forum** 다보스포럼(Davos Forum)이라고도 함. 1971년 1월 독일 출신의 제네바대학 경영학교수 클라우스 슈바브(Klaus Schwab)에 의해 창설된 유럽경영포럼(European Management Forum)으로 출발한 것으로 세계의 저명한 기업인 · 경제학자 · 저널리스트 · 정치인 등이 모여 세계경제에 대해 토론하고 연구하는 국제민간회의.

6) **feminism** (페미니즘, 여권신장운동) 여성해방 사상으로 성차별에 대해 시정을 요구하는 모든 사상 · 운동을 말한다. 예를 들면, 남녀동등권 또는 여권신장운동 등이 있다. 페미니즘은 근대의 사상으로서 시작되었다. '인간은 모두 평등하다'는 사상의 침투로 비로소 '모두' 속에 여성이 포함되어 있지 않다는 것의 부당성을 문제화할 수 있었기 때문이다. 따라서 페미니즘은 기본적으로 '남자와 동일한 평등'을 지향한다. 19세기 후반부터 20세기 초에 걸쳐 영국, 미국, 프랑스 등 서유럽 근대사회를 중심으로 일어난 제1기 페미니즘은 여성의 법적 권리의 확립을 목표로 참정권 획득운동으로서 위치한다. 이 시기에는 기존의 사회체제 내의 제도개혁으로 여성해방을 실현하고자 하는 자유주의적 페미니즘의 주장 외에 여성은 사회주의 사회의 달성에 의해 비로소 남성과 함께 해방된다고 주장한 사회주의적 페미니즘도 강한 영향력을 가지고 있었다.
1960년대 미국에서는 프리던(Betty Friedan)의 『여성다움의 신화』(1963)를 계기로 제2기 페미니즘 운동(이른바 Women's Live)이 시작되었다. 프리던은 경제적으로 혜택받은 중산계급의 주부들이 왜 일상적인 생활에서 만족하다고 생각을 하지 않는가, 왜 고독감이나 우울증에 시달리고 있는가를 주제화하여 그 원인을 강고한 성별 역할분담의 규범에서 찾았다. 프리던은 NOW(National Organization for Women)의 초대 회장으로서 전통적인 성별 역할 분담의 타파, 여성이 남성과 평등한 파트너르서 사회의 주류에 참가할 수 있는 권리를 요구하여 운동을 조직하였다. 이러한 미국에서의 움직임은 선진자본주의 국가로 파급되어 프랑스에서는 MLF(Mouvement de Liberation des Femmes)가 대두하여 인공임신중절의 합법화 등을 요구하는 운동을 전개하였다.
Women's Live의 운동 속에서 여성차별의 근본 원인을 제도가 아니라 성(남성과 여성의 성 관계)에서 찾는 근본적인 페미니즘의 사상이 등장하였다. 그 이론적인 기반이 된 밀레트(Kate Millett)의 『성의 정치학』(1970)은 일관되게 남성에 의한 여성의 성적 지배 · 성적 착취, 즉 성 관계라는 가장 개인적인 사항까지 지배/복종한다는 정치적 관계가 관철되어 있는 것을 고발하고 있다. 근본적인 페미니즘 이후 페미니즘은 '개인적인 것은 정치적이다'라는 슬로건에 단적으로 나타나 있듯이 제도를 지지하는 사회구조 자체가 성 관계라는 정치적 관계에 어떻게 규정되어 있는가를 고찰의 범위에 넣는 것을 불가결한 요건으로 하여 성립하고 있다.
1970년대 이후 여성이 가부장제와 자본제의 양방에서 2중으로 착취당하고 있는 사태를 '재생산 노동'이라는 개념에 의해 폭로하고, 성별 역할 분담 이데올로기의 해체를 목표로 한 마르크스주의 페미니즘이나 정신분석의 방법을 축으로 성적 차이의 성립 기반으로까지 거슬러 올라가 근대적 주체의 형성 과정을 분석하고자 하는 프랑스의 페미니즘(포스트모던 페미니즘) 등이 강한 영향력을 가지고 페미니즘 이론의 체계화가 진행되었다(네이버 지식백과, 21세기 정치학대사전).

9 martyrdom
순교

10 collective sentiment
집단 정서(심리)

11 oppressor
압제자, 억압자

12 common humanity
공통적 인간애

13 complex loyalty
복합적 충성심

14 caveat
(법률) 절차정지신청예고, 예고기재(記載), 경고

with the caveat (caution)
주의할 것

*martyrdom[9].

My own parents supported her election, and they expressed the *collective sentiment[10] of the 5060 generation when they explained to me why: they feel sorry for her and indebted to her, because she has been all alone.

I find that strange - nostalgia whitewashing the past. Park Geun-hye has never rated pity; she is a modern-day princess born to privilege inherited from a ruthless dictator[7)] . Yes, her father elevated South Korea's economy. But he also tortured dissidents and changed the constitution to keep himself in power. He left South Koreans thirsting for democracy, and while they were building it in the 1980s and '90s, they largely dismissed him as an *oppressor[11] — until his daughter returned, pulling on their heartstrings.

North and South Koreans share a soft spot for what we call "jung," a vague term that might best be translated as a collective sentiment of *common humanity[12] and warmth that binds people. Among my parents' generation, the 18 years under Park Chung-hee seem to have instilled a *complex loyalty[13] to him that is oddly parallel to the feeling that North Koreans had after Kim Il-sung's 46-year-long rule (with the *caveat[14], of course, that North Koreans never had democracy, before or since).

In any case, on either side of the 38th Parallel, we now

7) **ruthless dictator** 박정희를 가리킴.

have at the helm a daughter and a grandson of the two men[8)] who kept the halves of our nation pitted against each other through much of the cold war[9)].

We can only hope the dynamic will be different now. But despite her condemnation of the latest nuclear bomb test, Ms. Park's policy toward North Korea remains vague. South Koreans say her first duty is to rescue their *slowing economy[15]. But she cannot avoid for long the question of how she deals with North Korea. So we need to hear much more about how she proposes to reorder the relationship with the North so that *Korean souls[16] on both sides of the 38th Parallel[10)] at long last can move beyond the fears and misguided attachments left by a war that stopped, but did not end, in 1953.

nytimes.com February 25, 2013

15 slowing economy 경기침체

16 Korean souls 한국 사람들

8) **two men** 박정희와 김일성.

9) **cold war** (냉전) 제2차 세계대전 이후에 두 초강대국인 미국과 소련 간에 존재했던 적대감과 정치적 경쟁상태를 말한다. 이것은 정치적인 전복, 전략, 스파이 활동, 군소국가간의 국지전을 증대시키는 것 등과 관련이 있다. 그러나 이것은 전면전을 중지시켰다. 몇몇 논평가들은 가장 심각한 상호간의 의심과 적대감이 있었던 시기, 1945~55년을 냉전기간으로 간주하기도 한다. 또 어떤 사람들은, 냉전기간은 글라스노스트(Glasnost)와 페레스트로이카(Perestroika)의 도래와 1989년과 1990년의 동구의 군사적, 경제적 블럭의 해체로 종식되었다고 보고 있다(사회학사전, 사회문화연구소).

10) **38th Parallel** (38도선) When Japan surrendered in August 1945, the 38th parallel was established as the boundary between Soviet and American occupation zones. This parallel divides the Korean peninsula roughly in the middle. In 1948, this parallel became the boundary between the Democratic People's Republic of Korea (North Korea) and the Republic of Korea (South Korea), both of which claim to be the government of the whole of Korea. On 25 June 1950, after a series of cross-border raids and gunfire from both the Northern and the Southern sides, the North Korean Army crossed the parallel and invaded South Korea. This sparked a United Nations resolution against the aggression and the Korean War, with United Nations troops (mostly Americans) helping to defend South Korea.
After the Armistice ended the Korean War in 1953, a demarcation line was established through the middle of the Korean Demilitarized Zone. This new border crosses the 38th parallel, from the southwest to the northeast, and it now serves as the Military Demarcation Line between South Korea and North Korea(Wikipedia).

WORDS and STRUCTURES

down memory lane 옛날의, 그리운

a trip/walk down memory lane 추억 여행
His 1998 memoir is a delightful trip down memory lane.
그의 1998 회고록은 기억을 더듬어 가는 즐거운 여행이다.

in their 50s 50대(代)의

Today, in our society, when a person is in their 50s or 60s they are likely to retire.
요즘 우리사회에서는 사람이 50대나 60대에 있으면 은퇴하기 마련이다.

whose support at the polls ensured her election victory last December.
= ***and their*** support at the polls ensured her election victory last December.
그런데 그들의 선거에서의 지지가 지난 12월 그녀가 승리를 할 수 있게 했다.

ensure 보장하다, 확실히 하다

The book ensured his success. 그 책은 그의 성공을 보장해 주었다.

touchstone 시금석, (사물의 진가를 판가름하는) 시험, 기준

Job security has become the touchstone of a good job for many employees.
직업의 안전성이 많은 고용인들에게 좋은 직업을 가름하는 기준이 되었다.

rule 통치하다

The king reigns, but he does not rule.
왕은 군림하나 통치하지 않는다.

who was killed in 1974
= ***and she*** was killed in 1974

botched 잘못하거나 잘못 계획되어 실패한, 망가진

a botched attempt 망쳐버린 시도

weigh down ~을 (마음 · 기분을) 짓누르다

The responsibilities of the job are weighing her down.
그 일에 대한 책임감이 그녀를 짓누르고 있다.

just about 거의

Of course just about everyone now believes the previous punishment was far from sufficient.
물론, 지금 거의 모두가 이전의 처벌이 충분치 못하다고 생각한다.

anguish 괴로움, 비통

She seemed to be in great anguish at the moment.
그녀는 그때 무척 괴로워하는 것 같았다.

fright 놀람, 두려움

She was only unconscious, had fainted from shock and fright.
그녀는 의식을 잃었을 뿐이고 충격과 공포로 기절했다.

Park Chung-hee was the only leader we children had known
= Park Chung-hee was the only leader ***(whom)*** we children had known
(Park Chung-hee was the only leader + ***(and)*** we children had known ***him***)

with him gone 그가 죽었기 때문에

Mr. Shim was the only member of the ULD with an influential provincial head seat and with him gone, the party is likely to suffer with just four seats in the National Assembly.
심 지사는 자민련 소속 도지사로는 유일한데 그가 탈당함으로써 자민련은 국회 의석 4석만으로는 곤란해질 것 같다.

North Korea, ***where*** I was researching a book
= North Korea, ***and there*** I was researching a book

research a book

I was in London at the time researching a book on the British Conservative Party.
당시 필자는 영국 보수당에 관한 저서의 조사 작업을 위해 런던에 머물고 있었다.

rush out ~을 급히(서둘러) 만들어 내다

The editors rushed out an item on the crash for the late news.
편집부에서 심야 뉴스에 내보내기 위해 서둘러 그 충돌 사고에 대한 기사를 만들어 냈다.

reminiscent 생각나게 하는, 연상시키는

The event was reminiscent of the 1988 Summer Olympics and the 2002 World Cup, which also took place in the Korean capital.
그 행사는 한국의 수도 서울에서 열린 1988서울올림픽과 2002월드컵을 연상시켰다.

cast-cast-cast A as B A를 B로 그리다(묘사하다)

However, Charles has cast himself as an advocate for heritage, tradition and the environment.
그러나 찰스는 유산, 전통과 환경의 옹호자라고 자신을 그려왔다.

He cast himself as the innocent victim of a hate campaign.
그는 스스로를 비방질의 무고한 희생자라고 묘사했다.

whom South Korean history books have cast as the nation's ultimate first lady
= ***and*** South Korean history books have cast ***her*** as the nation's ultimate first lady
(whom = and her)

ultimate 최고의

Demographically speaking, Google is the ultimate choice.
이용자의 숫자를 놓고 볼때, 구글은 최고의 선택이다.

having never married or had children
= ***and she had*** never married or had children
그런데 그녀는 결코 결혼한 적도 없고 아이를 가진 적도 없었고

mother 어머니로서 돌보다

House work is the work that you do to keep your home clean and to mother the children living in it.
집안일이란 집안을 깨끗이 하고 아이들을 돌보기 위해 하는 가사일이다.

Emotional symbols to lean on
= ***They are*** emotional symbols to lean on
그것들은 기댈 수 있는 감정적 상징들이다.
(주어와 동사 생략)

lean on ~에 기대다, 의지하다

I want someone to lean on in hard times.
나는 힘들 때 기댈 수 있는 사람을 원한다.

in a nation ***that*** the World Economic Forum ranks 108th out of 135 in gender equality
nation과 동격의 that(세계 경제포럼이 양성평등에서 135개국 중에서 108위라고 평가하는 국가에서)

This woman, ***widely lauded*** as her country's first female president, is ***no*** symbol of latent feminism ***but*** of something far more traditional.
= This woman, ***and she was widely lauded*** as her country's first female president, is no symbol of latent feminism but of something far more traditional.

no(not) A but B A가 아니라 B

이 여성은(주어) 잠재적인 페미니즘의 상징이 아니라 훨씬 더 전통적인 어떤 것의 상징이다(동사).

only to do (결과) 결국 (~하기) 위한 것으로

I went to your house in the rain, only to find you out.
빗속에 너의 집에 갔는데, 공교롭게도 너는 외출 했더라.

carry a torch for somebody (특히 자기를 사랑하지 않는 사람에 대해) 연정을 불태우다

I carry a torch for her. 그 여자에게 반해있어요.

Are you still carrying a torch for him? 너 아직도 그를 생각하고 있어?

then become the mother ***for whom*** they had carried a torch
= then become the mother **+ *(and)*** they had carried a torch ***for her***
마침내 그들이 연정을 품어왔던 그 어머니가 되었다.

indebted 부채가 있는, 은혜를 입은, 신세 진

I'm indebted to you for your help during my illness.
내가 아팠을 때 도와주어 당신에게 신세를 졌다.

I find that strange. 나는 그것이 이상하다고 여긴다.
find+목적어+형용사(목적어를 ~라고 여기다)

whitewash ~에 백색도료를 바르다, ~의 결점(과실)을 감추다

His wife had wanted to whitewash his reputation after he died.
그의 아내는 그가 죽고 난 후에 그의 평판에 대해 눈가림을 하려고 했었다.

They tried to whitewash the incident.
그들은 사건을 축소, 은폐하려 했다.

rate ~할 가치(자격)가 있다, ~을 받을만하다(deserve)

The incident didn't even rate a mention in the press.
그 사건은 신문에서 언급할 가치조차 없었다.

a modern-day princess ***born*** to privilege ***inherited*** from a ruthless dictator
= a modern-day princess ***who was born*** to privilege ***which was inherited*** from a ruthless dictator
비정한 독재자로부터 물려받은 특권을 갖고 태어난 현대판 공주

leave + 목적어 + ~ing ~한 채로 놔두다, ~인 채로 남겨두다

Somebody has left the water running.
누군가 물을 틀어놓은 채로 두었다.

dismiss ~ as 치부하다, 간주하다

regard (A as B)
consider (A (as) B)
think of (A as B)
count (A as B)
look (up)on (A as B)

That piece of information became regarded as a groundless rumor.
그 정보는 근거 없는 소문으로 치부되었다.

heartstrings 심금(心琴), 깊은 애정(감정)

pull[tug] at a person's heartstrings
남의 심금을 울리다

soft spot 약점, 취약점; 특별한 애착

He has a soft spot for girls.
그는 여자에 약하다.

instil (주의 · 감정 등을) 서서히 불어넣다, (~에) 주입시키다(in, into)

The teacher instilled the idea of honesty in his students' mind.
그 교사는 학생들에게 정직의 개념을 심어주었다.

a complex loyalty to him ***that*** is oddly parallel to the feeling ***that*** North Koreans had after Kim Il-sung's 46-year-long rule
= a complex loyalty (to him) + ***(and) it*** (=a complex loyalty) is oddly parallel to the feeling + ***(and)*** North Koreans had ***it***(the feeling) after Kim Il-sung's 46-year-long rule
북한 사람들이 46년간의 김일성의 통치 후에 가졌던 감정과 이상하게도 비슷한 복합적인 충성심
that ***관계대명사***

at the helm 대표로

(항해) 키(의 손잡이), 조타장치, 지도(적 지위)
Park was at the helm of the firm during the turbulent 1960s through the 1980s.
박 명예회장은 격동의 60년대부터 80년대까지 포스코 회장직을 지냈다.

pit 싸우게 하다, 맞붙어 싸우다

The political parties are pitted against each other over tax cuts.
정당들은 세금감면을 둘러싸고 맞붙어 싸우고 있다.

remain + 형용사 여전히 ~하다

remains vague
여전히 불확실하다

at long last (오랜 기간이 지난 뒤에) 가까스로, 간신히, 마침내

At long last, bullet trains are coming to the US.
마침내 미국에 고속철도가 들어설 예정이다.

attachment 애착, 애정, 믿음

However, it is extremely rare to see a Buddhist monk spooling out his or her wisdom of compassion and attachment in English.

그러나 영어로 동정과 믿음에 관한 그들의 지혜를 풀어내는 스님을 보기란 굉장히 어렵다.

fears and misguided attachments ***left*** by a war ***that*** stopped, but did not end, in 1953
= fears and misguided attachments ***which were left*** by a war **+ *(and) it***(a war) stopped, but did not end, in 1953

1953년에 멈추었지만 끝나지 않았던 전쟁으로 남겨진 두려움과 잘못된 애정

Memo

04.

With Simple Actions and Dress, New Pope Shifts Tone at Vatican

VATICAN CITY - He stopped to pay his *hotel bill[1] a day after becoming pope. He wore simple black shoes and an ordinary wristwatch with a thick black band to his first *Mass[2] as *pontiff[3]. He rode in a minivan to dinner with the cardinals who elected him, affectionately telling them, "May God forgive you for what you've done."

Pope Francis began his first full day *in office[4] on Thursday with *private prayers[5] at a Roman *basilica[6] dedicated to the Virgin Mary[1)].

"Hopefully, the *Curia[7] will not eat him alive. I don't know how such a pastoral and humble man will deal with *entrenched[8] *Vatican bureaucracy[9]."

In an ancient institution where style often translates into substance, Francis[2)], in his first 24 hours as pope, has dramatically shifted the tone of the *papacy[10]. Whereas Benedict XVI[3)], the *pope emeritus[11], was a theologian who

1 hotel bill
호텔요금

2 Mass
미사, 예배

3 pontiff
로마교황(Pope)

4 in office
재임의, 재직의

5 private prayers
개인예배

6 basilica
성당

7 Curia = the Roman Curia, the central government of the Church
로마 쿠리아(교회 중앙정부)

8 entrenched
참호로 둘러싸인, 견고한

9 Vatican bureaucracy
바타칸(로마교황청) 관료

10 papacy
교황의 지위, 교황직

11 pope emeritus
명예교황

1) **Virgin Mary** 성모마리아(예수의 어머니). 그녀는 특히 Roman Catholics에 의해 존경을 받는다.

2) **Francis** (2013. 03. 13~) 프란치스코(제 266대 교황).

3) **Benedict XVI** (1927. 04. 16 ~) 베네딕트 16세(제 265대 교황) 2005~2013.

12 loafer loafer jacket
(패션용어) 로퍼 재킷

13 ermine-lined cloaks
흰 쪽제비 줄이 있는 망토

14 radical humility
철저한 겸손

15 Rev. = Reverend
성직자에 대한 경칭, 신부, 목사

16 Vatican Secretariat of State
로마교황청 사무국

17 patron saint
수호성인

18 careerism
출세 제일주의, 출세

19 side chapel
부속성당

20 the faithful
신도

favored red *loafers[12], *ermine-lined cloaks[13] and erudite homilies, reviving papal fashions from centuries past, Francis, the former Cardinal Jorge Mario Bergoglio[4)] of Buenos Aires, appeared Thursday to be sending a message of *radical humility[14].

"This choice indicates above all a style for the church: simplicity, poverty, rigor," said the *Rev.[15] Antonio Spadaro, the editor of La Civiltà Cattolica, a Jesuit journal close to the *Vatican Secretariat of State[16].

Francis, who chose the name of a medieval *patron saint[17] of Italy who came from a wealthy family and took a vow of poverty, is the first pope to come from the Jesuit order[5)], whose members take a vow of poverty and have traditionally shunned *careerism[18], instead focusing on service, education and engaging with the world.

On his first morning as pope, Francis slipped out of the Vatican to pray privately to the Virgin Mary in Santa Maria Maggiore, a Roman basilica dedicated to her. He also prayed in a *side chapel[19] where St. Ignatius Loyola, who founded the Jesuits, celebrated his first Christmas Mass.

On Thursday, Cardinal Jean-Pierre Ricard, the archbishop of Bordeaux, France, recalled how, soon after Francis greeted *the faithful[20] from the loggia[6)] at St. Peter's Basilica for the

4) **Jorge Mario Bergoglio** 교황이 되기 전의 교황의 이름.

5) **Jesuit order** (예수회) 종교개혁에 대항해서 카톨릭을 방어하고, 이교도들 사이에서 전도업무를 하기 위해 1534년 성 이그나티우스 로욜라에 의해 창설된 로마 카톨릭의 한 교단(파); 주로 교육과 학문에 헌신한다.

6) **loggia** ((英)로지아) 한 쪽 또는 그 이상의 면이 트여 있는 방이나 복도. 특히 주택에서 거실 등의 한쪽면이 정원으로 연결되도록 트여 있는 형태. 한쪽만 벽이 있는 복도.

first time as pope, he left with the cardinals to return to their residence during the *conclave[21].

"When he left to go back with us to Santa Marta, the staff moved us aside, because usually the pope descends alone in the elevator," Cardinal Ricard said. "And he said, 'No no, no, no, we can all get in.' And so we all got into the elevator, with the pope.

"And when we got to the bottom, he said, 'No, I am coming with you,' and he got in the bus with us, and the papal car left empty," he added. "I think this is the style of our new pope."

In a homily delivered in a Mass in the Sistine Chapel with the cardinals who elected him, Francis spoke of the need to build faith the way the apostle Peter[7)] built the church on the foundations of the *Gospels[22]. "When we don't walk, we stop," he said, as rows of cardinals in pale yellow *vestments[23] scrutinized him closely.

"When you don't build on stone, what happens becomes like what happens to children on the beach when they build sand castles. Everything falls down," he added.

Francis' more conversational tone, albeit dense in biblical allusions, came in contrast to the style of Benedict, whose speeches often expounded on the interplay between faith and reason.

On his way back to the Vatican after praying to the Virgin Mary, Francis stopped at the clerical residence in Rome where he had stayed before the conclave to collect his luggage and

21 conclave
(가톨릭)
(추기경이 모이는)
교황선거 비밀회의(장).
콘클라베

22 Gospels
복음서

23 vestment
예복. (교회) 성직복

7) **apostle Peter** 그리스도의 12제자중의 한 사람인 베드로 사도.

24 clergy
성직자들

25 audience
(국왕, 교황 등의) 공식회견, 알현

have an audience with (the Pope)
(교황)을 배알하다

26 cassock
성직자 등이 입는 검은색의 평상복, 설교복 밑에 입는 검은 비단 더블상의

27 surplice
(교회) 소매가 넓은 흰 성직자복

28 crippling
(병 · 장애 등이) 심한

29 sovereign debt crisis
국가부채 위기

30 name
임명하다, 지명하다

31 press office
(정부 · 정당 · 기업 등의) 홍보담당부서

32 the name he chose
새 교황의 이름으로 Francis를 선택함

to pay his bill. "He wanted to send a message" to the *clergy[24], the Vatican spokesman, the Rev. Federico Lombardi, said Thursday.

For an *audience[25] that he will hold with cardinals on Friday, the pope instructed them to wear plain black *cassocks[26], and not red with white lace *surplices[27].

Francis comes from Argentina, which was hit by a *crippling[28] *sovereign debt crisis[29] in 2001 from which it has not fully recovered.

Cardinal Philippe Barbarin of Lyon, France, recalled that he had asked Cardinal Bergoglio why he was not going to Rome last December when Benedict was *naming[30] more cardinals.

"And he told me that right now the situation in Argentina was too terrible; he couldn't leave Argentina," Cardinal Barbarin said. "For me, that was significant. In a moment where the country is going badly, he said, 'I have to be here.' He could have happily come to a party in Rome, but he didn't."

The Rev. Enzo Fortunato, the director of the *press office[31] at the Basilica of St. Francis in Assisi, Italy, where the new pope has an open invitation to visit, was thrilled at *the name he chose[32]. "I think this choice indicates the vitality of the church," he said. "St. Francis was a man of the church," and "simplicity and humility give breadth to the church," he added.

For Italians, the pope, who was born in Argentina to parents from the northern Italian region of Piedmont, may quickly become the most beloved Argentine since Diego Maradona, who played for the Napoli soccer club in the 1980s.

Already, they are praising his warmth and *common touch[33]. "He almost brought me to tears when he asked to be blessed by us, before blessing us," said Fabrizio Venanzoni, 21, an engineering student, as he stood in St. Peter's Square on Wednesday evening holding a sign that read, "We'll follow you, @pontifex," referring to the papal Twitter handle.

"And then he opened his speech with two simple words, 'Buona sera,' " or 'Good evening,' " Mr. Venanzoni added. "It made me feel like he is one of us, he is close to simple people. It made me hope that St. Peter's will no longer be a building, but a home for all those who have felt neglected by theologians and scholars."

33 common touch
서민성, 대중친화성

Reuters March 15, 2013

WORDS and STRUCTURES

Mass 1) 미사, 예배

The new pontiff's inaugural Mass was held a week later, on March 19.
신임교황의 취임미사가 1주일 후, 3월19일에 열렸다.

2) 대중의

We are talking about the world and the masses.
우리는 세상과 대중에 대해 이야기하고 있다.

3) 대량의, 대규모의

Customers can expect to pay about 37 million won if the car goes into mass production
소비자들은 그 자동차가 대량생산된다면 3천 7백 만원 정도를 지불할 수 있을 것으로 예상된다.

cardinal 1) 추기경

Pope(교황) – Cardinal(추기경) – Archbishop(대주교) – Bishop(주교) – Priest(사제) – Deacon(부제); Laity(평신도)
Monsignor: the title of a priest of high rank in the Catholic Church

2) 기본적인, 중요한

What are the four cardinal virtues?
네 가지의 주요 덕목은 무엇입니까?

at a Roman basilica ***dedicated*** to the Virgin Mary
= at a Roman basilica ***which was dedicated*** to the Virgin Mary

eat somebody alive ~을 잡아먹을 듯이 굴다

She seems like she is going to eat her daughter-in-law alive.
그녀는 그녀의 며느리를 잡아먹을 듯이 대한다.

erudite 학구적인, 유식(박식)한

There has been much erudite discussion about the origin of names.
이름의 기원에 관한 많은 학구적인 논의가 있어왔다.

homily 설교

In his homily Sunday, he urged young Catholics to keep God at the center of their lives and underlined the importance of Sunday Mass and receiving Holy Communion.
그는 일요일 설교에서 젊은 천주교도들이 하느님을 그들의 생활의 중심에 두기를 촉구했고 일요미사와 영성체를 받는 것의 중요성을 강조했다.

reviving papal fashions from centuries past,
= ***and they***(red loafers, ermine-lined cloaks and erudite homilies) ***revive*** papal fashions from centuries past,
그런데 그것들은 과거 수세기로부터 교황의 패션을 되살려놓고 있다.

Whereas Benedict XVI(, the pope emeritus,) ***was a theologian*** (who favored red loafers, ermine-lined cloaks and erudite homilies,) (reviving papal fashions from centuries past,) ***Francis***(, the former Cardinal Jorge Mario Bergoglio of Buenos Aires,) ***appeared*** Thursday to be sending a message of radical humility.
명예 교황인 베네딕트 16세가 과거 수세기로부터 교황의 패션을 부활시키면서 붉은 재킷과 흰족제비 줄이 있는 망토와 현학적인 설교를 좋아했던 신학자였던 반면에 이전에 브에노스 아이레스의 조지 마리오 베르고그리오 추기경이었던 프란시스는 목요일 철저한 겸손의 메시지를 브내는 것처럼 보였다.
Whereas + 주어(Benedict XVI) + 동사(was) + 보어(a theologian), 주어(Francis) + 동사(appeared)

take a vow 맹세하다, 서약하다

In Roman Catholicism, priests and nuns take a vow of celibacy.
로마 가톨릭교에서 신부와 수녀들은 금욕을 서약한다.

Francis(, who chose the name of a medieval patron saint of Italy who came from a wealthy family and took a vow of poverty,) ***is*** the first ***pope*** to come from the Jesuit order
프라시스, 그런데 그는 부유한 가문 출신이면서 가난의 서약을 했던 중세 이태리 수호성인의 이름을 선택했는데, 예수회 계열에서 나온 첫 교황이다
주어(Francis) + 동사(is) + 보어(pope)

whose members take a vow of poverty and have traditionally shunned careerism,
= ***and their*** members take a vow of poverty and have traditionally shunned careerism,
그런데 예수회 교인들은 가난의 서약을 하고 전통적으로 출세를 피했다(싫어했다)

instead ***focusing*** on service, education and engaging with the world
= instead ***they focused*** on service, education and engaging with the world
대신 그들은 봉사, 교육, 세상사에 참여하는 것에 집중했다.

We succeeded in ***slipping out of*** the meeting unnoticed.
우리는 그 집회에서 들키지 않고 몰래 빠져나오는데 성공했다.

a Roman basilica ***dedicated*** to her
= a Roman basilica ***which was dedicated*** to her
그녀에게 헌정된 로마대성당

in a side chapel ***where*** St. Ignatius Loyola, who founded the Jesuits, celebrated his first Christmas Mass
= in a side chapel ***and there*** St. Ignatius Loyola, who founded the Jesuits, celebrated his first Christmas Mass
부속 성당에서, 그런데 그곳에서 예수회를 성설했던 성 로욜라는 그의 첫 크리스마스 미사를 경축했다.

albeit dense in biblical allusions,
= ***though it(the tone) is*** dense in biblical allusions,
비록 대화 투의 어조가 성경의 암시 속에 응축되어 있다하더라도

the style of Benedict, ***whose*** speeches often expounded on the interplay between faith and reason

= the style of Benedict, ***and his*** speeches often expounded on the interplay between faith and reason

베네딕트의 스타일, 그런데 그의 연설들은 종종 신앙과 이성 사이의 상호작용에 관해 소상하게 설명했다.

deliver (연설 · 강연 등을) 하다

She is due to deliver a lecture on genetic engineering.

그녀는 유전 공학에 대해 강연을 하기로 되어 있다.

The way (that) 명사절 ~하는 식

I don't like the way he laughs. 그가 웃는 꼴이 마음에 안 든다

The way 부사절 ~하는 식에 따라, ~하는 식으로는

They will fail the way the others did. 다른 사람들이 실패한 것처럼 그들도 실패할 것이다.

scrutinize …을 정밀하게 조사하다, …을 빤히 쳐다보다

Vance was scrutinizing her closely.

밴스는 그녀를 자세히 관찰하고 있었다.

expound (이론 · 취지 등을) (남에게) 소상하게 설명하다, (경전 등을) 해설하다, 해석하다

He expounded on the events leading up to the revolution.

그는 혁명을 야기한 사건들에 대해 자세하게 설명했다.

hit crisis 위기가 덮치다

Then, a series of financial crises hit France, along with most of Europe.

그 후 일련의 재정위기가 유럽 대부분 지역과 더불어 프랑스를 덮쳤다.

Francis comes from Argentina, ***which*** was hit by a crippling sovereign debt crisis in 2001 ***from which*** it has not fully recovered.

= Francis comes from Argentina, ***and it*** was hit by a crippling sovereign debt crisis in 2001, ***and it***(Argentina) has not fully recovered ***from it***(a crippling sovereign debt crisis)

프란시스는 아르헨티나 출신인데, 아르헨티나는 2001년 심한 국가 부채위기가 덮쳤고, 그 위기에서 아직 완전히 회복하지 못하고 있다.

The ***Rev. Enzo Fortunato***(, the director of the press office at the Basilica of St. Francis in Assisi, Italy, ***where*** the new pope has an open invitation to visit,) ***was thrilled at*** the name he chose.

= The ***Rev. Enzo Fortunato***(, the director of the press office at the Basilica of St. Francis in Assisi, Italy, ***and there*** the new pope has an open invitation to visit,) ***was thrilled at*** the name ***which*** he chose.

그런데 그곳에서 새 교황은 언제와도 좋다는 초대를 받은 상태인데, 엔조 신부는 새 교황이 선택했던 이름에 흥분해 있다.

I have an ***open invitation*** to visit my friend in Japan.

나는 일본에 있는 친구에게서 언제 와도 좋다는 초대를 받은 상태이다.

thrilled (너무 좋아서) 황홀해 하는, 아주 흥분한, (신이 난)

He was thrilled at the prospect of seeing them again.

그는 그들을 다시 만날 생각에 몹시 흥분되었다.

simple = ordinary (명사 앞에서) 사람이 평범한

I'm a simple country girl.

나는 그저 평범한 시골 처녀일 뿐이다.

05.

Road to implosion?

North Korea angered its neighbors — South Korea, Japan and its ally China — and the United States when it conducted another nuclear test Tuesday in defiance of *U.N. resolutions[1]. The beleaguered *communist state[2] did so apparently in the *misguided belief[3] that *nuclear armament[4] would provide protection for its *regime[5] headed by the young leader Kim Jong-un.

Contrary to its wishes, however, North Korea may hasten its implosion by making a costly attempt to arm itself with nuclear bombs and long-range missiles. *Weapons of mass destruction[6] can hardly provide foolproof protection against an *ailing economy[7], as evidenced by the collapse of the Soviet Union[1)].

South Korea condemned the nuclear test as an "impermissible

1 U.N. resolutions
유엔 결의안

2 communist state
공산주의 국가

3 misguided belief
잘못된 믿음

4 nuclear armament
핵무장

5 regime
정권, 체제

6 weapons of mass destruction(WMD)
대량살상무기

7 ailing economy
병든 국가

1) **Soviet Union** (the ~) (소비에트 연방) 공식명 the Union of Soviet Socialist Republics(USSR) 소비에트 사회주의 공화국 연방, 1991년 해체됨.

8 highly provocative act
아주 도발적인 행동

9 forthcoming
다가오는, 뒤따르는, 예정된

10 U.S.-led U.N. sanctions
미국주도의 유엔 제재

11 subdued
억제된, 완화된

12 non-nuclearization
비핵화

13 nuclear proliferation
핵확산

14 its ally
북한의 동맹국 = 중국

15 denuclearization
비핵화

16 back
지지하다, 옹호하다

threat to peace and security both on the Korean Peninsula and in Northeast Asia." U.S. President Barack Obama, who called the test a "*highly provocative act[8]," hinted at *forthcoming[9] *U.S.-led U.N. sanctions[10] when he said, "The danger posed by North Korea's threatening activities warrants further swift and credible action by the international community."

A more *subdued[11] response came from China, which said, "It is China's firm stance to realize *non-nuclearization[12] for the Korean Peninsula and prevent *nuclear proliferation[13] and maintain peace and stability in Northeast Asia." Still, North Korea will do well not to take the comment lightly, given that *its ally[14] did not look the other way, as it had done before.

As one expert on China pointed out, Beijing, which is championing *denuclearization[15] for the Korean Peninsula, may regard the test as an insult and endorse U.N. sanctions this time, as it *backed[16] the U.N. sanctions that followed North Korea's December launch of a long-range missile.

2) **The United Nations Security Council** (UNSC, 유엔 안전보장 이사회) is one of the six principal organs of the United Nations and is charged with the maintenance of international peace and security. Its powers include the establishment of peacekeeping operations, the establishment of international sanctions, and the authorization of military action through Security Council resolutions; it is the only UN body with the authority to issue binding resolutions to member states. The Security Council held its first session on 17 January 1946.The Security Council consists of fifteen members. The great powers that were the victors of World War II— Russia, the United Kingdom, and the United States — along with France and China, serve as the body's five permanent members. These permanent members can veto any substantive Security Council resolution, including those on the admission of new member states or candidates for Secretary-General. The Security Council also has 10 non-permanent members, elected on a regional basis to serve two-year terms. The body's presidency rotates monthly between its members(Wikipedia).

As a *permanent member[17] of the U.N. Security Council[2)], China had on earlier occasions vetoed proposals for U.N. sanctions against North Korea for its provocative actions or threatened to veto tough-worded U.N. *draft resolutions[18] unless they had been watered down.

But Chinese support for the U.N. sanctions against the missile launch signaled a shift in China's North Korea policy. The change coincided with the *ongoing[19] *leadership transition[20] to Xi Jinping[3)]. Still, it is yet to be seen what action China will take when the U.N. Security Council moves to sanction North Korea for its latest nuclear test.

In addition to spearheading the adoption of tough U.N. resolutions, Washington may take action against the wayward communist state alone and together with its allies, such as South Korea and Japan.

It should not come as a surprise if Washington decides to tighten the economic noose around North Korea's neck. A bill banning food aid to North Korea is already awaiting action in the U.S. House of Representatives[4)].

17 permanent member
상임이사국

18 draft resolutions
결의안 초고

19 ongoing
계속하고 있는, 진행 중인

20 leadership transition
권력이양

3) **Xi jinping** (시진핑) 중국의 정치인. 저장성 · 상하이시 서기를 거쳐 당 중앙정치국 상구위원, 국가부주석, 중앙군사위원회 부주석을 맡았다. 2013년 3월 국가주석과 국가중앙군사위원회 주석에 선출되었다(두산백과).

4) **The United States House of Representatives** (미 의회의 하원) is one of the two houses of the United States Congress. It is frequently referred to as the House. The other house is the Senate(Wikipedia).

21 decades-long economic mismanagement 수 십 년간 이어져온 경제정책실패

North Korea had been pushing Washington to take retaliatory action when it openly said it had considered the United States as the potential target of attack when it conducted missile launches and nuclear tests.

It is not the United States alone that is withholding food aid to North Korea whose population is chronically underfed, with what scarce resources it holds in its possession diverted to developing weapons of mass destruction. Given a World Food Program[5)] report that North Korea has received no food aid from any country since its missile launch, the chronic food shortage will undoubtedly be exacerbated in the coming months.

Should North Korea collapse anytime in the future, it would be triggered by the weight of its own economic problems rather than any outside security threat. Long-range missiles and nuclear bombs would be of no help in deterring an implosion that could come as a consequence of *decades-long economic mismanagement[21]. North Korea should have learned a lesson from the disintegration of the Soviet Union in December 1991.

5) **World Food Program** (세계식량계획) 세계 식량안보와 국빈국의 농업개발 문제, 식량개발에 관한 정책토의, 식량원조 모금, 개발도상국의 식량지급 정책에 관한 지원을 하는 국제기구. 1961년 국제연합(UN)총회와 국제연합식량 농업기구(FAO)의 결정에 의해 설립되었으며 세계식량회의(WFC: World Food Council)의 결의를 신속하게 실행하기 위해 각국의 의견을 조정한다(한경 경제용어사전).

6) **Mikhail Gorbachev** (미하일 고르바초프) 러시아의 정치가로서 구 소련공산당 서기장과 최초의 대통령(재임 1990.3 ~ 1991.12.25)을 지냈다. 페레스트로이카(개혁)를 추진하여 소련 국내의 개혁과 개방뿐 아니라, 동유럽의 민주화 개혁 등 세계질서에도 큰 변혁을 가져왔다. 1990년 노벨평화상을 받았으며, 1991년 공산당을 해체하여 소련의 공산 통치사에 마침표를 찍었다(두산백과).

As he *rose to power[22] in 1985, Mikhail Gorbachev[6)] had tried to pull the Soviet Union out of chronic economic stagnation by adopting *glasnost[23] and *perestroika[24] for reform. But it was too late to reform the obsolete Soviet system and keep it from collapsing under its own weight.

Kim Jong-un, now 30, will do well to be taught about the Soviet demise as he is too young to have first-hand knowledge about it.

koreaherald.co.kr February 14, 2013

22 rise to power
집권하다

23 glasnost
(구소련의) 정보 공개, 글라스노스트, 개방

24 perestroika
페레스트로이카, 개혁, 소련공산당서기장 Mikhail Gorbachev의 개혁정책

WORDS and STRUCTURES

implosion 내파

Another possible scenario for which Seoul should prepare for is North Korea's implosion amid leadership confusion.
한국정부가 대비해야 할 또 하나의 가능한 시나리오는 북한이 지도력의 혼란 속에 내부에서 붕괴할지도 모른다는 것이다.

in defiance of (법 · 명령 따위)를 무시하여, 무릅쓰고

He became a singer in defiance of the family's tradition.
그는 집안의 전통을 무시하고 가수가 되었다.

beleaguered 포위된, 사면초가에 몰린

The beleaguered party leader was forced to resign.
사면초가에 몰린 당 대표는 어쩔 수 없이 사임을 해야 했다.

did so = conducted another nuclear test Tuesday in defiance of U.N. resolutions
유엔 결의안을 무시하고 화요일에 또 다시 핵실험을 했다.

apparently (문장 전체를 수식하여) 보기에, 외관상

I didn't see the accident, but apparently it was his fault.
나는 그 사고를 목격하지 못했지만 보기에는 그의 과실인 것 같다.

the misguided belief that
that = 동격의 that

provide protection 보호를 제공하다, 보호하다

It is clear that the primary duty of parents is to provide protection for our children.
부모의 일차적인 의무가 아이들을 보호하는 것임은 분명하다.

nuclear armament would provide protection for its regime ***headed*** by the young leader Kim Jong-un
= nuclear armament would provide protection for its regime ***(which is) headed*** by the young leader Kim Jong-un
핵무장이 젊은 지도자 김정은에 의해 영도되는 정권을 보호해 줄 것이다.

foolproof 아주 간단한, (계획 · 방법 등이) 확실한

The bank has a foolproof security system.
그 은행에는 확실한 안전장치가 있다.

Weapons of mass destruction can ***hardly*** provide foolproof protection against an ailing economy.
대량살상무기가 병든 국가에 대한 확실한 보호를 거의 해 줄 수 없다

as ***evidenced*** by the collapse of the Soviet Union
= as ***(it is) evidenced*** by the collapse of the Soviet Union
소련의 붕괴에 의해 그것이 입증되는 바와 같이

condemn (~ sb/sth (for/as sth) (보통 도덕적인 이유로) 규탄[비난]하다

The editor of the newspaper was condemned as lacking integrity.
그 신문의 편집자는 진실성이 부족하다는 비난을 받았다.

hint at 암시하다, 시사하다

Arafat and Peres hinted at breakthrough in peace talks Monday.
아라파트와 페레스는 월요일 평화회담에서 획기적인 타결 책을 시사했다.

U.S. President Barack Obama, ***who*** called the test a “highly provocative act”
= U.S. President Barack Obama, ***and he*** called the test a “highly provocative act”
call + A + B A를 B라고 부르다

The danger ***posed*** by North Korea’s threatening activities warrants further swift and credible action by the international community.”
= The danger ***(which is) posed*** by North Korea’s threatening activities warrants further swift and credible action by the international community.”
주어 danger 동사 warrant 목적어 action
북한의 위협적인 행위들로 야기된 위험은 국제사회의 추가의 신속하고 신뢰할 수 있는 행동을 정당화 한다.

proliferation 확산

Federal policy is changing to curb the proliferation of nuclear weapons.
연방 정부 정책은 핵무기 확산을 억제하는 쪽으로 바뀌고 있다.

still 그럼에도 불구하고, 그런데도

The weather was cold and wet. Still, we had a great time.
날씨는 춥고 궂었다. 그런데도 우리는 대단히 즐거운 시간을 보냈다.

do well to do ~하는 편(것)이 좋다

It is a foolish thing and you would do well not to repeat such aphorisms.
그것은 어리석은 짓이다 그러니 그런 격언들을 반복하지 않는 것이 좋을 것이다.

not to take the comment lightly 그 논평을 가볍게 받아들이지 않는 것

look the other way 못 본(모르는) 척하다, 무시하다

Prison officers know what's going on, but look the other way.
교도관들은 무슨 일이 벌어지는지 알고 있지만 모르는 척 한다.

as it had done before = as it had looked the other way
이전에 중국이 모르는 척 했었듯이

champion 옹호하다

President Lee was all about smiles as he championed the crowd at the Rio+20 Conference on Sustainable Development.
이 대통령은 지속가능발전에 관한 Rio+20 정상회의에서 청중들의 견해를 옹호하는 발언을 하면서 웃음이 만연했다.

endorse 지지하다

I wholeheartedly endorse his remarks.
저는 진심으로 그의 발언을 지지한다.

veto 거부하다

The mayor who is on a hot seat these days vetoed the ordinance.
요즘 책임이 막중한 시장은 그 법령을 거부했다.

provocative 도발적인, 자극적인

It isn't wise to ignore a regime with a propensity to engage in provocative actions.
도발적 행동의 경향이 있는 정권을 무시하는 것은 지혜롭지 못하다

draft resolution 결의안 초안

Even its traditional ally China has agreed to the draft resolution.
전통적으로 동맹국인 중국마저도 결의안 초안에 동의했다.

water down 물을 타다, (표현을) 약하게 하다

He tried to water down his remarks.
그 남자는 자신의 말을 적당하게 돌려 말하려고 했다.

unless they had been watered down
= ***if*** they(= tough-worded U.N. draft resolutions) had ***not*** been watered down
만일 거친 말로 되어있는 결의안 초고가 완화되지 않는다면

coincide 일치하다, 동시에 일어나다

The meeting coincides with the second anniversary of the death of two Korean high schoolgirls.
이번 회의는 미군에 의한 두 명의 여중생 사망사건 2주기와 때를 맞춰 열리고 있다.

be yet to do, have yet to do 아직 ~(하지) 않다

We have yet to see the full effect of this negative impact of technology.
우리는 아직 기술의 부정적인 영향의 완전한 효과를 보지 못했다.

spearhead ~의 선두에 서다

The media should spearhead a movement against the corrupt officials.
언론이 부패관리에 반대하는 운동에 앞장서야 한다.

wayward (사람 · 태도 등이) 고집불통인, 제멋대로인, 걷잡을 수 없는

China, however, rejected suggestions of taking a hard line with its wayward ally.
그러나 중국은 까다로운 동맹국(북한)에게 단호히 대처하자는 제안들을 거절했다.

come as a surprise 놀라움으로 다가오다

His stoicism should not come as a surprise.
그의 인내는 놀라운 일이 아니다.

if (= even if) (비록) …일지라도, (설사) …이라고 할지라도

noose 올가미

The government is stepping up its efforts to tighten the noose around the neck of smokers to help them kick the habit.
정부는 흡연자들이 담배를 끊는 것을 돕기 위해 이들에 대한 제약을 더욱 강화하기 위해 앞장서고 있다.

retaliatory 보복의

Without the threat of a retaliatory strike, countries can attack others at will.
보복공격의 위협 없이, 많은 나라들은 다른 나라들을 마음대로 공격할 수 있다.

withhold 보류하다, 중단하다

Delegations from nine other countries withheld approval because they lacked authority to sign.
다른 9개국대표단은 합의를 체결 할 권한이 없어 동의를 보류했다.

population 인구, 사람들, 주민

Koreans use more water than other foreign countries with large populations.
한국 사람들은 인구가 더 많은 다른 나라들보다도 더 많은 물을 쓰고 있다.

chronically 만성적으로

The chronically poor failed to benefit as the economy improved.
경제가 호전되었는데도 만성적으로 가난한 사람들은 이득을 얻지 못했다.

scarce resources 부족한 자원

Offering funds to these companies is just a waste of scarce resources.
이런 회사들에 자금을 제공하는 것은 단지 귀한 자원의 낭비에 블과하다.

It is not the United States alone ***that*** is withholding food aid to North Korea whose population is chronically underfed, with what scarce resources it holds in its possession diverted to developing weapons of mass destruction.
북한에 식량원조를 중단하려고 하는 것은 미국 뿐이 아닌데, 북한은 주민이 만성적으로 영양실조에 걸려 있고, 북한이 가지고 있는 참으로 부족한 자원도 대량살상무기개발로 돌리고 있다.

It is ~ that 강조 구문

It was a book that I bought yesterday. 어제 내가 산 것은 책이다.

It is he that deserves to be praised. 칭찬받아 마땅한 사람은 그이다.

North Korea ***whose*** population is chronically underfed
= North Korea, ***and its*** population is chronically underfed
(인구가 만성적으로 영양실조에 걸려있는 북한)

with + 목적어 + 보어(형용사, 분사, 부사구) ~한 상태로, ~하면서

He sat with his eyes closed.
그는 그의 눈을 감고 앉아있었다.

She left the kitchen with the kettle boiling.
그녀는 주전자 물이 끓는 것을 그대로 두고 부엌을 나갔다.

He stood with his back against the wall.
그는 등을 벽에 기댄 채 서 있었다.

with what scarce resources it holds in its possession ***diverted*** to developing weapons of mass destruction
(북한이 가지고 있는 참으로 부족한 자원도 대량살상무기개발로 돌리고)

divert 전용하다, 딴 데로 돌리다, 우회하다

King said that those types of foods are easily diverted by the military.
킹 특사는 그러한 종류의 식량은 군부로 흘러들어갈 가능성이 높다고 밝혔다.

given ~이 주어지면, ~라고 감안하면

Given time, it can be done.
시간만 있으면 될 수 있는 일이다.

exacerbate 악화시키다

Pollution and natural disasters exacerbate the situation.
오염과 자연재해는 이 상황을 더 악화시킨다.

Should North Korea collapse anytime in the future
= ***If North Korea should collapse*** anytime in the future
만일 장래 언젠가 붕괴한다면

deter 억제하다, 막다, 단념시키다

The death penalty deters crimes.
사형이 범죄를 억제한다.

It is to deter people from junk food.
그것은 정크푸드로부터 사람들을 단념시키는 것이다.

mismanagement 부실통치, 잘못된 경영, 실수

North Korea is currently in serious economic decline due to internal mismanagement and international sanctions.
북한은 현재 내부적 부실통치와 국제사회의 제재로 인해 심각한 경제침체를 겪고 있다.

stagnation 침체, 불황, 불경기

Recovery usually follows a period of economic stagnation.
경제회복은 주로 경기 침체기에 뒤 따른다.

obsolete 쇠퇴한, 쓸모없어진, 구식의(out of date)

As time passes, things change, and the things that cannot change are considered obsolete.
시간이 흐름에 따라 사물은 변하고 변할 수 없는 것들은 쓸모없는 것으로 여겨진다.

keep it ***from*** collaps***ing*** 소련이 붕괴되는 것을 막다

demise 사망, 서거, 소멸, (국가의) 종언

The 1980s saw the demise of communism in Eastern Europe.
1980년대에 동유럽에서 공산주의는 종말을 고했다.

first-hand 직접의

The news paper reporter made sure that she got first-hand information for her article.
그 신문기자는 직접들은 정보로 기사를 쓴 것이 확실하다고 말했다.

as he is ***too*** young ***to*** have first-hand knowledge about it.
그는 너무 어려 소련의 붕괴에 대해 직접적으로 알지 못하기 때문에

06.

China should abandon North Korea

North Korea's third nuclear test is a good moment for China to re-evaluate its longstanding alliance with *the Kim dynasty[1]. For several reasons, Beijing should give up on Pyongyang and press for the *reunification[2] of the Korean peninsula.

1 the Kim dynasty
김씨 왕조(북한을 가리킴)

2 reunification
재통일

3 geopolitical ally
지정학적 동맹국

First, a relationship between states based on ideology is dangerous. If we were to choose our allies on ideology alone, China's relationship with the west today would not exist. Although both countries are socialist, their differences are much larger than those between China and the west.

Second, basing China's strategic security on North Korea's value as a *geopolitical ally[3] is outdated. Even if North Korea was a useful friend during the cold war, its usefulness today is doubtful. Just imagine if the US, because of Pyongyang's development of nuclear weapons, came to see North Korea as a grave threat to its national security and launched a pre-emptive attack on it. Would China not be obliged to help North Korea based on our "alliance"? Would that not be drawing fire

4 safeguard
보호수단

5 shared sacrifice
공동의 희생

6 volunteer soldier
의용병

upon ourselves? If so, what useful "buffer" would be left to speak of? China's own strength and openness will be its most reliable *safeguard[4].

Third, North Korea will not reform and open up to the world. The international community once hoped that Kim Jong-eun would push reforms after taking power in 2011, and North Korea seemed to show signs of such a move. But even if he personally had the will to push small-scale reform, the country's ruling group would absolutely not allow him to do so. Once the door of reform opened, the regime could be overthrown. Why should China maintain relations with a regime and a country that will face failure sooner or later?

Fourth, North Korea is pulling away from Beijing. The Chinese like to view their relationship with Pyongyang through their *shared sacrifice[5] during the Korean war instead of reality. They describe it as a "friendship sealed in blood". But North Korea does not feel like this at all towards its neighbour.

As early as the 1960s, North Korea rewrote the history of the war. To establish the absolute authority of Kim Il-sung, its founder, North Korea removed from historical record the contribution of the hundreds of thousands of sons and daughters of China who sacrificed themselves to beat the UN troops back to the 38th parallel that now divides the peninsula. Many cemeteries commemorating the *volunteer soldier[6] heroes have been levelled, and Kim Il-sung was given all the credit for the offensive. For the North Korean people, shaking off the "Chinese bond" was seen as an expression of *independence and autonomy[7].

Last, once North Korea has nuclear weapons, it cannot be ruled out that the capricious Kim regime will engage in nuclear blackmail against China. According to Xue Litai of Stanford University, during former US president Bill Clinton's 2009 visit to Pyongyang, the North Koreans blamed the poverty of their economy on China's "selfish" strategy and American sanctions. Kim Jong-il, then leader, hinted that the motive for withdrawing from six-party talks[1)] on his country's *arms programme[8] was to free Pyongyang from Beijing. It was not directed against the US. He suggested that if Washington held out a helping hand, North Korea could become its strongest fortress against China. And Pyongyang revealed it could use a *nuclear arsenal[9] to coerce China.

7 independence and autonomy
독립과 자주(자율)

8 arms programme
= nuclear arms programme
핵무기개발계획

9 nuclear arsenal
핵무기

1) **The six-party talks** (6자 회담) aim to find a peaceful resolution to the security concerns as a result of the North Korean nuclear weapons program. There has been a series of meetings with six participating states: Republic of Korea, Democratic People's Republic of Korea, United States of America, People's Republic of China, Japan, and Russian Federation. These talks were a result of North Korea withdrawing from the Nuclear Non-Proliferation Treaty (NPT) in 2003. Apparent gains following the fourth and fifth rounds were reversed by outside events. Five rounds of talks from 2003 to 2007 produced little net progress until the third phase of the fifth round of talks, when North Korea agreed to shut down its nuclear facilities in exchange for fuel aid and steps towards the normalization of relations with the United States and Japan. Responding angrily to the United Nations Security Council's Presidential Statement issued on April 13, 2009 that condemned the North Korean failed satellite launch, the DPRK declared on April 14, 2009 that it would pull out of Six Party Talks and that it would resume its nuclear enrichment program in order to boost its nuclear deterrent. North Korea has also expelled all nuclear inspectors from the country(Wikipedia).

10 strategic alliance
전략적 제휴

11 pro-Beijing government
친 중국 정부

12 security assurances
안전보장

North Korea's development of nuclear weapons is, in part, based on the illusion that it can achieve an equal negotiating position with the US, and thereby force Washington to compromise. But it is entirely possible that a nuclear-armed North Korea could try to twist China's arm if Beijing were to fail to meet its demands or if the US were to signal goodwill towards it.

Considering these arguments, China should consider abandoning North Korea. The best way of giving up on Pyongyang is to take the initiative to facilitate North Korea's unification with South Korea. Bringing about the peninsula's unification would help undermine the *strategic alliance[10] between Washington, Tokyo and Seoul; ease the geopolitical pressure on China from northeast Asia; and be helpful to the resolution of the Taiwan question.

The next best thing would be to use China's influence to cultivate a *pro-Beijing government[11] in North Korea, to give it *security assurances[12], push it to give up nuclear weapons and start moving towards the development path of a normal country.

ft.com March 02, 2013

WORDS and STRUCTURES

alliance 동맹, 협력, 제휴

Seoul's alliance with Washington is the linchpin of the country's security policy.
한미동맹은 한국의 안보정책의 근간이다.

give up on (구어체) (글렀다고) ~을 단념하다

His teachers seem to have given up on him.
그의 선생님들이 그를 포기한 것 같다.

give up 포기(단념)하다, 그만두다, 끊다(smoking)

The doctor gave up the patient.
의사는 환자를 포기했다.

press 압박하다

Xiaobo devoted his entire life to advocating basic human rights and pressing for political reform in China.
샤오보는 그의 일평생을 기본인권 옹호와 중국의 정치적 개혁을 압박하는데 일생을 바쳤다.

a relationship between states ***based on*** ideology is dangerous
= a relationship between states ***(which is) based on*** ideology is dangerous
이념에 기반하고 있는 국가들 사이의 관계는 위험하다

If we were to choose our allies on ideology alone, China's relationship with the west today ***would*** not ***exist***.
만일 우리가 오로지 이념을 기반으로 해서 우리의 동맹국을 선택한다면 오늘날 중국의 서방과의 관계는 존재하지 않을 것이다.

가정법 과거 구문(현재사실과 반대)

If + 주어 + 과거동사 ~, 주어 + would + 동사원형

If I had the book, I could lend it to you.

만일 내가 그 책을 가지고 있다면 너에게 빌려줄 수 있을 것이다.

가정법 과거완료 구문(과거사실과 반대)

If + 주어 + had + 과거분사 ~, 주어 + would + have + 과거분사

If I had had the book, I could have lent it to you.

만일 내가 그 책을 가지고 있었더라면 너에게 빌려줄 수 있었을 것이다.

outdated 시대에 뒤진, 구식의

It will be a great benefit to students because many traditional textbooks are outdated.

기존의 교과서 대다수가 구식이기 때문에 그것은 학생들에게 많은 이득이 될 것이다.

pre-emptive attack 선제공격

The U.S. State Department announced that there is no exact evidence to prove that a North Korean pre-emptive attack was made on the sunken vessel.

미국무부는 북한이 침몰한 선박에 선제공격을 했다는 것을 증명할 정확한 증거는 어디에도 없다고 발표했다.

be obliged to + 동사원형 어쩔 수 없이 ~하다, ~할 의무가 있다

We will be obliged to take effective self-defense measures.

우리는 효과적인 자위 조치를 취하지 않을 수 없을 것이다.

draw fire 비난을 초래하다, 화를 자초하다

However, some of the government policies are drawing fire for hurting investor sentiment in the local capital markets.

하지만 정부의 정책 중에는 국내 자본시장에 대한 투자심리를 저해한다는 비난을 받는 것도 있다.

buffer 완충장치

The child was a buffer between the quarreling parents.
자식이 싸우는 부모사이에서 말리는 구실을 했다.

once 일단 ~하면, ~해버리면

Once you learn the basic rules, this game is easy.
일단 기본규칙을 알고 나면 이 게임은 쉽다.

pull away 떠나다

I hope the U.S. will pull away from the unilateral policies and try to balance it out.
나는 미국이 일방적 외교를 그만두고 균형을 취하길 희망한다.

sealed 밀봉된, 맺어진

Love sealed in blood is not easily forgotten.
피로 맺어진 사랑은 쉽게 잊혀 지지 않는다.

feel like ~하고 싶은 생각이 들다

I feel like some snacks. 나는 간식이 좀 먹고 싶다.

beat back 저지하다, 격퇴하다

The Russian guards reportedly beat back the Muslim rebel attack.
러시아 수비대가 회교 반군의 공격을 격퇴했다고 한다.

the hundreds of thousands of sons and daughters of China ***who*** sacrificed themselves to beat the UN troops back to the 38th parallel
= the hundreds of thousands of sons and daughters of China ***+(and) they*** who sacrificed themselves to beat the UN troops back to the 38th parallel
스스로를 희생해 UN군을 격퇴해서 38도선까지 되돌아가게 했던 수십만 명의 중국의 아들과 딸

the 38th parallel that now divides the peninsula
= the 38th parallel ***+(and) it*** now divides the peninsula
한반도를 나누고 있는 38도선

commemorate 기념하다, 기리다

Meanwhile, civic demonstrations commemorating the second anniversary of the death of the two high school girls are also anticipated, said the police.
한편 경찰은 여중생 사망 2주기를 추모하는 민간집회도 열릴 것으로 보인다고 말했다.

Many ***cemeteries*** commemorating the volunteer soldier heroes have been ***levelled***.
주어 cemeteries 동사 level
묘지가 평평하게 되었다(평장이 되었다).

give somebody the credit 누군가에게 영광을 주다

I think you have to give him credit for his bravery on the battlefield.
나는 전장에서의 그의 무공에 대해 공로를 치하해야 한다고 생각한다.

offensive 공격, 모욕적인, 불쾌한

The Bush-Putin summit comes at a time when the Kremlin is on the offensive.
부시-푸틴 정상회담은 크렘린이 공세를 취하고 있는 시기에 이루어졌다.

Citizens of the city have also been asked to report the use of offensive language, including swearing.
또한 그 도시의 시민들은 욕설을 포함하여 불쾌한 언어를 사용하는 경우를 보면 신고할 것을 요청 받았다.

shake off 떨쳐버리다

South Korea can't shake off its notoriety for working hours.
한국인의 긴 근로시간에 대한 악명을 떨쳐버릴 수 없다.

capricious 변덕스러운, 예측할 수 없는

Even though she is often capricious, she's very courteous and modest.
그녀는 가끔 변덕스럽기는 하지만 매우 예의바르고 겸손하다.

engage in 시작하다, 착수하다

He engaged in reconstruction efforts and publicized them across Iraq and elsewhere in the Arab world.
그는 재건작업에 착수하여 이를 이라크전역과 나머지 아랍세계에 널리 알렸다.

blackmail 공갈, 협박

Ahn's aides accused a Saenuri official of blackmail.
안의 보좌관들은 새누리당 관계자를 협박혐의로 고소했다.

blame 탓하다, ~탓으로 돌리다

People have blamed global warming on large corporations.
사람들은 지구 온난화를 대기업의 탓으로 돌려왔다.

coerce 압박하다

South Korea and China remain major aid donors despite some pressure by the United States to reduce the amount of assistance as a tool to coerce Pyongyang to return to the six-party talks.
한국과 중국은 북한의 6자회담 복귀를 압박하기 위해 지원을 줄이라는 미국의 요구에도 불구하고 최대의 지원국이다.

the illusion ***that*** it can achieve an equal negotiating position with the US
the illusion = that 이하(동격의 that)
북한이 미국과 동등한 협상 위치를 달성할 수 있다는 환상(착각)

twist a person's arm 남의 팔을 비틀다, 강요하다, 압력을 가하다

The dictator twisted his people's arm to make more money.
독재자는 돈을 더 벌기 위하여 사람들을 강제로 일을 시켰다.

goodwill 호의

The ancient Chinese sent messages of goodwill to their family and friends to celebrate the New Year.
고대 중국인들은 새해를 축하하기 위해 가족과 친구에게 호의적인 메시지를 보냈다.

Considering these arguments
= ***When we consider*** these arguments
우리가 이러한 주장들을 고려해 볼 때

initiative 주도권

I really need you to take the initiative on this.
나는 당신이 이 일에 정말로 주도권을 갖고 임했으면 한다.

facilitate 촉진하다

There are many who doubt that milk can actually facilitate physical growth.
우유가 실제로 신체의 성장을 촉진시킬 수 있다는 것을 의심하는 사람이 많다.

bring about (병 · 파멸을) 일으키다, (일을) 성취하다

Mr. Jones will bring about many changes in our office.
존스 씨는 회사에 많은 변화를 가져올 것이다.

undermine 약화시키다, 훼손하다

Indeed it undermines the very idea of democracy.
사실상 그것은 민주주의라는 바로 그 이념을 약화시킨다.

cultivate 조성하다, 구축하다

Home schooling also helps to cultivate family ties.
홈스쿨링은 또한 가족 간의 유대를 깊게 하는데 도움이 된다.

Memo

07.

The sequester[1)], explained

The *White House[1] has released its plan explaining how the sequester's *mandatory spending cuts[2] to *defense and domestic spending[3] will be implemented in 2013. Here's the background on what the sequester is, how it happened and what happens from here:

1 White House
백악관(미국대통령 관저)

2 mandatory spending cuts
강제적인 지출삭감

3 defense and domestic spending
국방과 국내지출

1) **sequester** (시퀘스터)는 '격리시킨다'는 의미를 담고 있는 시퀘스트레이션(Sequestration)의 줄임말이다. 원래는 소유권 분쟁 발생 시 법원의 재산 가압류 행위를 가리키는 법률 용어였지만 미국 연방 재정 자동 삭감 조처를 일컫는 말로 사용된다. 다음 회계연도에 허용된 최대 적자 규모 내로 예산을 짜지 못하면 시퀘스터에 의해 정부 재정지출을 자동 삭감해야 한다. 시퀘스터는 1985년 상원 의원 필 그램(텍사스), 워런 러드만(뉴햄프셔), 어니스트 홀링스(사우스캐롤라이나) 등이 주도해 제정한 '균형예산 및 긴급 적자 통제법(그램-러드만-홀링스 적자 감축법: GRH)'에 근거를 두고 있다. 시퀘스터로 미국은 1986년부터 매년 적자 규모를 축소해 1991년 균형예산 달성에 성공했지만 2000년 조지 W. 부시 정부의 출범 이후 다시 적자로 돌아섰다. 미국의 국가 채무는 2012년 16조 2070억 달러(국내총생산 대비 104.3%)에 달했는데, 미국을 빚더미에 올려놓은 주범은 국방비다. 전임 대통령 조지 W. 부시 행정부의 잇따른 전쟁 때문이다. 국가부채가 막대하게 늘어나자 미국 의회는 2011년 8월 '예산 통제법 2011'을 통과시켜 연방 정부 지출을 2013년 1월부터 향후 10년간 1조 2000억 달러 삭감하도록 했다. 2013년 3월 1일 오바마 행정부는 공화당과 최종 합의에 이르지 못해 시퀘스터를 발동했다. 이에 따라 미국은 2013년 850억 달러 예산 삭감을 시작으로 향후 10년간 1조 2000억 달러의 재정 지출을 자동으로 삭감하게 된다. 시퀘스터 발동으로 가장 큰 타격을 입을 것으로 예상되는 예산은 국방 예산이다. 국방부는 2013 회계연도가 끝나는 9월 30일까지 예산의 9퍼센트인 460억 달러의 지출을 줄여야 하는데, 이를 위해선 군수업체에 주는 돈을 줄이고 유지 보수 · 건설비도 대폭 깎아야 한다. 미국 정부는 국방 예산이 크게 줄면 일자리가 사라지고, 무기 수출이 늦어지고, 자국 경제는 물론 세계경제까지 나빠질 것이라고 주장하지만 정작 미국인들은 국방 예산 삭감을 바라고 있다. 여론조사에 따르면, 민주당 지지자 열 명 중 아홉 명이, 공화당 지지자들조차 열 명 중 일곱 명이 국방비를 줄여야 한다는 견해를 보였다. 시퀘스터 발동으로 단기적으로는 미국 경제에 충격이 클 것이라는 전망이 나오고 있지만 시퀘스터가 재정의 건전성을 확보하기 위한 안전장치라는 점에서 장기적으로는 미국 경제가 살아나고 달러화가 강세로 돌아설 가능성이 있다는 분석도 있다(네이버 지식백과, 트렌드 지식사전).

4 **defense spending**
국방비(방위비) 지출

5 **exempt**
면제된

What is the sequester?

It's a package of automatic spending cuts that's part of the Budget Control Act(BCA)[2], which was passed in August 2011. The cuts, which are projected to total $1.2 trillion, are scheduled to begin in 2013 and end in 2021, evenly divided over the nine-year period. The cuts are also evenly split between *defense spending[4] — with spending on wars *exempt[5] — and discretionary domestic spending, which exempts most spending on entitlements[3] like Social Security[4]

2) **Congressional Budget and impoundment Control Act** ((행정)의회예산 및 지출유예 통제법) The Budget Control Act of 2011 is a federal statute in the United States that was signed into law by President Barack Obama on August 2, 2011. The Act brought conclusion to the United States debt-ceiling crisis of 2011, which had threatened to lead the United States into sovereign default on or around August 3, 2011.
The law involves the introduction of several complex mechanisms, such as creation of the Congressional Joint Select Committee on Deficit Reduction(sometimes called the "super committee"), options for a balanced budget amendment and automatic budget sequestration(Wikipedia).

3) **entitlements** ((미)인타이틀먼트 프로그램) In the United States, an entitlement program is a type of "government program that provides individuals with personal financial benefits (or sometimes special government-provided goods or services) to which an indefinite (but usually rather large) number of potential beneficiaries have a legal right...whenever they meet eligibility conditions that are specified by the standing law that authorizes the program. The beneficiaries of entitlement programs are normally individual citizens or residents, although sometimes organizations such as business corporations, local governments, or even political parties may have similar special 'entitlements' under certain programs."Examples of entitlement programs at the federal level in the United States include Social Security, Medicare and Medicaid, most Veterans' Administration programs, federal employee and military retirement plans, unemployment compensation, food stamps, and agricultural price support programs.
Originally, the term "entitlement" in the United States was used to identify federal programs that, like Social Security and Medicare, got the name because workers became "entitled" to their benefits by paying into the system. In recent years the meaning has been used to refer also to benefits, like those of the food stamps program, which people become eligible to receive without paying into a system.Some federal programs are also considered entitlements even though the subscriber's "paying into the system" occurs via a means other than monetary, as in the case of those programs providing for veterans' benefits, and where the individual becomes eligible via service in the U.S. military(Wikipedia).

4) **Social Security** (사회보장연금) 사회의 구성원인 개인의 부상, 질병, 출산, 실업, 노쇠 등의 원인에 의해 생활이 곤궁에 처하게 될 경우에 공공의 재원으로 그 최저생활을 보장하여 주는 제도를 말한다. 이에는 사회부조와 사회보험의 두 가지가 있다. 사회부조는 국가 또는 공공단체가 생활비의 일부 또는 전부를 부조하는 제도이며, 생활곤궁자에 대해서만 부여되는 것이 보통이다. 사회보험은 본인 또는 이를 대신하는 자가 보험료를 적립하고 여기에 국가가 보조를 해주어 상기한 바와 같은 사유가 발생한 경우에는 연금 또는 일시금을 지급하는 제도이다(네이버 지식백과, 매일경제/매경닷컴).

and Medicaid[5], as the Bipartisan Policy Center[6] explains. The total cuts for 2013 will be $109 billion, according to the new White House report.

Under the BCA, the cuts were triggered to take effect beginning Jan. 1 if the supercommittee[7] didn't to agree to a $1.2 trillion *deficit-reduction package[6] by Nov. 23, 2011. The group failed to reach a deal, so the sequester was triggered.

6 deficit-reduction package 일괄 적자감축

7 across-the-board cuts 일괄 삭감

8 affected programs 복지프로그램

Why does everyone hate the sequester so much?

Legislators don't have any discretion with the *across-the-board cuts[7]: They are intended to hit all *affected programs[8] equally, though the cuts to individual areas will range from 7.6 percent to 9.6 percent (and 2 percent to Medicare providers). The indiscriminate pain is meant to pressure legislators into making a budget deal to avoid the cuts.

5) **Medicaid** (미국의 저소득층 의료보장제도) in the United States is a social health care program for families and individuals with low income and resources. The Health Insurance Association of America describes Medicaid as a "government insurance program for persons of all ages whose income and resources are insufficient to pay for health care." Medicaid is the largest source of funding for medical and health-related services for people with low income in the United States. It is a means-tested program that is jointly funded by the state and federal governments and managed by the states, with each state currently having broad leeway to determine who is eligible for its implementation of the program. States are not required to participate in the program, although all currently do. Medicaid recipients must be U.S. citizens or legal permanent residents, and may include low-income adults, their children, and people with certain disabilities. Poverty alone does not necessarily qualify someone for Medicaid(Wikipedia).

6) **The Bipartisan Policy Center(BPC)** (양당(공화당과 민주당) 정책 센터) is a non-profit organization that "drives principled solutions through rigorous analysis, reasoned negotiation, and respectful dialogue". It considers itself a think tank characterized by "politically balanced policy making with strong, proactive advocacy and outreach". The Center was founded in 2007 by former Senate Majority Leaders Howard Baker, Tom Daschle, Bob Dole, and George J. Mitchell(Wikipedia).

7) **Super Committee** ((정치)슈퍼위원회) 미국의 국가부채를 해결하기 위한 방안을 만들기 위해 2011년 8월 구성된 위원회.

9 top defense officials
국방부 고위 간부들

10 Democratic legislators
민주당 국회의원들

11 credit downgrade = credit (rating) downgrade
신용등급 하락

12 substantial cuts
상당한 삭감

13 establishment of the supercommittee
슈퍼위원회의 설치

14 on top of
~의 위에, 게다가

How would these cuts affect the country?

Since the details just came out, it's not entirely clear yet. But many *top defense officials[9] have warned that the cuts will lead the military to be "hollowed out." *Democratic legislators[10] have similarly warned about the impact on vital social programs. And defense, health care and other industries that are significantly dependent on federal spending say that major job losses will happen if the cuts end up taking effect.

At the same time, if legislators try to avoid the sequester without replacing it with real deficit reduction, the U.S. could face another *credit downgrade[11].

Why did Congress and the White House agree to the sequester in the first place?

The government was approaching its debt limit, which needed to be raised through a congressional vote or else the country would default in early August 2011. While Democrats were in favor of a "clean" vote without strings attached, Republicans were demanding *substantial cuts[12] in exchange for raising the debt limit.

President Obama and congressional leaders ultimately agreed to the BCA, which would allow the debt ceiling to be raised by $2.1 trillion in exchange for the *establishment of the supercommittee[13] tied to the fall-back sequester, as the Center for Budget and Policy Priorities[8)] explains. The deal also includes mandatory spending reductions *on top of[14] the sequester by putting caps on *non-entitlement discretionary spending[15] that will reduce funding by $1 trillion by 2021.

Who supported the debt-ceiling deal?

Party leaders, the White House and most members of Congress supported the debt-ceiling deal: The BCA passed on a 268-161 vote in *the House[16], with about one-third of *House Republicans[17] and half of House Democrats opposing it. It passed in *the Senate[18], 74-26, with six Democratic senators and 19 Republican senators opposing it.

Can the sequester be avoided?

Yes, but only if Congress passes another budget deal that would achieve at least $1.2 trillion in *deficit reduction[19]. Both Democrats and Republicans have offered proposals to do so, but there still isn't much progress on a deal. The political obstacles are the same as during the supercommittee negotiations: Republicans don't want to raise taxes to generate *revenue[20], while Democrats are reluctant to make dramatic changes to entitlement programs to *achieve savings[21].

What happens from here?

No one on *Capitol Hill[22] thinks any deal will happen before Election Day[9)]. After Nov. 6, Congress will have just a few weeks

15 non-entitlement discretionary spending
비 사회보장프로그램에 대한 자유 재량적 지출

16 the House = the House of Representatives
하원

17 House Republicans
하원 공화당의원

18 the Senate
상원

19 deficit reduction
적자감축

20 revenue
세입

21 achieve savings
비용절감을 달성하다

22 Capitol Hill
Washington, D.C.의 연방의회의사당이 있는 언덕 (미국연방의회)

8) **The Center on Budget and Policy Priorities**(CBPP, 예산 및 정책 우선순위 센터) is an American non-profit think tank that analyzes the impacts of budget policies and promotes effective approaches to reducing poverty. It was founded in 1981, and is based in Washington, D.C. The Center describes itself as a "policy organization...working at the federal and state levels on fiscal policy and public programs that affect low- and moderate-income families and individuals"(Wikipedia).

9) **Election Day**((미)대통령 선거일) 11월 첫 월요일 다음의 화요일.
General Election Day((미)총선거일) 4년마다 11월 첫 월요일의 다음 화요일.

23 payroll tax
원천소득세

24 unemployment benefits
실업수당(급여)

25 tax break
세제상의 우대 조치, 세금 우대

26 cumulative impact
누적된 영향, 점진적 충격

to come up with an alternative to the sequester. The challenge is complicated by the fact that the Bush tax cuts, the *payroll tax[23], *unemployment benefits[24] and a host of other *tax breaks[25] are all scheduled to expire Dec. 31. The *cumulative impact[26] of all of these scheduled cuts and changes is what's popularly known as the fiscal cliff[10)]. There's already talk of passing a short-term stopgap budget plan during the lame-duck session[11)] to buy legislators more time to come up with a grand bargain[12)].

washingtonpost.com February 22, 2013

10) **fiscal cliff** (재정절벽) 집행하던 예산이 갑자기 삭감되거나 중단되어 경제전반에 심각한 타격을 주는 현상을 말한다. 미국의 경우 2012년 말까지 민주·공화당 양당 간에 적자 감축 합의가 이루어지지 않으면 2013년 초부터 세제 감면 혜택들이 만료되면서 세금이 급격히 느는 반면 균형 예산안으로 인해 재정지출이 1조2000억달러 자동 삭감되게 돼 있다(네이버 지식백과, 한경 경제용어사전).

11) **lame-duck session** ((미)잔여 회기) 전 달 11월의 재선거에서 낙선한 국회의원들의 12월–3월(의회) 회기.

12) **grand bargain** (그랜드 바겐) 줄 것은 주고, 받을 것은 받는 '상호 주고 받는' 개념으로, 북한이 '비가역적 핵 폐기' 조치에 나서면 그에 상응하는 지원을 제공하겠다는 일종의 '빅딜(Big deal)' 개념으로 사용되고 있다. 이명박 정부는 2009년 9월 21일 미국외교협회에서 개최된 코리아소사이어티, 아시아소사이어티, 미국외교협회 등 3개 기관이 공동 주최한 오찬 간담회에 연설에서 "6자 회담을 통해 북핵 프로그램의 핵심 부분을 폐기하면 북한에게 확실한 안전보장을 제공하고 국제지원을 본격화하는 일괄타결, 즉 그랜드 바겐(grand bargain)을 추진해야 한다"고 언급했다(네이버 지식백과, 매일경제/매경닷컴).

WORDS and STRUCTURES

release 발표하다, 공개하다

The institute released the results of the survey on October 15.
그 기관은 설문조사 결과를 10월 15일에 발표했다.

mandatory 의무적인, 강제적인

Education experts and analysts agree that strict, mandatory reforms are needed.
교육전문가와 분석가들은 엄격하고, 의무적인 개혁이 필요 하다는데 동의한다.

implement 시행하다, 이행하다

For this reason guaranteeing 'refugee status' and implementing such policy is undesirable and cannot be justified under these grounds.
이러한 이유로 '난민지위'를 보장하고 그러한 정책을 시행하는 것은 바람직하지 않으며 이러한 토대 하에서 정당화될 수 없다.

a package of 일련의

The government is also considering granting a package of tax benefits to the nonprofit hospitals.
정부는 또 비영리 병원에 대해서는 일련의 세금 혜택을 부여하는 방안도 검토하고 있다.

the Budget Control Act(BCA), ***which*** was passed in August 2011
= the Budget Control Act(BCA), ***and it*** was passed in August 2011

impoundment (법률) 압수, 몰수, 압류

project 예상하다

The amount of resources which will be consumed by obesity is projected to be huge.
비만으로 인해 소비될 자원의 양은 엄청날 것으로 예상된다.

The cuts, ***which*** are projected to total $1.2 trillion, are scheduled to begin in 2013 and end in 2021
= The cuts, ***and they*** are projected to total $1.2 trillion, are scheduled to begin in 2013 and end in 2021
주어 cuts 동사 schedule
삭감, 그런데 그 삭감은 총 1조 2천억 달러로 예상되는데, 2013년에 시작해서 2021년에 끝나도록 계획되어 있다.

evenly 고르게, 균등히

Getting a date, we always split costs evenly.
데이트할 때에 우리는 항상 비용을 균등히 나눈다.

evenly divided

= ***and they(=cuts) are*** evenly divided 그런데 그 삭감이 균등하게 나누어진다

with spending on wars exempt 전비지출은 면제되고

discretionary 자유재량에 의한

You may be eligible for a discretionary grant for your university course.
당신의 대학 과정에 대해서는 자유재량에 의한 학자금을 받을 수 있을지도 모른다.

entitlement 자격(권리)

This may affect your entitlement to compensation.
이런 점이 당신의 보상 요구 자격에 영향을 줄 수도 있다.

cf. duration of entitlement to the National Pension 국민연금가입기간

take effect 효과가 나타나다, 발효되다

This bill will take effect next year.
이 법안은 내년부터 발효된다.

deficit reduction 적자 감축

The president sticks his neck out for deficit reduction.
대통령은 적자 감축에 모든 것을 걸고 있다.

reach a deal 합의에 이르다

The members of the association are said to have reached a deal after three hours of talks.
연합 회원들은 3시간의 토론 끝에 합의에 도달했다고 한다.

legislators 입법자, 입법부의 의원

Opposition legislators and activists also say the bills give conservative newspapers unfair benefits.
반대하는 의원들과 운동가들 또한 그 법안이 보수신문사에게 불공정한 이익을 가져다줄 것이라 말한다.

discretion 결정권, 자유재량

They used their discretion in deciding which task to do first
그들은 어떤 일을 먼저 할 것인가 결정하는데 재량권을 행사했다.

across the board 전반적인, 일괄적인

I just don't think a 10% across-the-board cut is the way to do it.
다만 전 부서의 인원을 10퍼센트 감축하는 것은 적절한 방법이라고 생각하지 않는다.

intend to do ~하려고 하다, 예정하다

The building was intended to be library.
그 건물은 도서관으로 쓸 예정이었다.

They are intended to hit all affected programs equally.
= ***The across-the-board cuts*** are intended to hit all affected programs equally.
일괄 삭감은 모든 영향을 받는 복지프로그램들에 똑같이 타격을 주게 되어있다.

indiscriminate 무분별, 무차별적인

Indiscriminate attacks by terrorists on civilians ares till occurring.
민간인에 대한 테러리스트들의 무차별적 공격이 여전히 일어나고 있다.

mean to do 의도하다, 예정하다, ~할 작정이다

He didn't mean to do it.
그는 그런 일을 할 생각은 아니었다.

pressure ~에 압박을 가하다

They pressured him into accepting the contract.
그들은 그에게 그 계약을 받아들이도록 압력을 가했다.

vital 중요한, 필수적인

Sleep plays a vital role in brain development and growth.
수면은 뇌 발달과 성장에 중요한 역할을 담당한다.

end up (doing) 결국 (~하게) 되다

She had always wanted to be an astronaut, but ended up becoming a lawyer.
그녀는 언제나 우주비행사가 되기를 원했지만, 결국 변호사가 되고 말았다.

its debt limit, ***which*** needed to be raised through a congressional vote
= its debt limit, ***and it***(debt limit) needed to be raised through a congressional vote
그런데 그 정부의 부채한도는 의회의 투표를 통해 올릴 필요가 있었다

default 채무불이행, 채무를 이행하지 않다

People who default on their mortgage repayments may have their home repossessed.
저당금을 갚지 않는 사람은 집을 몰수당할 수 있다.

or else 그렇지 않으면

Stop threatening me or else you'll be sorry for it.
나를 협박하는 건 이제 그만두라. 그렇지 않으면, 후회하게 될 것이다.

in favor of 찬성하여

Those in favor of the amendment said that flag burning is disrespectful.
그 수정안에 찬성하는 이들은 국기를 태우는 것이 무례하다고 말했다.

without strings attached 조건 없이

My parents gave me a computer without any strings attached.
나의 부모는 아무 교환 조건 없이 컴퓨터를 주었다.

debt ceiling 부채한도

U.S. politicians have been arguing over whether to raise the debt ceiling, or the amount of money the government is legally allowed to borrow.
미 정치가들은 부채한도 즉 정부가 합법적으로 빌릴 수 있는 총액을 높여야 할지에 대해 논쟁을 벌여왔다.

in exchange for ~대신에, 교환으로

Would you withdraw your demand in exchange for an additional order?
추가 주문에 대한 대가로 귀사의 요구를 철회해 주시겠습니까?

tied to 관련되다, 의지하다

We are not tied to that figure.
우리는 그 모형에 얽매여있지 않다.

fall-back 만일의 경우에 대비할 수 있는

Air drops are still being seriously considered as a fall-back measures.
만일을 대비한 조치 중 하나로 공중투하를 여전히 진지하게 고려하고 있다.

Of course, it is true that science has had its fallbacks.
물론 과학이 그 대비책을 가지고 있는 것은 사실이다.

put caps on 상한선을 두다, 제한하다

The government put a cap on its spending.
정부는 그것의 소비를 제한했다.

revenue 세입

Demand for welfare has skyrocketed while tax revenues have declined.
복지수요가 한없이 늘었지만 세입은 줄어드는 추세다.

come up with something (해답 · 돈 등을) 찾아내다(내놓다), 제시(제안)하다

She came up with a new idea for increasing sales.
그녀는 매출 증가를 위한 새로운 아이디어를 내놓았다.

tax break 세제상의 우대 조치, 세금 우대

Everyone wants bigger tax breaks and easier life.
모든 사람은 더 많은 세금우대조치와 좀 더 수월한 삶을 원한다.

expire 만기가 되다, 끝나다

My license expires on the first of May.
내 면허증은 5월 1일로 끝난다.

cumulative 누적하는

It is a cumulative effect of the evidence.
그것은 그 증거의 축적된 효과다.

stop gap 미봉책

However, many financial experts are calling the aid package merely a stop gap measure.
그러나, 많은 재정 전문가들은 원조정책이 그저 임시변통수단일 뿐이라고 말하고 있다.

buy time 시간을 벌다

The GNP accused the watchdog BAI of trying to shelter Lee and staging a lukewarm investigation to buy time.
한나라당은 감사원이 이 의원을 비호하고 시간을 벌기 위해 미온적인 수사를 벌이고 있다고 비난했다.

the Board of Audit and Inspection 감사원

Memo

08.

Economic Optimism vs. the Sequester

Most Americans haven't realized it yet, but there's a good deal of positive news about the economy. Four years after the nadir of the Great Depression[1)], disposable income, *consumer spending[1], and *corporate investment[2] are all expanding at a decent clip. Employers are hiring more workers, and, perhaps most importantly, the *housing market[3], which has been the biggest drag on the recovery, is finally turning around. In some neighborhoods, such as the *gentrifying[4] neck of Brooklyn[2)] where I live, things are already going kind of nuts. But it's more general than that. From Fort Lauderdale[3)] to

1 consumer spending
소비자의 지출

2 corporate investment
기업의 투자

3 housing market
주택시장

4 gentrify
고급 주택화하다

1) **The Great Depression** (of the 1930s) (1930년대의 경제 공황) 여기서는 2007-2009년의 미국의 금융위기를 가리킴.

2) **Brooklyn** 롱아일랜드 서쪽 끝에 위치하며, 이스트강 건너편에는 맨해튼이 있다. 뉴욕시의 5개 자치구 중에서 최대의 인구를 가지며, 주택지가 대부분을 차지한다. 그러나 서쪽의 연안부에는 항만시설과 양조 · 조선 · 식품가공 · 기계 · 화학 등의 공장이 많다.

3) **Fort Lauderdale** 미국 플로리다 주(州) 남동부에 있는 도시.

5 property
부동산, 재산

6 healthy growth
건전한 성장

7 falling unemployment
감소하고 있는 실업률

8 financial crisis
금융위기

9 unsustainable lending
지탱할 수 없는 대출

10 credit bubble
신용거품

11 extended
장기간에 걸친

12 nasty headache
심한 두통

13 default
채무를 불이행하다
(빚을 갚지 않다)

14 ravaged
파괴된

15 balance sheets
대차대조표, 잔고

16 debt-to-income ratio
총부채상환비율

Los Angeles, in areas where the crash was most intense, the number of sales is increasing, prices are rising, and there are even reports of shortages of available *properties[5].

If it weren't for what is happening in Washington, the United States would be poised for several years of *healthy growth[6] and *falling unemployment[7]. I say that as someone who spent years before the *financial crisis[8] of 2007-2009 warning about an *unsustainable lending[9] and *credit bubble[10], the unwinding of which was sure to be painful and *extended[11]. We've certainly had a *nasty headache[12]. But by paying down some of their debts, and *defaulting[13] on others that were never going to be repaid, Americans have, over the past few years, done much to repair their *ravaged[14] personal *balance sheets[15]. As the economics team at Goldman Sachs[4)] pointed out last week, the household *debt-to-income ratio[16] is now back to its 2003 level—a little over a hundred per cent. And with *interest

4) **The Goldman Sachs Group**, Inc. is an American multinational investment banking firm that engages in global investment banking, securities, investment management, and other financial services primarily with institutional clients.
Goldman Sachs was founded in 1869 and is headquartered at 200 West Street in the Lower Manhattan area of New York City, with additional offices in international financial centers. The firm provides mergers and acquisitions advice, underwriting services, asset management, and prime brokerage to its clients, which include corporations, governments and individuals. The firm also engages in market making and private equity deals, and is a primary dealer in the United States Treasury security market. It is recognized as one of the premier investment banks in the world, but has sparked a great deal of controversy over its alleged improper practices, including the loosening of financial industry underwriting guidelines which had been intact since the 1930s, and in particular its actions since the 2007-2012 global financial crisis(Wikipedia).

5) **The Federal Reserve System** (FRS, Fed 미국 연방 준비제도)는 미국의 중앙은행으로서 국가의 신용대부 및 통화에 관한 업무를 관장하며, 은행에 대해 감독하고 규제하는 기능을 담당한다. 워싱턴 D.C.(Washington, District of Columbia)에 소재하는 이사회(Board of Governors)와 12개의 연방 준비은행, 25개의 지사 및 이 제도에 가입한 5,900개 이상의 상업은행, 시중은행 등으로 구성되어 있다(네이버 지식백과, 미국 개황, 외교부).

rates[17] at historic lows (thanks to the Fed[5)]), the amount of money that people have to devote to *interest and principal repayment[18] has fallen sharply. In 2007, households were paying close to fifteen per cent of their incomes on servicing their debts; today, it's about 10.5 per cent—the lowest figure since 1983.

With the value of people's investments in *stocks[19] and *real estate[20] both rising, all of this means that the underlying outlook for consumer spending, which makes up more than two-thirds of *G.D.P.[21], is pretty good. And if demand for everything from household *furnishings[22] to vacations continues to expand, corporations could take some of the cash they have been hoarding during the past few years and spend it on building new properties and buying new equipment. In short, we could finally get what we've been waiting for since 2009: a self-sustaining recovery in which *capital investment[23] and consumer spending reinforce each other.

As I said, that's the good news. Unfortunately, we can't avoid the *fiscal gridlock[24] in Washington, which is now the single biggest threat to the recovery. Barring something unexpected, the so-called sequester will go into effect next week, bringing with it big cuts in defense and non-defense spending. Almost certainly, that blow to the economy will be followed by weeks of haggling over the budget, after which the two parties will return to arguing over raising the debt ceiling. (You thought that had been settled as part of the New Year's Day agreement

17 interest rates
금리, 이율

18 interest and principal repayment
이자와 원금 상환

19 stocks
주식

20 real estate
부동산

21 G.D.P (gross domestic product)
국내총생산

22 furnishings
세간, 비품
(가구 · 카펫 · 커튼 등)

23 capital investment
자본 출자, 설비 투자

24 fiscal gridlock
재정적 교착상태

to go over the fiscal cliff? Wrong. It was merely deferred until May.)

Contrary to the suggestions of some critics of the Obama Administration, the mere existence of political uncertainty isn't sufficient to derail economic growth. If firms see rising demand for their products, they will step up hiring and capital spending more or less regardless of what the politicians are doing. Ask the Italians. Until the euro crisis[6] hit, they'd enjoyed decades of decent growth despite having what seemed to be a new government in Rome every few months.

6) **The eurozone crisis** (유로위기)(often referred to as the euro crisis) is an ongoing crisis that has been affecting the countries of the eurozone since early 2009, when a group of 10 central and eastern European banks asked for a bailout. At the time, the European Commission released a forecast of a 1.8 per cent decline in EU economic output for 2009. The crisis made it difficult or impossible for some countries in the eurozone to repay or refinance their government debt without the assistance of third parties like the ECB or IMF. Banks in the eurozone were undercapitalised and have faced liquidity and debt problems. Additionally, economic growth was slow in the whole of the eurozone and was unequally distributed across the member states. Governments of the states most severely affected by the crisis have co-ordinated their responses with a committee dubbed "the Troika" formed by three international organisations: the European Commission, the European Central Bank and the International Monetary Fund(Wikipedia).

7) **fiscal-cliff** (재정절벽) The United States fiscal cliff was a situation that came into existence in January 2013 whereby a series of previously enacted laws would simultaneously come into effect. The Bush tax cuts of 2001, which had been extended for two years by the 2010 Tax Relief Act, were to expire on December 31, 2012, and planned spending cuts under the Budget Control Act of 2011 also came into play. That Act was enacted as a compromise to resolve a dispute concerning the United States debt ceiling and address the failure of the 111th Congress to pass a federal budget. Discretionary spending for federal agencies and cabinet departments would have been reduced through broad cuts referred to as budget sequestration. (Mandatory programs, such as Social Security, Medicaid, federal pay (including military pay and pensions) and veterans' benefits would have been exempted from the spending cuts.) The fiscal cliff would increase tax rates and decrease government spending through sequestration, and lead to an operating deficit (the amount by which government spending exceeds its revenue) which was projected to be reduced by roughly half in 2013. The previously enacted laws leading to the fiscal cliff had been projected to result in a 19.63% increase in revenue and 0.25% reduction in spending from fiscal years 2012 to 2013. The Congressional Budget Office (CBO) had estimated that the fiscal cliff would have likely led to a mild recession with higher unemployment in 2013, followed by strengthening in the labor market with increased economic growth(Wikipedia).

But the deadlock in Washington goes beyond creating uncertainty: it is having a substantial impact on taxes and government spending, which directly affect the economy. As part of the fiscal-cliff[7)] agreement, Congress raised taxes by upwards of a hundred and twenty-five billion dollars a year. (A failure to extend the *payroll-tax holiday[25] was largely responsible.) Among economic forecasters, there is general agreement that this will reduce 2013 G.D.P. by somewhere between 0.5 per cent and one per cent. If the sequester goes into effect—and it looks like it will—the economy will suffer another hit.

Quite how large a hit remains to be seen. According to the White House, the spending cuts would be eighty-five billion dollars in the remainder of this *fiscal year[26], with about two-thirds of the total coming out of the *Pentagon[27] budget. Eighty-five billion dollars is about 0.5 per cent of G.D.P. A negative shock of that size almost certainly wouldn't be sufficient to *tip[28] the economy back into a recession. But together with the impact of higher taxes and the spending cuts agreed to as part of the 2011 debt-ceiling deal between the

25 payroll-tax holiday 원천소득세(갑근세) 면세기간

26 fiscal year 회계연도(미국 정부에서는 9월 30일, 영국 정부에서는 3월 31일에 끝남)

27 Pentagon 미국 국방부

28 tip 뒤집어엎다, 쓰러뜨리다

8) **growth recession** (성장률 둔화) The term Growth Recession indicates a situation were growth is slow, but not low enough to be a technical recession, yet, unemployment increases since more jobs are lost than created. The term was created by Dr. Solomon Fabricant (New York University, National Bureau of Economic Research) and is recognized and cited more recently by business economists. Note that the term also has slightly different secondary meanings including a more general one that growth is below potential. However, the more specific meaning indicates the growth is weak and insufficient to provide jobs for those entering the labor market (see the Hoisington and Hunt reference). There may also be a third meaning referring to growth in which more jobs are actually being destroyed than created. In all cases the term indicates, Real GDP is expanding (slowly) but with job contraction, so the economy behaves or feels in many ways like a recession(Wikipedia).

29 Congressional Budget Office
(미)의회 예산국(CBO)

30 invoke
(법 · 규칙 등을) 들먹이다(적용하다), 호소하다

31 tax hike
세금인상

32 unemployment claims
실업수당청구

33 payrolls
급여

two parties, it does raise the danger of a "growth recession[8)]"—one in which G.D.P. continues to rise, but not by enough to prevent the unemployment rate from ticking back up above eight per cent. (Currently, the rate is 7.9 per cent.) Indeed, this is the sort of scenario that the *Congressional Budget Office[29] was *invoking[30] when it recently predicted that G.D.P. growth this year would be restricted to just 1.4 per cent.

Based upon my reading that the underlying state of the U.S. economy outside Washington is pretty positive, I'm more optimistic than the C.B.O. While retails sales barely grew in January, the fact that they held their own in the face of a substantial *tax hike[31] and higher gas prices was encouraging. Underpinning this strength is a gradually improving picture of the labor market, where, according to the Labor Department, employers added about two hundred thousand jobs a month between November and January. The upward trend appears to be continuing. In the past few weeks, the number of new applications for *unemployment claims[32] has hit a five-year low. As long as *payrolls[33] keep expanding, personal income will keep rising—in the past few months, it's been rising at an annual rate of about three per cent—which buttresses consumer spending.

Finally, there is the housing market and the construction industry, which some analysts think is now too small to give the economy much of a boost. I respectfully disagree. In December, new housing starts climbed more than ten per cent, to an annual rate of close to a million. That's about half the level *new starts[34] reached in 2005, at the peak of the housing boom, which means there is plenty of room for further growth. The population is still expanding, *mortgage rates[35] are low, and properties are more affordable than they were five years ago. As house prices continue to climb, the number of people trapped with "negative equity[9)]" will fall, banks will become more willing to lend, and the *all-too-familiar[36] upward spiral may well reappear in other parts of the country than Williamsburg[10)] and Cobble Hill[11)].

In short, the economy has quite a bit more momentum than many people realize. Largely thanks to the efforts of the Fed, financial conditions aren't just conducive to growth. As noted in a recent speech by Jeremy Stein, a Fed governor, they are potentially incendiary. But that's no justification for making the same mistake that Britain and many European countries made, and risking the recovery on the altar of *budget cutting[37] and *debt reduction[38]. While the contest between economic optimism and the effects of the fiscal cliff and sequester will be fascinating to watch, it's one that shouldn't have taken place to begin with. But don't try telling that to the Republicans.

newyoker.com February 22, 2013

34 housing starts (특정기간의) 주택건축 착공 수

35 mortgage rate 주택 담보대출의 금리

36 all-too-familiar 너무 친숙한

37 budget cutting 예산삭감

38 debt reduction 부채축소

9) **negative equity** (역 자산) 담보를 잡힌 주택의 가격이 갚아야 할 대출금 액수보다 낮은 상황. 담보물의 시장가치하락으로 인한 채무.

10) **Williamsburg** 미국 Virginia주 동남부에 있는 도시.

11) **Cobble Hill** 미국 New York주에 있는 Brooklyn 이웃 도시.

WORDS and STRUCTURES

nadir (어떤 상황에서) 최악의 순간(바닥)

Company losses reached their nadir in 1999.
회사 손실이 1999년에 바닥에 이르렀다.

disposable 자유롭게 사용할 수 있는, 이용 가능한

Gambling provides disposable income for a nation.
도박은 한 국가에게 이용 가능한 수입을 제공해 준다.

at a decent clip 상당한 속도로

By traveling at a good clip, we managed to get there before the wedding started.
우리는 아주 빠른 속도로 달렸기 때문에 결혼식이 시작되기 전에 거기에 도착할 수 있었다.

decent 상당한

In the end, despite the low value of the won, many companies earn decent profits.
결국, 원화의 낮은 가치에도 불구하고, 많은 기업들은 상당한 이익을 남긴다.

drag 장애물, 걸림돌

A strong won and high oil prices, however, could be a potential drag on the economy.
그러나 원화강세와 고유가가 우리 경제의 발목을 잡을 수 있다.

the housing market, ***which*** has been the biggest drag on the recovery, is finally turning around
= the housing market, ***and it*** has been the biggest drag on the recovery, is finally turning around
주택시장, 그런데 그 주택시장은 경기회복의 가장 큰 장애물인데, 마침내 돌아서고 있다.

go nuts 미치다, 아주 좋아하다

The kids go nuts over these little surprises.
아이들은 이런 작은 서프라이즈를 아주 좋아한다.

crash 폭락

The crash of 1929 precipitated the Great Depression of the 1930s.
1929년의 주가폭락이 1930년대의 (세계) 대공황을 재촉했다.

If it weren't for what is happening in Washington,
= ***But for*** what is happening in Washington,
만일 워싱턴에서 일어나고 있는 것이 없다면

poise (상태, 위치)를 유지하다

March figures supported optimism that the economy is poised to recover in the future.
3월 수치가 경제가 앞으로 회복될 것이라는 낙관론을 뒷받침 한다.

the unwinding of ***which*** was sure to be painful and extended
= ***and*** the unwinding of ***them***(unsustainable lending and credit bubble) was sure to be painful and extended
그런데 그것들(지탱할 수 없는 대출과 신용거품)을 해결하는 것은 확실히 고통스럽고 시간이 오래 걸렸다.

nasty 좋지 않은, 지독한

I really want to get rid of this nasty cold.
나는 정말 이 심한 감기가 나았으면 좋겠다.

pay down 상환하다

We will use this profit to pay down debt and invest in our core units.
우리는 이 수익금을 부채상환과 핵심 사업에 대한 투자에 사용할 것이다.

default 채무불이행

Foreign media predict that Greece will fail to secure revival on its own and declare national default sooner or later.
외신들은 그리스가 자력 회생을 못하고 조만간 디폴트(채무불이행)를 선언할 것으로 보고 있다.

repay 갚다, 상환하다

I've been repaying my house loan with an automatic withdrawal.
나는 주택융자금을 자동이체로 상환하고 있다.

But by paying down ***some*** of their debts, and defaulting on ***others that*** were never going to be repaid,
= But by paying down ***some*** of their debts, and defaulting on ***others + (and) they*** were never going to be repaid,
그렇지만 그들 빚 중의 약간은 상환하고(갚고), 결코 상환되지 못할 다른 빚은 채무불이행을 함으로써

Unemployment is at historic lows 실업률이 유래가 없을 정도로 낮다

the amount of money ***that*** people have to devote to interest and principal repayment has fallen sharply
= the amount of money ***+(and)*** people have to devote ***money*** to interest and principal repayment has fallen sharply
주어 amount 동사 fall
사람들이 이자와 원금 상환에 충당해야 하는 돈의 양이 급격히 줄어들었다.

service debts 이자를 갚다

The company can no longer service its debts.
그 회사는 더 이상 부채에 대한 이자를 갚을 수가 없다.

hoard 간직하다, 쌓아두다

But consumers across the region are not hoarding their money.
하지만 지역 소비자들이 돈을 쌓아두고만 있지는 않는다.

self-sustaining 자급하는, 자립하는

The family has a self-sustaining system of energy.
그 가족은 에너지 자급자족 시스템을 갖추고 있다.

reinforce 보강하다

We threw our energy into reinforcing the dike.
우리는 제방을 보강하는데 전력을 기울였다.

fiscal 재정의, 회계의

The government is committed to further efforts on fiscal policy and banking reforms.
정부는 앞으로 재정 정책과 금융 개혁에 더 많은 노력을 기울이겠다는 공약을 하고 있다.

gridlock 교통정체, 교착상태

Congress is in gridlock.
의회가 정체 상태에 빠져 있다.

barring ~이 없다면 (except for)

We should arrive in half an hour, barring at traffic congestion.
교통정체가 없다면, 우리는 30분 이내에 도착할 것이다.

go into effect 발효되다

The new rules will go into effect in August.
새로운 법안은 8월에 효력이 발효될 것이다.

haggling 흥정

I left him in the market haggling over the price of a shirt.
나는 시장에서 셔츠 값을 두고 실랑이를 벌이는 그를 두고 떠났다.

debt ceiling 부채한도

U.S. politicians have been arguing over whether to raise the debt ceiling, or the amount of money the government is legally allowed to borrow.
미 정치가들은 정부가 합법적으로 빌릴 수 있는 총액 즉 부채한도를 높여야 할지에 대해 논쟁을 벌여왔다.

derail (열차 · 전차 등을) 탈선시키다, (계획 · 협정 등을) 틀어지게(실패하게) 하다

Persistent household debt and slow job growth threaten to derail those projections.
계속되는 가계부채와 느린 일자리 증가세는 그러한 낙관적 전망에 위협요인이 되고 있다.

deadlock 교착 상태

European agriculture ministers failed to break the deadlock over farm subsidies.
유럽 국가들의 농림부 장관들이 농업 보조금을 둘러싼 교착 상태를 타개하지 못했다.

upwards of ~이상

Students are now finding ways around paying upwards of $1,000 a semester for books.
학생들이 이제 한 학기당 교재 값으로 천 달러가 넘는 돈을 내야 하는 것에 대해 방법을 찾고 있다는 것이다.

suffer hit(blow) 강타하다, 타격을 받다

The export industry suffered a major blow when the foreign exchange rate fell sharply.
수출업체가 환율 급락으로 된서리를 맞았다.

recession 경기 침체

There is no doubt that the current economic recession has made it difficult for young people to find a job.

현재의 경기침체로 젊은이들이 구직난을 겪고 있는 것은 의심의 여지가 없는 사실이다.

tick 똑딱거리며 지나가다, 움직이다

tick up 상승하다

Economic direction could be ticking back up.

경제 방향이 되돌려질 수 있을 것이다.

retails sales 소매 판매

Retails sales fell 1.8 percent last month from a year ago.

소매업종의 매출은 지난달에 1년 전보다 1.8퍼센트가 감소했다.

hold one's own 자기 지위(입장)를 고수하다, 꺾이지 않다

She was able to hold her own and promoted continuously.

그녀는 자기 지위를 고수할 수 있어서 계속해서 승진했다.

in the face of ~에도 불구하고, ~의 앞에서

She showed great courage in the face of danger.

그녀는 위험에 직면하여 큰 용기를 보여 주었다.

underpin 밑에서 떠받치다, 지지하다

Underpinning this success has been an exemplary record of innovation.

훌륭한 기록적 혁신이 이 성공의 토대를 이루고 있다.

unemployment claims 실업수당청구

New unemployment claims were flat or falling during the year until early July.
7월초까지 한 해 동안 신규 실업수당청구는 변동이 없거나 감소되었다.

hit low (증권 · 금융) 신 저점을 기록하다, 바닥을 치다

The government's popularity has hit a new low.
정부의 인기도가 또 다시 최저 수준을 갱신했다.

buttress ~에 버팀목을 대다, 강화하다

With the absence of a domestic consumption recovery, overseas sales have buttressed the world's 12th largest economy.
내수침체가 지속되고 있는 가운데 수출이 세계 12위의 경제대국인 우리나라의 버팀목 역할을 해오고 있다.

boost 격려, (신장시키는) 힘

Winning the competition was a wonderful boost for her morale.
그 대회에서의 우승이 그녀의 사기 진작에 큰 힘이 되었다.

there is the housing market and the construction industry, ***which*** some analysts think is now too small to give the economy much of a boost
= there is the housing market and the construction industry, ***and it*** some (analysts think) is now too small to give the economy much of a boost
노동시장과 건설업이 있는데 몇몇 분석가들이 생각하기로 그것은 너무나 작아 경제에 많은 활력을 줄 정도는 아니다.

respectfully 정중하게, 공손하게

Bids at less than 50 percent of our estimate are respectfully declined.
견적 가격의 반액 이하의 입찰은 정중히 사양 합니다.

affordable 입수 가능한, (가격 등이) 알맞은

There's a lot of affordable housing in this area.
이 지역에는 알맞은 가격에 살 수 있는 집이 많이 있다.

equity (한 회사의) 자기 자본, (자산의) 순수 가치

The corporation issued more stock and diluted the shareholders' equity.
그 회사는 증권을 더 발행하여 주주들의 지분을 줄였다.

upward spiral 연속상승

The upward spiral of inflation and wages had proved devastating without proper policy responses in earlier episodes of oil shocks.
과거 오일쇼크 당시 임금과 인플레율의 연속 상승은 적절한 정책 대응이 없을 경우 파괴적인 결과를 초래했다.

quite a bit more 상당히 더

That's quite a bit more than one beer.
맥주 한 병 보다는 상당히 더 마셔야 나오는 수치란다.

momentum (일의 진행에 있어서의) 탄력(가속도)

The fight for his release gathers momentum each day.
그의 석방을 위한 투쟁에 나날이 탄력(가속도)이 붙고 있다.

conducive 도움이 되는

Keeping early hours is conducive to good health. 일찍 자고 일찍 일어나면 건강에 좋다.

incendiary 선동적인, 자극적인, 방화의

Powell's speech is highly emotional and incendiary.
Powell의 연설은 매우 감정적이고 선동적이다.

Memo

09.

Obama Warns Sequester Will Cause Job Losses

Staking out his ground ahead of a fiscal deadline, President Barack Obama lashed out against Republicans on Tuesday, saying they are unwilling to raise taxes to reduce deficits and warning that the jobs of essential *government workers[1], from teachers to *emergency responders[2], are on the line.

Obama spoke as a March 1 deadline for automatic *across-the-board spending cuts[3] approached and with Republicans and Democrats in an apparent stalemate over how to avoid them.

Obama *cautioned[4] that if the $85 billion in immediate cuts -- known as the sequester -- occur, the full range of government would feel the effects. Among those he listed: *furloughed[5] *FBI[1)] agents[6], reductions in spending for *communities[7] to pay police and *fire personnel[8] and teachers, and decreased ability to respond to threats around the world.

1 government workers
정부직원(공무원)

2 emergency responders = first responders
긴급처치요원

3 across-the-board spending cuts
일괄지출 삭감

4 caution
경고하다

5 furlough
휴가

6 agents
요원들

7 communities
지역사회

8 fire personnel
소방대원

1) FBI(Federal Bureau of Investigation) 미국 연방 수사국.

9 unemployment rate
실업률

10 biggest corporations
대기업

11 House Republicans
하원 공화당 의원

12 undertake
(책임을 맡아서) 착수하다

13 tax code
세법

14 tax subsidy
조세보조

15 tax system
세금체계(세제)

16 rates
세율

17 revenue
세입

18 short-term resolution
단기 해결책

19 carrier
항공모함

He said the consequences would be felt across the economy.

"People will lose their jobs," he said. "The *unemployment rate[9] might tick up again."

"So far at least, the ideas that the Republicans have proposed ask nothing of the wealthiest Americans or the *biggest corporations[10]," Obama said. "So the burden is all on the first responders, or seniors or middle class families."

*House Republicans[11] have proposed an alternative to the immediate cuts, targeting some spending and extending some of the reductions over a longer period of time. They also have said they are willing to *undertake[12] changes in the *tax code[13] and eliminate loopholes and *tax subsidies[14]. But they have said they would overhaul the *tax system[15] to reduce *rates[16], not to raise *revenue[17].

Obama's remarks came a day after he returned to Washington from a three-day golfing weekend in Florida.

Congress is not in session this week, meaning no votes will occur before next week and complicating the ability to negotiate any *short-term resolution[18].

Obama said the anticipated cuts were already having an effect, noting that the Navy had already delayed the deployment of a *carrier[19] to the Persian Gulf[2)].

"Changes like this -- not well thought through, not phased

in properly -- changes like this affect our ability to respond to threats in unstable parts of the world," he said.

Obama wants to offset the immediate spending cuts through a combination of targeted spending cuts and increased *tax revenue[20]. The White House is backing a proposal unveiled last week by Senate Democrats that is in line with the president's principles.

But that plan has met an icy reception among Republicans, who oppose raising taxes to offset the cuts. GOP[3)] leaders say the president got the tax increases he wanted at the beginning of the year when Congress agreed to raise taxes on family income above $450,000 a year.

Obama called on congressional Republicans to compromise and accept the Senate Democrats' proposal.

The Democrats propose to generate revenue by plugging some tax loopholes. Those include *tax breaks[21] for the oil and natural gas industry and businesses that have sent jobs overseas, and by taxing millionaires at a rate of at least 30 percent.

20 tax revenue
세수입

21 tax break
세금 우대(감세) 조치

2) **The Persian Gulf** is located in Western Asia between Iran to the northeast and the Arabian Peninsula to the southwest. The Persian Gulf is an extension of the Indian Ocean(Gulf of Oman) through the Strait of Hormuz. The Shatt al-Arab river delta forms the northwest shoreline.
The Gulf was a battlefield of the 1980–1988 Iran-Iraq War, in which each side attacked the other's oil tankers. It is the namesake of the 1991 Gulf War, the largely air- and land-based conflict that followed Iraq's invasion of Kuwait(Wikipedia).

3) **GOP**(=Grand Old Party) 1880년 이래 미국공화당(Republican Party)의 별명.

22 House Speaker
하원 의장

23 the Senate
상원

24 deficit
적자

25 health care reform
건강보험 개혁

26 cost of living
생활비

27 chief of staff
대통령 수석보좌관

28 sharp austerity
심한 긴축재정

29 fragile economic recovery
취약한 경제회복

A spokesman for *House Speaker[22] John Boehner said the Ohio Republican agrees the sequester is a bad way to reduce spending, but put the onus for averting the cuts on Democrats.

"A solution now requires *the Senate[23] - controlled by the president's party - to finally pass a plan of their own," spokesman Brendan Buck said.

Meanwhile, a bipartisan proposal Tuesday by co-chairs of an influential deficit-reduction commission called for reducing the *deficit[24] by $2.4 trillion over the next 10 years, with much of the savings coming through *health care reform[25], closing tax loopholes, a stingier adjustment of Social Security's *cost of living[26] increases and other measures.

The proposal by former Republican Sen. Alan Simpson of Wyoming and Democrat Erskine Bowles, the former *chief of staff[27] for President Bill Clinton, calls for about one quarter of the savings to come from changes in health care programs and another quarter from revenue generated by tax changes.

In their plan, Bowles and Simpson say the automatic cuts scheduled for March 1 are too steep and could set back the economy.

"*Sharp austerity[28] could have the opposite effect by tempering the still *fragile economic recovery[29]. In order to protect the recovery, the sequester should be avoided and deficit reduction should be phased in gradually," they wrote.

Some Republicans, including House Budget Committee[4)] Chairman Paul Ryan, *R-Wis.[30], have advocated plugging loopholes, but as part of a discussion on a tax overhaul, not sequestration.

"Loopholes are necessary for tax reform," Ryan said Sunday on ABC's "This Week." "If you take them for spending, you're blocking tax reform and you're really not getting the deficit under control."

The sequester was first set to begin taking effect on Jan. 1. But as part of the "fiscal cliff" negotiations, the White House and *lawmakers[31] agreed to push it off for two months in order to create space to work on a larger *budget deal[32].

With little progress on that front in recent weeks, Obama is calling for the sequester to be put off again, though it's unclear whether another delay would have any impact on the prospects for a broader budget agreement.

cnbc.com February 22, 2013

30 R-Wis. = Republican, Wisconsin 위스콘신 주 공화당 국회의원

31 lawmakers 국회의원

32 budget deal = budget agreement 예산합의

4) **The U.S. House Committee** on the Budget, commonly known as the House Budget Committee, is a standing committee of the United States House of Representatives, the lower house of Congress. Its responsibilities include legislative oversight of the federal budget process, reviewing all bills and resolutions on the budget, and monitoring agencies and programs funded outside of the budgetary process. The committee briefly operated as a select committee in 1919 and 1921, during the 66th and 67th Congresses, before being made a standing committee in 1974.
In early December 2013, House Budget Committee Chairman Rep. Paul Ryan (R-Wis.) and Senate Budget Committee Chairwoman Sen. Patty Murray (D-Wash.) reached a two-year budget agreement that would prevent a government shutdown and bolster national defense priorities by providing relief for sequester cuts(Wikipedia).

WORDS and STRUCTURES

stake something out (울타리를 치거나 하여) ~이 자기 것임을 분명히 표시하다

The President staked out his position on the issue.
대통령이 그 쟁점에 대해 입장을 분명히 밝혔다.

lash out against ~을 맹렬히 비난하다

He lashed out against the President stating that he was not fit for the position.
그는 현 대통령이 직책에 걸맞지 않은 사람이라고 직격탄을 날렸다.

be unwilling to ~하고 싶어 하지 않다

I am unwilling to go. 나는 가고 싶지 않다.

on the line 위태로운

It appears that Seoul Mayor Oh Se-hoon's political career is on the line.
서울시장 오세훈의 정치경력이 위태로워 보인다.

stalemate 꼼짝할 수 없는 입장(상태), 막다른 궁지

The South has showed passive attitude to resolving the current stalemate.
남한은 현재의 난국을 푸는데 있어서 수동적인 태도를 보여 왔다.

with Republicans and Democrats in an apparent stalemate over how to avoid them
공화당과 민주당 국회의원들이 자동적인 일괄 지출삭감을 어떻게 피할지에 대해 명백하게 막다른 궁지에 몰리자

tick up (주가 등이) 상승하다

At an annualized rate, sales ticked up just 0.9percent.
연간 증가율로 환산하면 판매는 불과 0.9퍼센트 증가에 그쳤다.

House Republicans have proposed an alternative to the immediate cuts, ***targeting*** some spending and extending some of the reductions over a longer period of time
= House Republicans have proposed an alternative to the immediate cuts, ***and it targets*** some spending and extending some of the reductions over a longer period of time
하원 공화당 의원들은 즉각적인 삭감에 대한 대안을 제안했는데, 그 대안은 약간은 지출하고 삭감의 약간은 장기간에 걸쳐 연장하는 것을 목표로 한다.

loophole (법률 등의) 빠져나갈 구멍, 허점

Just because they found a loophole in the rules doesn't make it right.
이 규칙의 허점을 찾아냈다는 이유로 인해 (그들의 잘못이) 정당화 되지는 않는다.

overhaul ~을 철저히 점검(검사)하다, ~을 정비하다

The authorities should overhaul the project in order to avoid the same mistake again.
관련당국은 이런 실수를 반복하지 않기 위해 이번 계획을 철저히 검토해야 할 것이다.

phase in 단계적으로 도입하다

The new tax will be phased in over two years.
그 새 세금은 2년에 걸쳐 단계적으로 도입(시행)될 것이다.

not well thought through, ***not phased*** in properly
= (***and they***(changes) ***were) not well thought*** through, (***and they were) not phased*** in properly
변화들이 철저히 생각되지도 않았고, 적절하게 단계적으로 도입되지도 않았는데

offset ~을 상쇄하다, ~을 메우다

Many airlines worldwide have sought fare increases to offset the rise in fuel prices.
세계의 많은 항공사들은 연료가격 상승을 상쇄하기 위해 운임 인상을 도모해 왔다.

be in line with ~와 일치하다

The bank's official growth forecast was in line with the earlier prediction.
한국은행의 공식적인 성장전망은 당초 전망과 일치했다.

The White House is backing a proposal ***unveiled*** last week by Senate Democrats ***that*** is in line with the president's principles
= The White House is backing a proposal ***(which was) unveiled*** last week by Senate Democrats **+*(and) it*** is in line with the president's principles
백악관은 지난 주 상원 민주당 국회의원들에 의해 공개된 제안을 지지하고 있는데 그 제안은 대통령의 원칙과 일치한다.

the president got the tax increases he wanted at the beginning of the year
= the president got the tax increases ***(which)*** he wanted at the beginning of the year
= the president got the tax increases **+*(and)*** he wanted ***them*** at the beginning of the year
대통령은 올 해 초 그가 원했던 세금 증가를 달성했다.

call on A to B A가 B하도록 촉구(요구)하다

A vocal minority of legislators has called on the government to speed up compensations for the victims.
떠들썩한 소수파 의원들은 정부에 대해 희생자 보상을 조속히 하라고 촉구했다.

plug 막다

We must plug the existing loopholes and explore new and safe options.
우리는 현재의 허술한 구멍을 막아버리고 새롭고 안전한 선택사항에 대해 탐구해야한다.

tax break 세금 우대(감세) 조치

There are tax breaks for businesses that locate in rural areas.
시골 지역에 있는 사업체들에 대해서는 세금 혜택이 있다.

businesses ***that*** have sent jobs overseas
= businesses ***+(and) they*** have sent jobs overseas
해외로 일자리를 보냈던 기업들

onus 무거운 짐, 부담, 책임

The onus of making the decision fell on the manager.
그 결정을 내리는 책임은 지배인이 지게 되었다.

controlled by the president's party
= ***and it***(the Senate) ***is controlled*** by the president's party
그런데 상원은 대통령의 당(민주당)에 의해 통제를 받고 있는데

avert 돌리다, 피하다

The driver tried to avert the accident by bringing the car to a sudden halt.
운전자는 차를 급정거하여 그 사고를 피하려고 했다.

stingy 인색한, 몹시 아끼는

Disappointingly, Korea's economy has been stingy with spending for the disabled.
실망스럽게도 한국경제는 장애인에 대해 돈쓰는 것에 인색한 편이다.

steep 가파른, 급격한, 극단적인

Do not choose a hill that is too steep.
너무 가파른 경사는 피해라.

set back 저지(방해)하다, 지연시키다

The bad weather set back our plans by a whole week.
악천후 때문에 우리의 계획이 꼬박 일주일이나 지연됐다.

austerity (특히 국가적인 경제정책으로서의) 내핍, 긴축재정

Austerity can be counterproductive because it can slow the economy and reduce tax revenue.
긴축정책은 경제를 둔화시키고 세수를 줄이기 때문에 역효과를 낳을 수 있다.

temper 누그러뜨리다(완화시키다)

Justice must be tempered with mercy.
정의는 연민으로 완화되어야 한다.

fragile 취약한, 깨지기 쉬운, 부진한, 쉽게 영향을 받는

The rise threatens the price competitiveness of Korean exports, the sole engine of the nation's fragile economy.
원화강세는 한국의 취약한 경제를 홀로 이끌고 있는 수출의 가격경쟁력을 위협한다.

tax overhaul 세제개편

A radical overhaul of the tax system is necessary.
근본적인 세제 정비가 필요하다.

get the deficit under control 적자를 통제 하에 두다

I think I got this problem under control.
내가 이 문제를 통제하고 있다고 생각한다.

10.

Stepping Back From Capital Punishment

In December, the United Nations General Assembly[1)] voted overwhelmingly for a global moratorium on the *death penalty[1]. This fourth such vote in five years was supported by a record 111 nations.

Yet in the first month of 2013, Saudi Arabia beheaded nine people. In recent weeks, Yemen has sentenced a *juvenile offender[2] to death, fueling *hunger strikes[3] by scores of imprisoned children. Iran has reportedly begun imposing death sentences for *petty criminals[4] *accused[5] of robbery.

Elsewhere, a court in Indonesia, where there have been no *state executions[6] since 2008, sentenced a British grandmother to death for *drug trafficking[7] — reportedly to gasps of

1 death penalty = capital punishment 사형(제)

2 juvenile offender 청소년 범죄자

3 hunger strikes 단식투쟁

4 petty criminals 경범죄자

5 accused 기소된

6 state executions 국가적인 사형집행

7 drug trafficking 마약밀매

1) **The United Nations General Assembly**(UNGA, GA, or, from the French Assemblée Générale, "AG") (유엔 총회) is one of the six principal organs of the United Nations and the only one in which all member nations have equal representation. Its powers are to oversee the budget of the United Nations, appoint the non-permanent members to the Security Council, receive reports from other parts of the United Nations and make recommendations in the form of General Assembly Resolutions. It has also established a wide number of subsidiary organs(Wikipedia).

8 hangman = executioner 사형집행인

disbelief in the courtroom. Zimbabwe has hired a *hangman[8] after seven years of searching, while Sri Lanka, which has not carried out an execution since 1976, has reportedly recruited two executioners who are undergoing special training.

In the United States, the trend is toward fewer executions and death sentences, with more states repealing the death penalty. Nevertheless, in 2012 there were 43 executions and 77 death sentences.

Such developments make for grim reading. However, we at the International Commission against the Death Penalty[2)] — an independent body opposed to capital punishment in all cases — remain hopeful. It is clear that the world is becoming an increasingly lonely place for states that practice executions.

The United Nations call for a moratorium on executions is underpinned by a global trend toward abolition that has dramatically gathered pace in recent years. One hundred and five countries have repealed capital punishment in their laws and others no longer carry out executions.

According to the United Nations, over 150 countries have

2) **The International Commission against the Death Penalty** (ICDP or Commission)(사형제 반대 국제 위원회) was founded in Madrid in October 2010 as a result of a Spanish initiative. ICDP is an independent body composed of 15 commissioners who have experience in international law and human rights, and are committed to global abolition of capital punishment. Their experience, background, geographical representation and personal involvement towards abolishing the death penalty, enables them to engage with senior officials from different countries(Wikipedia).

abolished the death penalty in law or *practice[9]. All across humanity's diverse and sprawling community — encompassing all major cultures, religions and regions — there is growing understanding that this abhorrent practice has no place in modern *justice systems[10].

Quite simply, the death penalty does much harm and no good. It is inherently cruel, risks execution of the innocent, and is ineffective at deterring violent crime. States that have abolished capital punishment often have lower murder rates than those that have yet to do so.

Much remains to be done, not least because a handful of states remain willing to risk international outrage, controversy and isolation by persisting with this cruel, inhuman and *degrading[11] practice. Iran, Saudi Arabia and Yemen — all in the global spotlight in recent weeks — are accompanied by China, Iraq, North Korea and the United States as the world's most prolific executioners year on year.

As the United Nation's Human Rights Council[3] meets in Geneva on Monday, we are bringing together high-level government representatives to assess why and how the death penalty should be abolished. Our guests will include *foreign ministers[12] and *senior officials[13] from Argentina, Norway, Spain, Switzerland and other nations. We will also hear from

9 practice
관습

10 justice systems
사법제도

11 degrading
수치스러운

12 foreign ministers
외무장관

13 senior officials
정부고위 관리

3) **United Nation's Human Rights Council** 유엔 인권위원회.

14 deputy high commissioner
부(副)고등 판무관

15 secretary general
사무총장

Kyung-wha Kang, the U.N. *deputy high commissioner[14] for human rights, and the U.N. *secretary general[15], Ban Ki-moon.

Ultimately, experience from all over the world demonstrates that the death penalty is not just cruel, irrevocable and a violation of the right to life. It is a toxic and destructive punishment that damages society by endorsing violence and by causing injustice and suffering.

As more countries conclude that the only place for capital punishment is in the history books, the shrinking group of executing states looks set to become ever more isolated. The challenge for their leaders is to show political courage and foresight, and to bring their laws into the modern age by immediately suspending use of the death penalty, as a first step toward full abolition.

nytimes.com February 21, 2013

WORDS and STRUCTURES

capital punishment 사형, 사형제도

Some people think capital punishment is barbaric.
어떤 사람들은 사형제도는 야만적이라고 생각 한다.

overwhelmingly 압도적으로

They voted overwhelmingly against the proposal.
그들은 그 제안에 대해 압도적인 반대표를 던졌다.

moratorium 지불유예, 활동중단

The convention called for a two-year moratorium on commercial whaling.
그 총회는 상업적 고래잡이에 대해 2년간의 활동 중단을 요구했다.

record 기록적인

The highly polished girl band is expected to rack up record sales next year.
아주 세련된 소녀밴드가 내년에 기록적인 매출을 달성할 것으로 기대된다.

behead 목을 베다, 참수하다

In the end, they decided to behead Charles 1.
결국 그들은 찰스 1세를 교수형에 처하기로 결정했다.

sentence (형을) 선고하다

He was sentenced to 10 years' imprisonment but escaped before completing his sentence.
그는 10년 형을 선고받고 복역 중에 탈옥했다.

juvenile offender 청소년 범죄자

There is a growing second conviction rate for juvenile offenders.
청소년 범죄자들의 재범률이 점점 높아지고 있다.

fuel 부채질하다

Universities are blaming essay writing companies for helping to fuel the spread of plagiarism on campus.
대학들은, 에세이 쓰기 업체들이 대학에서의 표절행위확산을 부채질하고 있다고 비난했다.

scores of 다수의, 수십의

He drafted scores of bills in the next few years.
그는 이후 몇 년 사이에 수십 건의 법안을 초안했다.

imprison 수감하다, 가두다

The release of the party's long imprisoned leader was something of a surprise.
오랫동안 수감되었던 지도자의 석방은 놀라운 일이었다.

Yemen has sentenced a juvenile offender to death, ***fueling*** hunger strikes by scores of imprisoned children.

= Yemen has sentenced a juvenile offender to death, ***and it fueled*** hunger strikes by scores of imprisoned children

예멘은 한 청소년 범죄자에게 사형을 선고했는데 그것이 수십 명의 수감된 아이들로 하여금 단식투쟁을 부채질 했다.

petty criminal 경범죄자, 잡범

Petty criminals can be sent to jail for a maximum of four years under the new system.
경범죄자들은 새로운 제도 하에서 최대 4년 동안 감옥으로 보내질 수 있다.

drug trafficking 마약밀매

We need to completely root out drug trafficking.
마약 밀매를 뿌리 뽑아야 한다.

reportedly 보도에 따르면, 알려진 바에 의하면

The two have reportedly been going out with each other since January.
보도에 의하면, 이 둘은 1월부터 서로 사귀어 왔다고 한다.

gasps (숨이 막히는 듯) 헉(휴) 하는 소리를 냄

He gave a gasp of surprise.
그는 놀라서 헉 하는 소리를 냈다.

undergo 받다

They had to undergo intensive training everyday.
그들은 매일 강도 높은 훈련을 받아야 했다.

repeal 폐지하다

They tried to repeal the antiquated law.
그들은 그 낡은 법을 폐지하려 했다.

make for 도움이 되다, 기여하다

Constant arguing doesn't make for a happy marriage.
계속 다투는 것은 행복한 결혼 생활에 도움이 되지 않는다.

grim 단호한, 엄숙한

Life may be grim, but it offers small victories.
삶은 엄숙할 것이지만, 그것은 또한 작은 승리를 제공 한다.

underpin 지지하다, 뒷받침하다

The report is underpinned by extensive research.
그 보고서는 광범위한 실태 조사로 뒷받침되어 있다.

gather pace 증가하다, 가속화하다

We hope this trend will gather pace.
우리는 이 추세가 가속화되기를 바란다.

The United Nations call for a moratorium on executions is underpinned by a global trend toward abolition ***that*** has dramatically gathered pace in recent years
= The United Nations call for a moratorium on executions is underpinned by a global trend toward abolition **+*(and) it*** has dramatically gathered pace in recent years
주어 call 동사 underpin
사형집행 중단에 대한 유엔의 요청은 철폐 쪽으로의 세계적인 추세에 의해 지지를 받는데 그 추세는 최근에 극적으로 가속화 되었다

sprawling 제멋대로 뻗어나가는

The German government announced that it planned to privatize the sprawling autobahn highway system.
독일 정부는 널리 분포되어 있는 고속도로망을 민영화할 계획이라고 발표했다.

encompass 포함하다, 둘러싸다

The festival is to encompass everything from music, theater and ballet to literature, cinema and the visual arts.
그 축제는 음악, 연극, 발레에서 문학, 영화, 시각예술까지 모든 것을 포함할 것이다.

abhorrent 혐오스러운

They have been accused of committing abhorrent acts of sexual assaults on some defenseless women sleeping in a tent.
그들은 텐트 안에서 잠들어 있던 무방비상태의 여성들에게 가증스러운 성폭행을 저지른 혐의로 기소되었다.

justice system 사법제도

The jury system will help Korea develop a more democratic justice system.
배심제도는 한국이 좀 더 민주적인 사법제도를 발전시키는데 도움을 줄 것이다.

there is growing understanding ***that*** this abhorrent practice has no place in modern justice systems
동격의 that
이러한 혐오스러운 관습이 현대 사법제도에서 설 자리가 없다는 점증하는 이해가 있다

have yet to do 아직 ~하지 않았다

I have yet to call her because I was so busy.
나는 너무나도 바빠서 아직 그녀에게 전화를 하지 못했다.

States that have abolished capital punishment often have lower murder rates than ***those that have yet to do so***.
사형제를 철폐했던 나라들이 종종 아직 그렇게 하지 않았던 나라들 보다 낮은 살인률을 갖는다.

not least 특히

The documentary caused a lot of bad feeling, not least among the workers whose lives it described.
그 다큐멘터리는 많은 불쾌감을 자아냈는데, 특히 그것에 자신들의 생활이 묘사된 노동자들 사이에서 그랬다.

last but not least 마지막으로, 그렇지만 앞에 말씀드린 분(것)들과 마찬가지로 중요한(사람 · 사물을 열거하면서 마지막에 언급하는 것이 앞에 언급한 것 못지않게 중요함을 말하기 위해 씀)

Last but not least, I'd like to thank all the catering staff.
마지막으로(그러나 앞에 언급한 어느 분들 못지않게 중요한 분들인) 음식을 준비해 주신 분들께도 감사의 말씀을 꼭 드리고 싶다.

outrage 격분

The judge's remarks caused public outrage.
그 심판의 발언은 대중의 격분을 불러일으켰다.

prolific 다작의, 다산의

The most prolific serial killer in U.S. history has been sentenced to 48 consecutive life terms without the possibility of parole.
미국 역사상 가장 많은 희생자를 낸 연쇄살인범에게 감형 없이 48회에 걸쳐 종신형을 살도록 하는 선고가 내려졌다.

year on year 전년대비의, 전년 동기에 비해

The first-quarter figure plunged 14.2 percent year-on-year, the first drop in three years.
1분기 수치는 전년 동분기 대비 14.2% 떨어졌는데, 3년 만에 처음 감소세를 나타냈다.

bring together 소집하다, 모이게 하다

The meeting in Busan will bring together several heads of state.
부산에서 열릴 회의에는 여러 나라의 국가 지도자들이 참석할 예정이다.

irrevocable 취소할 수 없는, (법률 등이) 폐지할 수 없는, 돌이킬 수 없는

There remains an unforgivable and irrevocable risk of executing an innocent person, which explains why the right to life must not be limited in any way and under any excuses.
죄가 없는 사람을 사형시키는, 용서할 수 없으며 되 돌이킬 수 없는 위험이 남아있기 때문에, 어떠한 방법과 이유로도 생명권을 제한해서는 안 되는 것이다.

toxic 유독성의

The truth is there are other hundreds of toxic ingredients.
사실은 그밖에도 다른 수백 가지 유해성분들이 있다는 것이다.

endorse 지지하다, 배서하다(은행)

Meanwhile others have been busy endorsing candidates.
한편 다른 사람들은 후보자들을 지지하느라 바빴다.

look set to ~할 준비가 되어있다

The team look set to win Olympic gold.
그 팀은 올림픽 금메달을 따 놓은 당상인 것 같다.

foresight 통찰력, 선견지명

She has had the foresight to prepare herself financially in case of an accident.
그녀는 사고가 날 경우를 대비해서 재정적으로 준비를 하는 선견지명이 있었다.

Death Penalty

Liberal

The death penalty should be abolished. It is inhumane and is 'cruel and unusual' punishment. Imprisonment is the appropriate punishment for murder. Every execution risks killing an innocent person.

Conservative

The death penalty is a punishment that fits the crime of murder; it is neither 'cruel' nor 'unusual.' Executing a murderer is the appropriate punishment for taking an innocent life.

(studentnewsdaily.com February 25, 2013)

Memo

11.

Another Step Toward Fairness

Leon Panetta, the departing *secretary of defense[1], took an important step on Monday to improve *treatment[2] of gay[1)] and lesbian[2)] *military personnel[3] and their families.

He announced a limited expansion of *benefits[4] for same-sex partners, like access to military commissaries, *gyms[5] and various family-support programs on *bases and posts[6]. Same-sex partners will now be eligible for *identification cards[7] to allow them on base. Gay couples who are both in the military will be entitled to the same consideration for *joint-duty[8]

1 secretary of defense
국방장관

2 treatment
대우

3 military personnel
군 병력, 군 요원

4 benefits
수당, 보조금, 혜택

5 gyms = gymnasium
체육관

6 bases and posts
기지와 주둔지

7 identification cards
신분증

8 joint-duty
합동근무

1) **gay** 게이(gay)라는 말은 영어이며 '즐거운, 유쾌한, 기쁜, 행복한' 등의 사전적 의미를 가지고 있다. 주로 1960년대 서양에서 여성인권운동, 흑인인권운동과 더불어 동성애자의 인권운동이 활발하게 일어나면서 게이라는 용어가 새롭게 사용되었다. 게이는 남녀 동성애자를 아울러 일컫는 말이지만, 최근 들어서는 주로 남성 동성애자를 지칭하는 말로 쓰인다. 우리나라에서는 보통 게이는 남성 동성애자를, 레즈비언은 여성 동성애자를 나타내는 말로 구분되어 쓰인다. 동성애자 스스로 자신의 정체성을 긍정적, 적극적으로 수용한 결과 나타난 말인 호모 섹슈얼리티(homosexuality) 등의 정신분석학적 용어와는 구별된다. 한편, 동성애자, 양성애자(bisexual), 성전환자(transgender, transsexual) 등 성적소수자 전체를 퀴어(queer)라는 용어로 표현한다. 이성애자를 일반적이라고 보는 사회를 비판하는 취지에서 동성애자들은 자신들을 역설적으로 이반(二般 또는 異般)이라고 부르기도 한다(네이버 지식백과, 두산백과).

2) **A lesbian** is a female homosexual; a female who experiences romantic love or sexual attraction to other females. The term lesbian is also used with regard to sexual identity or sexual behavior, or as an adjective to characterize or associate nouns with female homosexuality or same-sex attraction(Wikipedia).

9 burial rights
매장권리(묻힐 권리)

10 national cemeteries
국립묘지

11 eligibility
자격

12 Pentagon
미 국방부 US Department of Defense

13 health care coverage
의료보험혜택

assignments as other couples.

Granting other benefits like *burial rights[9] at *national cemeteries[10] and *eligibility[11] for on-base family housing are said to remain under consideration.

The announcement adds to Mr. Panetta's solid record on equality during his time at the *Pentagon[12]. But the deplorable 1996 Defense of Marriage Act[3)], which prevents the federal government from recognizing same-sex marriages, stands in the way of full benefits like *health care coverage[13] and *off-

3) **The Defense of Marriage Act** (DOMA) (enacted September 21, 1996) is a United States federal law that allows states to refuse to recognize same-sex marriages granted under the laws of other states. Until Section 3 of the Act was ruled unconstitutional in 2013, DOMA, in conjunction with other statutes, had barred same-sex married couples from being recognized as "spouses" for purposes of federal laws, effectively barring them from receiving federal marriage benefits. DOMA's passage did not prevent individual states from recognizing same-sex marriage, but it imposed constraints on the benefits received by all legally married same-sex couples.
Initially introduced in May 1996, DOMA passed both houses of Congress by large, veto-proof majorities and was signed into law by President Bill Clinton in September 1996. By defining "spouse" and its related terms to signify a heterosexual couple in a recognized marriage, Section 3 codified non-recognition of same-sex marriages for all federal purposes, including insurance benefits for government employees, social security survivors' benefits, immigration, bankruptcy, and the filing of joint tax returns, as well as excluding same-sex spouses from the scope of laws protecting families of federal officers (18 U. S. C. §115), laws evaluating financial aid eligibility, and federal ethics laws applicable to opposite-sex spouses.
Clinton - along with key legislators - later advocated for DOMA's repeal. The Obama administration announced in 2011 that it had concluded Section 3 was unconstitutional and that although the administration would continue to enforce the law while it existed, it would no longer defend the law in court. In United States v. Windsor (2013), the U.S. Supreme Court declared Section 3 of DOMA unconstitutional under the Due Process Clause of the Fifth Amendment(Wikipedia).

4) **"Don't ask, don't tell" (DADT) was the official United States policy** on service by gays and lesbians in the military instituted by the Clinton Administration in February 28, 1994, when Department of Defense Directive 1304.26 issued on December 21, 1993, took effect, lasting until September 20, 2011. The policy prohibited military personnel from discriminating against or harassing closeted homosexual or bisexual service members or applicants, while barring openly gay, lesbian, or bisexual persons from military service(Wikipedia).

base housing allowances[14]. And even though the Pentagon's "don't ask, don't tell" policy[4)] ended in 2011, soldiers in same-sex unions are not eligible for the military's *family separation allowance[15] when they are deployed away from their spouse.

Achieving full equality for gay and lesbian service members requires repealing the marriage act, which *House Republicans[16] refuse to do. That means the task will be up to the *Supreme Court[17], which is scheduled to hear a challenge to the law's constitutionality next month.

The day before Mr. Panetta made his announcement, Charlie Morgan, a *chief warrant officer[18] in the *Army National Guard[19] who served in Kuwait, and a *named plaintiff[20] in a federal lawsuit challenging the Defense of Marriage Act's denial of equal protection, passed away after battling *breast cancer[21] for several years. She did not survive to see the unjust law fall. Now, her widow, Karen Morgan, is ineligible to receive *monthly survivor benefits[22] that *heterosexual military spouses[23] can count on to sustain them and their children.

nytimes.com February 22, 2013

14 off-base housing allowance
영외거주수당

15 family separation allowance
(군사) 가족별거수당

16 House Republican
하원공화당 국회의원

17 Supreme Court
대법원

18 chief warrant officer
선임준위(준사관)

19 Army National Guard
육군주방위군

20 named plaintiff
지명(정)된 (법률) (민사 소송의) 원고, 고소인

21 breast cancer
유방암

22 survivor benefits
유족보조금(수당)

23 heterosexual military spouses
이성 군인 배우자

WORDS and STRUCTURES

military personnel 군 병력, 군 장병

The United States disposed about 50 thousand military personnel in Japan.
미국은 현재 일본에 5만 여명의 미군을 배치하고 있다.

benefits 수당, 보조금, 혜택

Full-time employees are much more likely to have benefits coverage than are part-time employees.
정규 직원은 시간제 직원에 비해 부가수당 혜택을 받는 경우가 훨씬 더 많은 것 같다.

commissary (군대 · 교도소 등의) 매점

We don't have a commissary in our camp.
우리 기지에는 매점이 없다.

be eligible for 자격이 있다

To be eligible for the award, students must be enrolled full-time.
그 상을 받을 자격이 있기 위해서는 학생들은 정규 등록을 해야 한다.

joint-duty 합동근무

Katusas are on a joint duty with U.S. soldiers.
카투사는 미군과 합동 근무를 한다.

grant 부여하다, 허가하다

The city granted an honorary Busan citizenship to the actor on January 10.
그 도시는 1월 10일 부산 명예 시민권을 그 배우에게 부여했다.

deplorable 개탄스러운

It is deplorable that scandals should occur so often in the political circle.
정계에 부정 사건이 빈발하는 것은 매우 통탄할 일이다.

stand in the way of ~을 훼방 놓다, 막다

Don't stand in the way of progress.
길을 막고 서있지 마시오.

health care coverage 의료보험혜택

In his radio address, the President also reminded citizens that health care coverage will not be available for around half of all Americans under the age of 65 if nothing is done within the next 10 years.
오바마 대통령은 라디오 연설에서, 10년 안에 어떠한 대응도 하지 않는다면 65세 이하의 미국인들 중 절반은 의료보험의 혜택을 받지 못할 것이라고 시민들에게 상기시켰다.

repeal (법률) 폐지하다

The law was repealed two years ago.
그 법률은 2년 전에 폐지되었다.

Achieving full equality for gay and lesbian service members requires repealing the marriage act, ***which*** House Republicans refuse to do.
= Achieving full equality for gay and lesbian service members requires repealing the marriage act, ***and*** House Republicans refuse to do ***it***.
게이와 레즈비언 복무요원들에 대해 완전한 평등을 달성하는 것은 결혼법의 폐지를 필요로 하는데, 하원 공화당 국회의원들은 결혼법의 폐지를 거부한다.

challenge (적법성 등에 의문을 제기하는) 도전 (저항), 반론

Their legal challenge was unsuccessful.
그들의 법적 반론은 성공하지 못했다.

constitutionality 합헌성

They questioned the constitutionality of the law.
그들은 그 법률의 합헌성에 의문을 제기했다.

plaintiff (법률)(민사 소송의) 원고, 고소인

The jury found for(against) the plaintiff.
배심은 원고에게 유리(불리)한 평결을 내렸다.

pass away 사망하다(돌아가시다)

His mother passed away ten years ago.
그의 어머니는 10년 전에 돌아가셨다.

She did not survive to ***see*** the unjust law ***fall***.
그녀는 살아서 그 공정하지 못한 법률이 폐지되는 것을 보지 못했다.

sustain (필요한 것을 제공하여) 살아가게(지탱하게) 하다

The love and support of his family sustained him during his time in prison.
그가 교도소에서 형기를 사는 동안 가족의 사랑과 지지가 그를 지탱해 주었다.

monthly survivor benefits ***that*** heterosexual military spouses can count on to sustain them and their children
= monthly survivor benefits ***+(and)*** heterosexual military spouses can count on ***them***(monthly survivor benefits) to sustain them and their children
이성의 군인 배우자들이 그들과 그들의 가족이 살아가기 위해 의지할 수 있는 매월 받는 유족수당

Same-sex Marriage

Liberal

Marriage is the union of people who love each other. It should be legal for gay, lesbian, bisexual and transgender individuals, to ensure equal rights for all. Support same-sex marriage. Opposed to the creation of a constitutional amendment establishing marriage as the union of one man and one woman. All individuals, regardless of their sexual orientation, have the right to marry. Prohibiting same-sex citizens from marrying denies them their civil rights. [Opinions vary on whether this issue is equal to civil rights for African Americans.]

Conservative

Marriage is the union of one man and one woman. Oppose same-sex marriage.
Support Defense of Marriage Act (DOMA), passed in 1996, which affirms the right of states not to recognize same-sex marriages licensed in other states.
Requiring citizens to sanction same-sex relationships violates moral and religious beliefs of millions of Christians, Jews, Muslims and others, who believe marriage is the union of one man and one woman.

(studentnewsdaily.com February 25, 2013)

Memo

12.

The riddle of Europe's single currency with many values

The euro[1)] is not worth the same across the region – Spain and Germany have different currencies

A European Central Bank[2)] survey shows that households in northern Europe have a much lower *net wealth[1] than those in southern Europe. Average German net assets per household are just under €200,000, while they are €300,000 in Spain

1 net wealth
순 부

1) **euro** (유로화) 1999년부터 유통되기 시작해 2002년 7월부터 전면적으로 통용되기 시작한 유럽연합의 단일 화폐다. 1995년 12월 15일 스페인 마드리드에서 열린 EU정상회의에 참여한 15개 회원국들은 1999년 1월 유럽연합의 경제통화동맹(EMU : Economic and Monetary Union)을 출범시키고 단일통화의 명칭을 '유로(EURO)'로 하는 데 합의하였다. 그리고 유로화를 1999년 1월 1일 ~ 2001년 12월 31일까지의 과도기를 거쳐 2002년 1월 1일 ~ 6월 1일까지의 완결기간을 거친 후 전면적으로 통용하기로 확정하였다. 또한 EU는 EMU의 가입자격을 해당 국가정부의 재정적자를 국내총생산(GDP)의 3%로 제한하는 등 엄격히 규정하고 있다. 유로는 7종의 지폐와 8종의 동전으로 구성되며, 유로의 제작 · 발행은 각 국가가 독자적으로 실시하고 있다.
2002년 1월 유로 첫 시행에 참가한 국가는 벨기에 · 프랑스 · 독일 · 이탈리아 · 룩셈부르크 · 네덜란드 · 아일랜드 · 그리스 · 포르투갈 · 스페인 · 핀란드 · 오스트리아 등 12개국이며, 영국 · 덴마크 · 스웨덴 3개국은 자국 사정으로 불참했다. 이후 슬로베니아 · 몰타 · 키프로스 · 슬로바키아 · 에스토니아 등이 가입, 2013년 7월 현재 17개국에서 유통되고 있다. 유로화를 사용하는 이들 국가들을 일컬어 '유로랜드', '유로존'이라고 한다. 한편, 2013년 7월 유럽연합의 28번째 회원국이 된 크로아티아는 유로화로 대체되기 전까지는 자국 화폐인 쿠나를 사용한다.
EU회원국 중 유로화를 쓰지 않는 국가 : 덴마크, 스웨덴, 영국, 불가리아, 체코, 헝가리, 라트비아(2014년부터 사용 예정), 리투아니아, 폴란드, 루마니아, 크로아티아(네이버 지식백과, 시사상식사전).

2) **European Central Bank** (유럽 중앙은행) 유로를 사용하는 유럽연합(EU)의 중앙은행으로 2000년 설립됐다. 한국은행이나 미국 연방 준비제도이사회(FRB)처럼 기준금리를 조절해 유로 존 국가를 안정시키는 것이 핵심 기능이다. 2002년부터는 회원국의 금융정책의 집행권을 갖고 있다. 다만, 통화정책에 관해서는 각국의 통화당국이 최종 책임을 진다(네이버 지식백과, 한경 경제용어사전, 한국경제신문/한경닷컴).

2 Cypriot [sípriət]
키프로스 사람

3 counter-intuitive findings
반직관적인 조사 결과

4 exchange rates
환율

5 eurozone economies
유로 존 국가들

6 start of the eurozone
유로 존의 출발(1999년)

7 consumer prices
소비자물가

8 broadly
대체로, 대략적으로

9 wages and prices
임금과 물가

10 asset prices
자산 가격

11 property prices
부동산 가격

12 real estate
부동산

and €670,000 in Cyprus. No, this not a typo.

German newspapers screamed that poor Germans are bailing out rich *Cypriots[2]. This interpretation is wrong but the truth behind these *counter-intuitive findings[3] is even more disturbing. What the survey shows is not wealth differentials but the de facto *exchange rates[4] between the *eurozone[3)] economies[5]. They are not measures of net wealth but of imbalances. And they are enormous.

Since the *start of the eurozone[6], wages and *consumer prices[7] have remained *broadly[8] constant in Germany. In southern Europe, the general level of *wages and prices[9] has increased year in, year out. Over the period, this persistent inflation gap has led to a large discrepancy in *asset prices[10]. This is why an apartment in Milan costs much more than one in Munich, the city with the highest *property prices[11] in Germany. A German euro buys more *real estate[12] in Munich than an Italian euro buys in Milan.

3) **The Eurozone**, officially called the euro area, is an economic and monetary union (EMU) of 18 European Union (EU) member states that have adopted the euro (€) as their common currency and sole legal tender.
The Eurozone consists of Austria, Belgium, Cyprus, Estonia, Finland, France, Germany, Greece, Ireland, Italy, Latvia, Luxembourg, Malta, the Netherlands, Portugal, Slovakia, Slovenia, and Spain. Other EU states (except for the United Kingdom and Denmark) are obliged to join once they meet the criteria to do so. No state has left and there are no provisions to do so or to be expelled. Monaco, San Marino, the Vatican City and Andorra have formal agreements with the EU to use the euro as their official currency and issue their own coins. Other states, like Kosovo and Montenegro, have adopted the euro unilaterally, but these countries do not formally form part of the Eurozone and do not have representation in the ECB or the Eurogroup(Wikipedia).

In the frantic German debate about these figures, the focus is on *median wealth[13] – the statistic that pinpoints the exact middle if one were to rank households by wealth. Looking at the median, the gap becomes even more extreme. In countries with extremely large wealth differentials such as Germany, where a few super-rich people own a large share of the land and real estate, the median is significantly lower than the *mean[14].

13 median wealth
중간의 부, 평균 부

14 mean
평균

15 low property ownership rate
낮은 부동산 소유율

Measured in terms of the median, German households occupy the last place among all eurozone countries, with net wealth of a mere €51,000, while the median Cypriot household has net wealth of €267,000. The explanation for this gap is the *low property ownership rate[15] in Germany – well under 50 per cent. This means that the median German does not own a house, while the median Cypriot or Spaniard does.

The median is the statistic to quote when you want to say that your typical German is poorer than your typical Spaniard. But that is a meaningless statement because it is based on distributions within countries. If you want to compare across countries, it is better to take the mean. The gap is not quite as dramatic but it is still very large.

If mean German net wealth is €200,000 per household and mean Spanish net wealth is €300,000, and if I further believe that the Germans are not really less wealthy as a nation, measured per household, then this gap tells me the minimum

16 real exchange rates
실제 환율

17 monetary union
통화동맹

extent by which Germany and Spain would need to adjust their *real exchange rates[16].

In truth, the gap is likely to be larger. I happen to believe that your average German household is richer than the average Spanish household. If my assumption is right, then the imbalance between Germany and Spain, as expressed by those figures, would be even higher.

In a *monetary union[17], adjustment can only occur through real movements in wages and prices. Since Germany is not inflating, and is not likely to inflate in the future, I see no chance of that happening, even in the long run. My conclusion is that, in the long run, this adjustment will eventually happen through a nominal change in the exchange rates – which means that somebody has to quit the eurozone or resort to a parallel currency.

To put it another way: if the same unit of account[4)] gives us a higher wealth figure for Spain than for Germany, and when you also know that this cannot be true, then there must be something wrong with the unit of account. The other potential solution is that there could be a problem with the data, but I see no fault with the statistical techniques used by the ECB. Maybe they got the house prices wrong. Statisticians do have difficulty capturing the declines of house prices after

4) **unit of account** (money of account) (통화로서 발행되지 않는)(계산 화폐) 장부상으로만 쓰이는 화폐의 명칭.

*bubbles[18]. But this type of discrepancy could not account for such a wide gap.

Indeed, this view also ties in with anecdotal evidence. Looking back to 1999, my own experience was that restaurants and taxis in Berlin were cheaper than restaurants or taxis in Brussels or Paris, but the differences have now become extreme. Curiously, the price gap also affects *tradeable goods[19]: European *cross-border retail markets[20] are not working efficiently.

This leaves me to conclude that the unit of account is not really the same across the eurozone – that Spain and Germany have a different euro. This is also the reason why I believe southern Europeans have a rational reason to shift their *savings[21] to bank accounts in the north – because this would present the only way to preserve the value of their euros in the long run.

Of course, I would not expect the ECB or any other European institution to conclude that the euro is not the same in Germany as in Spain. It is their job to deny this. But the imposition of *capital controls[22] in Cyprus has set a precedent. It now has a new *currency[23]. I call it the Cypriot euro. According to the ECB's study, Germany also has its own currency – the German euro – and it is massively undervalued.

ft.com April 14, 2013

18 bubble
과열, 붕괴

19 tradeable goods
매매할 수 있는 상품

20 cross-border retail markets
국가 간 소매시장

21 savings
저금

22 capital controls
자본통제

23 currency
통화

WORDS and STRUCTURES

riddle 수수께끼, 난제

He thought he had solved a huge riddle of the universe.
그는 우주의 거대한 수수께끼를 풀었다고 생각했다.

net 순, 에누리 없는, 최종적인

Net sales were on the rise this year.
올해 순 매출은 증가했다.

net wealth 순 부

net assets 순 자산

typo (비격식) 오식, 오타(typographic error)

I think there's one typo on the test.
문제에 한 개의 오타가 있는 것 같다.

bail out (비격식) (경제적 위기에 처한 사람 · 회사 등을) 구제하다, 곤경을 벗어나게 하다

The three groups finally agreed to bail out the troubled country.
이 세 단체는 마침내 이 문제 많은 나라를 긴급구제해주기로 동의했다.

findings 결과, 결론

Surely, the finding is gloomy and disappointing.
분명히, 이러한 결과는 우울하고 실망스럽다.

disturbing 충격적인, 혼란스러운

This is terribly disturbing. 이것은 매우 충격적이다.

The title Sea of Japan is both incorrect and disturbing.
일본해라는 명칭은 옳지도 않을뿐더러 혼란을 주는 명칭이다.

de facto 사실상의, 실제상의

Everland is considered a de facto holding company of Samsung Group.
에버랜드는 삼성그룹의 사실상의 지주회사로 간주되고 있다.

exchange rate 환율

For the first time in 15 months, the won-dollar exchange rate hit a new yearly-low.
15개월 만에 처음으로, 원달러 환율이 연간 최저치를 기록했다.

economy (경제주체로서의) 국가

Colombia is now the third largest economy in South America.
콜롬비아는 현재 남아메리카에서 세 번째로 큰 경제대국이다.

What the survey shows is ***not*** wealth differentials ***but*** the de facto exchange rates between the eurozone economies.
not A but B A가 아니라 B다
그 조사가 보여주는 것은 부의 격차가 아니라 유로 존 국가들 사이의 사실상의 환율이다.

year in, year out 매년

year in and year out 해마다, 끊임없이

Many birds return to the same spot year in, year out(year after year).
많은 새들이 매년 같은 장소로 돌아온다.

persistent 지속적인, 계속하는

He added that Seoul will make persistent efforts for peace with the communist nation.
그는 남한은 북한과의 평화를 이룩하기 위해 지속적인 노력을 할 것이라고 덧붙였다.

discrepancy 불일치, 차이

There was a discrepancy between what they ordered and the bill they received.
그들이 주문한 것과 받은 계산서에는 차이가 있었다.

frantic 광적인, 제정신이 아닌

The savings of the wealthy and middle class, increasing far beyond the possibilities of sound investment, had been drawn into frantic speculation in stocks or real estate.
건전한 투자가능성을 훨씬 넘어서 증가되고 있던 부유층 및 중류층의 저축자금은 주식이나 부동산의 광적인 투기자금으로 끌려들어가고 있었다.

pinpoint (위치 · 시간을) 정확히 찾아내다(보여주다)

He was able to pinpoint on the map the site of the medieval village.
그는 지도에서 그 중세 마을 위치를 정확히 짚을 수 있었다.

a large share of 상당한 부분

It gets a large share of the world's trade.
그것은 세계무역의 상당한 부분을 차지하다.

mean 평균(의)

The mean annual rainfall was 800mm.
평균 연간 강수량은 800mm였다.

median German does not own a house, while the median Cypriot or Spaniard ***does***
does = own a house ***대동사*** *do*
중간의 독일인은 집을 소유하지 않지만 중간의 키프러스 사람들과 스페인 사람들은 집을 소유한다.

distribution 분배

Thus it will further exacerbate the unequal distribution of income in our nation.
따라서 그것은 한국에 불공평한 수입 분배를 더욱 악화시킬 것이다.

dramatic 급격한, 커다란

This year has seen a dramatic rise in profits for our company.
금년에 우리 회사는 현격한 이익증대가 있었다.

adjustment 조정

The opposition Democratic Party is willing to meet with the president to make necessary adjustments to the deal.
야당인 민주당은 협정에 필요한 조정을 하기 위해 기꺼이 대통령과 만날 것이다.

movement 변동

It is almost impossible to predict the oil price movement at the moment.
현재로서는 유가변동을 전망하기가 거의 불가능하다.

nominal 명목상의, 이름뿐인

He is the nominal leader of the party.
그는 그 정당의 명목상 대표이다.

to put it another way 달리 말하자면, 달리표현하면

He was too trusting - or, to put it another way, he had no head for business.
그는 사람들을 너무 잘 믿었다. 달리 표현하면, 그는 사업적인 머리가 없었다.

discrepancy 불일치, 차이

There is a discrepancy between spelling and pronunciation.
철자와 발음의 불일치가 있다.

tie in with 일치하다, 동시에 하게하다

I timed my holiday to tie in with my children's school holiday.
나는 휴가를 애들 방학과 일치하도록 시간을 짰다.

anecdotal 입증되지 않은, 일화적인

anecdotal evidence 입증되지 않은 증거

His speech is anecdotal evidence.
그의 말은 입증되지 않은 증거이다.

imposition (새로운 법률 · 세금 등의) 시행(도입)

To foster self-sufficiency, congressional leaders urged a policy of protectionism - imposition of restrictions on imported goods to foster the development of American industry.
경제적 자립을 촉진하기 위해 의회지도자들은 '보호무역주의' 정책 즉, 미국산업의 발전을 촉진하기 위해 수입품에 제한을 가하는 정책의 시행을 촉구했다.

set a precedent 선례를 만들다

The ruling set a precedent for future libel cases.
그 판결은 미래의 명예 훼손 사건들에 대한 선례를 만들었다.

13.

China enters era of slower growth

China has entered an era of slower growth and must adjust to the end of three decades of *double-digit[1] annual *economic expansion[2], the government warned on Monday.

Economic growth unexpectedly slowed to 7.7 per cent in the *first quarter[3] compared with a year ago, according to the National Bureau of Statistics[1)]. "After 30 years of high-speed economic growth, *potential productivity[4] in China has dropped," said Shen Laiyun, bureau spokesman. "During the *economic transformation period[5] of other countries, such as Germany, Japan and South Korea, their overall economic growth rates also fell to a lower level."

*Significantly[6] slower Chinese growth will affect economies across the world and hurt *exporters of raw materials[7] that have become reliant on surging Chinese demand over the past decade.

1 double-digit
두 자리 수의

2 economic expansion
경제성장

3 first quarter
1분기

4 potential productivity
잠재적 생산성

5 economic transformation period
경제체제 전환기

6 significantly
현저하게

7 exporters of raw materials
원자재 수출국

1) **National Bureau of Statistics of China** (중국) 중국 국가통계국.

8 commodity exporters
원자재 수출국

9 slowdown
(속도 · 활동의) 둔화

10 investment and exports
투자와 수출

11 domestic consumption
내수

12 agricultural and forestry goods
농 임산품

13 dairy products
유제품

14 growth potential
성장가능성(잠재력)

"For *commodity exporters[8] in places like Australia, Latin America and Africa, much slower Chinese growth is very bad news," said Frederic Neumann, co-head of Asian economic research at HSBC[2)]. "A lot of supply is coming on stream that was predicated on the idea that China would grow faster than 9 per cent forever."

Chinese officials have played down the significance of lower growth in recent weeks, saying the *slowdown[9] is partly due to efforts to rebalance the economy away from *investment and exports[10] towards *domestic consumption[11].

"I don't think China will be able to sustain a super-high or ultra-high speed of growth and that is not what we want," said Xi Jinping, president. "China's model of development is not sustainable, so it is imperative for us to speed up the transformation of the growth model."

Stock markets across Asia fell after the Chinese GDP[3)] figure was released on Monday morning. Currencies of countries that export heavily to China also tumbled. The Australian dollar dropped 0.6 per cent, while the New Zealand dollar shed 1 per cent against its US counterpart. New Zealand is a key exporter to China of *agricultural and forestry goods[12] such as lamb, *dairy products[13] and timber.Weaker *growth potential[14] will also force companies operating in China to reconsider their

2) **HSBC**(Hongkong and Shanghai Banking Corp.Lt.) 홍콩 · 상하이 은행 그룹.
3) **GDP**(gross domestic product) 국내 총생산.

business models, which often rely on high levels of debt and investment.

Most analysts had expected *the world's second largest economy[15] to grow by about 8 per cent in the first quarter after it rebounded in the middle of last year, growing 7.9 per cent in the fourth quarter.

But a weak *industrial sector[16] and disappointing *retail sales[17] *dragged down[18] growth even as China saw a *surge in credit[19], suggesting *monetary stimulus[20] is not having as much impact as before.

Echoing Beijing's warning, the World Bank[4)] on Monday said Chinese growth would slow to "between 6 and 7 per cent by the end of the decade", according to Bert Hofman, its chief Asia economist. In its half-yearly regional report, the bank said the Chinese economy would expand 8.3 per cent this year, but most analysts believe that forecast is optimistic.

Mr Sheng said he expected China to *meet[21] the annual growth target of 7.5 per cent set by China's new leaders earlier

15 the world's second largest economy
중국을 가리킴

16 industrial sector
산업부문

17 retail sales
소매판매

18 drag down
끌어내리다

19 surge in credit
신용등급 상승

20 monetary stimulus
금융적인 자극

21 meet
충족하다

4) **World Bank**(IBRD)(세계은행) 정식 명칭은 국제부흥개발은행(International Bank for Reconstruction and Development). 1944년의 브레튼우즈 협정에 기초해 1946년 6월에 발족한 국제 금융기관의 중심적 존재이며, 상업베이스로 장기의 하드 론(hard loan ; 조건이 엄격한 융자)을 행한다. 우리나라는 1955년에 가입했고 1970년 대표이사로 선임되었으며 1985년 10월 제40차 총회가 서울에서 개최되었다. 세계은행은 각국의 경제부흥과 개발촉진을 목적으로 설립되었는데 현재는 주로 개발도상국의 공업화를 위해 융자를 행하고 있다. 세계은행이 지원하는 개도국의 프로젝트 총 투자액은 연간 500~600억 달러 정도 규모로, 지역별로 중남미 지역이 가장 큰 수혜국이 되고 있다. 분야별로는 석유, 전력 등 에너지 분야에 큰 비중을 두고 있다. 세계은행의 융자방식은 전체융자액 가운데 50~55% 가량은 협조융자 방식으로 지원하고 그 재원은 2국간, 다자간 등 공적차관을 비롯해 각국의 수출신용과 상업차관에서 마련된다(네이버 지식백과, 매일경제/매경닷컴).

22 government figures
정부의 통계수치

23 employment figures
고용수치(취업률)

24 consumer inflation
소비자 인플레이션 (물가상승)

25 subdued
억제된

this year. If the economy grew at that rate or less in 2013, it would mark the slowest annual growth since 1990.

Beijing appears to be quite relaxed about slower growth, which has not triggered higher unemployment. More than 3m new jobs were created in urban areas in the first quarter, according to *government figures[22]. Mr Sheng said China's "*employment figures[23] stand in sharp contrast to those in the US and Europe".

*Consumer inflation[24] remains relatively *subdued[25], with an increase of 2.4 per cent in the first quarter from a year earlier.

ft.com April 15, 2013

WORDS and STRUCTURES

economies (경제 주체로서의) 국가

Youth unemployment is generally viewed as an important policy issue for many economies.
많은 국가들이 일반적으로 청년실업을 중요한 정책문제로 여긴다.

surging 급증하는

Illegal medical operations are surging these days.
요즘 불법 의료 시술 행위가 급증하고 있다.

commodity (경제)생필품, 물품, 원자재

The investment bank decided to buy commodities as a hedge against inflation.
그 투자은행은 인플레이션에 대한 대비책으로 원자재를 구매하기로 결정했다.

be/come on stream 가동 중이다(이용할 수 있다)

The new computer system comes on stream next month.
새 컴퓨터 시스템은 다음 달에 가동에 들어간다.

play down 과소평가하다

The Korean Counsellor in Bangkok also played down the report.
방콕 주재 한국영사도 이 보도를 심각하게 받아들이지 않았다.

tumble 추락하다, 굴러 떨어지다

Consumer sentiment also tumbled, falling from a two-year high in the first quarter.
소비심리 역시 하락해 1분기에 기록했던 2년 이래 최고수준에 미치지 못했다.

shed 빠지다

Between Dec. 29 and Jan. 6 this year, the country's foreign exchange rate shed 2.32 percent against the U.S. dollar.

올해 12월 29일부터 1월 6일까지 한국의 환율은 미 달러화에 대해 2.32퍼센트가 내렸다.

the New Zealand dollar shed 1 per cent against its US ***counterpart***

counterpart = dollar

뉴질랜드 달러는 미국 달러 대비 1%가 빠졌다(떨어졌다).

Weaker growth potential will also force companies operating in China to reconsider their business models, ***which*** often rely on high levels of debt and investment

= Weaker growth potential will also force companies operating in China to reconsider their business models, ***and they***(business models) often rely on high levels of debt and investment

약한 성장가능성은 또한 중국에서 가동 중인 회사들로 하여금 그들의 사업모델을 제고하도록 할 것인데, 그 사업모델은 종종 높은 수준의 부채와 투자에 의존한다.

a weak industrial sector and disappointing retail sales dragged down growth even as China saw a surge in credit, ***suggesting*** monetary stimulus is not having as much impact as before

= a weak industrial sector and disappointing retail sales dragged down growth even as China saw a surge in credit, ***and it suggests*** (that) monetary stimulus is not having as much impact as before

even as = even though

약한 산업부문과 실망스러운 소매판매는 비록 중국이 신용등급의 상승을 보인다하더라도 성장을 끌어내렸는데 그것은 금융적인 자극이 이전만큼 많이 영향을 미지고 있지 않다는 것을 암시한다.

he expected China to meet the annual growth target of 7.5 per cent ***set*** by China's new leaders earlier this year

= he expected China to meet the annual growth target of 7.5 per cent ***(which was) set*** by China's new leaders earlier this year

그는 중국이 올해 초 중국의 새 지도자에 의해 설정된 7.5%의 연 성장 목표를 충족할 것이라 기대했다.

Beijing appears to be quite relaxed about slower growth, ***which*** has not triggered higher unemployment

= Beijing appears to be quite relaxed about slower growth, ***and it***(slower growth) has not triggered higher unemployment

북경은 느린 성장에 대해 아주 느슨해 있는 것처럼 보이는데 느린 성장이 더 높은 실직을 유발하지는 않았다.

stand in sharp contrast to 뚜렷한(확연한) 대조를 보이다

The home stands in sharp contrast to the mansion on the U.S.

그 집은 미국의 대저택과는 뚜렷한 대조를 이루고 있다.

China's "employment figures stand in sharp contrast to ***those*** in the US and Europe"

= China's "employment figures stand in sharp contrast to ***those(employment figures)*** in the US and Europe"

중국의 취업률은 미국과 유럽의 취업률과 뚜렷한 대조를 보인다.

Memo

14.

*Justices[1] Consider Whether Patents on Genes Are *Valid[2]

The Supreme Court[1)] is poised to take up the highly *charged[3] question of whether human genes can be patented. But another question could *trump[4] it: Has the field of genetics moved so far so fast that whatever the court decides, it has come too late to the issue?

A Myriad Genetics[2)] scientist preparing samples for *DNA[5] sequencing[3)]. The Supreme Court will *hear a case[6] on Monday,

1 Justices
(연방) 최고재판소 판사

2 valid
유효한

3 charged
격론을 일으킬 만한

4 trump
(더 나은 말 · 행동으로 상대를) 이기다(능가하다)

5 DNA(deoxyribo nucleic acid)
(생명공학)생물의 유전현상에 큰 역할을 하는 핵산의 일종

6 hear a case
사건을 심리하다

1) **A supreme court** (대법원) is the highest court within the hierarchy of many legal jurisdictions. Other descriptions for such courts include court of last resort, instance court, judgment court, apex court, and highest court of appeal. Broadly speaking, the decisions of a supreme court are not subject to further review by any other court. Supreme courts typically function primarily as appellate courts, hearing appeals from decisions of lower trial courts, or from intermediate-level appellate courts(Wikipedia).

2) **Myriad Genetics**, Inc. is an American molecular diagnostic company based in Salt Lake City, Utah, United States. Myriad employs a number of proprietary technologies that permit doctors and patients to understand the genetic basis of human disease and the role that genes play in the onset, progression and treatment of disease. This information is used to guide the development of new molecular diagnostic products that assess an individual's risk for developing disease later in life (predictive medicine), identify a patient's likelihood of responding to a particular drug therapy and tailor a patient's drug dose to ensure optimal treatment (personalized medicine), and assess a patient's risk of disease progression and disease recurrence (personalized medicine). Myriad was the subject of scrutiny after it became involved in a lengthy lawsuit over its controversial patenting practices, which led to the landmark Supreme Court decision Association for Molecular Pathology v. Myriad Genetics(Wikipedia).

7 mutate
돌연변이가 되다

8 breast or ovarian cancer
유방암이나 난소암

9 monopoly
독점(권)

10 mutations
돌연변이

11 hearing
공판, 심리

12 microbe
미생물

13 detecting and combating diseases
질병을 찾아내고 질병과 싸우는 것

14 opponents
반대자

15 allies
협력회사

16 ruling
판결

17 upend
~을 뒤엎다

involving the company, on whether human genes can be patented.

The case, which will come before the court on Monday, involves patents held by Myriad Genetics on two human genes, which, when *mutated[7], give a woman a high risk of getting *breast or ovarian cancer[8]. The patents give Myriad a *monopoly[9] on testing for these *mutations[10], a highly lucrative business.

The *hearing[11] comes as rapid scientific advances are producing an explosion of new information about human genes, as well as those of animals, plants and *microbes[12], yielding new approaches to *detecting and combating diseases[13].

*Opponents[14] of gene patents say no company should have rights to what is essentially part of the human body. They contend that Myriad's monopoly has impeded medical progress and access to testing — in some cases denying patients their own genetic information.

Myriad and its *allies[15] in the biotechnology industry counter that a *ruling[16] that invalidates gene patents would *upend[17] three decades of patenting practice and undermine billions of dollars of investments to develop not only genetic tests but also biotech drugs, DNA-based vaccines and

3) **DNA sequencing** (디엔에이 염기서열 결정법) is the process of determining the precise order of nucleotides within a DNA molecule. It includes any method or technology that is used to determine the order of the four bases—adenine, guanine, cytosine, and thymine—in a strand of DNA. The advent of rapid DNA sequencing methods has greatly accelerated biological and medical research and discovery(Wikipedia).

*genetically modified crops[18].

"It would chill a wide range of important activities that benefit society," the Biotechnology Industry Organization[4)] said in a *friend of the court brief[19], one of about 50 such *briefs filed[20] in a sign of the case's potentially far-reaching consequences.

But while the debate continues, some experts say patents on human genes are actually fading in importance.

"Events *on the ground[21] have *overtaken[22] the law," said Dr. James P. Evans, a professor of genetics and medicine at the University of North Carolina. He said the impact of the Supreme Court's decision "will be much more ideological than it will be practical."

*For one thing[23], the Myriad patents *at issue[24] are due to expire over the next two years. And experts say a relatively small number of other diagnostic tests or drugs are protected by patents on single genes.

"I don't think this affects many patents that really matter to companies," said Robert Cook-Deegan, a professor at Duke University's Institute for Genome Sciences and Policy.

It is often said that one-fifth of the roughly 20,000 human genes are patented. But in a study, Christopher Holman, a professor of law at the University of Missouri, Kansas City,

18 genetically modified crops
유전자 변형 곡물

19 friend-of the-court brief
법정조언자의 개요

20 file a brief
소송사건 적요(개요)를 제출하다

21 on the ground
현장에서의

22 overtake
추월하다

23 for one thing
한 예를 든다면

24 at issue
문제가 되고 있는

4) **Biotechnology Industry Organization** (생명공학 산업 기구) is the largest trade organization to serve and represent the biotechnology industry in the United States and worldwide; its members include companies that make Pharmaceutical drugs, biofuels, industrial enzymes, and genetically modified crops. It was founded 1993 in Washington, D.C. and Carl B. Feldbaum was the president from BIO's founding until he retired in 2004, and was succeeded by James C. Greenwood. As of 2013, it represents 1,000 biotech companies in all 50 U.S. states, which employ 1.61 million Americans and support an additional 3.4 million jobs(Wikipedia).

25 isolated genes
분리된 유전자

found that many of those patents merely mentioned genes but would not block genetic testing, and many patents had been allowed to lapse.

Moreover, it will soon be possible to sequence a person's entire genome[5)] for less than the $4,000 that Myriad charges to analyze just two genes, which are called BRCA1 and BRCA2[6)]. And whole genome sequencing might not infringe patents on *isolated genes[25].

The case before the Supreme Court was filed in 2009 by the American Civil Liberties Union[7)] and the Public Patent Foundation[8)] on behalf of some medical societies, researchers and patients.

The question before the court is whether isolated human

5) **genome** [(유전학) 게놈] 생물의 생활기능을 유지하지 위한 최소한의 유전자 군을 함유하는 염색체의 한 세트.

6) **BRCA1 and BRCA1** are a human gene and its protein product, respectively. The official symbol (BRCA1, italic for the gene, nonitalic for the protein) and the official name (breast cancer 1, early onset) are maintained by the HGNC. Orthologs, styled Brca1 and Brca1, are common in other mammal species. BRCA1 is a human tumor suppressor gene(to be specific, a caretaker gene), found in all humans; its protein, also called by the synonym breast cancer type 1 susceptibility protein, is responsible for repairing DNA.
BRCA1 and BRCA2 are normally expressed in the cells of breast and other tissue, where they help repair damaged DNA or destroy cells if DNA cannot be repaired. They are involved in the repair of chromosomal damage with an important role in the error-free repair of DNA double-strand breaks. If BRCA1 or BRCA2 itself is damaged by a BRCA mutation, damaged DNA is not repaired properly, and this increases the risk for breast cancer. Thus, although the terms "breast cancer susceptibility gene" and "breast cancer susceptibility protein" (used frequently both in and outside the medical literature) sound as if they describe an oncogene, BRCA1 and BRCA2 are normal; it is their mutation that is abnormal(Wikipedia).

7) **American Civil Liberties Union** (ACLU)(미국 시민 자유 연맹).

8) **Public Patent Foundation**, or PUBPAT(공립 특허재단), is a non-profit organization that seeks to limit perceived abuse of the United States patent system. It was founded in 2003 by Dan Ravicher. As of 2004, there was growing concern by many technology professionals over the number of patents granted that are either too trivial to deserve protection, or duplicate existing or expired patents. It usually works by petitioning the United States Patent and Trademark Office to review patents that are suspected of being invalid somehow or another, usually by prior art(Wikipedia).

genes are products of nature, and therefore ineligible for patents, or are sufficiently different from the genes found inside the body's cells.

The *plaintiffs[26] won the first round when Judge Robert W. Sweet of Federal District Court[9)] in Manhattan said that isolated DNA was the same as DNA in the body in what really mattered — the genetic information it carries.

But Myriad prevailed at the United States Court of Appeals for the Federal Circuit[10)], twice, by 2-to-1 decisions. One of the majority opinions said that DNA was a *chemical[27], not an information medium, and that disconnecting DNA from the *chromosome[28] changed it enough structurally to qualify for patenting.

The plaintiffs, appealing to the Supreme Court, are *challenging[29] this. "Under this rationale, a kidney 'isolated' from the body would be patentable, gold 'isolated' from a stream would be patentable and leaves 'isolated' from trees would be patentable," they say in their brief.

Myriad and allies argue that patents can and have been granted on products derived from nature — like the *immune-suppressing drug[30] rapamycin, which comes from a bacterium — as long as sufficient *inventiveness[31] is involved.

26 plaintiff
원고

27 chemical
화학물질

28 chromosome
염색체

29 challenge
이의를 제기하다

30 immune-suppressing drug
면역억제 약물

31 inventiveness
창의성, 독창성

9) **Federal District Court** (미국 연방 지방법원) 연방 법원의 관할 하에 있는 지방법원.

10) **The United States Court of Appeals for the Federal Circuit** (Federal Circuit; in case citations, Fed. Cir. or C.A.F.C.)(미국 연방 특별 행정고등법원) is a United States court of appeals headquartered in Washington, D.C.. The court was created by Congress with passage of the Federal Courts Improvement Act of 1982, which merged the United States Court of Customs and Patent Appeals and the appellate division of the United States Court of Claims, making the judges of the former courts into circuit judges. The Federal Circuit is particularly known for their decisions on patent law, as they are the only appellate level court with the jurisdiction to hear patent case appeals(Wikipedia).

32 seed companies
종자회사

33 venture capitalists
벤처 투자가

34 advisory committee
자문위원회

Briefs in support of the plaintiffs were submitted by the American Medical Association[11)], AARP[12)], and various consumer and patient advocacy groups. Supporters of Myriad include drug companies, biotech *seed companies[32] and *venture capitalists[33]. Diagnostic companies appear split.

The Obama administration, breaking with longstanding policy of the Patent and Trademark Office[13)], says isolated genes should not be patentable. They are medically useful, it says in its brief, "precisely because isolated DNA operates in exactly the same way in a laboratory as it does in its natural environment."

If the Supreme Court, which has shown a recent tendency to rein in patenting, were to say genes cannot be patented, the impact could depend on how the opinion was worded. Drugs, vaccines or crops might still be protectable even without patents on genes because other steps are involved in their creation.

An *advisory committee[34] to the Health and Human Services Department[14)] said in a 2010 report that gene patents were

11) **The American Medical Association** (AMA)(미국 의학협회), founded in 1847 and incorporated in 1897,is the largest association of physicians—both MDs and DOs—and medical students in the United States(Wikipedia).

12) **AARP**, Inc., formerly the American Association of Retired Persons(전(全) 미 퇴직자 협회), is a United States-based non-governmental organization and interest group, founded in 1958 by Ethel Percy Andrus, PhD, a retired educator from California, and based in Washington, D.C. It is a membership organization for people age 50 and over(Wikipedia).

13) **The United States Patent and Trademark Office** (PTO or USPTO)(미국 특허청) is an agency in the U.S. Department of Commerce that issues patents to inventors and businesses for their inventions, and trademark registration for product and intellectual property identification. The USPTO is "unique among federal agencies because it operates solely on fees collected by its users, and not on taxpayer dollars". Its "operating structure is like a business in that it receives requests for services—applications for patents and trademark registrations—and charges fees projected to cover the cost of performing the services [it] provide[s]"(Wikipedia).

not necessary to spur development of genetic tests. There are about 50 tests offered for mutations that cause *cystic fibrosis[35], for instance, despite the lack of the *exclusivity[36] that patents provide.

The committee did find instances in which patents inhibited patients' access to testing.

Ellen T. Matloff, director of cancer genetic counseling at the Yale Cancer Center and a plaintiff in the case, described a woman with a history of breast and ovarian cancer who *tested negative[37] for BRCA mutations on Myriad's test in early 2006. Ms. Matloff said Myriad refused to let Yale researchers look for mutations, in this patient or others, that they suspected the test missed.

Myriad later introduced a supplemental test to detect genetic changes missed by its main test, but the woman's *insurer[38] would not pay for it until last October. By then, the woman's daughter had developed breast cancer that might have been detected at a more treatable stage had the women known about the mutation.

Ms. Matloff did not identify the woman and her daughter to protect their privacy.

Mark C. Capone, the president of Myriad Genetic Laboratories, said the company had no knowledge of any discussion with Yale.

He said Myriad had invested $500 million to make a success of BRCA testing. He said 18,000 researchers had published

35 cystic fibrosis
(병리) 낭포성 섬유증

36 exclusivity
독점권

37 test negative
음성반응을 보이다

38 insurer
보험회사

14) **Health and Human Services Department** = Department of Health and Human Services(보건사회 복지부).

39 thicket
덤불, 얽힘

40 start-up
신생기업

41 tumor
종양

42 outlier case
국외자 소송

43 alleged
주장된, 알려진

10,000 papers on those genes, a sign that research was not being hindered.

Myriad made $405.5 million from BRCA testing in its last fiscal year, accounting for more than 80 percent of its revenue.

One concern going forward is that a *thicket[39] of patents on individual genes will impede development of newer tests that look at multiple genes or of whole genome sequencing.

InVitae, a *start-up[40] developing a single test for all rare inherited diseases, filed a brief arguing against gene patents for this reason. Ambry Genetics already offers a test for 14 genes that raise the risk of breast cancer, but it leaves out the two most important genes because they are patented by Myriad.

But Dr. Evans said that in general, whole genome sequencing is taking off, apparently unimpeded by patents. And cancer centers are already sequencing many genes from patients' *tumors[41] to help determine the best drugs to use.

Dr. Cook-Deegan of Duke, along with Timothy Caulfield of the University of Alberta and some other researchers, argued in a recent essay that the Myriad case "stands as an example of the power of an anecdote or *outlier case[42] rather than definitive proof of systemic problems" with gene patents.

"In total," they wrote in the journal Genome Medicine, "the available evidence tells us that the *alleged[43] harms (and, for that matter, the suggested benefits) of human gene patenting have been overstated and oversimplified."

nytimes.com April 14, 2013

WORDS and STRUCTURES

poised (…할) 태세를 갖춘, 준비가 된

The economy is poised for recovery.
경제는 회복될 준비가 되어 있다.

The case, ***which*** will come before the court on Monday, involves patents ***held*** by Myriad Genetics on two human genes, ***which, when mutated***, give a woman a high risk of getting breast or ovarian cancer.

= The case, ***and it***(the case) will come before the court on Monday, involves patents ***(which were) held*** by Myriad Genetics on two human genes, ***and they***(two human genes), when ***(they are)*** mutated, give a woman a high risk of getting breast or ovarian cancer.

그 소송은 월요일에 법정 앞에 서게 될 것인데, 두 개의 인간 유전자들에 대해 미리아드 유전회사가 보유하고 있는 특허들을 포함한다. 그런데 두 개의 인간 유전자들은 돌연변이가 되면 여성에게 유방암이나 난소암에 걸릴 높은 위험이 있다.

lucrative 돈벌이가 되는, 수지맞는(profitable)

These days medical tourism is emerging as a lucrative business in Korea.
요즘 한국에서 의료관광이 수익성 좋은 사업으로 부상하고 있다.

microbe 미생물

For instance, microbe hunters were a large part of the first two decades.
예를 들면, 미생물 탐구가들은 첫 20년 동안 큰 부분을 차지했다.

deny 주지않다

in some cases denying patients their own genetic information
몇몇 경우에는 환자들에게 그들 자신의 유전적 정보를 주지 않는

counter 저지하다, 반박하다

However, North Korea did not make any moves to counter the exercise.
하지만, 북한은 훈련을 저지하기 위한 어떠한 움직임도 보이지 않았다.

I tried to argue but he countered that the plans were not yet finished.
내가 따지려고 했지만 그가 그 계획들은 아직 끝난 게 아니라고 반박했다.

ruling 판결, 결정

At this point it is unclear why the Seoul based university gave up trying to overturn the initial ruling.
이 시점에서 왜 서울을 근거로 한 대학이 처음 판결을 뒤집으려는 노력을 포기했는지가 의문이다.

invalidate ~을 무효로 하다, ~의 법적 효력을 없애다

Still, the court did nothing to invalidate the passage of the bill.
그러나 법원은 법안을 무효화시키기 위한 어떤 조치도 취하지 않았다.

undermine 약화시키다

Indeed democracy undermines the very idea of democracy.
사실상 민주주의는 민주주의의 생각을 약화시킨다.

chill 얼어붙게 하다

But regrettably, Lee's tougher stance has chilled Seoul-Pyongyang ties by linking economic assistance to progress in the North's denuclearization.
하지만 유감스럽게도, 이명박 대통령의 완고한 입장은, 경제적 원조와 북한비핵화진전(진행)을 연계시킴으로써 남북한의 관계를 얼어붙게 했다.

friend-of the-court 법정조언자

Ten other states filed friend-of-the-court briefs supporting the case.
10개의 다른 주들이 그 소송을 지지하는 법정조언자의 개요를 제출했다.

file 소송을 제기하다

His wife, Maria Shriver, filed for divorce, which ended their 25 years of marriage.
그의 아내, 마리아 슈라이버는 그들의 25년 결혼을 끝내는 이혼소송을 제기했다.

far-reaching 지대한 영향을 가져올

far-reaching consequences/implications 지대한 영향을 미칠 결과

at issue 논쟁중인, 문제가 되고 있는

That's what's at issue here, not just the airport site.
비단 공항 부지 문제뿐만이 아니라, 바로 이런 것이 여기서 문제가 되고 있는 것이다.

be due to do ~할 예정인, ~하기로 되어있는

They are due to arrive here soon. 그들은 곧 여기에 오기로 되어있다.

lapse 시간이 경과하다, 만료되다

His house was broken into a week after his insurance policy had lapsed.
그의 집은 보험증권의 계약이 소멸된 후 일주일 만에 털렸다.

infringe 침해하다

Then again various civic groups suggested that disclosing such detailed personal data will infringe upon the human rights of the offenders.
한편 여러 시민단체들은 그러한 상세한 개인정보를 공개하는 것은 범죄자들의 인권을 침해하는 것이라고 제안했다.

on behalf of ~을 대표(대신)하여

Lee's managing company Key East made an official statement on behalf of the actress.
이의 소속사 키 이스트는 그녀를 대신하여 공식발표를 했다.

prevail 이기다

Finally, she prevailed and became the firs telected female head-of-state in Africa.
마침내, 그녀는 이겼고 아프리카의 첫 여성국가원수로 선출되었다.

appeal 항소하다

Samsung is expected to appeal the U.S. court verdict.
삼성은 미국법원의 이 평결에 대해 항소할 예정이다.

challenge 이의를 제기하다

Congress rejected this plan and challenged Lincoln's right to deal with the matter without consultation.
그러나 연방의회는 이 계획을 거부했고, 또 연방의회와 협의 없이 이 문제를 다룰 수 있는 대통령의 권한에 이의를 제기했다.

break with ~와 관계를 끊다

He seemed to break with art being used as a tool of a movement.
그는 운동의 도구로서의 미술에서 탈피하는 듯했다.

rein 통제하다, 제어하다

The government is also preparing various measures to rein in increasing influence by foreign investors over the local economy.
정부는 또 국내경제에 대해 늘어나고 있는 외국인투자자의 영향력을 제어하기 위해 여러 가지 대책을 준비하고 있다.

word 말로 표현하다

She worded her ideas carefully.
그녀는 조심스러운 말로 자신의 생각을 표현했다.

develop 일으키다

Previously, scientists knew of only one gene, called APOE4, which increases the risk of developing the most common form of the disease.
이전에 과학자들은 가장 흔한 종류의 질병을 일으킬 확률을 높이는 APOE4라는 유전자만 알고 있었다.

the woman's daughter had developed breast cancer that might have been detected at a more treatable stage had the women known about the mutation
had the women known about the mutation = if the women had known about the mutation
(가정법 과거완료 구문)
그녀의 딸은 만일 그 여성들이 돌연변이에 대해 알았었더라면 더 치료단계에서 탐지될 수 있었을지도 모르는 유방암에 걸렸었다.

account for 차지하다

Smart Beach service accounted for 60 percent of the total sales on the beach.
스마트 비치서비스는 해변에서의 총 판매 중 60%를 차지한다.

leave out 빼다, 제외하다

He was left out of the national judo team.
그는 국가 유도 팀에서 제외되었다.

stand as an example 실례가 되다

Hur's life mirrors the hardships physically-challenged people experience in South Korea and stands as an example of over coming them.
허씨가 살아온 인생역정은 한국에 사는 신체장애자들이 겪는 고역을 반영하는 것이며 그런 고역을 극복한 실례가 되고 있다.

overstate 과장하다

I must not overstate the case.
이 문제를 너무 부풀려 얘기해서는 안 되겠다.

*On June 13, 2013, in a unanimous decision, the Supreme Court invalidated Myriad's claims to isolated genes. The Court held that merely isolating genes that are found in nature does not make them patentable.

Embryonic Stem Cell Research

Liberal

Support the use of embryonic stem cells for research. It is necessary (and ethical) for the government to fund embryonic stem cell research, which will assist scientists in finding treatments and cures for diseases. An embryo is not a human. The tiny blastocyst (embryos used in embryonic stem cell research) has no human features. Experimenting on embryos/embryonic stem cells is not murder. Embryonic stem cells have the potential to cure chronic and degenerative diseases which current medicine has been unable to effectively treat. Embryonic stem cells have been shown to be effective in treating heart damage in mice.

Conservative

Support the use of adult and umbilical cord stem cells only for research. It is morally and ethically wrong for the government to fund embryonic stem cell research. Human life begins at conception. The extraction of stem cells from an embryo requires its destruction. In other words, it requires that a human life be killed. Adult stem cells have already been used to treat spinal cord injuries, Leukemia, and even Parkinson's disease. Adult stem cells are derived from umbilical cords, placentas, amniotic fluid, various tissues and organ systems like skin and the liver, and even fat obtained from liposuction. Embryonic stem cells have not been successfully used to help cure disease.

(studentnewsdaily.com February 25, 2013)

15.

Woods's Odd Journey Through Golf's Majors[1)]

Tiger Woods on the 18th green, where he finished the Masters *tied for fourth[1], still five years *removed[2] from his last major title.

For Tiger Woods, the long, strange journey through golf's majors since his 2009 crash into a *fire hydrant[3] continues. And it is getting odder all the time.

Woods has played in 11 major championships in the post-marital-scandal period of his career, and in that time he has thrown away opportunities to win his 15th major with

1 tie for fourth
공동 4위

2 removed
떨어진, 먼

3 fire hydrant
소화전

1) **The men's major** golf championships, commonly known as the Major Championships, and often referred to simply as the majors, are the four most prestigious annual tournaments in professional golf. In order of their playing date, the current majors are:

- April – Masters Tournament (weekend ending 2nd Sunday in April) – hosted as an invitational by and played at Augusta National Golf Club in the U.S. state of Georgia.
- June – U.S. Open (weekend ending with the 3rd Sunday in June) – hosted by the USGA and played at various locations in the United States.
- July – The Open Championship (weekend containing the 3rd Friday in July) – hosted by The R&A, an offshoot of The Royal and Ancient Golf Club of St Andrews, and always played on a links course at one of nine various locations in the United Kingdom.
- August – PGA Championship (3rd or 4th weekend after the Open Championship) – hosted by the Professional Golfers' Association of America and played at various locations in the United States(Wikipedia).

4 break in
길들이다, 훈련시키다

5 give away
(좋은 기회 등을) 놓치다

6 news conference
기자회견

7 verbosity
말이 많음, 수다

8 imprecision
부정확성

9 self-imposed penalty
자진하여 하는 (스스로 과한) 벌칙

10 snicker
낄낄(킬킬) 웃다

wayward tee shots, poor wedge play and especially with sloppy putting. He has lost tournaments because he wasn't healthy. He has lost because he was distracted. He has lost because he was reworking his swing or *breaking in[4] a new caddie or a new coach.

But at this year's Masters, he may have *given away[5] his chance for a fifth green jacket with words he spoke to reporters. Or he may have given it away by the drop of a ball that was one to three feet off.

That leaves him with no one to blame but himself, yet it is a bizarre turn of events for a player never known for his postround *news conference[6] *verbosity[7] or for *imprecision[8] with basic golf rules.

"We always lose more tournaments than we win," Woods said Sunday night. "You can ask 'what if' after every tournament that we lose. I guess this is another one."

But in this case, the "what if" will linger because Woods's march toward Jack Nicklaus[2)]'s 18 career major championship victories remains stalled at 14, and perhaps for one of the most peculiar reasons — an unintentional *self-imposed penalty[9].

Asked about that Sunday, Woods smiled. He actually *snickered[10] from time to time after his final round.

"It's a funny game," he said. "Things happen."

2) **Jack Nicklaus** (잭 니클라우스)(born January 21, 1940), nicknamed "The Golden Bear", is an American professional golfer. He is widely regarded as the greatest professional golfer of all time, winning a total of 18 career major championships, while producing 19 second place and 9 third place finishes in them, over a span of 25 years. Nicklaus focused on the major championships, and played a selective schedule of regular PGA Tour events, yet still finished with 73 victories, third on the all-time list(Wikipedia).

To *recount[11] some of those things, Woods finished Sunday's round at five under par for the tournament, good enough for a *fourth-place tie[12] that was four shots behind the *eventual winner[13], Adam Scott, who defeated Ángel Cabrera in a *playoff[14].

Woods could have played his way into that playoff with a 66 on Sunday. He missed multiple makable putts for birdie. He had chances to lower his score Saturday as well and squandered them. In the end, he did not summon one of those Sunday-at-the-Masters *charges[15].

Not *insignificantly[16], three other golfers scored lower.

But it is also inescapable that the tournament turned when Woods's exceedingly accurate third shot at the 15th hole Friday *clanked[17] off the flagstick and bounced into the pond in front of the green. With the ball in the air, Woods was staring at a birdie that would put him in the tournament lead.

After the unlucky flagstick episode, he made bogey. And then came the rules bungle heard round the golf world and a two-stroke penalty. Altogether, that one 87-yard wedge shot Friday might have been a four-stroke turnaround.

It is all *speculative[18], but there is nothing uncertain about the circumstances that led to the two-stroke penalty. If Woods had not mentioned to reporters after his round that he wanted to *back up[19] two yards on his second attempt to put a ball on the 15th green Friday, there would be no penalty.

The Masters rules officials had determined there was no violation. There were two rules officials standing near the 15th green Friday, as there are at every hole. They were watching

11 recount
이야기하다,
상세히 얘기하다

12 fourth-place tie
공동 4위

13 eventual winner
최종 우승자

14 play-off
(동점일 때의) 재 시합,
연장전, 챔피언결정전

15 charge
흥분, 감동

16 insignificant
(←insignificantly)
대수롭지 않은, 사소한,
하찮은

17 clank
탕 소리 나게 하다

18 speculative
추측에 근거한

19 back up
후진하다

20 gaffe
실수

closely, but neither saw anything inappropriate about Woods's drop. And Woods did not realize his *gaffe[20].

Adding to the drama, it also now appears that Woods may have dropped his ball very near where he had played his first shot from, anyway. A photographer for The Augusta Chronicle took pictures of both approach shots while standing in the same position alongside the green. In light of several divot marks just behind and near Woods, it appeared Woods may have been standing in the same place both times even if he thought he had backed up. It is up to the player to call a violation on himself, and if he thinks he backed up two yards, then his word is enough for the penalty to be assessed.

On Sunday, Woods acknowledged he had seen the photos.

"I saw them," he said. "Maybe not as much as I thought. But it was certainly not as close as the rule says."

He was asked if the flagstick shot was the most frustrating outcome he had experienced in a major championship.

"I've had a few," he answered. "But that's certainly up there."

3) **Augusta National** Golf Club, located in Augusta, Georgia, is one of the most famous golf clubs in the world. Founded by Bobby Jones and Clifford Roberts on the site of the former Fruitland (later Fruitlands) Nursery, the course was designed by Jones and Alister MacKenzie and opened for play in January 1933. Since 1934, it has played host to the annual Masters Tournament, one of the four major championships in professional golf, and the only major played each year at the same course. It was the number one ranked course in Golf Digest's 2009 list of America's 100 greatest courses and is currently the number ten ranked course on Golfweek Magazine's 2011 list of best classic courses in the United States, in terms of course architecture.
The golf club's exclusive membership policies have drawn criticism, particularly its refusal to admit black members until 1990, a former policy requiring all caddies to be black and its refusal to allow women to join. In August 2012, it admitted its first two female members, Condoleezza Rice and Darla Moore. The golf club has defended the membership policies, stressing that it is a private organization(Wikipedia).

And with an *unforced[21] smile, Woods turned around and walked toward the Augusta National[3)] clubhouse.

If golfers had numbers on their backs like other athletes, Woods would have been wearing No. 14. It goes with him everywhere now. The player who once won majors so easily, and did so with élan, talent and skill, is not only not winning those tournaments now, he is also running into new and highly inventive ways to lose them.

It may just be a cycle within a prodigious career. But as Tiger Woods walked away from his eighth consecutive Masters and 11th consecutive major without a victory, the path before him seemed to be growing narrower and shorter and still not quite the same since that path was blocked by a symbolically weighty fire hydrant.

nytimes.com April 14, 2013

21 unforced
강제적이지 않은, 자연스러운

WORDS and STRUCTURES

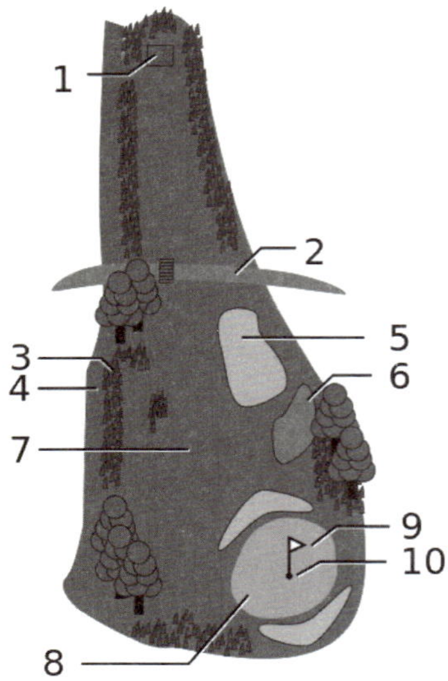

Typical elements of a hole on a golf course:

1. teeing ground	2. water hazard	3. rough	4. out of bounds
5. sand bunker	6. water hazard	7. fairway	8. putting green
9. flagstick	10. hole		

Numeric term

Condor(-4) : Four strokes under par
Albatross or Double Eagle(-3) : Three strokes under par
Eagle(-2) : Two strokes under par
Birdie(-1) : One stroke under par
Par(0)(E) : Equal to par
Bogey(+1) : One stroke over par
Double bogey(+2) : Two strokes over par
Triple bogey(+3) : Three strokes over par

wayward 불규칙한, 일정치 않은, 변덕스러운; erratic

Mary is a gifted but wayward player.
메리는 재능은 있지만 실력이 일정하지가 않은 선수이다.

sloppy (태도, 일이) 부주의한, 되는 대로의

He does sloppy work.
그는 일을 되는대로 한다.

distracted 마음이 산란해진, 주의가 산만한

She was distracted by the students chasing around.
뛰어다니는 학생들 때문에 그녀는 정신이 산란했다.

with words he spoke to reporters 그가 기자들에게 한 말 때문에

bizarre 기괴한, 괴상한

There were many guesses as to the reason for her sudden bizarre behavior.
그녀의 갑작스런 기괴한 행동에 대한 이유로 많은 추측이 있었다.

linger 지속되다, 남아있다

Perhaps the event will linger long in our memory.
그 사건은 오래도록 우리의 기억에 남을 것이다.

(these) things happen 이런 일은 흔히 있는 일이다

'Sorry - I've spilt some wine.' 'Never mind. These things happen.
"죄송해요. 제가 포도주를 좀 흘렸어요." "신경 쓰지 마세요. 늘 있는 일인 걸요."

summon 끄집어내다, 불러일으키다

He did not summon one of those Sunday-at-the-Masters charges.
그는 마스터스의 일요일의 감동을 불러 일어키지 못했다.

bungle 실책, 서투른 솜씨

Their pay was late because of a computer bungle.
컴퓨터 처리 실수로 그들의 급료가 늦어졌다.

assess 부과하다

The U.S. Transportation Department announced that Toyota is expected to pay the full amount of the assessed fine within 30 days if it wishes to avoid going to court against the U.S. government.
미국교통부는 도요타는 미국정부와 법정에 가지 않으려면 30일안에 부과된 벌금을 다 내야한다고 발표했다.

élan 기세, 격한 열정

As a prime minister, she had a certain elan.
총리로서 그녀는 확실한 열의가 있었다.

prodigious 거대한, 놀라운, 엄청난

On Saturday, they showed their prodigious capacity for RedBull.
토요일 그들은 레드불 팀에 맞서 엄청난 역량을 보여주었다.

16.

Royal baby born: It's a boy

LONDON – A royal baby boy was born Monday to Prince William and his wife, the former Kate Middleton, after weeks of anticipation and excitement among fans of the royal family over the arrival of a new *heir to the British throne[1].

The child was born at 4:24 p.m. London time, about 10½ hours after Catherine, the Duchess of Cambridge[1)], entered St. Mary's Hospital in central London in the *early stages of labor[2]. Palace officials said the infant weighed 8 *pounds[3], 6 *ounces[4].

*Barring[5] tragedy – or revolution – he is destined one day to *reign over[6] Britain and the 15 other nations, including Australia and Canada, that recognize the *British monarch[7] as *head of state[8]. The child takes his place in the *line of succession[9] behind the *heir apparent[10] and his grandfather, Prince Charles[2)], and father, William[3)].

In a historic change, the baby was guaranteed to be third

1 heir to the British throne
영국왕위계승자

2 early stages of labor
산통의 초기단계

3 pound
중량의 단위, 기호 lb., 약 453그램; 영국의 화폐단위

4 ounce
중량의 단위 1/16 파운드, 기호 oz, 28.35 그램

5 barring
~을 제외하고, ~이 없다면

6 reign over
~을 다스리다, 통치하다

7 British monarch
영국국왕

8 head of state
국가수반, 국가원수

9 line of succession
왕위 계승서열

10 heir apparent
법정추정 상속인

1) **The Duchess of Cambridge** = wife of the future King of England (케임브리지 공작부인) 영국의 차세대 왕세자비.

11 male offspring
남자자손

12 elbow aside
밀어제치다, 밀어내다

in line regardless of gender. A new rule being ratified by the 16 "realms" removes the automatic right of *male offspring[11] to leapfrog over older sisters on to the throne, a formula that held for centuries.

The infant - no name has been announced - *elbows aside[12] William's younger brother, Prince Harry[4)], who has now been demoted to fourth in line.

2) **Charles**, Prince of Wales(Charles Philip Arthur George; born 14 November 1948), is the eldest child and heir apparent of Queen Elizabeth II. Known alternatively in Scotland as Duke of Rothesay and in South West England as Duke of Cornwall, he is the longest-serving heir apparent in British history, having held the position since 1952. He is also the oldest heir to the throne since 1714.
Charles was born at Buckingham Palace as the first grandchild of King George VI and Queen Elizabeth. He was educated at Cheam and Gordonstoun Schools, which his father, Prince Philip, Duke of Edinburgh, had attended as a child, as well as the Timbertop campus of Geelong Grammar School in Victoria, Australia. After earning a bachelor of arts degree from Trinity College, Cambridge, Charles served in the Royal Navy from 1971 to 1976.
In 1981, he married Lady Diana Spencer and they had two sons, Prince William, Duke of Cambridge(born 1982), and Prince Harry(born 1984). In 1996, the couple divorced, following well-publicised extra-marital affairs. The following year, the former Princess of Wales died in a car crash. In 2005, he married Camilla Parker Bowles in a civil ceremony followed by a televised blessing service. Camilla uses the title Duchess of Cornwall(Wikipedia).

3) **Prince William**, Duke of Cambridge(William Arthur Philip Louis; born 21 June 1982), is the elder son of Charles, Prince of Wales, and his first wife Diana, Princess of Wales. His paternal grandparents are Queen Elizabeth II and Prince Philip, Duke of Edinburgh. He is second in line to succeed his grandmother, after his father.
Prince William was educated at four schools in the United Kingdom and obtained a degree from the University of St Andrews. He spent parts of a gap year in Chile, Belize, Tanzania, and Kenya, where he has lived and holidayed several times. Prince William has also taken Kiswahili studies at universities in Kenya and Tanzania. He also completed training as an officer (eventually being commissioned as a lieutenant in the Blues and Royals Regiment), and a pilot (earning his wings by completing pilot training at Royal Air Force College Cranwell) in the British military. He then underwent helicopter flying training in order to become a full-time pilot with the Search and Rescue Force.
Prince William married Catherine Middleton, on 29 April 2011 at Westminster Abbey. Hours prior to the event, Buckingham Palace announced that he would be created Duke of Cambridge, Earl of Strathearn, and Baron Carrickfergus. Their first child, Prince George of Cambridge, was born on 22 July 2013.
Following the end of his more than seven-and-a-half years of full-time service with the British armed forces, in early 2014, from early January to late March, Prince William attended a series of seminars, lectures, and meetings in agricultural management at the University of Cambridge(Wikipedia).

The newborn is Queen Elizabeth II's[5)] third *great-grandchild[13]. The queen, who celebrated 60 years on the throne last year, is Britain's longest-serving monarch after Victoria[6)], who died in 1901.

Following tradition, the public announcement of the House of Windsor's[7)] newest arrival was withheld until the queen and senior members of the royal family were notified. It was then posted on paper on an easel at Buckingham Palace[8)] and on social media networks worldwide.

The child's name could take much longer to be unveiled. The world didn't learn of William's name until a week after his

13 great-grandchild
증손자

4) **Prince Harry** (Henry Charles Albert David; formally styled Prince Henry of Wales; born 15 September 1984), known as Captain Harry Wales in his military role, is the younger son of Charles, Prince of Wales, and Diana, Princess of Wales. His paternal grandparents are Queen Elizabeth II and Prince Philip, Duke of Edinburgh. His stepmother is Camilla, Duchess of Cornwall. He stands fourth in line to succeed his grandmother as monarch of the Commonwealth realms, preceded by his father, elder brother Prince William, Duke of Cambridge, and nephew Prince George of Cambridge.
After an education at schools in the United Kingdom and spending parts of his gap year in Australia and Lesotho, Harry chose a military career, undergoing officer training at Royal Military Academy Sandhurst. He was commissioned as a second lieutenant into the Blues and Royals of the Household Cavalry Regiment, serving temporarily with his brother, and completed his training as a troop leader. In 2007–2008 he served for 77 days in Helmand, Afghanistan. but he was pulled out following publication of the story in an Australian magazine. He returned to Afghanistan for a 20-week deployment in 2012-2013 with the Army Air Corps(Wikipedia).

5) **Elizabeth II** (Elizabeth Alexandra Mary; born 21 April 1926) is the constitutional monarch of sixteen realms of the 53-member Commonwealth of Nations. She is also Head of the Commonwealth and Supreme Governor of the Church of England(Wikipedia).

6) **Victoria** (Queen Victoria) 영국의 여왕(1819-1901).

7) **The House of Windsor** (1917년 이래 현 영국 왕실의 공식명칭) is the royal house of the United Kingdom and the other Commonwealth realms. It was founded by King George V by royal proclamation on 17 July 1917, when he changed the name of the British Royal Family from the German Saxe-Coburg and Gotha(a branch of the House of Wettin) to the English Windsor, due to the anti-German sentiment in the British Empire during World War I. The most prominent member of the House of Windsor is its head, Queen Elizabeth II, who is the reigning monarch of 16 Commonwealth realms(Wikipedia).

8) **Buckingham Palace** is the London residence and principal workplace of the monarchy of the United Kingdom. Located in the City of Westminster, the palace is often at the centre of state occasions and royal hospitality. It has been a focus for the British people at times of national rejoicing(Wikipedia).

birth in 1982. Britain's *bookmakers[14] have been taking bets for months as to the new royal *moniker[15], the most popular choices for a boy being George and James. A very outside shot was given to the name Hashtag.

The birth gives another *PR[16] *boost[17] to a *royal household[18] already enjoying a *surge in popularity[19], fueled *in great part[20] by the very modern romance between William and Kate, who were *college sweethearts[21]. A few public *missteps[22] and naked Harry photos notwithstanding, the dark days that descended on the monarchy after the shocking death of the baby's grandmother, Princess Diana, in a 1997 car crash are mostly a *distant memory[23].

*Retailers[24] are rubbing their hands over *estimates[25] that the royal birth could add more than $350 million to Britain's sluggish economy through sales of *memorabilia[26] such as the mugs bearing the slogan "Born to Rule." That could help compensate for lost productivity from the national holidays declared for the queen's *jubilee[27] last year and William and Kate's wedding in 2011.

Many Britons were expected to *raise a glass[28] *in honor of[29] the birth, or perhaps just to beat the unusual *heat wave[30] gripping the country. The mercury hit the high 80s[9)]

9) Fahrenheit 화씨, Celsius 섭씨
섭씨온도 = (화씨온도−32) × 5/9
화씨온도 = (9/5×섭씨온도) + 32

14 bookmaker
(비격식 bookie)
(경마의) 마권 업자

15 moniker
인명, 별명

16 PR
홍보(public relations)

17 boost
신장, 증가

18 royal household
(소속 직원을 포함하는)
왕실

19 surge in popularity
인기급증

20 in great part
많이

21 college sweethearts
캠퍼스커플

22 misstep
실수, 잘못

23 distant memory
아득한(희미한) 추억

24 retailer
소매상인

25 estimates
예상액, 추정치

26 memorabilia
수집품(기념품)

27 jubilee
기념일
diamond jubilee
(60주년),
golden jubilee
(50주년),
silver jubilee
(25주년)

28 raise a glass
축배를 들다

29 in honor of
~을 기념하여,
~을 축하하여

30 heat wave
장기간의 혹서

in London on Monday, baking the *hordes of[31] reporters and photographers camping out in front of St. Mary's Hospital, near Paddington Station.

The duchess was booked into the private hospital's exclusive Lindo Wing, where *delivery[32] of a baby costs more than $7,500. Cameras have been *trained[33] on the entrance for weeks in hopes of catching a glimpse of the pregnant duchess being *whisked[34] inside. The royal couple avoided the *media circus[35] by reportedly entering through a side gate about 6 a.m. Monday.

But now the wait is for the couple to appear on the hospital steps holding their newborn, echoing the moment when William was first presented for public inspection outside the same hospital by Charles and Diana.

latimes.com July 22, 2013

31 hordes of
수많은

32 delivery
출산, 분만

33 train
준비하다,
채비를 갖추다

34 whisk
민첩하게 움직이다

35 media circus
(판매 부수, 시청률
신장을 노린)
매스미디어의 흥미
위주 보도, 집중보도

WORDS and STRUCTURES

labor 출산, 진통

The labor pains started a few days before my due dat.
진통이 예정일 보다 며칠 앞서 시작되었다.

be destined to 운명의, 예정된

She was destined to be a great singer from childhood.
그녀는 어릴 때부터 위대한 가수가 될 운명이었다.

Britain and the 15 other nations, including Australia and Canada, ***that*** recognize the British monarch as head of state.
= Britain and the 15 other nations, including Australia and Canada, ***and they***(Britain and the 15 other nations) recognize the British monarch as head of state.
호주와 캐나다를 포함해서 영국과 15개의 다른 국가들은 영국국왕을 국가원수로 인정한다.

ratify 승인하다, 비준하다

The Seoul-Washington free trade agreement, signed in 2007, was ratified by U.S. Congress and Korea's National Assembly, respectively, in 2011.
2007년 체결된 한미자유무역협정(FTA)이 2011년 한미 양국의회에 의해 각각 비준되었다.

realm 왕국

In January 1215, the barons vowed that they would stand fast for the liberty of the church and the realm, demanding that King John confirm the Charter of Liberties.
1215년 1월 귀족들이 교회와 왕국의 자유를 위해서 싸우기로 맹세하면서 존이 자유의 헌장을 인정하길 요구하였다.

leapfrog (더 높은 위치, 등급으로) 뛰어 넘다

The win allowed them to leapfrog three teams to gain second place.
그 우승으로 그들은 세 팀을 뛰어넘어(제치고) 2위를 차지했다.

withhold 보류하다

Delegations from nine other countries withheld approval because they lacked authority to sign.
다른 9개국 대표단은 합의를 체결할 권한이 없어 동의를 보류했다.

take bets 내기를 걸다

Bookmakers are currently taking bets on the marriage being over by Christmas.
마권업자들은 크리스마스까지 그 결혼생활이 끝나게 될 것이라는 것에 현재 내기를 걸고 있다.

hashtag

(인터넷)해시태그, 소셜네트워크 서비스(SNS: social network service)인 트위터에서 '# 특정단어' 형식으로, 특정 단어에 대한 글이라는 것을 표현하는 기능

fuel 가중하다, 부채질하다

There has been a recent resurgence of neo-Nazi, racial hate crime in Russia, partly fuelled by the terrorist activity in the Chechen region of the country.
최근 러시아에서 신나치주의와 인종차별범죄가 부활해왔고, 부분적으로 체첸에서 테러리스트활동에 의해 부채질되었다.

a surge in popularity, ***fueled*** in great part by the very modern romance between William and Kate, ***who*** were college sweethearts
= a surge in popularity, ***(and it***(a surge in popularity) ***is) fueled*** in great part by the very modern romance between William and Kate, ***and they*** were college sweethearts
인기급증은 윌리엄과 케이트 사이의 바로 그 현대적인 로맨스 때문에 가중되었는데, 그 둘은 캠퍼스 커플이었다.

notwithstanding ~에도 불구하고(in spite of)

현재분사로 간주되어 목적어 뒤에 위치시키는 구문도 가능함
He is very active, his age notwithstanding.
= His age notwithstanding, he is very active.
그의 나이에도 불구하고 그는 아주 활동적이다.

descend on/upon somebody/something (때로는 예상치 못하게, 대규모로) ~에 몰려들다

Hundreds of football fans descended on the city.
수백 명의 축구 팬들이 그 도시에 몰려들었다.

the dark days that descended on the monarchy after the shocking death of the baby's grandmother, Princess Diana, in a 1997 car crash ***are*** mostly ***a distant memory***
주어 days 동사 are 보어 memory
그 아이의 할머니 다이애나 공주의 1997년 자동차 충돌로 인한 충격적인 죽음 이후 군주에 대해 몰려들었던 암울한 날들은 대개 아득한 추억이다.

sluggish 부진한, 느린, 침체된

Currently, the American economy is very sluggish.
현재 미국 경제는 침체되어 있다.

memorabilia 기억할 만한 일

Some of you may have many pieces of Mickey Mouse memorabilia.
몇몇은 미키마우스 관련 수집품을 여러 개 갖고 있을지도 모른다.

jubilee (특히 25주년이나 50주년) 기념일

The couple celebrated their golden jubilee, 50 years of marriage.

그 노부부는 결혼 50주년을 자축했다.

Royal Baby's Birth Certificate

BIRTH		Entry No. 207
Registration district Westminster		Administrative area
Sub-district Westminster		City of Westminster
CHILD		
1. Date and place of birth Twenty second July 2013 St Mary's Hospital Praed Street Westminster		
2. Name and surname His Royal Highness Prince George Alexander Louis of Cambridge		3. Sex Male
FATHER		
4. Name and surname His Royal Highness Prince William Arthur Philip Louis Duke of Cambridge		
5. Place of birth Paddington Westminster	6. Occupation Prince of the United Kingdom	
MOTHER		
7. Name and surname Catherine Elizabeth Her Royal Highness The Duchess of Cambridge		
8.(a) Place of birth Reading	8. (b) Occupation Princess of the United Kingdom	
9.(a) Maiden surname MIDDLETON	9. (b) Surname at marriage if different from maiden surname —	
10. Usual address (if different from place of child's birth) Kensington Palace London W8 4PU		
INFORMANT		
11. Name and surname (if not the mother or father) —	12. Qualification Father	

Memo

17.

Bezos, Amazon's Founder, to Buy The Washington Post

The Washington Post[1)], the newspaper whose reporting helped topple a president and inspired a generation of journalists, is being sold for $250 million to the founder of Amazon.com[2)], Jeffrey P. Bezos, in a deal that has shocked the industry.

Donald E. Graham, *chairman and chief executive[1] of The Washington Post Company, and the third generation of the Graham family to lead the paper, told the staff about the

1 chairman and chief executive 회장 겸 최고경영자

1) **The Washington Post** is an American daily newspaper. It is the most widely circulated newspaper published in Washington, D.C., and was founded in 1877, making it the area's oldest extant newspaper.
Located in the capital city of the United States, the newspaper has a particular emphasis on national politics. Daily editions are printed for the District of Columbia, Maryland and Virginia.
In the early 1970s, in the best known episode in Post history, reporters Bob Woodward and Carl Bernstein led the American press's investigation into what became known as the Watergate scandal; reporting in the newspaper greatly contributed to the resignation of President Richard Nixon. The newspaper has won 47 Pulitzer Prizes.
On August 5, 2013, Jeff Bezos agreed to purchase the newspaper for $250 million in cash, completing the transaction on October 1, 2013. The newspaper is owned by Nash Holdings LLC, a holding company created for the acquisition and controlled by Bezos(Wikipedia).

2) **Amazon.com** 1994년 7월, 월가의 펀드매니저이던 제프 베조스(Jeff Bezos)가 아마존닷컴을 설립하였다. 1995년 인터넷 서점 서비스를 시작해 큰 성장을 이루었다. 이후 아마존은 음반, 의류, 주방용품, 장난감, 차량용품, 소프트웨어, 컴퓨터 등 다양한 영역으로 사업을 확장하였다(네이버 지식백과, 시사상식사전).

sale late Monday afternoon. They had gathered together in the newspaper's auditorium *at the behest of[2] the publisher, Katharine Weymouth, his niece.

"I, along with Katharine Weymouth and our *board of directors[3], decided to sell only after years of familiar newspaper-industry challenges made us wonder if there might be another owner who would be better for the Post (after a transaction that would be in the best interest of our *shareholders[4])," Mr. Graham said in a *written statement[5].

In the auditorium, he closed his remarks by saying that nobody in the room should be sad — except, he said, "for me."

The announcement was greeted by what many *staff members[6] described as "shock," a reaction shared in *newsrooms[7] across the country as one of the *crown jewels[8] of newspapers was surrendered by one of the industry's royal families.

In Mr. Bezos, The Post will have a very different owner, a technologist whose fortunes have risen in the last dozen years even as those of The Post and most newspapers have struggled. Through Amazon, the *retailing giant[9], he has helped *revolutionize[10] the way people around the world consume — first books, then expanding to all kinds of goods and more recently in *online storage[11], electronic books and online video, including a recent spate of original programming.

In the meeting, Mr. Graham stressed that Mr. Bezos would purchase The Post in a personal capacity and not *on behalf of[12] Amazon the company. The $250 million deal includes all of the *publishing businesses[13] owned by The Washington

2 at the behest of
~의 명령에 따라

3 board of directors
이사회

4 shareholders
주주

5 written statement
진술서

6 staff members
직원들

7 newsroom
(신문사 · 방송 스튜디오의) 뉴스 작성실

8 crown jewels
왕권 상징 보석

9 retailing giant
대규모 소매업체

10 revolutionize
대변혁(혁신)을 일으키다, 혁신시키다

11 online storage
(컴퓨터)온라인 기억 장치

12 on behalf of
~을 대신(대표)하여

13 publishing businesses
출판업

Post Company, including the Express newspaper, The Gazette Newspapers, Southern Maryland Newspapers, Fairfax County Times, El Tiempo Latino and Greater Washington Publishing.

The Washington Post company plans to hold on to Slate magazine, The Root.com and Foreign Policy. According to the *release[14], Mr. Bezos has asked Ms. Weymouth to remain at The Post along with Stephen P. Hills, *president and general manager[15]; Martin Baron, *executive editor[16]; and Fred Hiatt, editor of the editorial page.

Mr. Bezos, who did not attend the meeting at The Post on Monday, said in a statement that he had known Mr. Graham for the past decade and said about Mr. Graham that "I do not know a finer man." Ms. Weymouth said that in negotiating this deal, Mr. Bezos made it clear he was not purely focused on profits.

The sale, at a price that would have been unthinkably low even a few years ago, represents the end of eight decades of ownership by the Graham family of The Post since Eugene Meyer bought The Post at auction on June 1, 1933. His son-in-law Philip L. Graham served as president of the paper from 1947 until his death in 1963. Then Graham's widow, Katharine Graham, oversaw the paper through the publication of the Pentagon Papers[3)] alongside The New York Times and its *coverage[17] of Watergate, the political scandal that led to the resignation of Richard Nixon and also a *starring role[18] for the newspaper in the film, "All The President's Men[4)]."

The Post's daily *circulation[19] peaked in 1993 at 832,332, according to the Alliance for Audited Media[5)]. But like

14 release
발표

15 president and general manager
사장 겸 총지배인

16 executive editor
편집장

17 coverage
(신문 · 텔레비전 · 라디오의) 보도(방송)

18 starring role
주연

19 circulation
(신문 · 잡지의) 판매 부수

20 flagship headquarters
주력 본부

21 regulatory filing
공시

22 pay rent to
~에 임대료를 지불하다

23 somber mood
엄숙한 분위기

most newspapers, it has suffered greatly from circulation and advertising declines. By March, the newspaper's daily circulation had dropped to 474,767.

The company became pressed enough for cash that Ms. Weymouth announced in February that it was looking to sell its *flagship headquarters[20]. According to a *regulatory filing[21] associated with the sale, Mr. Bezos will *pay rent to[22] The Post Company on the space for up to three years.

As of 2012, the newsroom, which once had more than 1,000 employees, had fewer than 640. People there on Monday described the *mood as "somber"[23] with "a lot of people kind

3) **The Pentagon Papers** (국방부 비밀 보고서), officially titled United States – Vietnam Relations, 1945–1967: A Study Prepared by the Department of Defense, is a United States Department of Defense history of the United States' political-military involvement in Vietnam from 1945 to 1967. The papers were discovered and released by Daniel Ellsberg, and first brought to the attention of the public on the front page of The New York Times in 1971. A 1996 article in The New York Times said that the Pentagon Papers had demonstrated, among other things, that the Johnson Administration "systematically lied, not only to the public but also to Congress."
More specifically, the papers revealed that the U.S. had secretly enlarged the scale of the Vietnam War with the bombings of nearby Cambodia and Laos, coastal raids on North Vietnam, and Marine Corps attacks, none of which were reported in the mainstream media. In June 2011, the entire set of the Pentagon Papers was declassified and publicly released(Wikipedia).

4) **All The President's Men** (대통령의 사람들) 워터게이트 사건을 취재하던 〈워싱턴 포스트〉의 두 젊은 기자, 밥 우드워드와 칼 번스타인의 고군분투를 그린 1976년 작품. 이들이 익명의 취재원 딥스로트의 도움을 받아, 워터게이트빌딩 난입 사건 피의자들로부터 닉슨의 최측근으로까지 범위를 좁혀가며 독자적인 수사를 벌이는 과정이 이야기의 중심을 이룬다. 배우 로버트 레드퍼드가 제작과 주연을 겸했고, 앨런 J. 파큘러가 연출을, 고든 윌리스가 촬영을 맡았다. 저널리즘과 정치의 생리를 균형감 있게 담아내 정치 스릴러의 수작으로 평가받는다(네이버 지식백과, 세계영화작품사전).

5) **The Alliance for Audited Media** (AAM) is a non-profit organization located in Arlington Heights, Illinois, that connects North American media companies, advertisers and ad agencies. Founded in 1914 as the Audit Bureau of Circulations (ABC), the AAM is a leading source of cross-media verification and information services, providing standards, audit services and data for the advertising and publishing industries. It is one of more than three dozen such organizations operating worldwide, affiliated with the International Federation of Audit Bureaux of Circulations (IFABC).
AAM independently verifies print and digital circulation, mobile apps, website analytics, social media, technology platforms and audience information for newspapers, magazines and digital media companies in the U.S. and Canada(Wikipedia).

of in disbelief."

In an interview in July, Mr. Graham was cagey about the family's future in the business. "I'll just fall back on the same answer," he said, adding, "In family companies you have judgments about the family and you have professional judgment. The family control of The Washington Post Company over the years, I think, has been a *healthy thing[24]."

In an e-mail Monday, Ms. Weymouth, who replaced her uncle as *publisher[25] in 2008, talked about the effect of the sale on her family: "Yes — we knew the sale was coming. This was a process that was months in the making. It is, of course, sad for the family — we have been incredibly honored to have been a part of The Post for the past 80, but we have always understood that this is a *public trust[26] and our focus was on ensuring that it would remain strong for generations of readers to come."

The Post is not the only newspaper to move to new ownership. The New York Times Company announced early Saturday morning that it had sold its New England Media Group, which includes The Boston Globe, for $70 million, a fraction of the $1.1 billion the Times company paid for just The Globe in 1993. Ken Doctor, an analyst at Outsell, said that the Post sale reflected a broader trend of newspaper ownership returning to local investors rather than large, *publicly traded enterprises[27].

"Newspapers are not really much creatures of the marketplace anymore," said Mr. Doctor. "They're not *throwing off[28] much in profits. They need shelter from the

24 healthy thing
바람직한 일

25 publisher
발행인

26 public trust
자선 신탁, 공익 재단

27 publicly traded enterprises
주식공개회사, 상장기업

28 throw off
떨쳐버리다, 벗어던지다

29 quarterly financial statements
분기별 재무제표와 보고

30 1953 Plymouths in Cuba
쿠바의 1953년형 자동차

31 collaborations
협력, 제휴

32 iconic
~의 상징(아이콘)이 되는

pressure of *quarterly financial statements and reports[29].”

Newspaper analysts also said that the sale seems to be good news for the future of The Post. Alan D. Mutter, a newspaper consultant who writes the blog Reflections of a Newsosaur, said that for the first time someone with a native digital background was purchasing a major newspaper rather than an old-time businessman who would try to restore The Post to its earlier heyday and treat it “like *1953 Plymouths in Cuba[30].”

While Mr. Bezos may be purchasing The Post separate from Amazon, Mr. Mutter predicted that there could be *collaborations[31] between the brands, like The Post's content appearing on every Kindle[6)] or Post video content appearing on Amazon.

“This is a guy who literally has invested in building rockets because he thinks it's a good idea. I believe he's bought the newspaper because he wants to re-envision the enterprise and The Post is an *iconic[32] world brand,” said Mr. Mutter about Mr. Bezos. “He knows something about building iconic world brands.”

Shortly after the announcement, Leonard Downie, the Post's former executive editor, sat down at the Caribou Coffee store down the block from the newsroom he once led and contemplated a future where the Grahams no longer own the newspaper.

6) **Kindle** 인터넷 서점 아마존이 2007년 11월 발매한 전자책 단말기(e-book reader)로, 아마존의 킨들 스토어에서 구입한 전자책과 신문 · 잡지, 그리고 사전을 이 단말기를 통하여 읽을 수 있다. 두 번째 버전인 킨들 2(2009년 출시), 킨들 DX(2009년 출시) 등 꾸준히 업그레이드 된 후속모델이 개발되고 있다. 킨들 스토어에는 종이책보다 3~5배 가량 저렴한 전자책이 구비되어 있으며, 킨들 이용자들은 원하는 전자책을 다운로드하여 볼 수 있다(네이버 지식백과, 두산백과).

Mr. Graham had called Mr. Downie, now a vice president at The Post Company, earlier in the day. "I was completely shocked," Mr. Downie said. "I could hardly say anything."

Mr. Downie arrived at the paper nearly 50 years ago, and for all of the time since, the Graham family has been at the center of the newspaper — and more broadly, he said, at the center of journalism in Washington.

"The important thing about the Grahams for me," he said, referring to Ben Bradlee, his predecessor as executive editor, "is that starting with Ben and with me, and I assume my successors, is that the news decisions were always ours, but the Grahams were always behind us."

nytimes.com August 05, 2013

WORDS and STRUCTURES

topple 넘어지다; 넘어뜨리다

The show of support follows recent moves to topple the embattled leader.
이 날의 대통령 지지 시위는 궁지에 몰린 대통령을 축출하려는 최근의 움직임에 뒤이은 것이다.

gather together ~을 모으다, 집합하다

People gathered together and listened to the critic's criticism with a bite.
사람들은 한자리에 모여서 비평가의 날카로운 비평을 들었다.

transaction 거래, 매매

Other terms of the transaction were not disclosed.
그 외의 거래 조건들은 밝혀지지 않았다.

greet 맞다, (특정한) 반응을 보이다, 받아들이다

The team's win was greeted as a major triumph.
그 팀의 우승은 주요한 승리로 받아들여졌다.

surrender 항복(굴복)하다, (권리 등을) 포기하다(내주다/넘겨주다)

He agreed to surrender all claims to the property.
그는 그 재산에 대한 모든 권리를 포기하기로 동의했다.

struggle (~와) 싸우다, (~에게서 벗어나려고) 발버둥을 치다

I struggled and screamed for help.
나는 버둥거리며 도와(살려) 달라고 비명을 질렀다.

a technologist ***whose*** fortunes have risen in the last dozen years even as ***those*** of The Post and most newspapers have struggled

= a technologist ***+(and) his*** fortunes have risen in the last dozen years even as ***fortunes*** of The Post and most newspapers have struggled

최신과학기술 전문가, 그런데 비록 포스트지와 대부분의 신문사들이 발버둥치고 있었는데도 지난 12년간에 그의 재산은 불어났다.

spate ~ of something (보통 불쾌한 일의) 빈발, 범람

The bombing was the latest in a spate of terrorist attacks.

그 폭탄 공격은 빈발하던 테러 공격 행위들 중 가장 최근의 것이었다.

purchase 구매(입)하다, 인수하다

YouTube was purchased by Google in 2006 for $1.65 billion.

2006년에는 구글이 16억5천만 달러에 유튜브를 인수하였다.

hold on to something (자기에게 유리한 것을) 고수하다, (팔거나 주지 않고) 계속 보유하다

You should hold on to your oil shares.

당신은 석유 주식들을 계속 보유해야 한다.

ask + 목적어 + to + 동사원형 ~에게 ~하라고 요구(청)하다

Mr. Bezos has asked Ms. Weymouth to remain at The Post.

베조씨는 Ms. 웨이마우스에게 포스트에 남아있도록 요청했다.

oversee (작업 · 활동이 제대로 이뤄지는지) 감독하다

A team leader was appointed to oversee the project.

그 사업을 감독하도록 팀장이 임명되었다.

suffer from ~로 고통 받다

She suffered from a feeling of alienation from others.
그녀는 다른 사람들로부터 느끼는 소외감 때문에 괴로웠다.

pressed (for something) (특히 시간 · 돈이) 충분하지 않은(궁한)

I'm really pressed for cash at the moment.
내가 지금 당장은 정말 현금이 궁하다.

be looking to do something ~할 길을 찾고(모색하고) 있다

The government is looking to reduce inflation.
정부에서는 인플레이션을 줄일 길을 찾고 있다.

The company became pressed enough for cash that Ms. Weymouth announced in February that ***it*** was looking to sell its flagship headquarters.
it = the company
그 회사는 Ms. 웨이마우스가 2월에 그 회사의 주력 본부를 팔려는 길을 찾고 있었다고 발표할 정도로 자금 압박을 받게 되었다.

as of ~ ~일자로, ~현재

As of the 10th, your new extension is 123.
10일부터 당신 내선 번호는 123번이다.

cagey (about something) (무엇에 대해) 말을 안 하는, 비밀스러운

Tom is very cagey about his family. 토니는 자기 가족 얘기를 잘 안 한다.

fall back on somebody/something ~에 기대다(의지하다)

I have a little money in the bank to fall back on.
나는 은행에 의지할 돈이 좀 있다.

have judgement 판단력이 있다, 판단을 내리다

King Solomon was famous for having the good judgment.
솔로몬 왕은 현명한 판단을 내리는 것으로 유명했다.

effect of the sale ***on*** her family
그 매각이 가족에 미칠 영향

This was a ***process*** that was months in the ***making***.
이것은 처리하는데 수개월이 걸렸다.

fraction 부분, 일부

Only a small fraction of a bank's total deposits will be withdrawn at any onetime.
언제든 어느 한 번에는 은행 총 예금액의 적은 일부만을 인출할 수 있게 될 것이다.

heyday 전성기, 한창때

In its hey day, the company ran trains every fifteen minutes.
전성기에는 그 회사가 15분마다 기차를 운행했다.

envision (특히 앞으로 바라는 일을) 마음속에 그리다(상상하다)

They envision an equal society, free of poverty and disease.
그들은 가난과 질병이 없는 평등한 사회를 마음속에 그리고 있다.

Memo

18.

*Cybersecurity[1]: A View From the Front

TALLINN, Estonia — The changes in the digital world today represent a dramatically sped-up version of the changes the world underwent in a century of industrialization. It is a *paradigm transformation[2] of our world: Notions of a nation's size, wealth, power, *military might[3], population and *G.D.P.[4] mean something altogether different from what they meant a generation ago.

These relations are in *constant flux[5], and old assumptions no longer hold. Today, a small, poor East European country can be a world leader in e-governance[1)] and cybersecurity.

1 Cybersecurity
사이버보안

2 paradigm transformation
틀(패러다임) 전환(변형)

3 military might
군사력

4 GDP(gross domestic product)
국내 총생산

5 constant flux
끊임없는 흐름

1) **e-governance** (전자정부) Several dimensions and factors influence the definition of e-governance or electronic governance. The word "electronic" in the term e-governance implies technology driven governance. E-governance is the application of information and communication technology (ICT) for delivering government services, exchange of information communication transactions, integration of various stand-alone systems and services between government-to-customer (G2C), government-to-business (G2B), government-to-government (G2G) as well as back office processes and interactions within the entire government framework. Through e-governance, government services will be made available to citizens in a convenient, efficient and transparent manner. The three main target groups that can be distinguished in governance concepts are government, citizens and businesses/interest groups. In e-governance there are no distinct boundaries. Generally four basic models are available - government-to-citizen (customer), government-to-employees, government-to-government and government-to-business(Wikipedia).

6 annual reports
연차(연례) 보고서

7 third year in a row
3년 연속

8 ministries
(정부의 각) 부처

In February, the United Nations praised Estonia's e-Annual Report system, by which entrepreneurs can submit *annual reports[6] electronically, as the "best of the best" e-Government application of the past decade. Last autumn, Freedom House[2)] ranked Estonia first in Internet freedom for the *third year in a row[7] (the United States and Germany were second and third).

At the same time, Estonia is also remembered as the first publicly known target of politically motivated cyberattacks in April 2007, which inundated the Web sites of Parliament, banks, *ministries[8], television stations and other organizations.

Disruptive as the attacks were, they were by today's standards primitive, consisting of "distributed denial of service[3)]" attacks (DDoS), which essentially overload servers with signals from hijacked, hacker[4)]-controlled PCs. Six years later, as computing power and IT dependency have increased

2) **Freedom House** is a U.S.-based non-governmental organization(NGO) that conducts research and advocacy on democracy, political freedom, and human rights. Freedom House was founded in October 1941. Wendell Willkie and Eleanor Roosevelt served as its first honorary chairpersons. It describes itself as a "clear voice for democracy and freedom around the world".
The organization's annual Freedom in the World report, which assesses each country's degree of political freedoms and civil liberties, is frequently cited by political scientists, journalists, and policy-makers. Freedom of the Press and Freedom of the Net, which monitor censorship, intimidation and violence against journalists, and public access to information, are among its other signature reports(Wikipedia).

3) **distributed denial of service**(DDoS) (디도스) 무의미한 데이터를 여러 대의 컴퓨터에 동시전송 함으로써 인터넷에 연결된 수십, 수백 대의 컴퓨터를 해킹하는 것.

4) **hacker** (해커) ①컴퓨터를 이용하여 소프트웨어 작품을 만들어 내는 사람. ②타인의 컴퓨터에 불법으로 접속하여 컴퓨터에 고장을 일으키거나 컴퓨터에 수록된 정보를 변조 또는 파괴하는 사람. 원래는 MIT 공대에서 컴퓨터 프로그래밍에 열중하는 개발자들을 지칭하는 좋은 의미로 출발했으나 일반적으로는 부정적인 의미로 널리 사용되고 있다. 이에 대해 해커들은 남의 보안 시스템에 몰래 침입하여 불법 행위(크래킹)를 하는 사람들을 구분하여 크래커(cracker)라는 이름을 붙였다. 그러나 최근에는 해커와 크래커를 구분하지 않고 해커로 통칭하여 부정적 의미로 더 많이 사용하고 있다(네이버 지식백과, IT용어사전).

hugely, cyberattacks are far more *sophisticated[9] and our *vulnerabilities[10] are far greater.

Yet those attacks were a blessing — Estonia took cybersecurity seriously earlier than most. In 2008, NATO[5)] opened its Cooperative Cyber Defense Center of Excellence[6)], to enhance NATO's cyberdefense capability, in Tallinn.

Cybersecurity needs to be taken seriously by everyone. We continue to think of cyberthreats in military or classical *warfare terms[11], when in fact cyber can simply render the military paradigm irrelevant. The whole information and communication technologies(ICT)[7)] infrastructure[8)] must be regarded as an "ecosystem" in which everything is interconnected. It functions as a whole; it must be defended as a whole.

Today, almost everything we do depends on a digitized system of one kind or another. Our critical infrastructure — our electrical, water or energy production systems and

9 sophisticated
정교한

10 vulnerabilities
취약성

11 warfare terms
전투용어

5) **NATO**(North Atlantic Treaty Organization)(나토) 북대서양 조약 기구.

6) **Cooperative Cyber Defense Center of Excellence** (최고 사이버 방어 협력 센터) 암호명 K5로 일컬어진다.

7) **Information and communications technology**(ICT)(정보통신기술) is often used as an extended synonym for information technology(IT), but is a more specific term that stresses the role of unified communications and the integration of telecommunications (telephone lines and wireless signals), computers as well as necessary enterprise software, middleware, storage, and audio-visual systems, which enable users to access, store, transmit, and manipulate information(Wikipedia).

8) **infrastructure** (공공기반시설) 경제활동의 일반적인 기초를 제공하는 자본설비의 총칭이고 사회 자본으로도 불린다. 여기에는 의료, 교육, 주택 등 생활기반과 관련되는 사회 인프라스트럭처와 도로, 치수, 통신 등, 생산기반과 관련되는 산업 인프라스트럭처가 있다.

12 traffic management 교통관리

13 defense forces 방위군

*traffic management[12] — essentially interacts with, and cannot be separated from, our critical information infrastructure — private Internet providers, lines of telecommunications and the Supervisory Control and Data Acquisition(Scada)[9)] systems that run everything from nuclear power plants to delivery of milk to our supermarkets.

Understanding that cybersecurity means defending the entirety of our societies, we need to re-examine many assumptions of security. In cyberwarfare, it is much harder to identify the attacker, and therefore to know how to retaliate.

In a modern digitalized world it is possible to paralyze a country without attacking its *defense forces[13]: The country can be ruined by simply bringing its Scada systems to a halt. To impoverish a country one can erase its banking records. The most sophisticated military technology can be rendered irrelevant. In cyberspace, no country is an island.

This requires rethinking some of our core philosophical notions of modern society: the relations between the public and private spheres, between privacy and identity.

9) **Supervisory Control and Data Acquisition** 집중 원격감시 제어시스템 또는 감시 제어 데이터 수집 시스템이라고도 하는 SCADA시스템의 감시 제어기능을 말한다. SCADA시스템은 통신 경로상의 아날로그 또는 디지털 신호를 사용하여 원격장치의 상태정보 데이터를 원격소 장치(remote terminalunit)로 수집, 수신 · 기록 · 표시하여 중앙 제어 시스템이 원격 장치를 감시 제어하는 시스템을 말하며 발전 · 송배전시설, 석유화학 플랜트, 제철공정 시설, 공장 자동화 시설 등 여러 종류의 원격지 시설 장치를 중앙 집중식으로 감시 제어하는 시스템이다(네이버 지식백과, 매일경제).

At a time when the greatest threats to our privacy and the security of our data come from criminal hackers and foreign countries (often working together), we remain fixed on the idea that Big Brother[10)], our own government, is the danger.

This may have been true in the past, when only *national governments[14] had the ability to monitor citizens. Today, as we know, a single hacker can access the most *intimate details[15] of your digital and nondigital life, your finances and your *correspondence[16].

This is a clear case of market failure[11)]. A bank that builds *identity theft[17] and *fraud[18] into the cost of doing business is an example of market failure. A *power company[19] that treats a cyber-induced *power outage[20] as an *act of God[21], no different from a tornado or earthquake, demonstrates market failure.

If the private sector is unwilling to take the necessary steps to guarantee the *integrity[22] of its online activities, the government must step in to fulfill its most fundamental task — to ensure the security of its citizens; that is, to provide them with a *secure identity[23].

14 national governments 중앙정부

15 intimate details 은밀한 세부사항

16 correspondence 서신

17 identity theft 개인의 금융정보를 이용하여 사기를 치려는 신용도용 범죄

18 fraud 사기

19 power company 전력회사

20 power outage 전력 공급 정지, 정전

21 act of God (예측 · 예방 불가능한) 천재(天災), 불가항력

22 integrity = data integrity (컴퓨터)데이터완전성 (입력된 데이터가 변경, 파괴되지 않은 상태)

23 secure identity 안전한 신원(신분)

10) **Big Brother** (빅브라더) 정보의 독점으로 사회를 통제하는 관리 권력, 혹은 그러한 사회체계를 일컫는 말이다. 사회학적 통찰과 풍자로 유명한 영국의 소설가 조지 오웰(1903~1950)의 소설 《1984년》에서 비롯된 용어이다. 긍정적 의미로는 선의 목적으로 사회를 돌보는 보호적 감시, 부정적 의미로는 음모론에 입각한 권력자들의 사회통제를 뜻한다(네이버 지식백과, 한경 경제용어사전).

11) **market failure** (시장실패) 시장이 자유롭게 기능하도록 맡겨둘 때 효율적인 자원 배분을 달성하지 못하는 경우를 말한다. 시장실패는 크게 △공공재 △외부효과 △독과점 등의 이유로 발생한다. 공공재는 시장 기구에 맡기면 사회적으로 바람직한 수준보다 과소 생산된다. 외부효과는 한 사람의 행위가 제3자의 경제적 후생에 영향을 미치는 현상으로 환경오염이나 발명 등이 한 예이다. 독과점은 한 사람이나 소수의 사람들이 시장가격에 대해 임의로 영향을 미치는 상태로 역시 효율적인 자원배분을 저해한다(네이버 지식백과, 한경 경제용어사전).

24 breaches
위반

25 fake identity
가짜(위조) 신분(증)

26 three-digit security code
세 자리 보안암호

27 secure online transactions
안전한 온라인 거래

28 guarantor
보증인

29 body
단체, 조직

30 encrypted transfer of information
암호화된 정보전송

31 thus far
지금까지는

Identity lies at the core of security online. Virtually all *breaches[24] of computer security involve a *fake identity[25], be it stealing a credit card number or accessing the internal documents of the European Commission[12)]. A *three-digit security code[26] on the back of a credit card does not provide you with a secure identity, nor does an ordinary computer password. The fundamental question is whether you can be sure the person you interact with online is who he claims he is.

The key to all online security is a secure online identification system. But a nebulous fear of an imagined Big Brother prevents citizens in many places from adopting a smart-chip-based access key that would afford them *secure online transactions[27].

In Estonia, the government has become the *guarantor[28] of secure transactions online, while identity is authenticated by a *body[29] independent of the government. We use a two-factor identification system in which the ID is protected by both a chip and a password. A binary key or public key infrastructure guarantees securely *encrypted transfer of information[30]. *Thus far[31], our system has proved secure. Even during the DDoS attacks of 2007, our digital government system remained online and intact.

12) **European Commission**(유럽연합 집행위원회)는 유럽 통합과 관련된 조약을 수호하고 유럽연합(EU, European Union)의 행정부 역할을 담당한다. 유럽연합 관련 각종 정책을 입안하고 유럽연합의 이익을 수호하는 유럽 통합의 중심 기구이다(네이버 지식백과, 유럽연합 개황, 외교부).

Precisely because we offer a verifiable and reliable identification system, Estonia has gone further than any other country in investing in digitizing the basic processes of society. A quarter of the *electorate votes[32] online; 95 percent of *tax returns[33] are done online, and 95 percent of *prescriptions are filled[34] online.

By the end of 2012, Estonians gave more than a hundred million digital legal signatures. Citizens, as legal owners of their own data, have access to their digital medical and dental records. And we have more and more e-services available every year.

In the future, we hope to connect our digital services and make them *interoperable[35] with our neighbors in Northern Europe. In the longer run, we're looking toward uniting systems in all of Europe. Ultimately, government data will move across borders as freely as e-mail and Facebook and follow the international flows of commerce and trade.

The job of cybersecurity is to enable a globalized economy based on the free movement of people, goods, services, capital and ideas. This can only be accomplished if identities are secure.

Undoubtedly the most effective means by which our societies could be safeguarded from cyberattacks would be to *roll back the clock[36] — to go back to the pen, typewriter, paper and mechanical switch. We should give up on mobile

32 electorate vote
유권자 투표

33 tax returns
소득세 신고

34 ill a prescription
약을 조제하다

35 interoperable
컴퓨터 시스템이나 프로그램이상호 정보 교환이 가능한

36 roll back the clock
시계를 거꾸로 돌리다

37 cyberinsecurity
사이버 불안전성

38 enabler
조력자

phones, iPads, online banking, social media, Google searches — everything we have become accustomed to in the modern world. But that won't happen.

Cybersecurity is not just a matter of blocking bad things a cyberattack can do; it is protecting all the good things that **cyberinsecurity*[37] can prevent us from doing. Genuine cybersecurity should not be seen as an additional cost, but as an *enabler[38], guarding our entire digital way of life.

nytimes.com April 11, 2013

WORDS and STRUCTURES

a dramatically sped-up version of the changes the world underwent in a century of industrialization

= a dramatically sped-up version of the changes ***(which)*** the world underwent in a century of industrialization

= a dramatically sped-up version of the changes **+*(and)*** the world underwent ***them***(changes) in a century of industrialization

세계가 한 세기의 산업화에서 겪었던 변화의 아주 가속화한 유형

inundate ~을 침수시키다

The shock wave will be an economic tsunami that will inundate the world economy.

그 충격파는 세계경제를 침수시키는 경제 쓰나미가 될 것이다.

primitive 원시적인 단계의

A spear is a primitive weapon.

창은 원시적인 무기이다.

hijack (차량, 특히 비행기를) 납치하다, (자신의 목적이나 관심사를 홍보하기 위해 특히 회의를) 장악(이용)하다

The plane was hijacked by two armed men on a flight from London to Rome.

그 비행기는 런던에서 로마로 비행하던 도중 두 명의 무장 괴한에게 납치되었다.

Disruptive as the attacks were, they were by today's standards primitive, ***consisting*** of "distributed denial of service" attacks (DDoS), ***which*** essentially overload servers with signals from hijacked, hacker-controlled PCs.

= ***Though the attacks were disruptive***, they were (by today's standards) primitive, ***and they***(attacks) ***consisted*** of "distributed denial of service" attacks (DDoS), ***and they***(DDoS attacks) essentially overload servers with signals from hijacked, hacker-controlled PCs

형용사 + as + 주어 + 동사 = Though + 주어 + 동사 + 형용사(양보절)
비록 그 공격들이 파괴적이라 하더라도 오늘날의 기준으로 볼 때 원시적인 단계에 있었는데, 그 공격들은 디도스 공격으로 구성되어 있었고, 디도스 공격은 본질적으로 장악된 해거의 통제를 받는 PC로부터 오는 신호들로 서브에 과부하를 건다.

earlier than most = earlier than most countries 대부분의 나라들 보다 일찍

render (어떤 상태가 되게) 만들다(하다)

Hundreds of people were rendered homeless by the earthquake.
수백 명의 사람들이 그 지진으로 집을 잃게 되었다.

of one kind, or another 이런저런

We've all got problems of one kind or another.
우리 모두가 이런저런 문제를 안고 있다.

almost everything we do depends on a digitized system of one kind or another
= almost everything ***(which)*** we do depends on a digitized system of one kind or another
= almost everything ***+(and)*** we do ***it*** depends on a digitized system of one kind or another
우리가 하는 거의 모든 것은 이러저런 디지털화된 체계에 의존한다.

critical (앞으로의 상황에 영향을 미친다는 점에서) 대단히 중요한

Your decision is critical to our future.
당신의 결정은 우리의 장래에 대단히 중요하다.

retaliate 보복하다

But if there is any action, we will retaliate.
어떠한 조치가 있다면 우리는 보복할 것이다.

paralyze 마비시키다

Their long-term goal is to paralyze and destroy drug trafficking organizations.
그들의 장기 목표는 마약 밀매 조직을 마비시키고 파괴시키는 것이다.

bring~to a halt ~을 정지(중지, 중단)시키다

One strong man brought a broken-down old car to a halt.
한 힘센 남자는 망가진 중고차를 정지시켰다.

impoverish 빈곤(가난)하게 하다

Brown is determined to impoverish the middle classes.
브라운은 중산층을 가난하게 만들려고 결심했다.

build A into B A를 B의 일부로 만들어내다

We are trying to build those factors into the core competence.
우리는 그런 요소들을 핵심역량으로 만드는 중이다.

A power company ***that*** treats a cyber-induced power outage as an act of God, no different from a tornado or earthquake, demonstrates market failure.

= A power company ***+(and) it*** treats a cyber-induced power outage as an act of God, no different from a tornado or earthquake, demonstrates market failure.

주어 power company 동사 demonstrate
사이버로 인한 정전을 태풍이나 지진과는 다른 천재로 간주하는 전력회사가 시장실패를 예증한다.

be it stealing a credit card number or accessing the internal documents of the European Commission

= ***if it***(a fake identity) ***be stealing*** a credit card number or accessing the internal documents of the European Commission

만일 위조 신분자가 신용카드번호를 훔치거나 유럽연합 집행위원회의 내부문서에 접근하려고 한다면

nor does an ordinary computer password
= and an ordinary computer password ***does not provide*** you with a secure identity
또한 보통의 컴퓨터 암호도 안전한 신분을 제공하지 못한다.

interact 소통하다(교류하다)

Teachers have a limited amount of time to interact with each child.
교사들이 아동 개개인과 소통할 수 있는 시간의 양은 제한되어 있다.

The fundamental question is whether you can be sure the person you interact with online is who he claims he is
= The fundamental question is whether you can be sure the person ***(whom)*** you interact with online is who he claims he is
= The fundamental question is whether you can be sure the person ***+(and)*** you interact with ***him*** online is who he claims he is
근본적인 질문은 우리가 온라인으로 소통하고 있는 그 사람이 실제의 그인지 확신할 수 있는가 하는 것이다.

nebulous 흐릿한, 모호한

It is a very nebulous concept in lots of ways.
이것은 여러모로 아주 모호한 개념이다.

afford 주다, 제공하다

The transaction afforded him a good profit.
그 거래는 그에게 많은 이득을 주었다.

authenticate 진짜임을 증명하다

The letter has been authenticated by handwriting experts.
그 편지는 필체 전문가들에 의해 진짜임이 밝혀졌다.

intact (하나도 손상되지 않고) 온전한, 전혀 다치지 않은

Most of the house remains intact even after two hundred years.
그 집은 200년이 지났는데도 대부분이 온전하다.

become accustomed to + 명사 ~하는데 익숙해지다

Dogs and cats that are not familiar with each other will require sometime to become accustomed to each other.
서로 친하지 않은 개와 고양이는 서로 친숙해지기까지 약간의 시간이 필요하다.

Cybersecurity is not just a matter of blocking bad things a cyberattack can do
= Cybersecurity is not just a matter of blocking bad things ***(which)*** a cyberattack can do
= Cybersecurity is not just a matter of blocking bad things ***+(and)*** a cyberattack can do ***them***
사이버 보안은 단지 사이버 공격이 할 수 있는 나쁜 것들을 막는 문제가 아니다.

it is protecting all the good things ***that*** cyberinsecurity can prevent us from doing
= it is protecting all the good things ***+(and)*** cyberinsecurity can prevent ***them*** us from doing
그것은 사이버 불안전성이 좋은 것들을 하지 못하게 하는 모든 좋은 것들을 보호하는 것이다.

Memo

19.

Medical Progress, Social Progress, and Legal Regression

The abortion laws[1)] passed last week in North Dakota[2)] are troubling first and foremost because they restrict women's freedom to control their own bodies. More insidiously, they criminalize **selective abortion*[1], which means that a woman cannot choose to *terminate a pregnancy[2] because she knows the *fetus[3] has a *genetic abnormality[4], or to select for other characteristics, such as gender. The very use of the world "selective" here indicates how right the pro-choice movement[3)] has been to emphasize "choice." All abortion is selective, and whether a woman has selected not to have a baby at all or has

1 selective abortion
선택적 낙태(유산)

2 terminate a pregnancy
예정일보다 빨리 인공적으로 출산시키다. 임신중절수술을 하다

3 fetus
(임신 9주 후의) 태아
cf. embryo 배아
(인간의 경우는 수정 후 첫 8주까지의 태아)

4 genetic abnormality
유전적 기형

1) **Abortion law** (낙태법) is legislation and common law which pertains to the provision of abortion. Abortion has been a controversial subject in many societies through history because of the moral, ethical, practical, and political power issues that surround it. It has been banned frequently and otherwise limited by law. However, abortions continue to be common in many areas where they are illegal; abortion rates are similar in countries where the procedure is legal and in countries where it is not according to the World Health Organization (WHO), due to unavailability of modern contraceptives in areas where abortion is illegal. The number of abortions worldwide is declining due to increased access to contraception according to WHO. Almost 2/3 of the world's women currently reside in countries where abortion may be obtained on request for a broad range of social, economic or personal reasons. Abortion laws vary widely by country. Seven countries (in Latin America and Europe) ban the procedure entirely(Wikipedia).

2) **North Dakota**(ND)(미국 중북부 캐나다와 국경을 접하고 있는 39번째 주(州)) 속칭 the Sioux State.

selected not to have a particular baby is not a matter the state should parse. No one should be forced to have a child she doesn't wish to have.

Both *anti-abortionists[5] and *disability activists[6] have sometimes suggested that women should defer to "nature" and have whatever baby they conceive. The *bioethicist[7] William Ruddick calls this the "*'hospitality' view of women[8]." The *proposition[9] is that we do not have and should not *exercise volition[10] in the making of children; *pregnancies[11] are an *arranged marriage[12] we are not free to buck. Yet a study a few years ago concluded that women who do not make use of *prenatal testing[13] or who choose to keep pregnancies they know will lead to children with disabilities "were judged more responsible, more to blame, and less deserving of both sympathy and social aid subsequent to *giving birth to[14] a *disabled child[15] than were women to whom testing was not made available." The hospitality view is *oppressive[16], but so is the rush to social judgment.

I have written in my most recent book, "Far From the Tree," about the rich experience many parents find in children with conditions against which people often select. I would

5 anti-abortionists 낙태 반대론자
6 disability activists 장애자 권익보호 활동가
7 bioethicist 생명윤리학자
8 'hospitality' view of women 접대 여성관
9 proposition 명제, 진술
10 exercise volition 자유의지를 행사하다
11 pregnancy 임신
12 rranged marriage 중매결혼
13 prenatal testing 태아기 검사
14 give birth to (아이)를 낳다
15 disabled child 장애아
16 oppressive 강압적인, 억압적인

3) **The United States pro-choice movement** (also known as the United States abortion-rights movement)(임신중절 합법화를 찬성하는, 낙태에 찬성하는 운동) is the United States part of a broader sociopolitical global abortion-rights movement, supporting the view that a woman should have the legal right to elective abortion, meaning the right to terminate her pregnancy. The pro-choice movement includes a variety of organizations, with no single centralized decision-making body. There are diverse arguments and rationales for the pro-choice stance.
A key point in abortion rights in the United States was the U.S. Supreme Court's 1973 decision in Roe v. Wade, which struck down most state laws restricting abortion which decriminalized and legalized elective abortion in various states(Wikipedia).

never propose to anyone—even to myself—that such parents' rapture constitutes an *imperative[17] to bring similar children into the world.

I do see a problem, however, in the speed with which women who have no *prior exposure to[18] the conditions in question are expected to make these decisions. Women often terminate a pregnancy without knowing what life would be like with and for an *anomalous child[19]. It is worth publicizing the satisfaction that the experience may entail, so that the pro-choice movement becomes the *pro-informed-choice*[20] movement. Others have already pointed out that if we want people to keep these pregnancies, we might start by providing better services for *people with disabilities[21]; our neglect of decent care is a *national disgrace[22], and is ignored in North Dakota's new *statutes[23].

There is *muddle[24] from both sides on abortion after *prenatal diagnosis[25]. The women I interviewed, whether they had carried such children to term or had terminated, described intense pressure pushing them away from their *natural inclination[26]. The *political right[27] conflates choice and abortion, implying that most women will terminate, eliminating *disabled populations[28] whose lives have value. It also *honeys[29] the story of *challenging parenthood[30]; having a child with severe disabilities can be rewarding, but it is also difficult, and denying the difficulty is a *disservice[31]. The political left conflates access to abortion and abortion itself. In this view, the "responsible" choice is to prevent the suffering a disabled child will endure. But all children suffer,

17 imperative 책무

18 prior exposure to ~에의 사전노출

19 anomalous child 정상이 아닌 아이

20 *pro-informed-choice* 잘 알고 내린(하는) 선택, 정보에 근거를 둔 선택을 찬성하는

21 people with disabilities 장애인

22 national disgrace 국가적 수치

23 statutes 법규, 법령

24 muddle 혼란스러움

25 prenatal diagnosis 출생 전 진단, 태아 검진

26 natural inclination 타고난 성향, 천성

27 political right 정치적 우파

28 disabled populations 장애인

29 honey 꿀로 달게 하다

30 challenging parenthood 도전적인(저항하는) 부모 되기

31 disservice 폐, 해

32 procreative race
출산(생식)력이 있는 종족

33 putative suffering
추정상의 고통

34 smoke screen
연막, 위장

35 would-be parents
부모가 되려는 사람, 장래의 부모

36 erroneously
잘못되게, 틀리게

37 variant body
변종의 신체

38 lobby
(정치적인) 로비(활동) (영향력 행사)

39 the would-have-been-aborted
낙태 받을 가능성이 있었던 사람들

40 terminations
임신중절 수술

41 humanitarian breakthrough
인도주의적 대전환

42 eugenic
우생학적인, 우수한 자손을 만드는

43 founding principle
토대가 되는 원리

and we remain a *procreative race[32]. The *putative suffering[33] of disabled children can be a *smoke screen[34]. *Would-be parents[35] often imagine the suffering *erroneously[36]; they confuse how it feels to lose an ability (to be suddenly bereft of hearing) with how it feels to live healthily with a *variant body[37] (to be deaf all your life). Further, they confuse their own discomfort with their child's.

A *lobby[38] of *the would-have-been-aborted[39] militate against *terminations[40]; some have greeted the North Dakota laws as a *humanitarian breakthrough[41]. I can empathize with their concern, because I suspect my parents would have considered termination very seriously if they had somehow known I would be gay. I imagine a *eugenic[42] world in which medical advances could allow parents to abort fetuses destined to be like me in this regard, and the thought makes me sad. Still, choice is the hallmark and *founding principle[43] of democracy, and I would champion people's right to it. I would do so with a firm belief that choice strengthens families no matter what choice they make.

4) **Down syndrome**(DS)(다운증후군) or Down's syndrome, also known as trisomy 21, is a genetic disorder caused by the presence of all or part of a third copy of chromosome 21. It is typically associated with physical growth delays, characteristic facial features and mild to moderate intellectual disability. The average IQ of a young adult with Down syndrome is 50, equivalent to the mental age of an 8 or 9 year old child, but this varies widely.
Down syndrome can be identified during pregnancy by prenatal screening followed by diagnostic testing, or after birth by direct observation and genetic testing. Since the introduction of screening, pregnancies with the diagnosis are often terminated.
Down syndrome is the most common chromosome abnormality in humans, occurring in about 1 per 1000 babies born each year. It is named after John Langdon Down, the British doctor who fully described the syndrome in 1866. Some aspects of the condition were described earlier by Jean-Étienne Dominique Esquirol in 1838 and Édouard Séguin in 1844.The genetic cause of Down syndrome—an extra copy of chromosome 21—was identified by French researchers in 1959(Wikipedia).

Both opponents and supporters of the right to selective termination tend to consider people who want to terminate — but choice is equally valuable to women who want to continue their pregnancies. Of the five thousand five hundred children born with Down syndrome[4)] in the United States each year, about six hundred and twenty-five are born to women who had a prenatal diagnosis. I have interviewed many such women, and, without exception, they were glad they had been able to think about the pregnancy and make a positive, affirming decision to keep it. Tierney Temple Fairchild, whose fetus had a prenatal Down syndrome diagnosis, wrote, in words I quote in my book, "I had a choice, and I chose life. Does that make me pro-choice or pro-life? Our political parties tell us we can't have it both ways.... I chose life, but I am thankful I had the choice."

North Dakota's *legislation[44] attempts to interfere in the race between medical and social advancement. On the medical front, it's getting easier and easier to pick up genetic conditions earlier and earlier. At the same time, on the social front, people with *genetic anomalies[45] who were once *hidden away[46] in darkness and left to die young are writers, actors, activists. New strategies for early intervention have allowed people with Down syndrome to *secure accomplishments[47] that were once unimaginable; some are living independently; *life expectancies[48] have soared. People with forms of deafness that can be detected prenatally are members of a thriving deaf culture. People with *achondroplastic dwarfism[49], also detectable prenatally, are more readily accepted than ever

44 legislation
법률제정, 입법행위

45 genetic anomalies
유전적 이상

46 hide a person away
아무를 빼돌리다

47 secure accomplishments
업적을 얻어내다

48 life expectancies
기대수명

49 achondroplastic dwarfism
연골형성 부전 왜소증

50 accommodations
숙박시설

51 tyrannical laws
압제적인 법

before, with more *accommodations[50] than ever before. We need only to bear collective witness to these changes. It will get harder to select against people in these categories not because of *tyrannical laws[51], but because we see so much more joy in their lives.

newyorker.com 2013-04-13

WORDS and STRUCTURES

first and foremost 다른 무엇보다도 더

He does a little teaching, but first and foremost he's a writer.
그는 가르치는 일도 좀 하지만 다른 무엇보다도 그는 작가이다.

insidiously 은밀하게, 모르는 사이에

It is probable that the fatal disease began insidiously months ago.
그 치명적 병은 아마 수개월 전 알지 못하는 사이에 시작된 것 같다.

criminalize (새로운 법을 통과시켜 무엇을) 불법화하다

The use of opium was not criminalized until fairly recently.
아편 사용은 꽤 최근까지만 하더라도 불법이 아니었다.

terminate 끝나다, 끝내다

Your contract of employment terminates in December.
당신의 고용 계약은 12월에 끝난다.

After a lot of agonizing she decided to terminate the pregnancy.
그녀는 수많은 번민 끝에 낙태하기로 결심했다.

choose to + 동사원형 (~하기를) 결정하다, 결심하다

He choose to run for the election. 그는 선거에 출마하기르 결심했다.

parse 구성요소로 분석하다, 구문해석하다, …을 세밀히 조사하다

I can't work out how to parse the code correctly.
나는 어떻게 그 암호를 정확히 분석하는지 알아낼 수가 없다.

whether a woman has selected not to have a baby at all or has selected not to have a particular baby is not a matter the state should parse

= whether a woman has selected not to have a baby at all or has selected not to have a particular baby is not a matter ***(which)*** the state should parse

= whether a woman has selected not to have a baby at all or has selected not to have a particular baby is not a matter ***+(and)*** the state should parse ***it***(the matter)

여성이 전혀 아이를 가지지 않기로 했거나 특별한 아이를 가지지 않기로 했는지는 주가 해석해야하는 문제가 아니다.

No one should be forced to have a child she doesn't wish to have

= No one should be forced to have a child ***(whom)*** she doesn't wish to have

= No one should be forced to have a child ***+(and)*** she doesn't wish to have ***him***(a child)

어느 누구도 그녀가 가지고 싶지 않은 아이를 가지도록 강요받아서는 안 된다.

defer to somebody/something ~을 따르다

We will defer to whatever the committee decides.

우리는 위원회의 결정이 어떻게 나오든 그 결정을 따를 것이다.

conceive (아이를) 가지다(임신하다)

She is unable to conceive.

그녀는 아이를 가질 수 없다.

should have ***whatever baby*** they conceive

= should have ***any baby +(and)*** they conceive ***it***(baby)

그들이 임신하는 아이는 어떤 아이든 가져야 한다.

buck 저항하다, 반대하다

Thai Buddhism is well known for bucking convention.
태국불교는 관습을 거스르는 것으로 잘 알려져 있다.

pregnancies are an arranged marriage we are not free to buck
= apregnancies are an arranged marriage ***(which)*** we are not free to buck
= pregnancies are an arranged marriage **+*(and)*** we are not free to buck ***it***(the arranged marriage)
임신은 우리가 마음대로 반대할 수 없는 중매결혼이다.

women ***who*** choose to keep pregnancies they know will lead to children with disabilities "were judged more responsible,
= women **+*(and) they*** choose to keep pregnancies ***(which)*** (they know) will lead to children with disabilities "were judged more responsible,
= women **+*(and) they*** choose to keep pregnancies **+*and they***(pregnancies) (they know) will lead to children with disabilities "were judged more responsible,
임신이 장애가 있는 아이로 이어질 것이라는 것을 알고도 임신을 유지하기로 결정한 여성들은 더 책임감이 잇는 것으로 판명되었다.

be to blame ~에 대하여 책임이 있다

The emergence of the Internet and short revenues in advertising are also to blame.
인터넷의 등장과 광고의 수익감소도 책임이 있다.

subsequent to (전치사) ~다음에(뒤에)

There have been further developments subsequent to our meeting.
우리 회의 뒤에 추가로 다른 일들이 전개되었다.

so is the rush to social judgment
= the rush to social judgment is also oppressive
성급한 사회적 판단도 또한 강압적이다.

about the rich experience many parents find in children with conditions against which people often select

= about the rich experience ***(which)*** many parents find in children with conditions ***against which*** people often select

= about the rich experience **+*(and)*** many parents find ***it***(the rich experience) in children with conditions **+*(and)*** people often select ***against them***(conditions)

사람들이 종종 선택하지 않는 조건을 가진 아이들에게서 많은 부모님들이 발견하는 풍부한 경험에 관하여

rapture 황홀감

He listened to the music with an expression of pure rapture on his face.

그는 얼굴에 완전히 황홀감에 빠진 표정으로 음악을 들었다.

what life would be like with and for an anomalous child

정상이 아닌 아이에게서 삶이 어떠할지를

publicize (일반 사람들에게) 알리다, 광고(홍보)하다

They flew to Europe to publicize the plight of the refugees.

그들은 난민들의 곤경을 널리 알리기 위해 유럽으로 날아갔다.

decent (수준, 질) 괜찮은, 제대로 된

This would allow underprivileged families to afford decent care.

이것은 혜택을 받지 못하는 가정에 제대로 된 보살핌 받을 수 있게 할 것이다.

term 기한, 만기

The pregnancy went to full term.

임신이 달이 다 차게 되었다.

whether they had carried such children to term or had terminated,

그들의 아이를 만기출산 하였건, 임신중절 하였건

conflate 융합하다, 하나로 합치다

Many Christians would conflate occultism with Paganism, but the two are fundamentally distinct labels.

많은 기독교인들이 신비주의를 이교주의와 하나로 보려고 하지만, 그 둘은 근본적으로 다른 말이다.

The political right conflates choice and abortion, ***implying*** that most women will terminate, ***eliminating*** disabled populations ***whose lives*** have value

= The political right conflates choice and abortion, ***and it implies*** that most women will terminate, ***and it eliminates*** disabled populations ***+(and) thier lives*** have value

it = The political right conflates choice and abortion

it = most women will terminate

정치적 우파는 선택과 낙태를 합치고 있는데, 그것이 함축하고 있는 것은 대부분의 여성들이 임신중절을 할 것이라는 것이고 그것은 그들의 삶이 가치가 있는 장애인을 죽이는 것이다.

rewarding 보람 있는

It's not a very exciting job but it's rewarding.

그다지 재미있는 직업은 아니지만 보람 있는 일이다.

to prevent the suffering a disabled child will endure

= to prevent the suffering ***(which)*** a disabled child will endure

= to prevent the suffering ***+(and)*** a disabled child will endure ***it***(the suffering)

장애아가 겪을 고통을 예방하는 것

bereft of ~을 빼앗긴, ~을 상실한(잃은)

She is bereft of all happiness.

그녀는 모든 행복을 빼앗겼다.

discomfort (신체적인) 불편

For most of us, the discomfort is only temporary.

우리 중 대부분에게 있어 불편은 단지 일시적인 것일 뿐이다.

militate against ~을 방해하다, 악영향을 미치다

His bad manners will militate against his success in business.
무례한 태도가 사업성공에 있어 방해가 될 것이다.

greet ~ as 받아들이다, 반응을 보이다

The team's win was greeted as a major triumph.
그 팀의 우승은 주요한 승리로 받아들여졌다.

empathize with ~에 마음으로부터 공감하다

I can empathize with her.
나는 그 여자에 공감할 수 있다.

still 그런데도, 그럼에도 불구하고

The weather was cold and wet. Still, we had a great time.
날씨는 춥고 궂었다. 그런데도 우리는 대단히 즐거운 시간을 보냈다.

hallmark (전형적인) 특징

Accuracy is a hallmark of good scholarship.
정확성은 훌륭한 학문의 특징이다.

champion ~을 위해 싸우다, …을 옹호하다

He has always championed the cause of gay rights.
그는 항상 동성애자 인권이라는 대의를 위해 싸워 왔다.

consider (특히 남의 감정을) 고려하다(감안하다)

You should consider other people before you act.
행동을 하기 전에 다른 사람들을 고려해야 한다.

interfere 간섭(참견)하다

She didn't want to interfere in family problems.
그녀는 가족의 문제에 간섭하기를 원치 않았다.

bear witness to ~라는 증거를 제시하다, ~을 입증(증명)하다

Can you bear witness to your innocence?
당신의 결백함을 입증할 수 있나요?

Abortion

Liberal

A woman has the right to decide what happens with her body. A fetus is not a human life, so it does not have separate individual rights. The government should provide taxpayer funded abortions for women who cannot afford them. The decision to have an abortion is a personal choice of a woman regarding her own body and the government must protect this right. Women have the right to affordable, safe and legal abortions, including partial birth abortion.

Conservative

Human life begins at conception. Abortion is the murder of a human being. An unborn baby, as a living human being, has separate rights from those of the mother. Oppose taxpayer-funded abortion. Taxpayer dollars should not be used for the government to provide abortions. Support legislation to prohibit partial birth abortions, called the "Partial Birth Abortion* Ban"

(studentnewsdaily.com February 25, 2013)

Memo

20.

Nelson Mandela dies

Nelson Rolihlahla Mandela[1)], the father of the nation, died on December 5 2013 at the age of 95.

President Jacob Zuma[2)] made the announcement from the Union Buildings[3)] in Pretoria on Thursday night. He said Mandela passed away at 8:50 pm at his home in Houghton, Johannesburg, surrounded by his wife, Graça Machel and members of his family.

Zuma said Mandela would have a *state funeral[1] and that flags would fly *half-mast[2] from December 6 until after the funeral. Zuma called on South Africans to "recall the values for which Madiba[4)] fought".

1 state funeral
국장(國葬)

2 half-mast
반기(半旗)의 위치
(조의를 나타내는)

1) **Nelson Rolihlahla Mandela** 넬슨 롤리랄라 만델라(1918년 7월 18일~2013년 12월 5일)는 남아프리카공화국에서 아파르트헤이트(Apartheid)가 철폐된 후 처음으로 실시된 평등선거에서 대통령에 당선된 인물이다. 남아프리카공화국 최초의 흑인대통령으로 선출되기 전에는 아프리카민족회의(ANC, African National Congress)의 지도자로서 백인정권의 극단적 인종차별정책에 맞선 투쟁을 이끌었던 인권운동가였다(네이버 지식백과, 남아프리카공화국 개황).

2) **Jacob Gedleyihlekisa Zuma** (born 12 April 1942) is the President of South Africa, elected by parliament following his party's victory in the 2009 general election. He was reelected in the 2014 election(Wikipedia).

3) **Union Buildings** 남아프리카공화국의 행정수도 프리토리아(Pretoria)에 있는 정부청사 및 대통령 집무실. 1910년 11월에 착공하여 1913년에 완공하였다. 밝은 사암(砂岩)으로 된 건물로서 남아프리카 건축물 가운데 걸작으로 손꼽힌다(네이버 지식백과, 두산백과).

3 hospitalize
입원시키다

4 recurring lung infection
되풀이하여 발생하는 폐 감염(폐렴)

5 the Presidency
= the office of the president 대통령 궁

6 court affidavits
법정진술서

7 the former statesman
이전의 정치가 (만델라를 가리킴)

8 assisted-breathing
호흡 보조장치

9 permanent vegetative state
지속적 식물인간 상태

10 improvement
회복, 호전

11 pneumonia
폐렴

12 treatment
치료

13 death bed
임종(의 자리)

14 speculation
추측

Mandela was *hospitalised[3] on June 8 with a *recurring lung infection[4]. Initial reports from *the Presidency[5] suggested Mandela was stable, although his condition was serious. But on June 23, the Presidency announced that Mandela's condition had deteriorated and he was critical.

*Court affidavits[6] soon confirmed that *the former statesman[7] was on an *assisted-breathing[8], life support machine. More reports emerged about Mandela in the days that followed — that he was in a "*permanent vegetative state[9]" — although the presidency denied these, maintaining that he was "critical yet stable".

On his 95th birthday, July 18, Zuma announced an *improvement[10] in Mandela's health. Mandela was discharged from hospital in September and transported to his home in Houghton. In November, his family said he remained "quite ill", but his *pneumonia[11] had cleared up. Zuma visited Mandela on November 18 and said he was still in a critical condition, but that he continued to respond to *treatment[12].

On December 3, his daughter, Makaziwe Mandela, said the former president was "strong" and "courageous", although he was "on his *death bed[13]". Mandela's grandson, Ndaba Mandela, said his grandfather was "not doing well", although, "he is still with us".

His declining health has been the subject of *speculation[14] over the past few years. He was diagnosed and treated for

4) **Madiba** 만델라의 존칭, 그의 씨족 명 Xhosa에서 파생됨.
Madiba generation 만델라가 남아프리카 다민족 사회의 첫 대통령이 되었을 때인 1994년경에 태어난 세대

*prostate cancer[15] in 2001 but made a full recovery. In 2011, he *was admitted to hospital[16] following a severe *respiratory infection[17] and a year later underwent a scheduled surgery for a longstanding *abdominal complaint[18].

Mandela was plagued by recurring *lung ailments[19] in recent years. He spent 18 days in hospital at the end of 2012 and, despite receiving home-based *high care[20] thereafter, was back in hospital in March and April 2013.

There were *renewed[21] fears for his health when he returned to hospital in June. Despite assurances from the presidency that he was in a "serious but stable" condition, South Africans began preparing themselves for the worst as Mandela's family members flocked to Johannesburg[5)], *struggle stalwarts[22] paid visits to the *icon[23], and the world's media gathered in Qunu[6)], Houghton and at the Pretoria hospital where he was treated.

The much-loved Mandela, known *affectionately[24] as Tata

15 prostate cancer
전립선암

16 be admitted to (a) hospital
병원에 입원하다

17 respiratory infection
호흡기 감염

18 abdominal complaint
복부 질환(통증)

19 lung ailments
폐 질환

20 high care = high standards of care
높은 수준의 치료

21 renewed
(관심) 재개된, 새로워진

22 struggle stalwarts
투쟁 당원들(지지자들)

23 icon
(특정한 사상, 생활방식 등의 상징으로 여겨지는) 우상(아이콘), 여기서는 만델라를 가리킴

24 affectionately
애정을 담고, 친근하게

5) **Johannesburg**[dʒouhǽnisbə̀:rg] also known as Jozi, Joburg, Joni, eGoli or Joeys, abbreviated as JHB, is the largest city in South Africa, by population. Johannesburg is the provincial capital of Gauteng, the wealthiest province in South Africa, having the largest economy of any metropolitan region in Sub-Saharan Africa. The city is one of the 50 largest urban agglomerations in the world, and is also the world's largest city not situated on a river, lake, or coastline(Wikipedia).

6) **Qunu** is a small rural village in South Africa's Eastern Cape Province. The previous President of South Africa, Nelson Mandela was born near Qunu in the village Mvezo next to the M'bashe river. He grew up in Qunu after his father was deposed as the chief of Mvezo. After his retirement, Mandela returned to Qunu. In his autobiography, Long Walk to Freedom, Mandela describes Qunu as the place where he spent the happiest moments of his childhood.
The remains of three of Mandela's children was originally buried here, but was exhumed by one of his grandsons, Mandla Mandela. Mandla reburied the remains in Mvezo, the village of which he was chief. On 3 July 2013 the Eastern Cape high court ruled that the remains should be moved back to Qunu. Shortly after this, king Buyelekhaya Dalindyebo relieved Mandla of his duties.
On 15 December 2013, Mandela was buried in Qunu following a state funeral, on his family's property in a spot he personally selected(Wikipedia).

25 ancestral home
조상전래의 집

26 life imprisonment
종신형

27 iconic speech
상징이 되는 연설

Madiba, became increasingly frail and retired from public life in 2004 at the age of 85.

Mandela's last public appearance was a brief one, at the end of the Soccer World Cup in 2010. Since then, he has split his time between his home in Houghton and his *ancestral home[25] in Qunu in the Eastern Cape.

Mandela became the symbol of the struggle against apartheid[7)] after he was convicted in the Rivonia Trial[8)] of charges of sabotage[9)] and was sentenced to *life imprisonment[26] on Robben Island[10)].

At the end of his trial, Mandela gave a now *iconic speech[27] in which he said: "I have fought against white domination,

7) **apartheid**[əpɑːrtaɪt;əpɑːrteɪt] (아파르트헤이트) 남아프리카공화국의 공용어의 하나인 아프리칸스어(Afrikaans : (남아프리카의) 공용 네덜란드 말)로부터의 격리 또는 분리를 의미하고, 일반적으로는 남아프리카공화국에서 제2차 세계대전 후 채용하여 1991년에 폐지될 때까지 실행되었던 백인 우위의 인종차별정책을 말한다.
1991년 아파르트헤이트의 근간법의 폐지, 1992년 백인 유권자의 투표에 의한 개혁 속행을 거쳐 1993년의 모든 정당에 의한 모든 인종평등의 원칙에 기초하여 공동 통치를 결정한 헌법의 채택으로 17세기 중반의 네덜란드인 이주이래 3세기 반 동안 계속되어 온 남아프리카의 백인 소수지배가 막을 내렸다(네이버 지식백과, 21세기 정치학 대사전).

8) **The Rivonia Trial** was a trial that took place in South Africa between 1963 and 1964. Ten leaders of the African National Congress (ANC) were charged (and eight eventually convicted) on four broad charges: (a) recruiting persons for training in the preparation and use of explosives and in guerrilla warfare for the purpose of violent revolution and committing acts of sabotage; (b) conspiring to commit these acts and to aid foreign military units when they [hypothetically] invaded the Republic; (c) acting in these ways to further the objects of communism; and (d) soliciting and receiving money for these purposes from sympathizers outside South Africa.
Among other consequences, the trial led to the imprisonment of ANC leader (and future President of South Africa) Nelson Mandela and the other convicted defendants on life sentences, of which Mandela actually served 27 years. Mandela's speech from the dock was to prove an influential statement of his political beliefs(Wikipedia).

9) **sabotage** (사보타지) 프랑스어의 사보(sabot; 나막신)에서 나온 말로 중세 유럽 농민들이 영주의 부당한 처사에 항의해 수확물을 사보로 짓밟는 데서 연유했다. 우리나라에서는 흔히 태업(怠業)이라고 번역되는데 실제로는 태업보다 범위가 넓다. 태업은 노동자가 고용주에 대해 형식적으로는 일을 하면서 몰래 작업능률을 저하시키는 것을 말하지만, 사보타지는 쟁의 중에 기계나 원료를 고의적으로 파손하는 행위도 포함된다(네이버 지식백과, 매일경제/매경닷컴).

10) **Robben Island** (로벤 섬) Cape 반도의 난바다의 작은 섬; 남아프리카 공화국 정부가 정치범을 수용하는 데 씀.

and I have fought against black domination. I have cherished the ideal of a democratic and free society in which all persons live together in harmony and with equal opportunities. It is an ideal, which I hope to live for and to achieve. But *if needs be[28], it is an ideal for which I am prepared to die."

Mandela, a *key figure[29] in the African National Congress[11)], who helped found the party's *youth league[30] and *armed wing[31], Umkhonto weSizwe, was imprisoned for 27 years before he was finally released in 1990 at the age of 71.

Mandela was awarded the Nobel Peace Prize in 1993, together with former president F.W. De Klerk[12)], for the "peaceful termination of the apartheid regime and for *laying the foundations[32] for a new democratic South Africa". A year later, he was elected president in the country's first democratic election.

28 if needs be
= if it is necessary
필요하다면

29 key figure
핵심인물

30 youth league
청년동맹

31 armed wing
무장단체

32 lay the foundations for
~에 대한 토대를 놓다

11) **African National Congress**(ANC)(아프리카 민족회의) 남아프리카공화국 백인정권의 인종차별 정책에 대항해온 흑인해방운동조직이다. 1912년 창설되어 반(反) 아파르트헤이트조직 중 가장 오랜 역사를 가지고 있다. 처음엔 인도의 간디주의의 영향을 받아 비폭력 노선을 기조로 했으나, 1960년의 흑인폭동 등을 계기로 비합법화 되자 점차 무장노선으로 기울었다. 특히 1970년대 후반 이후 백인정권의 '당근과 채찍' 정책에 반발, 흑인 각층의 반(反) 아파르트헤이트 의식의 고양과 함께 게릴라 활동이 도시권에까지 확대되었다.
그러나 1990년 2월 ANC의 지도자 넬슨 만델라가 27년 만에 감옥에서 풀려난 후 곧이어 무력투쟁중단을 선언했다. 1993년 12월 인종차별을 철폐하는 새 헌법이 의회에서 통과되었고, 1994년 5월 총선에서 아프리카민족회의는 60% 이상의 득표로 압승을 거둬 최초의 흑인정권을 출범시켰다(네이버 지식백과 시사상식사전).

12) **Frederik Willem de Klerk**(born 18 March 1936), was the seventh and last State President of apartheid-era South Africa, serving from September 1989 to May 1994. De Klerk was also leader of the National Party (which later became the New National Party) from February 1989 to September 1997.
De Klerk brokered the end of apartheid, South Africa's racial segregation policy, and supported the transformation of South Africa into a multi-racial democracy by entering into the negotiations that resulted in all citizens, including the country's black majority, having equal voting and other rights. He won the Félix Houphouët-Boigny Peace Prize in 1991, the Prince of Asturias Award in 1992 and the Nobel Peace Prize in 1993 along with Nelson Mandela for his role in the ending of apartheid(Wikipedia)

33 broker
(국가 간의 협상을)
중개(재)하다

34 Foundation
재단

He stepped down from the presidency in 1999 after one term in office but continued with a busy public schedule. He *brokered[33] negotiations for peace in Rwanda, established the Mandela-Rhodes[13)] *Foundation[34] for educational scholarship, and launched the 46664 Aids fundraising foundation.

Mail & Guardian 2013-12-05

13) **Rhodes**(Cecil John Rhodes)(로즈)(1853–1902) 영국 태생의 남아프리카 정치가.

WORDS and STRUCTURES

pass away 사망하다(돌아가시다)

His mother passed away last year. 그의 어머니는 작년에 돌아가셨다.

surrounded by his wife,
= ***and Mandela was surrounded*** by his wife,

call on/upon somebody to do …에게 ~하도록 요구(부탁)하다

He called on me to make a speech.
그는 나에게 연설을 부탁했다.

Zuma ***called on*** South Africans ***to*** "recall the values ***for which*** Madiba fought"
= Zuma called on South Africans to "recall the values **+*(and)*** Madiba fought ***for them***(the values)"
주마는 남아아프리카 국민들에게 만델라가 싸웠던 가치들을 상기하도록 요구했다.

deteriorate 악화되다, 더 나빠지다

Her health deteriorated rapidly, and she died shortly afterwards.
그녀는 건강이 급속도로 악화되어 그 후 곧 죽었다.

critical 위태로운, 위독한

One of the victims of the fire remains in a critical condition.
그 화재 피해자들 중 한 명은 위독한 상태이다.

discharge from hospital/job ~에서 떠나는 것을 허락하다, 해고하다

Patients were being discharged from the hospital too early.
환자들을 병원에서 너무 빨리 퇴원시키고 있었다.

clear up 질병 등이 없어지다(사라지다)

Has your rash cleared up yet?
두드러기 난 거 다 없어졌니?

be doing well (질병 후에) 회복 중이다, (출산 후에) 건강하다

Mother and baby are doing well. 산모와 아기 둘 다 건강하다.

longstanding 오랫동안에 걸친, 다년간의

They have been trying to capitalize on the longstanding so called special relationship between the two countries.
그들은 양국 간에 오랫동안 지속되어 온 소위 각별한 관계를 이용해 오고 있다.

plague 괴롭히다

The team has been plagued by injury this season.
그 팀은 이번 시즌에 부상 때문에 골치를 썩이고 있다.

flock (많은 수가) 모이다, 떼 지어 가다

Thousands of people flocked to the beach this weekend.
이번 주말에는 수천 명의 사람들이 해변으로 몰렸다.

frail (특히) 노인이 노쇠한

Mother was becoming too frail to live alone.
어머니는 혼자 사시기 힘들어질 정도로 노쇠해지고 있었다.

convict 유죄를 선고하다, 기소하다

According to sources, approximately 200 members of the vicious cult have been convicted.
정보에 따르면, 이 잔인한 교파의 회원 약 200명이 유죄판결을 받았다.

cherish (마음속에) 간직하다

I still cherish the telegram I received from her.
나는 그녀가 보낸 전보를 아직도 간직하고 있다.

It is an ideal, ***which*** I hope to live for and to achieve
= It is an ideal, ***and*** I hope to live for ***it***(the ideal) and to achieve ***it***(the ideal)
그것은 이상이고, 나는 그 이상을 위해 살고 그 이상을 성취하기를 희망한다.

it is an ideal ***for which*** I am prepared to die
= it is an ideal **+*(and)*** I am prepared to die ***for it***(the ideal)
내가 그것을 위해 죽을 각오가 되어 있는 이상이다.

Memo

21.

Margaret Thatcher: the lady and the land she leaves behind

Whether you were for her or against her, Margaret Thatcher[1)] set the agenda for the past three and a half decades

1) **Margaret Hilda Thatcher**, Baroness Thatcher(13 October 1925 – 8 April 2013), was the Prime Minister of the United Kingdom from 1979 to 1990 and the Leader of the Conservative Party from 1975 to 1990. She was the longest-serving British Prime Minister of the 20th century and is the only woman to have held the office. A Soviet journalist called her the "Iron Lady", a nickname that became associated with her uncompromising politics and leadership style. As Prime Minister, she implemented policies that have come to be known as Thatcherism.
Originally a research chemist before becoming a barrister, Thatcher was elected Member of Parliament (MP) for Finchley in 1959. Edward Heath appointed her Secretary of State for Education and Science in his 1970 government. In 1975, Thatcher defeated Heath in the Conservative Party leadership election to become Leader of the Opposition and became the first woman to lead a major political party in the United Kingdom. She became Prime Minister after winning the 1979 general election.
Upon moving into 10 Downing Street, Thatcher introduced a series of political and economic initiatives intended to reverse high unemployment and Britain's struggles in the wake of the Winter of Discontent and an ongoing recession. Her political philosophy and economic policies emphasized deregulation (particularly of the financial sector), flexible labour markets, the privatization of state-owned companies, and reducing the power and influence of trade unions. Thatcher's popularity during her first years in office waned amid recession and high unemployment until the 1982 Falklands War brought a resurgence of support, resulting in her re-election in 1983.
Thatcher was re-elected for a third term in 1987. During this period her support for a Community Charge (referred to as the "poll tax") was widely unpopular and her views on the European Community were not shared by others in her Cabinet. She resigned as Prime Minister and party leader in November 1990, after Michael Heseltine launched a challenge to her leadership. After retiring from the Commons in 1992, she was given a life peerage as Baroness Thatcher, of Kesteven in the county of Lincolnshire, which entitled her to sit in the House of Lords. After a series of small strokes in 2002, she was advised to withdraw from public speaking, and in 2013 she died of another stroke in London at the age of 87(Wikkipedia).

1 public arena
공적인 분야

2 disposed of
버리다 . 처리하다

3 electoral liability
선거 책임자

4 defined
~의 경계를 정하다

5 to an extraordinary degree
과도할 정도로

6 refine
개선하다

7 shape
형성하다

8 formidable
강력한

9 landmarks
획기적 사건

of British politics. All the debates that matter today in the *public arena[1], whether in economics, social policy, politics, the law, the national culture or this country's relations with the rest of the world, still bear something of the imprint she left on them in her years in office between 1979 and 1990. More than 20 years after her party *disposed of[2] her when she had become an *electoral liability[3], British public life is still *defined[4] *to an extraordinary degree[5] by the argument between those who wish to continue or *refine[6] what she started and those who want to mitigate or turn it back. Just as in life she *shaped[7] the past 30 years, so in death she may well continue to shape the next 30. These are claims that can be made about no other modern British prime minister. She was in many ways the most *formidable[8] peacetime leader this country has had since Gladstone[2)].

The fact that Mrs Thatcher was Britain's first and so far only woman major party leader, chosen entirely on merit, and then Britain's first woman prime minister, were of course huge *landmarks[9]. But her gender, though fundamental to her story, was in the end secondary. It was at least as significant, in the

2) **William Ewart Gladstone**(29 December 1809 - 19 May 1898), was a British Liberal politician. In a career lasting over sixty years, he served as Prime Minister four separate times(1868-74, 1880-85, February-July 1886 and 1892-94), more than any other person. Gladstone was also Britain's oldest Prime Minister, 84 when he resigned for the last time. He had also served as Chancellor of the Exchequer four times(Wikkipedia).

3) **Tory party** (영국 보수당의 전신인 잉글랜드 정당) 찰스 2세(Charles II) 시대인 1678년부터 1681년 사이에 왕위 계승을 둘러싸고 벌어진 자격 논쟁에서 국교인 성공회 교도가 아니라 가톨릭 교도였던 왕의 아우 요크 공작 제임스(나중의 제임스2세)의 즉위를 인정하는 사람들을 '토리'라고 부른 데서 연유했다. '토리(Tory)'는 아일랜드어의 'toraidhe'에서 유래했는데, '불량' 혹은 '도적'이라는 뜻이다. 한편 즉위를 인정하는 자들은 즉위를 인정하지 않는 자들을 가리켜 휘그'(Whig)라고 불렀는데, 스코틀랜드어로 '모반자', '말 도둑'이라는 의미였다(네이버 지식백과, 네이버 기관단체사전: 정치행정 분야).

evolution of the late 20th-century Tory party[3], that she came from a petit-bourgeois[4] background, a shopkeeper's daughter, though the man she *overthrew[10] in 1975, Ted Heath[5], had similarly middling origins and John Major[6] an even humbler start. There was something of the rebel and outsider about her, as well as much that was *stultifyingly[11] conventional.

Mrs Thatcher's transcendent quality, however, was that she was a political warrior. She had a love of political combat, a *zealotry[12] for the *causes[13] she believed in, a *reluctance[14] to

10 overthrow
전복시키다

11 stultifyingly
멍청할 정도로

12 zealotry
열성, 열광

13 causes
대의

14 reluctance
싫음, 꺼림

4) **Petite bourgeoisie** (소시민) also petty bourgeoisie (literally small bourgeoisie), is a French term (sometimes derogatory) referring to a social class comprising semi-autonomous peasantry and small-scale merchants whose politico-economic ideological stance is determined by reflecting that of a haute (high) bourgeoisie with which the petite bourgeoisie seeks to identify itself, and whose bourgeois morality it strives to imitate(Wikipedia).

5) **Sir Edward Richard George Heath**(9 July 1916 – 17 July 2005) was Prime Minister of the United Kingdom from June 1970 to February 1974 and Leader of the Conservative Party from 1965 to 1975.
Despite losing two general elections in quick succession, Heath vowed to continue as leader of his party. In February 1975, however, his former Education Secretary Margaret Thatcher challenged and defeated Heath to win the leadership. Returning to the backbenches, Heath became an active critic of Thatcher's policies as leader and, from 1979, as Prime Minister. He remained a backbench MP until retiring in 2001, serving as the Father of the House for his last nine years in Parliament. Outside of politics, Heath was a world-class yachtsman and a musician of near-professional standard. He was also one of only four British Prime Ministers never to have married(Wikipedia).

6) **Sir John Major**(born 29 March 1943) is a British Conservative politician who served as Prime Minister of the United Kingdom and Leader of the Conservative Party from 1990 to 1997. He previously held the posts of Chancellor of the Exchequer and Foreign Secretary in the Thatcher Government and was the Member of Parliament for Huntingdon from 1979 to 2001. Although, according to Malcolm Rifkind, Major proved "a great disappointment to Thatcher", he was her preferred choice as successor as she expected that she would "continue in control of the country as a backseat driver". Within weeks of becoming Prime Minister, Major presided over British participation in the Gulf War in March 1991 and claimed to have negotiated "Game, Set and Match for Britain" at negotiations over the Maastricht Treaty in December 1991. Despite the British economy being in recession, he went on to lead the Conservatives to a fourth consecutive election victory, winning the most votes in British electoral history with over 14 million in the 1992 general election albeit with a much reduced majority in the House of Commons. He remains to date the last Conservative Leader to win an outright majority at a general election(Wikipedia).

15 consensus
합의, 의견일치

16 predecessor
전임자

17 proof positive
확증

18 audacity
대담성

19 top job
여기서는 수상 직을 의미함

20 senior figures
고위인사, 원로 인사

21 patronise
깔보는 듯한 태도로 대하다, 아랫사람 대하듯 하다

22 made a difference
차별을 두다

23 biographer
전기 작가

24 pellucid
투명한

25 sceptical
회의적인

listen to advice, a conviction that she was always right and never wrong, and a scorn for *consensus[15] that set her apart from almost all her *predecessors[16] and, with the occasional exception of Tony Blair, from those who came after.

Mrs Thatcher was *proof positive[17] that personality matters in politics. As a young minister she did not seem destined for greatness. Even her election as Tory leader was something of a surprise, though her *audacity[18] in going for the *top job[19] while so many more *senior figures[20] hesitated was an indication of what was to come. Early on in her leadership, she was much *patronised[21] by male colleagues and adversaries. But as the social democratic consensus faltered in the 1970s and then cracked in the 1980s she rode the wind of history with an opportunist's brilliance. A Britain led by Willie Whitelaw or Michael Heseltine would have faced most of the same challenges that the one led by Mrs Thatcher faced. But the response would have been completely different. For good or ill, she *made a difference[22].

The late Guardian columnist and Thatcher *biographer[23] Hugo Young, reflecting on her overthrow in 1990, identified five large events that would not have happened the way they did without her.

The first was the Falklands war[7)] of 1982, which Young described as "a prime example of ignorance lending *pellucid[24] clarity to her judgment". Surrounded by *sceptical[25] men who had fought in the second world war[8)] and knew what combat involved, she went for it. The result was an astonishing and *absurd[26] military triumph followed by an electoral one, which elevated Mrs Thatcher from the ordinary to the extraordinary.

A second, which would not have been possible without the authority conferred by the first, was the dethroning of trade union power. Once again, against the instincts of ministers – and the *grandest of grandees[27], Harold Macmillan[9)] – who all preferred compromise to *confrontation[28], she fought the miners' strike to the bitterest of finishes, in a contest that was always about industrial strategy rather than just coal.

26 absurd
터무니없는, 말도 안 되는

27 grandest of grandees
귀족들 중의 최고귀족

28 confrontation
대치, 대립

7) **The Falklands War** (Spanish: Guerra de las Malvinas), also known as the Falklands Conflict, Falklands Crisis and the Guerra del Atlántico Sur (Spanish for "South Atlantic War"), was a ten-week war between Argentina and the United Kingdom over two British overseas territories in the South Atlantic: the Falkland Islands and South Georgia and the South Sandwich Islands. It began on Friday 2 April 1982 when Argentina invaded and occupied the Falkland Islands (and, the following day, South Georgia and the South Sandwich Islands) in an attempt to establish the sovereignty it has long claimed over them. On 5 April, the British government dispatched a naval task force to engage the Argentine Navy and Air Force before making an amphibious assault on the islands. The conflict lasted 74 days and ended with the Argentine surrender on 14 June 1982, returning the islands to British control. 649 Argentine military personnel, 255 British military personnel and 3 Falkland Islanders died during the hostilities(Wikipedia).

8) **World War II** (WWII or WW2), also known as the Second World War, was a global war that lasted from 1939 to 1945, though related conflicts began earlier. It involved the vast majority of the world's nations—including all of the great powers—eventually forming two opposing military alliances: the Allies and the Axis. It was the most widespread war in history, and directly involved more than 100 million people from more than 30 different countries. In a state of "total war", the major participants threw their entire economic, industrial, and scientific capabilities behind the war effort, erasing the distinction between civilian and military resources. Marked by mass deaths of civilians, including the Holocaust, the Three Alls Policy, the strategic bombing of enemy industrial and/or population centers, and the first use of nuclear weapons in combat, it resulted in an estimated 50 million to 85 million fatalities. These made World War II the deadliest conflict in human history(Wikipedia).

9) **Maurice Harold Macmillan**, 1st Earl of Stockton(10 February 1894 – 29 December 1986) was a British Conservative politician and statesman who served as the Prime Minister of the United Kingdom from 10 January 1957 to 18 October 1963(Wikipedia).

29 articulate
주창하다,
말로 표현하다

30 privatise
민영화하다

Arguably even more important than these headline events was the third example, the conduct of economic policy. There had been a New Right[10)] before Mrs Thatcher, but it was the ideas of Friedrich von Hayek[11)], as *articulated[29] to her by a series of domestic rightwing ideologues, on which she seized. It was Mrs Thatcher, abetted by her chancellors Sir Geoffrey Howe and Nigel Lawson, who drove the policy that the public sector was an unproductive burden on the wealth-creating sector and on taxpayers, and must therefore be reduced and *privatised[30]. It was she who insisted that the chief aim of government economic policy should be price stability, and that it should not give priority to reducing unemployment or to stimulating demand.

And it was she again who seemed to believe, far more than

10) **New Right** (뉴라이트, 신우익) 1980년대에 등장하여 영국의 대처, 미국의 레이건 행정부의 정책기조를 이룬 사상으로, 자유주의와 보수주의가 결합된 사상이다. 개혁적인 보수성향을 가지고 있어 신보수주의라고 불리기도 한다. 즉, 보수우파(라이트)를 계승하되 새로이 태어나겠다는 뜻을 담고 있다. 신우파 이념에 속하는 신자유주의(new freedom)와 신보수주의(neo-conservatism)로 대체하여 사용하기도 한다. 뉴라이트에서 자유주의는 개인주의 · 제한적인 작은 정부 · 자유시장이라는 전통적인 자유주의의 가치로 구성되어 있고, 보수주의는 사회 · 종교 · 도덕적 보수주의에 기초한 사회적 질서와 권위의 확립을 강조한다. 케인즈파의 복지국가론을 비판하고, 공공정책을 위한 시장기구의 부활과 시민권의 제한을 주장한다. 또한 신보수주의의 경우 국가개입의 축소, 작은 정부 지향, 시장기구 옹호, 인위적 평등지향 배제, 재산권 우선 등의 특징을 보인다(시사상식사전, 지식엔진연구소).

11) **Friedrich von Hayek** (8 May 1899 - 23 March 1992), born in Austria-Hungary as Friedrich August von Hayek and frequently known as F. A. Hayek, was an Austrian, later turned British, economist and philosopher best known for his defense of classical liberalism. In 1974, Hayek shared the Nobel Memorial Prize in Economic Sciences (with Gunnar Myrdal) for his "pioneering work in the theory of money and economic fluctuations and ~ penetrating analysis of the interdependence of economic, social and institutional phenomena".
Hayek is an economist and major political thinker of the twentieth century. Hayek's account of how changing prices communicate information which enables individuals to coordinate their plans is widely regarded as an important achievement in economics. He also contributed to the fields of systems thinking, jurisprudence, neuroscience, and the history of ideas(Wikipedia).

those around her, that the market economy required not a minimal state to protect it but a strong state, marked by everything from the abolition of local government autonomy to the *enhancement[31] of police powers, intolerance towards gay rights, the broadcasting ban on Sinn Féin[12)], and increased defence spending. She made enemies without flinching, and they reciprocated. Her rule was marked by the most serious urban riots of the 20th century, one of the most divisive strikes in recent times, and the century's most audacious prime ministerial assassination attempt, which thankfully she survived.

Mrs Thatcher's unique mark was also felt in the two confrontations that ultimately undid her. The first was the *poll tax[32], which was disastrous, unjust and was her policy alone. The poll tax came to embody a prime minister who ruled from conviction not sense, and who did not care about, indeed gloried in, a confrontation that destroyed the Tory party in Scotland and may indirectly come to destroy the union she otherwise championed. Similarly, and less easily

31 enhancement
향상, 증대

32 poll tax
인두세

12) **Sinn Féin** (an Irish republican political party active in both the Republic of Ireland and Northern Ireland. The name is Irish for "ourselves" or "we ourselves", although it is frequently mistranslated as "ourselves alone". Originating in the Sinn Féin organisation founded in 1905 by Arthur Griffith, it took its current form in 1970 after a split within the party (the other party is the Workers' Party of Ireland), and has been associated with the Provisional Irish Republican Army. Gerry Adams has been party president since 1983.
Sinn Féin is currently the second-largest party in the Northern Ireland Assembly, where it has four ministerial posts in the power-sharing Northern Ireland Executive, and the fourth-largest party in the Oireachtas, the parliament of the Republic. Sinn Féin also received a plurality of Northern Ireland votes in the 2010 United Kingdom general election, although the Democratic Unionist Party won more seats(Wikipedia).

33 pragmatic
실용(주의)적

34 acerbic
가혹한, 신랄한

35 strident
공격적인,
귀에 거슬리는

36 disruptive
분열시키는, 파괴적인

37 overmighty
= excessively mighty

disposed of after her fall, was Europe. Mrs Thatcher began her prime ministership as a *pragmatic[33], if often *acerbic[34], European. But as she became a bigger figure on the world stage, feted both by Mr Reagan[13)] and by Mikhail Gorbachev[14)], she became increasingly *strident[35] and *disruptive[36] towards Europe. Her style became the policy, cementing the love affair with an already *overmighty[37] press but with disastrous effects for her leadership (which was ended by Sir Geoffrey's resignation over the issue), her party (which became obsessed with the subject) and for Britain. Except for Mr Blair[15)] in his early years, every British leader since has felt Mrs Thatcher at his shoulder in dealings with Europe, to the lasting national loss.

13) **Ronald Wilson Reagan**(February 6, 1911 - June 5, 2004) was an American actor and politician. He was the 40th President of the United States (1981-89). Prior to his presidency, he served as the 33rd Governor of California (1967-75)(Wikipedia).

14) **Mikhail Sergeyevich Gorbachev**(born 2 March 1931) is a former Soviet statesman. He was the seventh and last leader of the Soviet Union, having served as General Secretary of the Communist Party of the Soviet Union from 1985 until 1991, and as the country's head of state from 1988 until its dissolution in 1991 (titled as Chairman of the Presidium of the Supreme Soviet from 1988 to 1989, as Chairman of the Supreme Soviet from 1989 to 1990, and as President of the Soviet Union from 1990 to 1991). He was the only general secretary in the history of the Soviet Union to have been born after the October Revolution(Wikipedia).

15) **Anthony Charles Lynton "Tony" Blair**(born 6 May 1953) is a British Labour Party politician who served as the Prime Minister of the United Kingdom from 1997 to 2007. He was the Member of Parliament (MP) for Sedgefield from 1983 to 2007 and Leader of the Labour Party from 1994 to 2007. Blair led Labour to a landslide victory in the 1997 general election, winning 418 seats, the most the party has ever held. The party went on to win two more elections under his leadership: in 2001, in which it won another landslide victory, and in 2005, with a reduced majority(Wikipedia).

16) **Downing Street**(다우닝가) 외무부와 내무부 등이 있고, 10번지에는 총리관저, 11번지에는 재무장관 관저가 있다. 영국의 근대 내각제도가 확립된 18세기부터 줄곧 총리관저가 이곳에 있었으므로 다우닝가는 영국정부의 대명사로도 사용되며, 역사상 가장 유명한 도로의 하나이다. 다우닝가라는 명칭은 왕정복고(王政復古)의 공신 G.다우닝(1623~1684)이 이 지역에 건물을 지어 재무부에 대여한 데서 유래한다(네이버 지식백과, 두산백과).

When she arrived in Downing Street[16)] in 1979 she talked about replacing discord with harmony. She may briefly have meant it, but the harmony she sought *in the long term[38] was one whose terms were set overwhelmingly in the interests of the British business class[17)] as she perceived them. She disdained the public realm and presided over the growth of the *cult[39] of marketplace success as the foundation of a good society – a low-tax, home-owning, privatised, high-carbon, possessive, individualist, *winner-takes-all[40] financial model whose failure haunts the choices still facing this country today. Much was wrong with the Britain she inherited in 1979, undemocratic union power among them, and many things, though not wrong in themselves, were unsustainable without radical change, including some nationalised *utilities[41]. Britain would have had to alter radically in the 1980s and 90s, and the process would have been hard and controversial. But, as Germany and other northern nations have shown, *economic dynamism[42] has been possible without the squandering of *social cohesion[43] that Mrs Thatcher promoted.

In the last analysis, though, her *stock in trade[44] was *division[45]. By instinct, inclination and effect she was a *polariser[46]. She glorified both individualism and the *nation

38 in the long term
장기적으로 보아

39 cult
(생활 방식 · 태도 · 사상 등에 대한) 추종(숭배)

40 winner-takes-all
승자독식

41 utilities
(수도 · 전기 · 가스 같은) 공익사업

42 economic dynamism
경제적 활력

43 social cohesion
사회적 결속, 응집

44 stock in trade
상투적 수단

45 division
분열

46 polarizer
편광자, 분열시키는 사람

17) **Business class** is a travel class available on many commercial airlines and rail lines, known by brand names which vary by airline or rail company. In the airline industry, it was originally intended as an intermediate level of service between economy class and first class, but many airlines now offer business class as the highest level of service, having eliminated first class seating. Business class is distinguished from other travel classes by the quality of seating, food, drinks, ground service and other amenities. Full business class is usually denoted 'J' or 'C' with schedule flexibility, but can be many other letters depending on circumstances(Wikipedia).

47 nation state
민족국가

48 atomism
원자론(주의)(만물을 개별 요소로 분리하여 분석할 수 있다고 보는 주의)

49 unleash
속박을 풀다

state[47], but lacked much feeling for the communities and bonds that knit them together. When she spoke, as she often did, about "our people", she did not mean the people of Britain; she meant people who thought like her and shared her prejudices. She abhorred disorder, decadence and bad behaviour but she was the empress ruler of a process of social and cultural *atomism[48] that has fostered all of them, and still does.

The governments that followed have struggled to put a kinder and more cohesive face on the forces she *unleashed[49] and to create stability and validity for the public realm that yet remains. New Labour[18)] offered a first response. The coalition is attempting a second draft in grimmer circumstances, and there will be others. There can certainly be no going back to the failed postwar past with which Margaret Thatcher had to

18) **The Labour** Party is a centre-left political party in the United Kingdom. It grew out of the trade union movement and socialist political parties of the nineteenth century and has been described as a broad church; the party contains a diversity of ideological trends from strongly socialist, to more moderately social democratic.
Founded in 1900, the Labour Party overtook the Liberal Party in general elections during the early 1920s and formed minority governments under Ramsay MacDonald in 1924 and 1929–31. The party was in a wartime coalition from 1940 to 1945, after which it formed a majority government under Clement Attlee. Labour was also in government from 1964 to 1970 under Harold Wilson and from 1974 to 1979, first under Wilson and then James Callaghan.
The Labour Party was last in national government between 1997 and 2010 under Tony Blair and Gordon Brown, beginning with a landslide majority of 179, reduced to 167 in 2001 and 66 in 2005. Having won 258 seats in the 2010 general election, the party currently forms the Official Opposition in the Parliament of the United Kingdom. Labour has a minority government in the Welsh Assembly, is the main opposition party in the Scottish Parliament and has 13 MEPs in the European Parliament, sitting in the Socialists and Democrats group. The Labour Party is a full member of the Party of European Socialists and Progressive Alliance, and continues to hold observer status in the Socialist International. The current leader of the party is Ed Miliband MP(Wikipedia).

wrestle. But there should be no going back to her own failed answer either. She was an exceptionally *consequential[50] leader, in many ways a very great woman. There should be no dancing on her grave but it is right there is no state funeral either. Her legacy is of public division, private selfishness and a cult of greed, which together shackle far more of the human spirit than they ever set free.

guardian.co.uk April 08, 2013

50 consequential 결과로서 일어나는, 필연적인

WORDS and STRUCTURES

set the agenda 의제를 정하다, 현안을 제시하다

Does television set the agenda on foreign policy?
텔레비전이 외교 정책에 대한 현안을 제시하는가?

arena 장, 무대, 영역, 분야

Furthermore the government has reinforced investment in the arena of science and research.
더군다나 한국정부는 과학과 연구 분야에 투자를 아끼지 않고 있다.

All the debates that matter today in the public arena still bear something of the imprint she left on them in her years in office between 1979 and 1990
= All the debates that matter today in the public arena still bear something of the imprint ***(which)*** she left on them in her years in office between 1979 and 1990
= All the debates that matter today in the public arena still bear something of the imprint ***+(and)*** she left ***it***(the imprint) on them in her years in office between 1979 and 1990
오늘날 공적 분야에서 문제가 되는 모든 논란들은 그녀가 1979년과 1990년 사이에 재직하고 있었던 동안에 그러한 것들에 남긴 어떤 흔적을 여전히 가지고 있다.

matter 중요하다

The only strength that matters is strength of mind and heart.
단 한 가지 중요한 힘은 정신과 마음의 힘이다.

leave an imprint on ~에 자국을 남기다

She had left the imprint of her stiletto heels all over the floor.
그녀는 바닥 전체에 스파이크 힐 자국을 남겼다.

mitigate 완화시키다, 누그러뜨리다

South Koreans have quickly taken steps to mitigate the effects.
한국인들은 이러한 결과를 완화시키려는 조치를 신속하게 취해왔다.

just as A~, so B~ A가 ~하는 것과 꼭 같이 B도 ~한다

Just as adults undergo daily stress, so do kids today.
어른이 매일 스트레스를 받는 것처럼 현대의 어린이들도 스트레스를 받고 있다.

may well do (~하는 것도) 당연하다

She may well be wrong and other people may well take a different view.
그녀가 틀렸을 가능성도 있고, 다른 사람들이 그녀와 생각이 다를 수도 있을 것이다.

She was in many ways the most formidable peacetime leader this country has had since Gladstone.
= She was in many ways the most formidable peacetime leader ***(whom)*** this country has had since Gladstone.
= She was in many ways the most formidable peacetime leader +***(and)*** this country has had ***her***(leader) since Gladstone.
그녀는 많은 면에서 이 나라가 글래드스톤 이후에 가져왔던 가장 강력한 평화 시의 지도자였다.

on merit = according to merit 공적에 따라, 실력으로

I want to get the job on merit.
나는 실력으로 그 직장에 취직하고 싶다.

The fact that Mrs Thatcher was Britain's first and so far only woman major party leader, ***chosen*** entirely on merit, and then Britain's first woman prime minister, were of course huge landmarks
= The fact that Mrs Thatcher was Britain's first and so far only woman major party leader, ***(and she was) chosen*** entirely on merit, and then Britain's first woman prime minister, were of course huge landmarks

주절의 주어 fact와 woman prime minister 동사 were

The fact = that 주어(Mrs Thatcher) + 동사(was)

대처 여사가 영국의 첫 그리고 오로지 실력으로 선출된 지금까지의 유일한 여성 다수당의 당수였다는 사실과 그 후 영국의 첫 여성 수상이 된 것은 물론 거대한 획기적인 사건들이다.

stultifying(←stultifyingly) (격식)(사람을) 멍청하게 만드는

They have the stultifying effects of work that never varies.

그것들은 결코 변화가 없는 일의, 사람을 멍청하게 만드는 효과가 있다.

transcendent 초월적인, 탁월한

His transcendent ability made him a famous person.

그의 탁월한 능력이 그를 유명한 사람으로 만들었다.

come after ~의 뒤를 잇다, 뒤에 오다

The United Kingdom, France, Japan and Canada all came after.

영국, 프랑스, 일본, 캐나다가 그 뒤를 이었다.

proof positive 확증

This is proof positive that he stole the money.

이것은 그가 그 돈을 훔쳤다는 움직일 수 없는 증거이다.

audacity 대담성

His audacity is far out of reason.

그의 대담성은 도리에 어긋난다.

what was to come

She was frightened and apprehensive of what was to come.

그녀는 장차 다가올 일이 두렵고 염려되었다.

falter 비틀거리다

The Chinese economy is not showing any sign of faltering.
중국경제가 흔들리고 있다는 조짐은 없다.

A Britain led by Willie Whitelaw or Michael Heseltine would have faced most of the same challenges that the ***one*** led by Mrs Thatcher faced.
= A Britain led by Willie Whitelaw or Michael Heseltine would have faced most of the same challenges that the ***Britain*** led by Mrs Thatcher faced.
가정법 과거완료 구문(would + have + 과거분사)
윌리 화이트로나 마이클 해즐타인이 이끈 영국은 대처 여사가 이끈 영국이 직면했던 것과 같은 대부분의 도전에 직면했었을 것이다.

for good or ill 좋든 나쁘든

Once the boss gives us an order, for good or ill, we must follow.
상사가 명령을 내리면, 좋든 나쁘든 우리는 따라야 해.

five large events that ***would not have happened*** the way they did ***without her***
가정법 과거완료
without her = if it had not been for her
그녀가 없었더라면 사건들이 발생했던 방식으로 발생하지 않았을 다섯 가지 큰 사건들

go for ~을 택하다

I think I'll go for the steak.
나는 스테이크로 할까한다.

grandee 최고 귀족

All the local grandees attended the opening of the new hospital.
그 지방의 모든 명사들이 새 병원의 개원식에 참석했다.

prefer A to B B보다 A를 선호하다

Newly-bred women prefer public life to marriage.
요즘 여성들은 결혼보다는 사회에 진출하기를 원한다.

confrontation 대치, 대립

She wanted to avoid another confrontation with her father.
그녀는 아버지와 또 다시 대립하는 것은 피하고 싶었다.

arguably (충분한 근거를 갖고) 주장하건대, 거의 틀림없이(흔히 비교급이나 최상급 형용사 앞에 나옴)

He is arguably the best actor of his generation.
그가 자기 세대 중 가장 훌륭한 배우라는 것은 거의 틀림없다.

seize on (아이디어, 기회를) 이용하다, ~에 달려들다

The rumours were eagerly seized upon by the local press.
그 소문을 지역 신문이 열심히 달려들어 다루었다.

abet 부추기다, 선동하다

She was unwilling to abet him in the swindle he had planned.
그녀는 그가 계획한 사기를 치라고 그를 부추기는 것이 내키지 않았다.

price stability 물가안정

The central bank is monitoring core prices to attain its main goal of price stability.
한은은 물가안정 목표 달성을 위해 근원 물가를 모니터하고 있다.

without flinching 조금도 꿀리지 않고

He met my gaze without flinching.
그는 조금도 움츠러들지 않고 내 시선을 맞받았다.

reciprocate 응수하다, 보답하다

I wasn't sure whether to laugh or to reciprocate with a remark of my own.
나는 웃어야 할지 내 나름대로의 말로 응수를 해야 할지 확신이 안 섰다.

undo 원상태로 돌리다, 몰락시키다, 무너뜨리다

No doubt Mrs. Merkel would have to contend with the same forces that undid Mr. Schroeder.
의문의 여지없이 메르켈 의장이 슈뢰더를 몰락시킨 같은 세력들과 싸워야할 것이다.

glory in ~을 대단히 기뻐하다

She gloried in her new-found independence.
그녀는 새롭게 찾은 독립을 대단히 기뻐했다.

champion 옹호하다

President Lee was all about smiles as he championed the crowd at the Rio+20 Conference on Sustainable Development.
이 대통령은 지속가능 발전에 관한 Rio+20 정상회의에서 청중들의 견해를 옹호하는 발언을 하면서 웃음이 만연했다.

acerbic 사람이나 그의 말이 가혹한, 신랄한

The letter was written in her usual acerbic style.
편지는 그녀가 늘 쓰는 신랄한 어투로 쓰여 있었다.

fete (공식적으로) 환영(환대)하다

She's also been feted as the beautiful singer with a face to match in women's glossies like W Magazine and Mademoiselle.
그녀는 또한 W Magazine이나 Mademoiselle과 같은 여성지에 나와도 손색이 없는 얼굴을 가진 아름다운 가수라는 찬사를 받기도 했다.

strident 귀에 거슬리는, 공격적인

She was increasingly seen as a strident feminist.
그녀는 점점 더 공격적인 페미니스트로 인식되었다.

be obsessed with ~에 사로잡혀 있는, 강박관념에 시달리다

So don't be too obsessed with the fortune-teller's predictions.
그러니까 점쟁이의 예언에 너무 사로잡혀 있지 마라.

as ~이긴 하지만

He was a foreigner, as I knew from his accent.
비록 내가 그의 말투로부터 알긴 했지만 그는 외국인이다.

the harmony she sought in the long term was one ***whose*** terms were set overwhelmingly in the interests of the British business class as she perceived them

= the harmony ***(which)*** she sought in the long term was ***one***(the harmony) ***+(and) its*** terms were set overwhelmingly in the interests of the British business class as she perceived ***them***(its terms)

= the harmony ***+(and)*** she sought ***it***(the harmony) in the long term was one(the harmony) ***+(and) its*** terms were set overwhelmingly in the interests of the British business class as she perceived ***them***(its terms)

장기적으로 보아 그녀가 추구했던 조화는 그녀가 비록 그것들을 지각하였기는 하였지만 압도적으로 영국의 비즈니스 클래스의 이익에 고정되어 있었던 조화였다

disdain 경멸하다, 무시하다

He disdained to answer her rude remarks.
그는 그녀의 무례한 말에 대답할 가치가 없다고 생각했다.

haunt 괴롭히다

Her obsession for a boy haunted me as if I were faulty or incomplete.
남자아이에 대한 지나친 집착은 마치 내가 뭔가 잘못됐거나 모자란 아이라는 느낌이 들만큼 나를 괴롭혔다.

squander 낭비하다

He squandered all his fortune on gambling.
그는 도박으로 전 재산을 들어먹었다.

in the last analysis 결국(은), 요는

In the last analysis, walking home would be the most reasonable way.
결국에는 집으로 걸어가는 것이 가장 합리적인 방법일 것이다.

stock in trade 상투수단

Famous people and their private lives are the stock-in-trade of the popular newspapers.
유명인들과 그들의 사생활은 대중적인 신문들의 상투적인 요소이다.

glorify 미화하다

He denies that the movie glorifies violence.
그는 그 영화가 폭력을 미화한다는 것을 부인 한다.

knit together 결합하다

The two families were knit together by marriage.
두 집안은 결혼으로 결합되었다.

decadence 타락, 퇴폐

Decadence among the leadership was rampant.
지도층의 타락이 만연했다.

coalition 연립 정부, 연정

The two political parties broke their coalition and disunited.
두 정당은 연합을 해체하고 분열하였다.

grim 암담한, 냉혹한

All things considered, the forecast looks grim this year.
모든 면을 고려해 볼 때 금년도 전망은 어두워 보인다.

There can certainly be no going back to the failed postwar past ***with which*** Margaret Thatcher had to wrestle
= There can certainly be no going back to the failed postwar past **+*(and)*** Margaret Thatcher had to wrestle ***with it***(the failed postwar past)
마가렛 대처가 싸워왔던 그 실패한 전후의 과거로 분명히 되돌아갈 수 없다.

shackle 족쇄(쇠고랑)을 채우다, 구속하다

The hostage had been shackled to a radiator.
그 인질은 라디에이터에 쇠고랑이 채워져 있었다.

22.

Scandal in South Korea Over Nuclear Revelations

SEOUL, South Korea — Like Japan, resource-poor South Korea has long relied on *nuclear power[1] to provide the cheap electricity that helped build its miracle economy. For years, it *met[2] one-third of its electricity needs with nuclear power, similar to Japan's level of dependence before the 2011 disaster at its Fukushima plant[1)].

Seoul city employees used fans on Friday to cope with power shortages. The closing of *nuclear reactors[3] has set off a

1 nuclear power
원자력, 원자력 발전

2 meet
(필요, 요구) 충족시키다

3 nuclear reactor
원자로

1) **The Fukushima Daiichi Nuclear Power Plant** is a disabled BWR nuclear power plant located on a 3.5-square-kilometre (860-acre) site in the towns of Okuma and Futaba in the Futaba District of Fukushima Prefecture, Japan. First commissioned in 1971, the plant consists of six boiling water reactors (BWR). These light water reactors drove electrical generators with a combined power of 4.7 GWe, making Fukushima Daiichi one of the 15 largest nuclear power stations in the world. Fukushima I was the first nuclear plant to be designed, constructed and run in conjunction with General Electric, Boise, and Tokyo Electric Power Company(TEPCO).
The plant suffered major damage from the magnitude 9.0 earthquake and tsunami that hit Japan on March 11, 2011. The incident permanently damaged several reactors making them impossible to restart. Due to the political climate, the remaining reactors will not be restarted. The disaster disabled the reactor cooling systems, leading to releases of radioactivity and triggering a 30 km evacuation zone surrounding the plant; the releases continue to this day. On April 20, 2011, the Japanese authorities declared the 20 km evacuation zone a no-go area which may only be entered under government supervision(Wikipedia).

4 faked safety tests
가짜(위조) 안전검사

5 undermine
손상시키다

6 anonymous tip
익명의 정보

7 indict
기소하다

8 on charge of
~의 혐의로

9 raid
급습하다

campaign to save energy.

Now, a snowballing scandal in South Korea about bribery and *faked safety tests[4] for critical plant equipment has highlighted yet another similarity: experts say both countries' nuclear programs suffer from a culture of collusion that has *undermined[5] their safety. Weeks of revelations about the close ties between South Korea's nuclear power companies, their suppliers and testing companies have led the prime minister to liken the industry to a mafia.

The scandal started after an *anonymous tip[6] in April prompted an official investigation. Prosecutors have *indicted[7] some officials at a testing company on charges of faking safety tests on parts for the plants. Some officials at the state-financed company that designs nuclear power plants were also indicted *on charges of[8] taking bribes from testing company officials in return for accepting those substandard parts.

Worse yet, investigators discovered that the questionable components are installed in 14 of South Korea's 23 nuclear power plants. The country has already shuttered three of those reactors temporarily because the questionable parts used there were important, and more closings could follow as investigators wade through more than 120,000 test certificates filed over the past decade to see if more may have been falsified.

In a further indication of the possible breadth of the problems, prosecutors recently *raided[9] the offices of 30 more suppliers suspected of also providing parts with faked quality certificates and said they would investigate other testing companies.

"What has been revealed so far may be the *tip of an iceberg[10]," said Kune Y. Suh, a professor of nuclear engineering at Seoul National University.

With each new revelation, South Koreans — who, like the Japanese, had grown to believe their leaders' *soothing claims[11] about nuclear safety — have become more jittery. Safety is the biggest concern, but the scandals have also caused economic worries. At a time of slowing growth, the government had loudly promoted its plans to become a major builder of nuclear power plants abroad.

The scandal, Professor Suh said, "makes it difficult to continue claiming to build reliable nuclear power plants cheaply."

South Koreans say they are already *suffering for the industry's sins[12]. The closing of the three reactors, in addition to another three *offline[13] for *scheduled maintenance[14], has led the country's leaders to order a nationwide energy-saving campaign in the middle of a particularly muggy summer. At university campuses, students have deserted the libraries for cooler Internet cafes, and major corporations have turned down air-conditioning.

President Park Geun-hye has *kept off[15] her own air-conditioning even when she hosted foreign guests, including Mark Zuckerberg[2)], the *chief executive[16] of Facebook. And

10 tip of an iceberg
빙산의 일각

11 soothing claims
진정시키는 주장

12 suffer for one's sins
저지른 죄로 처벌을 받다

13 offline
가동 중지

14 scheduled maintenance
정기유지보수
(미리 설정된 계획에 따라 실시하는 보수로서, 고장 예방을 위해 주기별로 검사하거나 보수하는 것)

15 keep off
차단하다

16 chief executive
대표, 책임자

2) **Mark Elliot Zuckerberg**(born May 14, 1984) is an American computer programmer, Internet entrepreneur, and philanthropist. He is best known as one of five co-founders of the social networking website Facebook. As of April 2013, Zuckerberg is the chairman and chief executive of Facebook, Inc. and his personal wealth, as of April 2014, is estimated to be $25.3 billion. Mark Zuckerberg receives a one-dollar salary as CEO of Facebook(Wikipedia).

17 sound
이상이 없는

18 supply chain
공급과정, 공급망

19 activate emergency measures
긴급장치를 작동하게하다

some entrepreneurs have capitalized on the troubles, selling "cool scarves" made of a special fabric that, after being dipped in water, keeps wearers cool for hours. But the modeling and creativity have not stopped the grousing, or alleviated anger at the industry.

Critics of South Korea's nuclear industry say there were plenty of warning signs.

Last year, the government was forced to shut down two reactors temporarily after it learned that parts suppliers — some of whom were later convicted — had fabricated the safety-test certificates for more than 10,000 components over 10 years. But the government emphasized at the time that those parts were "nonessential" items and that the industry was otherwise *sound[17].

As it turned out, the problems went much deeper.

The investigation that began this spring suggested that the oversight within the *supply chain[18] may also be more deeply compromised. A company that was supposed to test reactor parts skipped portions of the exams, doctored test data or even issued safety certificates for parts that failed its tests, according to government investigators. And this time the parts involved included more important items. Among the parts that failed the tests were cables used to send signals to *activate emergency measures[19] in an accident.

"This is not a simple negligence or mistake; this is a deliberate fabrication by those who were supposed to safeguard the reliability of parts," said Kim Yong-soo, a professor of nuclear engineering at Hanyang University in

Seoul. "It raises serious questions about the immune system of our nuclear power industry."

Although much remains unclear with the investigations *under way[20], experts say they know enough to pinpoint the underlying cause of the scandal: an industry that is even more highly centralized than Japan's, with poor oversight on the relations among the major players.

While Japan has a small number of utilities that provide nuclear power, South Korea has just one: the state-run Korea Electric Power Corporation, or Kepco. One of its subsidiaries, Korea Hydro & Nuclear Power, runs all the plants. Another, Kepco Engineering & Construction, designs them and is tasked with inspecting parts from suppliers and vetting the safety certificates they include from testing companies.

Over the years, senior retirees from the two subsidiaries have found jobs with parts suppliers and testing companies or invested in them, according to industry data submitted to the National Assembly.

In a culture where honoring *personal ties[21] is often considered more important than following regulations, the porous borders among the members of the supply chain resulted in what government officials and industry experts call an "*entrenched chain of corruption[22]." Important school and hometown connections among the groups further cemented the collusive links, they said. And then there is the *lure[23] of bribery, which has often *lubricated[24] relationships between South Korean parts suppliers and their buyers in various industries.

20 under way
진행 중인

21 personal ties
인맥

22 entrenched chain of corruption
깊게 뿌리 박힌 부패사슬

23 lure
유혹

24 lubricate
기름을 치다, 매끄럽게 하다

25 Ministry of Trade, Industry and Energy
통상 산업부

26 opaque
투명하지 않은

27 picked up the main line
대표전화를 받다

28 bribery charges
뇌물혐의

29 ensure contracts
계약을 보장하다

30 self-purification measures
자정 조치

"In the past 30 years, our nuclear energy industry has become an increasingly closed community that emphasized its specialty in dealing with nuclear materials and yet allowed little oversight and intervention," the government's *Ministry of Trade, Industry and Energy[25] said in a recent report to lawmakers. "It spawned a litany of corruption, an *opaque[26] system and a business practice replete with complacency."

In the current scandal, Korea Hydro officials are accused of ordering Kepco E & C to ignore faked certificates from the testing firm Saehan Total Engineering Provider Company. The testing company's top officials and investors included current and former employees from Kepco E & C or their family members. (Although the company was called for comment several times in recent days, no one *picked up the main line[27].)

But the problems appear to go beyond testing. At the home of one of the Korea Hydro officials, investigators found boxes of cash amounting to several hundred thousand dollars. Investigators tracing the origin of the money recently arrested officials of Hyundai Heavy Industries, a major parts supplier, on *bribery charges[28]. Prosecutors said the money was meant to *ensure contracts[29] for Hyundai Heavy and appeared not to be part of the scandal over testing certificates.

In a statement jointly issued in June, Korea Hydro, Kepco E &C and two other state-financed nuclear industry companies promised "*self-purification measures[30]." To "root out corruption arising from collusive ties," they said they would make it mandatory for senior officials to make *public their personal assets[31], ban all employees from buying stocks in suppliers or getting jobs there after retirement, and reduce the retirement package benefits for those fired for corruption.

Amid a *public uproar[32], the government fired the heads of both the Kepco subsidiaries. It also promised to enact new laws and tighten regulations to ban retirees from the two subsidiaries from getting jobs at suppliers and test agencies.

Political opposition parties, which control some seats on the Nuclear Safety and Security Commission3) — the top nuclear *watchdog[33], which has long been criticized as being too cozy with the industry — recently added two critics of nuclear power to the *regulatory[34] group. But many worry the changes, and promised changes, will not be enough.

After last year's scandal, the government had vowed to keep parts suppliers found to have falsified documents from bidding[35] again for 10 years. But in February, Korea Hydro imposed only a six-month penalty for such suppliers. And nuclear opponents say that more fundamental changes are needed in the regulatory system, pointing out that one of the government's main regulating arms, the Korea Institute of Nuclear Safety4), gets 60 percent of its annual budget from Korea Hydro.

Some go further, saying ordinary South Koreans will have to change their own expectations before real change can occur.

31 public their personal assets
개인재산을 공개하다

32 public uproar
비난 여론

33 watchdog
감시인

34 regulatory
(산업 · 상업 분야의) 규제(단속)력을 지닌

35 bid
입찰하다

3) **Nuclear Safety and Security Commission** (원자력 안전 위원회) 원자력의 생산과 이용에 따른 방사선 재해로부터 국민을 보호하고, 공공의 안전과 환경보전에 이바지하기 위하여 2011년에 설치된 중앙행정기관.

4) **Korea Institute of Nuclear Safety** (한국 원자력 안전기술원) 방사선 재해로부터 국민의 건강과 국토환경을 보호하기 위해 1981년에 정부출연으로 설립한 원자력 안전규제 전문기관.

36 guzzle
마구 마셔대다,
마구 사용하다

The nuclear industry, they say, was built around the notion that South Korea's industries needed inexpensive power, leading Kepco to build plants quickly and operate them cheaply.

"South Koreans have *guzzled[36] cheap electricity while turning a blind eye to the safety concerns of their nuclear power plants," said Yang Lee Won-young, a leader at the Korean Federation for Environmental Movement[5)]. "They may end up paying dearly."

nytimes.com August 03, 2013

5) **The Korea Federation for Environmental Movements**(KFEM)(한국 환경운동연합) is a non-profit organization in South Korea that focuses on environmentalism.
The group was founded in April 1993 as a federation of eight environmental groups, the largest being the Korean Anti-Pollution Movement Association. KFEM activities include raising awareness of environmental issues(Wikipedia).

WORDS and STRUCTURES

revelation (비밀 등을) 드러냄, 폭로

The company's financial problems followed the revelation of a major frauds candal.
주요한 사기사건 스캔들의 폭로 뒤에 그 회사의 재정적인 문제가 이어졌다.

it met one-third of its electricity needs with nuclear power, ***similar*** to Japan's level of dependence before the 2011 disaster at its Fukushima plant
= it met one-third of its electricity needs with nuclear power, ***(and it is)*** similar to Japan's level of dependence before the 2011 disaster at its Fukushima plant.
한국은 전기수요의 1/3을 원자력으로 충당하고 있는데 그것은 후쿠시마 원전에서의 2011년 재난 이전의 일본의 원자력 의존수준과 유사하다.

needs 수요

They eat more than 30 kilograms of bamboo every day to meet their energy needs.
그들은 에너지 수요를 맞추기 위해서 매일 대나무 30킬로그램 이상을 먹는다.

set off (일련의 사건 · 과정을) 유발하다 (일으키다)

Panic on the stock market set off a wave of selling.
주식 시장에서의 공포감이 매도 사태를 유발했다.

collusion 공모, 유착

Collusion between politics and business is rampant. 정경유착이 만연하고 있다.

prompt 촉구하다

A separate report from the Korea International Trade Association prompted the government to be better prepared for a worst-case energy scenario.
별도의 한국무역협회 보고서는 정부가 최악의 에너지 시나리오를 대비할 것을 촉구했다.

indict 기소하다

He was indicted on charges of fraud and embezzlement and breach of bioethics.
그는 사기와 횡령, 생명윤리법 위반의 죄로 기소되었다.

worse yet 게다가, 설상가상으로

Worse yet, residents near by some burial sites have complained about environmental contamination.
설상가상으로 매몰지 주변 주민들은 환경오염으로 인한 불평을 토로하고 있다.

component 부품

All this shows that the power supply for this winter will most likely hit a snag until the defective components of the reactors are replaced in December.
이 모든 것은 12월에 원전의 결함부품이 교체될 때까지 이번 겨울의 전력공급에 차질이 생길 가능성이 거의 확실하다는 것을 보여 준다.

wade through 애쓰며 나아가다, 간신히 돌파하다

You have to wade through a lot of stuff to find anything good.
좋은 것을 찾기 위해서는 많은 물건을 다 뒤져봐야 한다.

breadth 폭, 효과

We are also taking into consideration the breadth of the possible negative impact on the market caused by the sale.
우리는 또한 이번 매각으로 시장에 미치는 부정적인 영향의 효과도 고려하고 있다.

jittery 신경질적인, 초조해하는

Imbibing too much caffeine can cause you to feel jittery, irritable, dehydrated, and even interrupt your sleep pattern at night.
너무 많은 카페인의 섭취는 신경과민, 짜증, 탈수를 느끼게 하며 심지어 수면습관에 영향을 끼치기도 한다.

maintenance 점검, 정비

The server is currently down for maintenance.
그 서버는 현재 점검을 위해 중단되었다.

muggy 후텁지근한, 무더운

The weather is humid, sticky, muggy, and sweltering.
날씨는 습하고, 끈적거리고, 찌는듯하고 무덥다.

desert 비우다

The house appeared to be deserted.
그 집은 빈 것 같았다.

chief executive 대표, 책임자

I want to be Chief Executive Officer in the future.
나는 장래에 최고경영자가 되고 싶다.

capitalize on ~을 활용하다(기회로 삼다), 이용하다

Wise investors capitalize on opportunities in the market to earn their money.
현명한 투자자는 돈을 벌기위해 시장에서의 기회를 이용한다.

grouse 투덜대다, 불평하다

Will you stop grousing? It looks as good as new.
투덜대지마! 새 것 처럼 보이는데

alleviate 경감하다, 완화하다

The U.N.'s most important objective is to alleviate world poverty.
유엔의 가장 중요한 목적은 세계의 빈곤을 완화하는 것이다.

convict 유죄를 선고하다

Approximately 200 members of the vicious cult have been convicted.
이 잔인한 교파의 회원 약 200명이 유죄판결을 받았다.

fabricate 조작하다, 위조하다

The nation's movement in the fields tumbled when Hwang was found to have fabricated his research in 2005.
그 분야에서의 한국의 움직임은 황이 2005년에 그의 연구를 조작했음이 발견됐을 때 휘청거렸다.

oversight 관과, 실수

That was an oversight on my part. I'll correct it right away.
그것은 제 실수이다. 즉각 시정 하겠다.

compromise (무분별한 행동으로) ~을 위태롭게 하다

She had already compromised herself by accepting his invitation.
그녀는 이미 그의 초대를 받아들임으로써 자신을 위태롭게 만든 상태였다.

doctor 변조하다, (문서, 증거) 조작하다

Experts suspected the police evidence might have been doctored.
전문가들은 경찰의 증거가 변조되었을지도 모른다고 의심했다.

be supposed to ~하기로 되어 있다, ~할 의무가 있다

We were supposed to meet at seven.
우리는 일곱 시에 만날 예정이었다.

You're supposed to buy a ticket, but not many people do.
표를 사야 하는 것으로 되어 있지만 그렇게 하는 사람들이 많지 않다.

subsidiary 자회사

A holding company has a controlling interest in its subsidiary company.
지주회사는 자회사의 이익을 통제한다.

vet 진료하다, (사람, 물건)을 검사하다, 상세히 조사하다

Government experts vetted information about the new drug.
정부의 전문가들은 그 새 약물의 정보를 면밀히 검토했다.

porous 구멍이 많은

His arguments were as porous as a leaky boat.
그의 주장은 아주 허점투성이였다.

collusive 공모한, 담합에 의한

He broke the chain of collusive links between politicians and businessmen.
그는 정경유착의 고리를 끊었다.

spawn (알)을 낳다, ~의 원인이 되다, ~을 야기시키다

The senator's careless remarks spawned public outrage and calls for resignation.
상원의원의 부주의한 발언이 대중의 격노와 사퇴요구를 낳았다.

litany 장황한 설명(이야기)

a litany of 많은

There is a litany of reasons for getting cheap scooters.
값싼 스쿠터를 구입할 많은 이유가 있다.

replete 가득한

This car has an engine replete with the latest technology.
이 차는 최신의 기술로 완비된 엔진을 갖고 있다.

complacency 자기만족, 자기도취

Complacency will turn victory into defeat quickly.
자만은 승리를 패배로 그것도 급속히 바꾸어 놓을 것이다.

charge 혐의, 기소

He had been confined since October while awaiting trial on bribery charges.
그는 뇌물수수혐의로 재판을 기다리며 10월부터 수감 중이었다.

retirement package benefits 퇴직 수당

After an employee has been employed for at least 20 years, he is entitled to take an early retirement package.
한 직원이 적어도 20년 동안 근무한 후에야, 조기퇴직제도의 자격이 주어진다.

enact laws 법률을 제정하다

Many states enacted laws to improve the conditions under which people lived and worked.
많은 주들이 국민들의 생활과 근로조건을 개선하기 위한 법률들을 제정했다.

23.

America's problem is not political gridlock

With last week's *release[1] of the president's budget, Washington has once again descended into partisan squabbling. In the US today, there is pervasive concern about the basic functioning of democracy. Congress is viewed less favourably than ever before in the history of *opinion polling[2]. There is widespread revulsion at *political figures[3] seemingly unable to reach agreement on *measures[4] to reduce future *budget deficits[5]. Pundits and politicians alike condemn "gridlock". Angry movements, such as Occupy Wall Street[1)] and the Tea Party[2)], are present and still active on the extremes of both sides of the political spectrum.

The A-List provides *timely[6], insightful comment on the topics that matter, from globally renowned leaders, *policymakers[7] and commentators.

Meanwhile, *profound changes[8] are redefining the global order. *Emerging economies[9], led by China, are converging towards the west. Beyond the current economic *downturn[10] lies the even more serious challenge of the rise of technologies,

1 release
발표, 공개

2 opinion poll
여론조사

3 political figures
정치인

4 measure
조치

5 budget deficits
재정적자

6 timely
시기적절한, 때맞춘

7 policymakers
정책입안자

8 profound change
(영향 · 느낌 · 경험 등이) 엄청난(깊은) 변화

9 Emerging economies
개발도상국

10 downturn
(경기)하강, 침체

11 ageing population
노령인구

12 ample experience
충분한(풍부한) 경험

13 unfeasible
가능하지 않은,
달성할 수 없는

which may raise average productivity but will displace large numbers of workers. Public debt is increasing in a way that is without precedent except in times of total war. A combination of an *ageing population[11] and the rising prices of health and education will put pressure on future budgets.

Anyone who has worked in a political position in Washington has had *ample experience[12] with great frustration. Almost everyone in US politics feels there is much that is essential yet *unfeasible[13] in the current environment. Many

1) **Occupy Wall Street**(OWS)(월가 시위) is the name given to a protest movement that began on September 17, 2011, in Zuccotti Park, located in New York City's Wall Street financial district.
The Canadian, anti-consumerist, pro-environment group/magazine Adbusters initiated the call for a protest. Media awareness helped inspire Occupy protests and movements around the world.
The main issues raised by Occupy Wall Street were social and economic inequality, greed, corruption and the perceived undue influence of corporations on government—particularly from the financial services sector. The OWS slogan, "We are the 99%", refers to income inequality and wealth distribution in the U.S. between the wealthiest 1% and the rest of the population. To achieve their goals, protesters acted on consensus-based decisions made in general assemblies which emphasized direct action over petitioning authorities for redress.
The protesters were forced out of Zuccotti Park on November 15, 2011. After several unsuccessful attempts to re-occupy the original location, protesters turned their focus to occupying banks, corporate headquarters, board meetings, foreclosed homes, and college and university campuses.
On December 29, 2012, Naomi Wolf of The Guardian newspaper provided U.S. government documents which revealed that the FBI and DHS had monitored Occupy Wall Street through its Joint Terrorism Task Force, despite labelling it a peaceful movement. The New York Times reported in May 2014 that declassified documents showed extensive surveilliance and infiltration of OWS-related groups across the country(Wikipedia).

2) **Tea Party** (미국의 보수주의 유권자 단체) 기성 정치권이 아닌 일반 시민의 주도로 확산되고 있는 미국의 풀뿌리정치운동으로, 1773년 미국 독립전쟁 당시 영국에 대한 조세저항운동의 진원이었던 보스턴 티파티에서 따온 명칭이다. 티파티는 월가와 부실 대기업에 대한 오바마 대통령의 구제금융 지원에 항의하기 위해 2009년 결성된 모임이다. 티(TEA)는「세금을 낼 만큼 냈다(Taxed Enough Already)」는 의미의 약어로, 이 모임은 전형적인 보수 이념을 표방하며 작은 정부를 지향한다.
최근 세금을 늘려 큰 정부를 만들려는 오바마 행정부의 국정운영에 반대하는 보수성향 유권자들을 일컫는 말로 사용된다. 2010년 미국 중간선거에서 당선된 공화당 하원의원의 3분의 1인 초선의원 80여 명 중 절반 이상이 티파티 소속이다(네이버 지식백과, 시사상식사전).

yearn for a return to an imagined era when *centrists[14] in both parties negotiated *bipartisan[15] compromises that moved the country forward. Yet fears about the functioning of the US government have been a recurring feature of the political landscape since Virginian Patrick Henry[3)]'s 1791 assertion that the spirit of the revolution had been lost.

It is sobering to contrast today's concern about political paralysis with that which gripped Washington during the early 1960s. Then, the *prevailing diagnosis[16] was that a lack of cohesive and responsible parties for voters to choose from precluded the clear electoral mandates necessary for decisive action. While there was a flurry of legislation passed in the 1964-66 period after a *Democratic electoral landslide[17], Vietnam[4)] and Watergate[5)] followed, all leading to President Jimmy Carter's declaration of a crisis of the national spirit.

14 centrist
중도주의자

15 bipartisan
양당의

16 prevailing diagnosis
지배적인 진단

17 Democratic electoral landslide
(선거에서) 민주당의 대승리

3) **Patrick Henry**(May 29, 1736 – June 6, 1799) was an American attorney, planter and politician who became known as an orator during the movement for independence in Virginia in the 1770s. A Founding Father, he served as the first and sixth post-colonial Governor of Virginia, from 1776 to 1779 and from 1784 to 1786.
Henry led the opposition to the Stamp Act of 1765 and is remembered for his "Give me liberty, or give me death!" speech. Along with Samuel Adams and Thomas Paine, he is regarded as one of the most influential champions of Republicanism and an invested promoter of the American Revolution and its fight for independence.
After the Revolution, Henry was a leader of the anti-federalists in Virginia. He opposed the United States Constitution, fearing that it endangered the rights of the States as well as the freedoms of individuals; he helped gain adoption of the Bill of Rights. By 1798 however, he supported President John Adams and the Federalists; he denounced passage of the Virginia and Kentucky Resolutions as he feared the social unrest and widespread executions that had followed the increasing radicalism of the French Revolution.
As a married man, Henry was an expanding landowner. By 1779, along with his cousin and her husband, Henry owned a 10,000-acre (40 km2) plantation known by the name of Leatherwood. He is also recorded to have purchased up to 78 slaves. In 1794 he and his wife retired to Red Hill Plantation, which had 520-acre (2.1 km2) in Charlotte County that was also a functioning tobacco plantation(Wikipedia).

18 rose-tinted
= rose-colored
장밋빛의

19 rapport
관계, 교감

20 impeach
탄핵하다

21 House of Representatives
(미국) 하원

Despite the *rose-tinted[18] view today, there was hardly high *rapport[19] in Washington during Ronald Reagan's presidency. During his time in office Bill Clinton worked hard at compromising with a US Congress controlled by Republicans, only to be *impeached[20] by the *House of Representatives[21].

Throughout American history, division and slow change have been the norm rather than the exception. While often frustrating, this has not always been a bad thing.

4) **The Vietnam War**, also known as the Second Indochina War, and known in Vietnam as the Resistance War Against America or simply the American War, was a Cold War-era proxy war that occurred in Vietnam, Laos, and Cambodia from 1 November 1955 to the fall of Saigon on 30 April 1975. This war followed the First Indochina War and was fought between North Vietnam—supported by the Soviet Union, China and other communist allies—and the government of South Vietnam—supported by the United States and other anti-communist allies. The Viet Cong (also known as the National Liberation Front, or NLF), a lightly armed South Vietnamese communist common front aided by the North, fought a guerrilla war against anti-communist forces in the region. The People's Army of Vietnam (aka the North Vietnamese Army) engaged in a more conventional war, at times committing large units into battle(Wikipedia).

5) **Watergate** (워트게이트 사건) 1973년 초부터 1974년 8월 닉슨대통령이 사임할 때까지 미국의 네트워크 텔레비전 뉴스를 장악했던 사건. 이 사건을 폭로해서 스캔들로 만드는 데 영웅적인 기여를 한 사람들은 '워싱턴 포스트'지의 우드워드(Bob Woodward)와 번스타인(Carl Bernstein)이었지만 그것을 전국적으로 알려서 부각시킨 것은 텔레비전이었다. 즉 워터게이트 사건의 발생과 그 후의 은닉과정에서 닉슨 행정부가 한 역할에 대한 상원특별조사위원회의 조사(1973년 봄에 시작해서 가을에 끝남)와 하원법사위원회의 닉슨 대통령에 대한 탄핵에 대한 열띤 논의(1974년 7월 24일–30일 방송)를 텔레비전이 중계하면서부터 사건이 세상에 본격적으로 알려지기 시작했다. 워터게이트 사건을 다루는 데 있어서 '워싱턴 포스트'에 버금가는 큰 역할을 한 것은 CBS 뉴스였다. CBS 뉴스는 가장 용기있고, 밀도 높은 보도를 했으며, '워싱턴 포스트'에 요긴하고 믿을만한 정보를 주기도 했다. 당시 가장 큰 텔레비전 사건은 상원의 워터게이트 청문회에 대한 3대 네트워크나 PBS의 보도였다. 사건과 관련된 모든 인물을 소개했으며, 버터필드(Alexander Butterfield)로부터 닉슨이 오벌 오피스(Oval Office)에서 나누는 모든 이야기를 녹음했다는 폭탄 선언을 받아냈던 것이다. 결국 닉슨에게서 그 테이프를 받아냄으로써 이 테이프가 탄핵 과정의 길을 연 셈이다. 1973년 봄, 여름, 가을 13주 동안 워트게이트 청문회는 낮 시간 텔레비전의 큰 화제가 되었으며, 밤에도 PBS에서 재방송을 하여 많은 시청자를 끌었다. 청문회는 3월 17일에 시작해서 37주 동안 계속되었으며 11월 15일 마감했다. 3대 네트워크가 돌아가며 거의 300시간 동안 방송한 이 청문회로 인해 발생한 광고 시간과 방송 시간의 손실을 값으로 치자면 약 1,000만 달러였다고 한다. 미국 전체 가구의 85%가 이 청문회를 전부 또는 일부 시청했다. 1974년 3월 9일 하원탄핵위원회에서 닉슨 대통령에 대한 탄핵을 논하는 토론회가 시작되어 7월 30일 끝났으며, 닉슨은 8월 8일 사임을 발표하는 방송을 했는데, 16분짜리 이 연설을 1억 1,000만 시청자가 지켜봄으로써 역대 대통령의 연설 중에서 시청률이 제일 높은 것이 되었다(네이버 지식백과, 매스컴대사전).

There were probably too few checks and balances as the US entered the Vietnam and Iraq wars[6)]. There should have been more checks and balances in place before the huge *tax cuts[22] of 1981, 2001 and 2003, or to avert the many *unfunded[23] entitlement expansions of the past few decades. Most experts would agree that it is a good thing that politics thwarted the effort to establish a guaranteed annual income in the late 1960s and early 1970s and the effort to put in place a "*single-payer" healthcare system[24] during the 1970s.

The great mistake of the gridlock theorists is to suppose that all progress comes from legislation and that more legislation consistently represents more progress. While these are seen as years of gridlock, consider what has happened in the past five years.

The US moved faster to contain a systemic financial crisis than any country facing such an episode has done in the past generation. Through all the *fractiousness[25], enough change has taken place that without further policy action, the *ratio of debt[26] to *gross domestic product[27] is expected to decline for the next five years. Beyond that, the outlook depends largely

22 tax cuts
감세

23 unfunded
자금(재원)이 없는

24 single payer healthcare system
단일보험자 체제

25 fractiousness
다루기 힘듦,
괴팍스러움

26 ratio of debt
부채비율

27 gross domestic product(GDP)
국민 총 생산

6) **The Iraq War** was an armed conflict in Iraq that consisted of two phases. The first was an invasion of Iraq starting on 20 March 2003 by an invasion force led by the United States. It was followed by a longer phase of fighting, in which an insurgency emerged to oppose the occupying forces and the newly formed Iraqi government. Roughly 96.5 percent of the casualties suffered by the U.S.-led coalition were suffered during the second phase, rather than the initial invasion. The U.S. completed its withdrawal of military personnel in December 2011, during the ninth year of the war. However, the insurgency is ongoing and continues to cause thousands of fatalities. Throughout the armed conflict, the United States never formally declared war on Iraq, making the war a military action(Wikipedia).

28 universal healthcare
일반 의료보험

29 financial regulation
금융규제

30 metrics of performance
업적평가지표

31 pessimism
비관론

32 prophecies
예언

on healthcare costs - but their growth has slowed to the rate of GDP growth for three years now - the first such slowdown in half a century. At last, *universal healthcare[28] has been passed and is now being implemented. Within a decade it is likely that the US will no longer be a net importer of fossil fuels. *Financial regulation[29] is not in a fully satisfactory place but has received its most substantial overhaul in 75 years. Most schools and teachers are for the first time evaluated on objective *metrics of performance[30]. Gay marriage has become widely accepted across the states.

No comparable list can be put forth for Japan or countries in western Europe. Yes, change comes rapidly to some of the authoritarian societies of Asia. But it may not endure and may not always be for the better.

Anyone prone to *pessimism[31] about the US would do well to ponder the alarm with which it viewed the Soviet Union after it launched the Sputnik satellite[7)] or Japan's economic rise in the 1980s and the early 1990s. One of America's greatest strengths is its ability to defy its own *prophecies[32] of doom.

7) **Sputnik satellite** 소련이 1957년 10월 4일 발사한 사상 최초의 인공위성. 스푸트니크란 러시아어로 '위성'이란 뜻이며, 서구에서는 보통 '소련의 인공위성'이라는 의미로 쓰이고 있다. 스푸트니크의 성공적인 발사는 미국을 비롯한 서방진영에 소련의 맹렬한 추격에 대한 일종의 위기의식을 불러일으켰다. 직경 58cm, 중량 83.6kg, 표면에 4개의 봉상 안테나를 달고 2대의 무선 송신기로 내부 온도와 압력의 측정치를 송신했다. 근지점 227km, 원지점 941km의 타원궤도를 비행했다. 발사 로켓은 소련 최초로 대륙간 탄도미사일의 개량형이었다. 스푸트니크 1호는 다음해인 1958년 1월 4일 대기권에 들어와서 소멸했다. 스푸트니크 2호는 1957년 11월 3일 라이카견(犬) 한 마리를 태우고 발사, 그 생리 상태를 측정해 인간우주비행의 가능성을 탐색하는 실험을 개시했다. 스푸트니크 3호는 1958년 5월 15일 발사. 1,327kg라는 당시로서는 경이적인 중량으로 대기층의 밀도, 자장, 태양 방사선 등의 광범한 공간 관측을 실시했다(네이버 지식백과, 매스컴대사전).

None of this is to say that the US does not face huge challenges. But these are not due to structural obstacles. They are about finding solutions to problems such as rising inequality and climate change – where we do not quite know the way forward. This is not a problem of gridlock – it is a problem of vision.

ft.com 2013-04-13

WORDS and STRUCTURES

gridlock (교차점에서의 자동차의) 교통정체, 교통마비상태, (특히 정치에서) 꼼짝달싹 못하는 상태

This removes the dangers of political gridlock.
이것은 정치적 교착상태에 빠질 위험이 없다.

descend into 빠져들다

The country was descending into chaos.
그 나라는 서서히 혼란 속으로 빠져들고 있었다.

partisan squabbling 당파적 싸움

The National Assembly will have another chance tomorrow to prove it is the hall of popular sentiment, not partisan squabbling.
국회는 내일 당파적 다툼이 아닌 민의를 위한 전당임을 입증할 또 한번의 기회를 가지게 된다.

pervasive 널리 퍼지는, 만연하는

Television is the most pervasive influence in American daily lives.
텔레비전은 미국인들의 일상에 가장 큰 영향을 준다.

revulsion 혐오, 반감

She felt a deep sense of revulsion at the violence.
그녀는 그 폭력 행위에 깊은 혐오감을 느꼈다.

seemingly 겉보기에는

Therefore, these latest concessions are seemingly insincere.
따라서, 이러한 최근의 양보는 겉보기에도 진실 되지 못하다.

pundit 전문가

Political pundits say there even may be a revolution.
정치 전문가들은 혁명이 일어날 수도 있다고 말한다.

A-list (주로 명사 앞에 씀) 최고의, 일류의

He only invited A-list celebrities to his parties.
그는 자기 파티에 최고 유명인사만 초대했다.

emerging economies 개발도상국(developing countries)

Thus, nations, particularly the emerging economies, are also engaging in an international image pageant.
따라서 각국, 특히 개발도상국들이 국제적인 이미지 선전무대에 나서고 있는 것이다.

converge towards ~쪽으로 모이다

Thousands of supporters converged on London for the rally.
수천 명의 지지자들이 그 집회에 참석하기 위해 런던으로 모여들었다.

Emerging economies, ***led*** by China, are converging towards the west
= Emerging economies, ***(and they***(emerging economies) ***are) led*** by China, are converging towards the west
중국을 주도로 개발도상국들이 서방을 향해 모여들고 있다.

downturn (경기)하강, 침체

Who in the world can put an end to this sharp economic downturn?
도대체 이 심각한 경제침체에 종지부를 찍을 사람이 누구일까?

without precedent 전례 없이

This course of action is quite without precedent. 이런 행동 방침은 전례가 없다.

yearn 갈망하다

City dwellers sometimes yearn to see the nature and beauty of a scenic countryside.
도시 거주자들은 때때로 경치가 아름다운 전원의 자연과 미를 보기를 갈망하기도 한다.

sobering 번쩍 정신이 들게 하는, 심각하게 만드는

It is sobering to realize that this is not a new problem.
이것이 새로운 문제가 아님을 깨닫게 되니 정신이 번쩍 든다.

cohesive 응집력이 있는

The United States struggled to find a cohesive policy toward Syria, preferring to resort to standard operating procedures.
미국은 표준적인 외교 절차에 호소하는 편을 선택하여 응집력 있는 정책을 찾기 위해 애썼다.

preclude ~하지 못하게 하다, 불가능하게 하다

Lack of time precludes any further discussion.
시간이 부족해서 더 이상 논의하는 것이 불가능하다.

mandate 위임, 권한부여

The election victory gave the party a clear mandate to continue its programme of reform.
선거에서의 승리로 그 당은 개혁 프로그램을 계속할 수 있는 확실한 권한을 부여받았다.

a flurry of 일련의

A flurry of labor unrest is expected to hit the nation's key industries this week.
이번 주 일련의 노동계파업이 국내 주요업계에서 발생할 전망이다.

only to do 그 결과는 ~뿐

The girl cried hard only to madden her mom more.
소녀는 심하게 울었지만 그 결과 엄마만 더 화나게 했을 뿐이다.

checks and balances (권력의)견제와 균형

Autocracies can potentially be transparent and have checks and balances.
독재국가는 잠재적으로 투명하고 견제와 균형이 있을 수 있다.

avert 피하다, 돌리다

Investigators believe he reversed his stance to avert accusations of wrong doing.
수사관들은 민씨가 불법행위 혐의를 피하기 위해 입장을 바꾼 것으로 믿고 있다.

entitlement (program) (미 정부의)복지후생(계획)

duration of entitlement to the National Pension 국민연금 가입기간

thwart 훼방 놓다, (계획 · 목적)을 좌절시키다

Engagement is best policy to thwart anachronistic act.
포용이 시대착오적 행동을 막는 최선의 정책이다.

put in place 취하다

New measures must be put in place as soon as possible to stabilize the stumbling currency market.
위태로운 통화시장을 가능한 빨리 안정화시키기 위해 이제 조치가 취해져야 한다.

contain 방지하다, 억제하다

Doctors are working hard to contain the spread of cholera.
의사들은 콜레라의 확산을 방지하기 위해 열심히 일하고 있다.

implement 시행하다, 실시하다

When new policies are implemented money will be cut in other areas.
새로운 정책이 실시되면, 예산은 다른 분야에서 삭감되게 된다.

overhaul 점검, 정비

A radical overhaul of the tax system is necessary.
근본적인 세제 정비가 필요하다.

put forth (안건 · 문제 등을) 내다, 제출하다

These columns often put forth a distinct and consistent point of view week after week.
이런 칼럼들은 종종 매주 독특하고 일관성 있는 관점을 제시한다.

for the better 보다 나은 쪽으로

Sometimes a brilliant idea can change the world for the better.
가끔은 멋진 아이디어가 세상을 더 살기 좋은 곳으로 변화시킬 수 있다.

be prone to ~하기 쉽다

If you do not wish to be prone to anger, do not feed the habit.
쉽게 화내고 싶지 않다면 그런 습관을 키우지 말라.

do well to do ~하는 것이 온당(현명)하다

He would do well to concentrate more on his work.
그가 자기 일에 더 집중을 하는 것이 온당할 것이다.

with alarm 불안한 마음으로

She walked after him with alarm.
그녀는 불안한 마음으로 그를 뒤따라갔다.

Anyone prone to pessimism about the US would do well to ponder the alarm ***with which*** it viewed the Soviet Union after it launched the Sputnik satellite

= Anyone prone to pessimism about the US would do well to ponder the alarm **+*(and)*** it viewed the Soviet Union ***with it***(the alarm) after it launched the Sputnik satellite

미국에 대해 비관적이기 쉬운 사람은 누구든지 소련이 스푸트니크 위성을 발사한 후 미국이 소련에 대해 가지고 있었던 그 경각심을 깊이 생각하는 것이 좋을 것이다.

석 종 환

경상대학교 영어영문학과 졸업
계명대학교 대학원 박사과정 수료(문학박사)
런던대학교(SOAS) 수학
인디애나대학교 언어학과 방문교수
경상대학교 국제어학원장
현재 경상대학교 영어영문학과 교수

편 · 역서

『단어의 음운구조』 공역(한국문화사)
『해설 영문독해』 공편(경상대학교출판부)

논문

「음운론적 지배와 음절구조」(1996)
「영어의 어두자음군 분석」(2000)
「영어 강세이론에서 외운율성의 운명」(2004)
「CVCV와 영어의 음절구조」(2009)
「영어합성어의 분류」(2011)
「영어의 외심합성어 분석」(2013)
「영어등위합성어의 분류」(2014) 외 다수

Current English

초판 1쇄 인쇄 · 2014년 8월 20일
초판 1쇄 발행 · 2014년 8월 25일

엮은이 · 석종환
펴낸이 · 권순기 | 경영 · 김명주
책임편집 · 김종길 | 디자인 · 느티나무

펴낸곳 · 경상대학교출판부
주소 · 경남 진주시 진주대로 501
전화 · 055)772-0801~2
FAX · 055)772-0809
E-mail · gspress@gnu.ac.kr
등록 · 1989년 1월 7일 제16호

ISBN 978-89-6257-090-8 13740

©경상대학교출판부, 2014

• 저자와의 협의 하에 인지를 생략합니다.
• 경상대학교출판부의 서면 동의 없이 무단전제 및 복사를 금합니다.

값 14,800원

이 도서의 국립중앙도서관 출판예정도서목록(CIP)은 서지정보유통지원시스템 홈페이지(http://seoji.nl.go.kr)와 국가자료공동목록시스템(http://www.nl.go.kr/kolisnet)에서 이용하실 수 있습니다. (CIP제어번호 : CIP2014024109)

외래에서 바로 통하는

근골격 영상 판독 가이드

JN444620

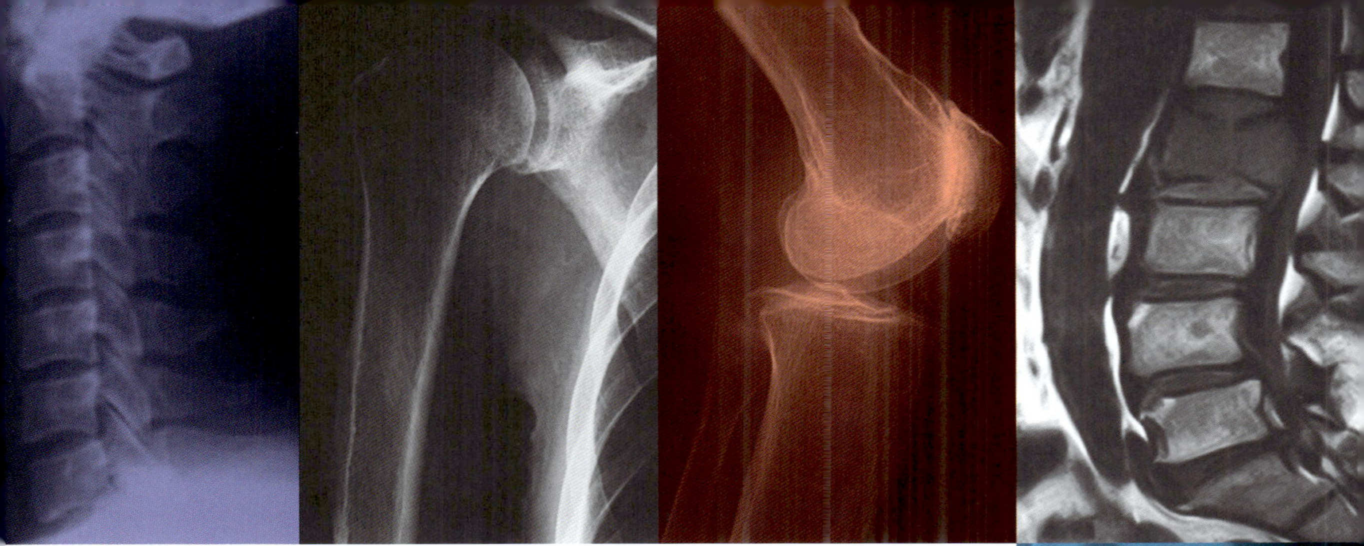

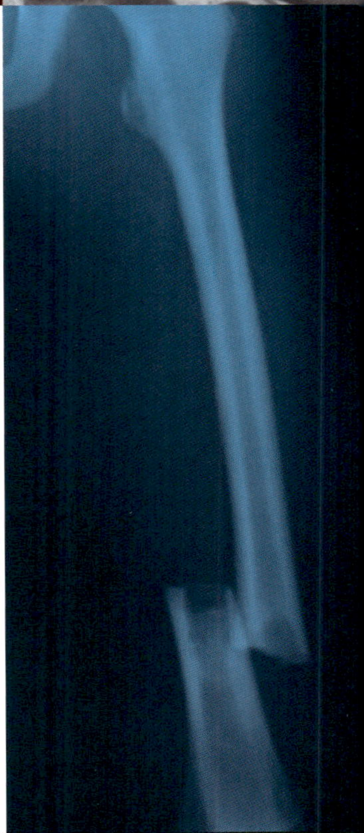

외래에서 바로 통하는

근골격 영상 판독 가이드

Kazumasa Nakada

정효준·서준원 옮김 | 김연스 감수

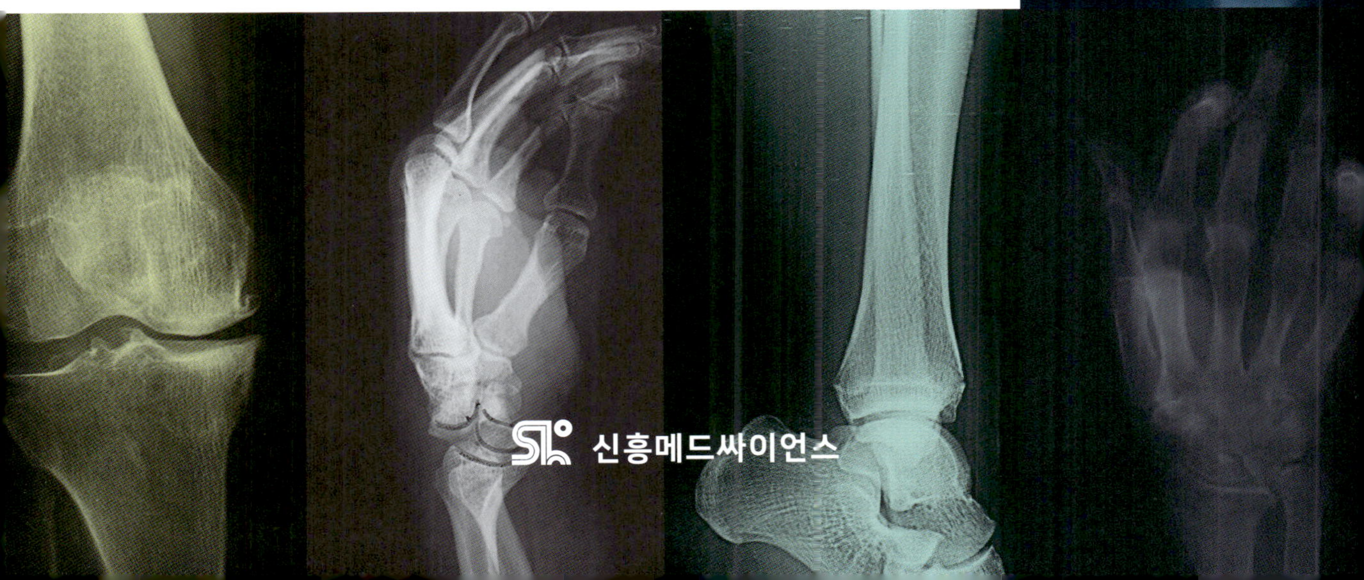

신흥메드싸이언스

Authorized translation from the Japanese language edition, entitled
《ジェネラリストBOOKS》整形画像読影道場
ISBN 978-4-260-03833-1
編著:仲田 和正
published by IGAKU-SHOIN LTD., TOKYO Copyright ⓒ 2019
All Rights Reserved. No part of this book may be reproduced or transmitted in any form or by any means, electronic or mechanical, including photocopying, recording or by any information storage retrieval system, without permission from IGAKU-SHOIN LTD.

Korean language edition published by ShinHeung Medscience, Inc. Copyright ⓒ 2022

외래에서 바로 **통**하는
근골격 영상 판독 가이드

발 행	2022년 1월 10일
지 은 이	Kazumasa Nakada
옮 긴 이	정 효 준·서 준 원
감 수	김 연 수
발 행 인	홍 성 혁
발 행 처	신흥메드싸이언스
디 자 인	박 은 경
주 소	서울시 강서구 마곡중앙1로 10, 907호 (마곡동 한일노벨리아타워)
등록번호	제318-2007-000077호
전 화	02-6956-8670
팩 스	02-6956-8671
홈페이지	www.shmed.co.kr
I S B N	978-89-6498-077-4 93510
정 가	35,000원

* 이 책의 저작권은 **IGAKU-SHOIN LTD.**,와 저작권 계약을 한 ㈜**신흥메드싸이언스**에 있으며 저작권법에 따라 한국에서 보호를 받는 저작물이므로 내용 또는 화보의 무단 전재와 복제를 금합니다.

* 파본이나 낙장이 있는 책은 교환해 드립니다.

옮긴이 서문

임상의학을 처음 배우던 시절, 선배에게 물려받은 책에서 가장 중요하다고 표시된 부분은 당연하게도 가장 치명적인 질환과 가장 흔한 질환이었습니다.

의원에서 근골격계 일차진료를 하고 있는 지금도 환자가 호소하는 증상이나 소견을 보고 가장 먼저 머릿속에 떠올리는 것도 바로 그것입니다. 지금 여기서 처치나 대응이 가능한 질환과 그렇지 않은 질환을 구별하는 것이 우선이라고 생각하기 때문입니다.

이를 위해서는 이학적 검사, X-ray, 초음파 검사 등 현재 가능한 검사와 진단적 치료 등을 통해 특정 증상을 유발하는 질환을 빠르게 감별하는 것이 중요합니다.

이 책은 그러한 내용을 간략하게 담고 있으며, 보기 편하게 편집되어 있습니다. 바쁜 일상 진료 중 길잡이가 되기를 바랍니다. 저도 이 책의 번역을 계기로 앞으로 핵심을 놓치지 않고 실수를 줄이기 위해 더욱 노력하겠습니다. 감사합니다.

2022년 1월
수재활의학과의원
정 효 준

감수의 글

정형외과 수련을 마치고 제 8군단 특공대대에서 군의관으로 근무를 시작하였을 때, 모든 분과를 아우르는 일차진료를 해야 한다는 부담감과 두려움을 경험한 적이 있습니다.

지식과 경험의 부재가 두려움을 만드는 것이고, 이는 학문의 수련과 경험의 축적으로 극복하는 수밖에 없지만, 다른 사람의 귀중한 경험을 간접적으로 체험하고 이를 고찰하여 나의 것으로 만들 수 있다면 훨씬 효율적으로 목표하는 경지에 이를 수 있을 것입니다.

이 책은 저자가 오랜 세월 경험하였던 정형외과 일차 진료현장을 생생하게 묘사하고 있으며, 독자들로 하여금 국경을 초월하는 흥미로운 증례를 경험하게 해줍니다.

좋은 책을 경험하게 해주신 정효준 원장님께 깊이 감사드리며 이 책을 추천합니다.

2022년 1월

서울통정형외과의원
원장 김 연 수

서문

수련의 시절, 덴류강 상류의 산간벽지에 있는 진료소를 처음 견학했을 때 무릎 통증과 요통, 사지 외상 등 정형외과 질환이 많다는 사실에 놀랐다. 내과, 소아과, 정형외과적 소양이 있다면 벽지에서 마주치는 질환의 80~90%에 대처할 수 있음을 실감했다. 벽지에 도움이 되는 의사가 되는 것이 필자의 바람이었기 때문에, 그전까지는 외과를 지망했지만, 이를 계기로 정형외과 의사가 되기로 결심했다.

내과, 소아과도 수련을 받아야 하지만, 그 이후에는 독학으로 지식을 넓힐 수 있다. 그러나 외과 계열은 스승을 따라 꾸준히 실력을 연마해야 한다. 이러한 이유로 정형외과 수련을 받고, 내과 계열은 스스로 공부해 벽지에 이바지하는 의사가 되기로 했다.

한 지방도시의 외과의사회에서 정형외과 질환에 대한 강의를 의뢰받은 적이 있다. 외과의사회에서 정형외과 강의가 필요한 이유를 물으니, 소화기외과를 전문으로 내걸어도 일단 '외과'로 개원하면 대부분의 환자는 정형외과 질환으로 내원하기 때문에 정형외과 지식이 가장 필요하다는 답변을 들었다.

일차진료 현장에서 정형외과 지식과 근골격계 영상판독 능력은 필수적이다. 미국 의료소송에서 가장 흔한 것이 골절을 놓치는 경우이다. 이 책에서는 의원급 외래진료에서 수요가 많은 정형외과 질환에 집중하고 불필요한 내용은 배재하여, 진료에 즉시 적용할 수 있는 X-ray 지식을 정리했다. 일상 진료 중 이 책 정도의 지식이 있다면 그다지 곤란하지 않을 것이라고 확신한다. 사진은 필자가 지금까지 축적해온 2,000장 정도의 teaching file에서 엄선했다.

2019년 3월

니시이즈 켄이쿠카이 병원장
Kazumasa Nakada

목차

COLUMN

SPECIAL LECTURE

LEVEL UP을 위한 연습문제

제1장

근골격계 질환 진찰의 기본

일반적인 내과 외래 진료에서 정형외과적(근골격계) 증상을 호소하는 경우가 적지 않다. 통증을 호소하는 부위에 X-ray를 촬영하는 일도 있을 것이다. 그런데, 그 X-ray의 이상 소견을 놓치고 있었을지도 모른다. 판독할 때의 포인트를 숙지하고, 의심을 한다면 저절로 이상 부위가 보일 것이다. 그래서 이 책에서는 내과계 선생님들에게 필요한 X-ray 판독의 포인트를 근골격계 질환을 중심으로 전달하고자 한다. 필요에 따라 CT나 MRI 등의 관련 영상도 제시하며, 때로는 내과적인 판독 포인트도 소개할 것이다. '꾸준한 반복 학습'을 통해 함께 배워봅시다.

골절의 발생기전

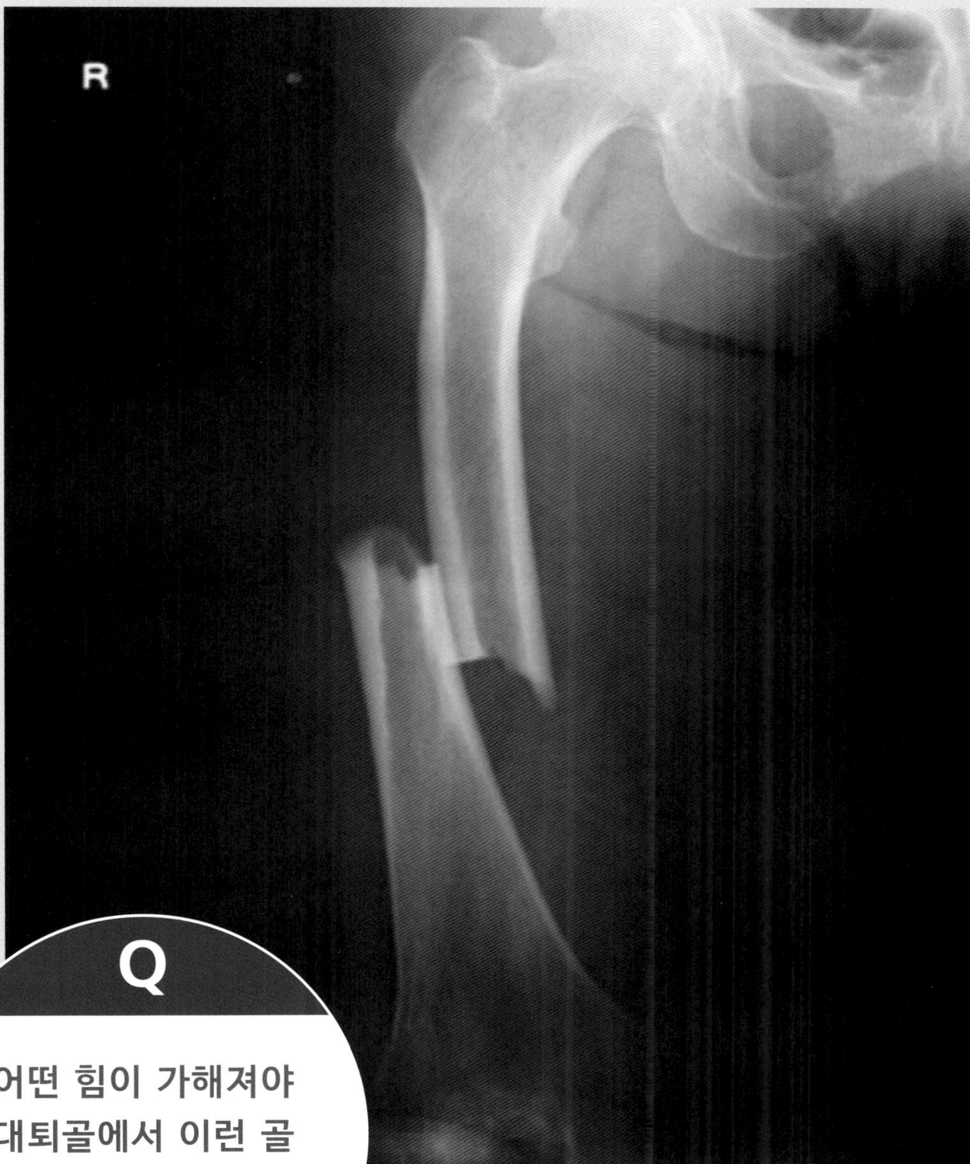

70세 · 여성

Q

어떤 힘이 가해져야 대퇴골에서 이런 골절이 발생할까?

첫 번째 주제는 골절이다. 미국의 의료 소송에서는 '골절을 놓치는 것'이 자주 문제가 된다. 이전 의사의 진료에서 '골절은 없다'고 했는데, 다음 의사의 진료에서 '골절'이라고 진단한다면 큰 불신을 야기할 것이다. 내과계 의사라도 골격 X-ray를 판독할 수 있어야 한다. 또한, 골절의 기전을 이해하고 있으면, 환자의 전신 상태나 다른 부위의 손상을 가늠하는데 도움이 될 수 있다. 예를 들어 X-ray에서 확인되는 골절이 고에너지 손상이라고 판단될 때는 다발성 외상을 의심하게 될 것이다.

오이로 알 수 있는 골절의 기전

골절은 X-ray를 보면 어떤 힘이 작용했는지 대략 예상할 수 있다. 필자는 'Rockwood and Green's fractures in adults'[1)]에서 골절의 기전에 대한 설명을 읽고 오이를 이용하면 골절을 재현할 수 있지 않을까라고 생각했다.

골절은 오이로 쉽게 재현할 수 있다. 실제로 오이를 준비하고 두 사람이 실험해 보도록 한다.

옆에서 약하게 혹은 강하게(그림 1)

우선 한 사람이 오이를 수평으로 잡고 다른 한 사람이 가볍게 손날로 내려쳐 부러뜨린다(뼈에 퍽하고 물체가 충돌: tapping fracture). 그러면 오이는 **횡골절**(transverse fracture)이 된다. 즉, 장관골

Dr. Nakata는 실제로 가라테 검은띠 보유자이다. 하지만 오이 실험은 유단자가 아니어도 쉽게 할 수 있다!

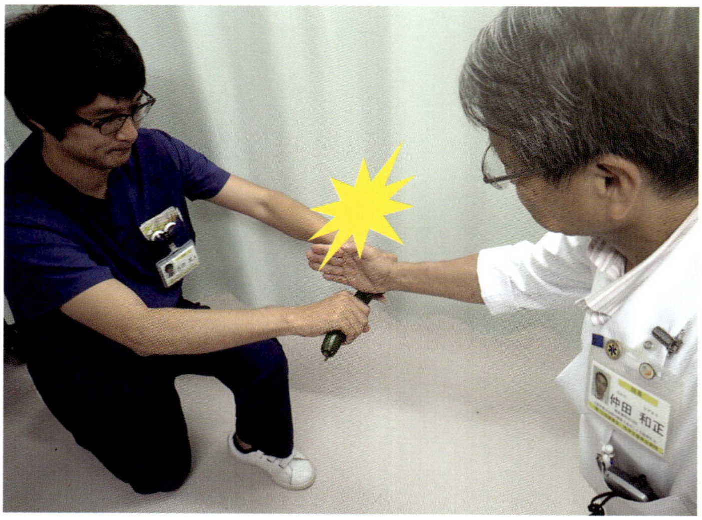

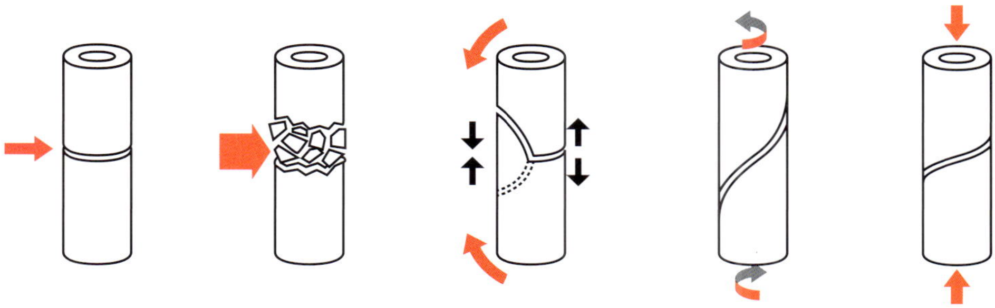

그림 1 골절의 기전

(long bone)에 옆에서 물체가 충돌하면 횡골절이 되는 것이다.

마찬가지로 오이를 수평으로 잡고 이번에는 있는 힘껏 손날로 내려친다. 그러면 오이는 산산조각이 난다. 즉, 장관골에 강한 에너지가 작용하면 **분쇄골절**(comminuted fracture)이 되는 것이다.

비틀기, 구부리기(그림 1)

다음은 오이를 양손으로 잡고 비틀어 본다. 그러면 **나선골절**(spiral fracture)이 된다(그림 2, 3).

또한, 오이를 천천히 양손으로 구부려서 부러뜨려본다(그림 4). 이러한 굴곡 모멘트는 지렛대(lever)의 길이에 비례하므로 가늘고 긴 뼈의 사람은 굵고 짧은 사람보다 골절의 위험이 높다.

횡골절+사골절

오이를 굴곡시키면 그림 4b와 같은 골절이 된다. 장력(tension)이 가해지는 위쪽은 **횡골절**이, 압박력(compression)이 가해지는 아래쪽은 **사골절**(oblique transverse fracture)이 된다.

뼈는 장력(tension)보다는 압박력(compression)에 강하므로, 우선 처음에 장력이 가해지는 쪽(tension side)에서 골절이 시작되어 오이에 대해 수직으로 부러진다. 압박력이 가해지는 쪽은 그림 4b와 같이 주골절선에 어긋나는 경우가 많고 제3 골편(나비형 골편)이 생기기도 한다[1].

따라서, p3의 X-ray는 이러한 **굴곡력에 의한 사골절**이다. 오른쪽 다리를 축으로 왼쪽 다리로 가드레일을 넘으려다 경사면 때문에 왼쪽 다리가 지면에 닿지 못하고 왼쪽으로 쓰러지며(그림 4) 딛고 있던 우측 대퇴골에 내측으로 굴곡력이 작용하여 골절된 것이다.

그림 2 오이 실험 ❶ (비틀기)

먼저 세로로 균열이 발생하고(➡) 그곳에서 골절이 시작되어 나선골절이 된다.

그림 4 오이 실험 ❷ (굴곡)

위쪽은 횡골절이, 아래쪽은 사골절이 된다.

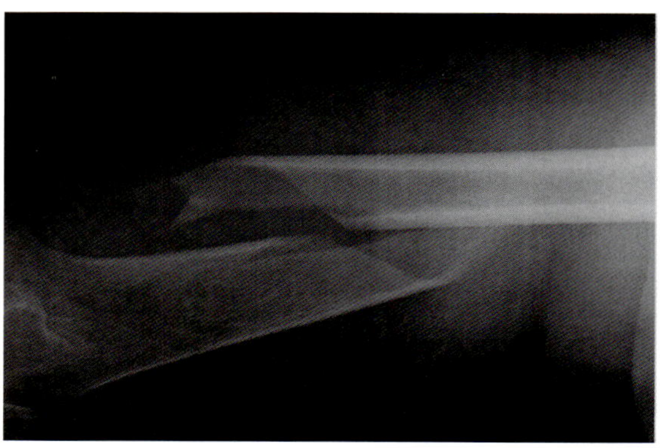

그림 3 나선골절(대퇴골)

청소를 하다 상체를 비틀면서 넘어졌다.

그림 5 앞 페이지 증례의 수상 기전

축압이 가해지면

사골절만은 오이로 실험할 수 없다. 사골절은 축 방향의 압박력이 가해져 발생한다. 오이는 뼈보다 강도가 약하기 때문에 세로로 바닥에 부딪히면 부서진다.

그림 6은 33세 · 남성으로 거푸집 목수인데 한쪽 무릎을 세우고 작업 중 크레인에 매달린 베니어판 30장이 등 뒤로 쓰러져 가슴이 무릎에 닿으며 하퇴골에 축압이 가해져 사골절이 발생한 것이다. 즉, 사골절은 축압에 의해 발생한다.

족관절 골절의 기전

이제까지의 내용을 '반복 학습'에서 정리하였다. '장력(당기는 힘)이 작용하면 횡골절이 된다'는 것을 알고 있으면, 족관절 골절의 기전도 이해할 수 있다. **그림 7**은 발목 외반(발바닥이 바깥쪽을 향함)에 의한 내과 횡골절과 외과 사골절이다. 내과로 당기는 힘이 가해져 횡골절이 된 것이다.

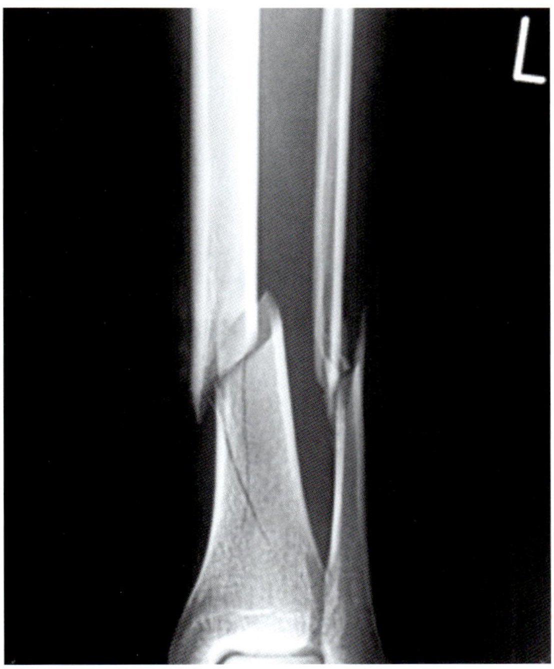

그림 6 축압에 의한 사골절(하퇴골)
33세 · 남성, 거푸집 목수. 한쪽 무릎을 세우고 작업하던 중 등 뒤로 베니어판 30장이 쓰러졌다.

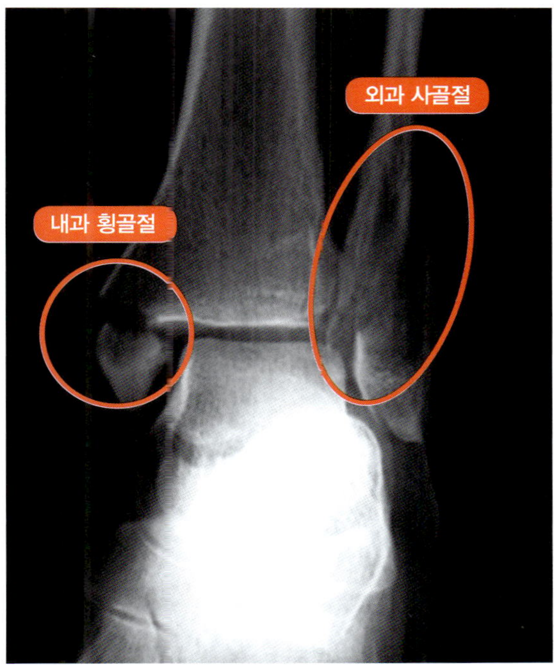

그림 7 발목 외반에 의한 내과 횡골절, 외과 사골절
발목 외반(발바닥이 바깥쪽을 향함)에 의해 내과 횡골절과 외과 사골절이 발생했다.

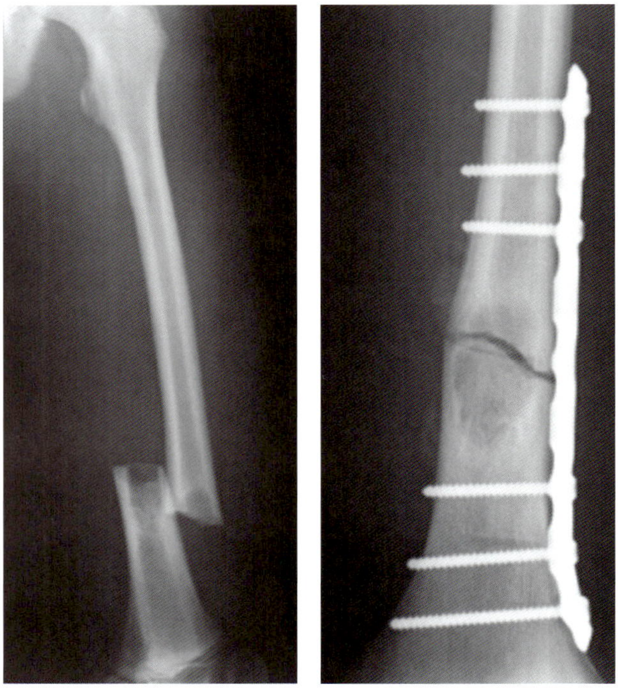

그림 8 **골내 농양에 의한 병적 골절**
골내 농양(Brodie 농양)에 의한 횡골절. 오른쪽은 플레이트 고정 후 사진이다.

또한, 횡골절은 **병적 골절**로도 발생할 수 있다. 그림 8은 대퇴골에 농양(Brodie 농양*)이 있어 횡골절을 일으킨 증례이다. 횡골절이 보인다면 병적 골절일 가능성도 염두에 둔다.

* **Brodie 농양** : 1832년, Brodie[2] 는 장기간 지속되는 다리 통증을 호소하는 환자들의 경골 내에서 주변의 골경화를 동반한 농양을 발견하여 보고하였다. Brodie 농양은 아급성 골수염으로 인해 발생한 골내 농양으로 여겨진다. 매우 서서히 발병하며, 임상 증상이 거의 없다. 국소적인 통증, 압통이나 발적, 종창 등이 발생하는 경우도 많지만, 이러한 증상이나 CRP · WBC 상승 등의 감염증을 시사하는 소견을 보이지 않는 경우도 있다. 특히 10대 남성에 흔하다. 원인균은 *Staphylococcus aureus*가 대부분을 차지하며 병소 소파, 골이식 등을 요한다. 재발은 드물며, 예후는 양호하다.

반복 학습

❶ 뼈 옆에서 물체가 충돌하면 **횡골절**이 된다.

❷ 뼈 옆에서 큰 에너지가 작용하면 **분쇄골절**이 된다.

❸ 굴곡력이 작용하면 장력이 작용하는 쪽은 **횡골절**, 압박력이 작용하는 쪽은 **사골절**이 된다. 힘이 강하면 **제3 골편(나비형 골편)**이 생긴다.

❹ 비트는 힘이 작용하면 **나선골절**이 된다.

❺ 축압이 작용하면 **사골절**이 되며, 오이로는 실험할 수 없다.

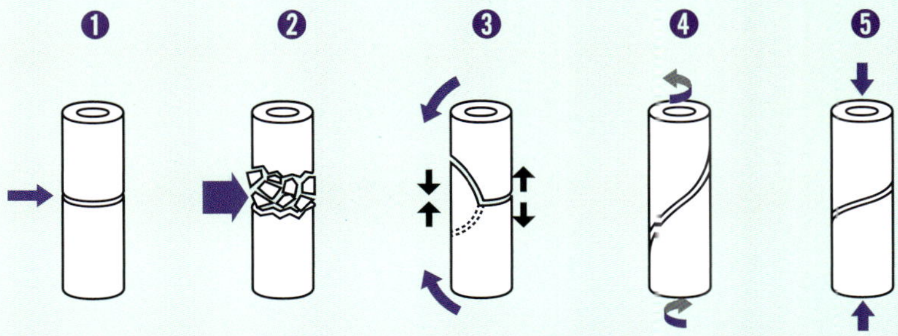

따라서 X-ray로 골절을 보면 어느 방향으로부터 어떤 힘이 가해졌는지 대략 예측할 수 있다. 특히 분쇄골절은 고에너지 외상이므로 전신을 확인할 필요가 있다.

참고문헌

1. Jo MJ, et al : Biomechanics of fractures and fracture fixation. Bucholz RW (ed) : Rockwood and Green's fractures in adults. Lippincott-Raven Publishers, pp3-16, 2014.
2. Brodie BC : An account of some cases of chronic abscess of the tibia. Med Chir Trans 17:239-249, 1832.
3. 仲田和正：手・足・腰診療スキルアップ. シービーアール, 2015.

경추의 신경지배

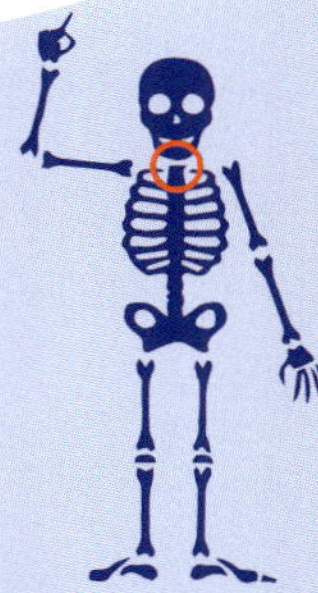

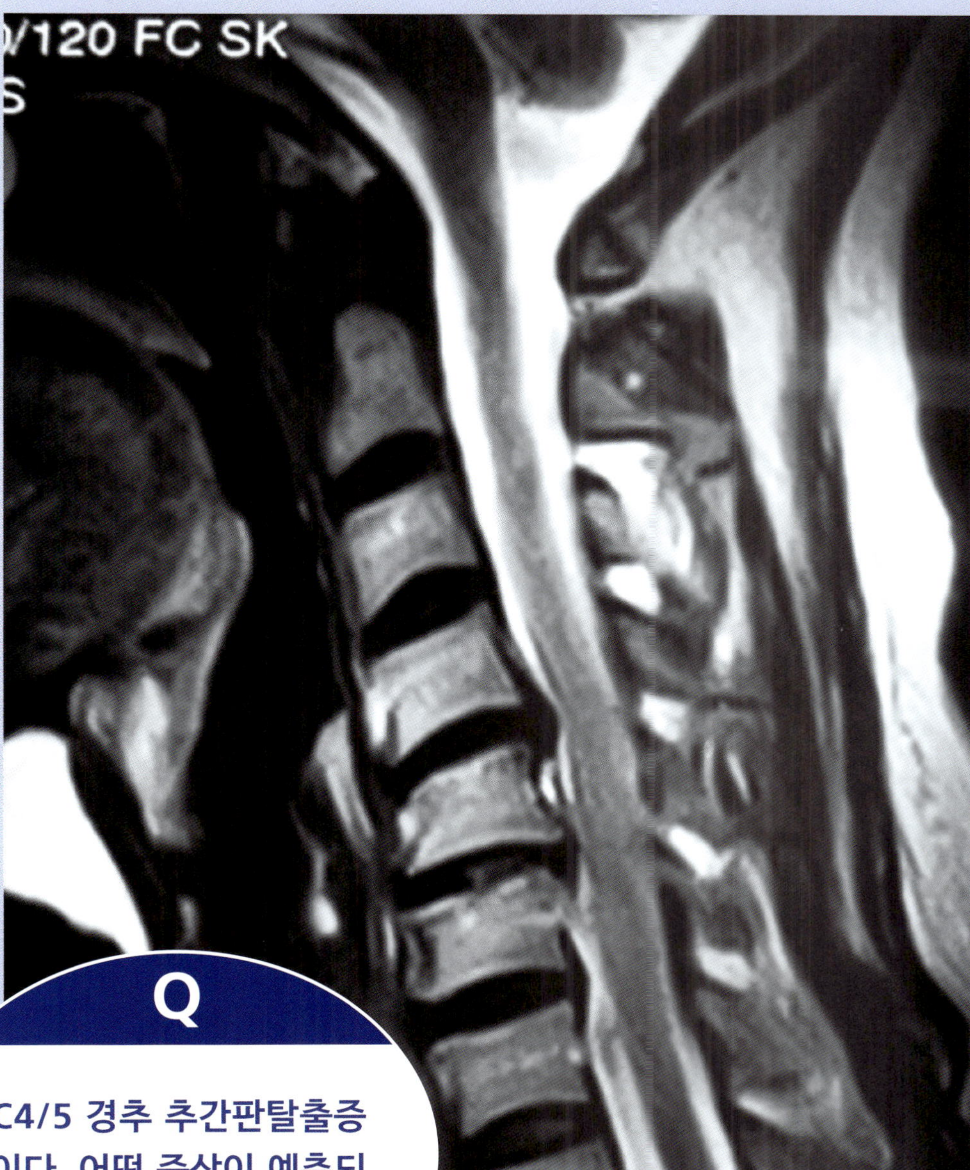

Q

C4/5 경추 추간판탈출증이다. 어떤 증상이 예측되는가?

53세 · 여성

앞 페이지의 경추 MRI 영상에서는 C4/5의 추간판에 돌출이 있다. C4/5 추간판 레벨에서 나오는 신경근은 C5이다. C5 신경근은 C5 추체의 위에서부터 나와 있다. C5 운동신경은 어깨 거상과 팔꿈치 굴곡을 지배한다. 또한, C5와 C6 신경근에서 유래하는 방사통은 승모근에서 견관절에 이르는 부위에 나타난다.

이 환자는 '직접적인 원인 없이 왼쪽 어깨의 거상이 어려워지고 또한, 왼쪽 팔꿈치의 굴곡이 약해져 있으며, 왼쪽 승모근부터 어깨에 걸쳐 나타나는 통증'을 호소하고 있었다.

어느 신경근에 병변이 생기면 어디에 어떤 증상이 나타나는지를 기억해 두면 큰 도움이 된다. 여기에서는 경추의 신경지배를 '체조'로 암기해보자.

'신경' 체조 제1번!

운동신경지배

❶ 몸통에 석 삼(三)자 새기기

'위(흉강)와 아래(복강)를 나누는 **횡격막의 신경지배는 3**'이라고 기억한다(그림 1). 정확히는 C3~C5이다.

❷ 양손 머리 위로! Victory! 사인은 'V'♪

V는 로마 숫자로 5이므로 '**상지 거상(견관절 굴곡)은 C5**'로 기억한다(그림 2).

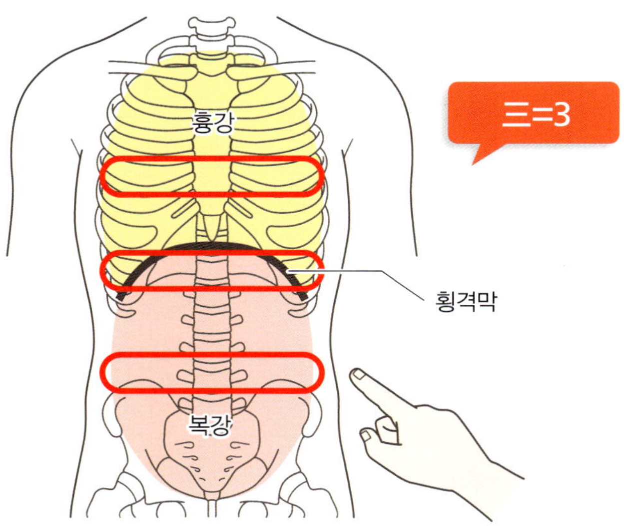

그림 1 횡격막은 C3(~C5) 신경

❸ 다섯 손가락으로 자기 뺨 때리기!

다섯 손가락을 쫙 펴고(5), 팔을 굽혀 힘껏 본인의 뺨을 때리며 '**주관절 굴곡도 C5**'로 기억한다(그림 3). 뺨을 맞은 충격으로 기억한다.

❹ 손목을 젖히며 OK!♪

'**수관절 배굴은 C6**'이다. 손가락으로 OK(6자 모양) 사인을 만들며, 수관절을 배굴시킨다(그림 4).

❺ 고양이 앞발로 '야옹'♪

'**수관절 장굴은 C7**'이다. 손목을 굽혀(7자 모양) 마네키네코처럼 앞으로 흔들며 '야옹'(그림 5). 이것으로 평생 기억해 둘 수 있을 것이다.

❻ '칙칙!' 잽을 날리자!♪

'**주관절 신전도 C7**'이다. 칙(7)! 칙(7)! 하고 팔을 뻗으며 기억한다(그림 6).

❼ 두 손 곱게 모으고 '팔'아보고 있네~♪

'**손가락 굴곡은 C8**'이다. 양손을 맞잡으면 '8'로 보인다(그림 7).

❽ 차표 한 장 손에 끼우고~

'**손가락 벌림/모음은 T1**'이다. 차표 한 장(1)을 손가락 사이에 끼운다고 기억한다(그림 8).

감각신경지배

손가락의 감각신경은 '**무지(엄지)와 검지가 C6**'이다. 이것도 OK(6자 모양) 사인을 손가락으로 만들어 기억한다(그림 9).

중지는 C7, 소지는 C8이다. 즉 '**무지에서 하나씩 건너뛰며** 6→7→8'로 기억한다(그림 10). 이 신경지배는 일정하므로, 진단의 지표로써 중요하다(➡ p23).

또한, 경추 유래의 통증에 대하여 C5 · C6 신경근 유래의 방사통은 '승모근에서 어깨'에 걸쳐 느끼는 경우가 많으며, C7 · C8 신경근 유래의 방사통은 '견갑골 혹은 견갑골 사이'에서 느끼는 경우가 많다(그림 11). 먼저 주먹으로 어깨 위쪽을 톡톡 치며 '5! 6!', 다음으로 주먹을 등 뒤로 돌려 등 위쪽을 두드리며 '7! 8!'이라고 구호를 외치며 기억한다(그림 12).

그림 2 **상지 거상은 C5 신경**
양팔을 V자로 거상, V는 로마 숫자로 '5'.

그림 3 **주관절 굴곡은 C5 신경**
다섯손가락을 쫙 펴고 팔을 굽혀 힘껏 뺨을 때린다(팔꿈치를 굽히며).

그림 4 **수관절 배굴은 C6 신경**
손가락으로 OK(6자 모양) 사인을 만들며 수관절을 배굴. 또한, 무지와 검지의 감각도 C6.

그림 5 **수관절 장굴은 C7 신경**
손목을 굽히며 '야옹(고양이 발, 7자 모양)'.

그림 6 **주관절 신전은 C7 신경**
칙!칙!(7)하며 팔을 뻗는다.

그림 7 **손가락 굴곡은 C8 신경**
두 손을 모으면(옆에서 볼 때) 8자로 보인다.

그림 8 **손가락 벌림/모음은 T1 신경**
손가락 사이에 차표 한 장(1)을 끼운다.

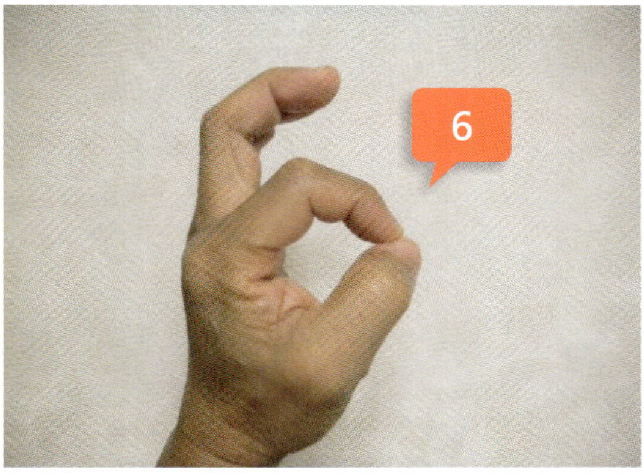

그림 9 무지와 검지의 감각은 C6 신경

OK(6자 모양) 사인으로 기억한다.

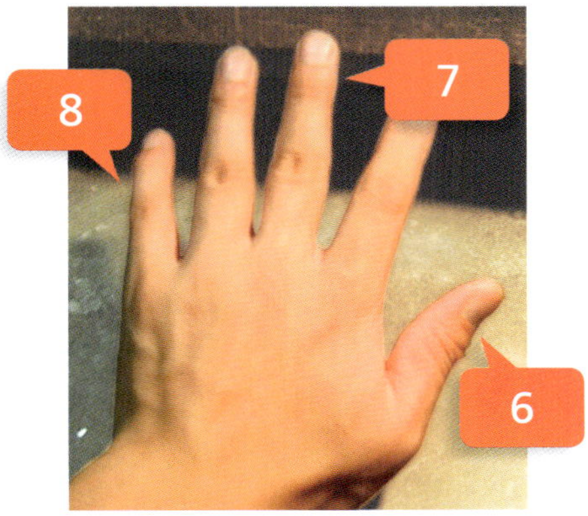

그림 10 무지에서 하나씩 건너뛰며 C6, C7, C8 신경

엄지가 C6, 하나씩 건너뛰며 중지는 C7, 소지는 C8로 기억한다. 이 신경지배는 일정하므로 진단의 지표로써 중요하다!

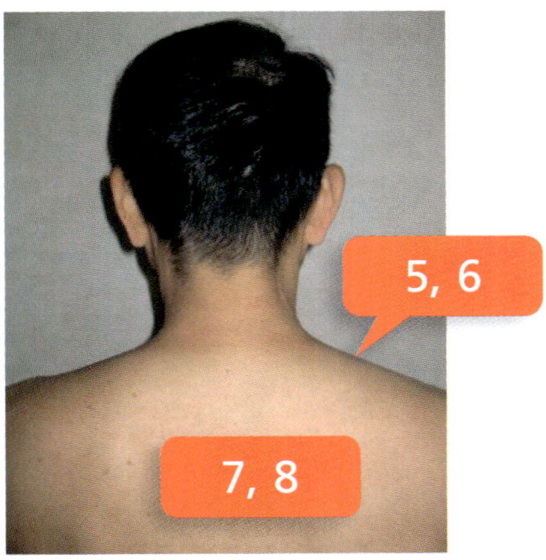

그림 11 방사통의 위치

C5, C6 신경근 유래는 승모근 부근, C7, C8 신경근 유래는 견갑골 혹은 견갑골 사이에서 느껴진다.

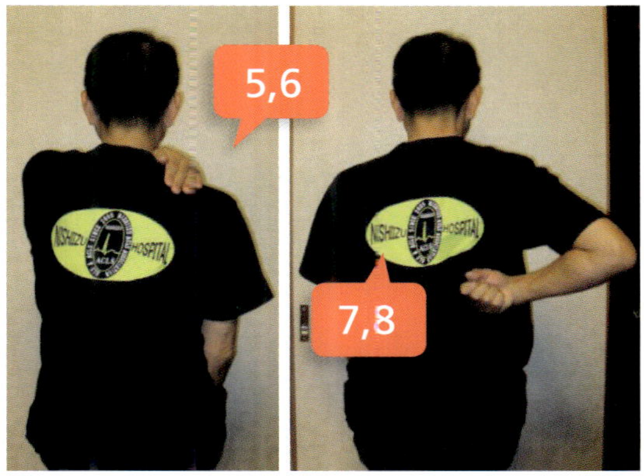

그림 12 승도근 부근은 C5, C6 신경, 견갑골 부근은 C7, C8 신경

어깨 위를 두드리며 '5, 6', 주먹을 등 뒤로 돌리고 '7, 8'.

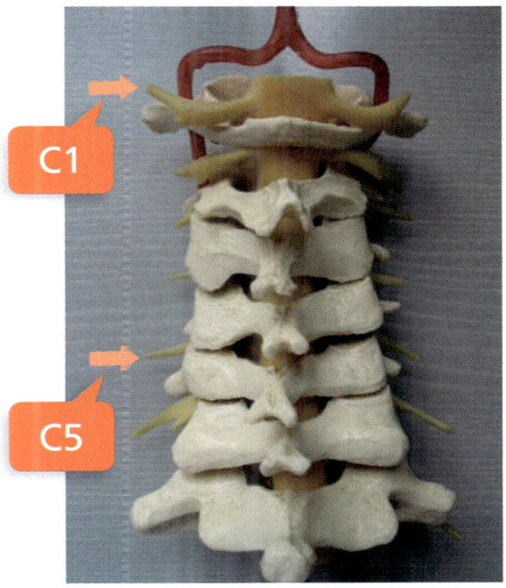

그림 13 경추 신경근은 위로부터, 요추 신경근은 아래로부터

C1 신경근은 C1 추체의 위로부터, C5 신경근은 C5 추체의 위로부터 나온다. 경추신경은 8개, 경추 추체는 7개이므로 흉추와 그 이하 동일 신경근은 추체의 아래로부터 나온다. 예를 들어 L4 신경근은 L4 추체의 아래로부터 나온다. 이것을 '위는 위, 아래는 아래'로 외운다.

'위는 위, 아래는 아래'

앞에서 설명한 대로 경추 신경근은 동일 추체의 위에서 나온다. 그러나 흉추 이하에서는 신경근이 동일 추체의 아래에서 나온다. 이것은 경추 신경근은 8개 있지만, 경추는 7개 밖에 없기 때문이다. 따라서 요추의 L5 신경근은 L5 추체의 아래에서 나온다.

다시 말해, 경추 신경근은 동일 추체의 위에서, 요추 신경근은 동일 추체의 아래에서 나오는 것이다. 이것을 '위는 위, 아래는 아래'로 기억한다(그림 13).

반복 학습

❶ 상지 거상(V)은 C5 신경, 주관절 굴곡도 C5 신경(다섯손가락을 쫙 펴고 팔을 굽혀 자신의 뺨을 때린다).

❷ 손목을 젖히며 손가락으로 OK(수관절 배굴은 C6 신경) 또한, 무지와 검지의 감각은 C6 신경.

❸ 손목을 굽히며 '야옹'(수관절 장굴은 C7 신경).

❹ 칙칙! 팔을 뻗는다(주관절 신전은 C7 신경).

❺ 두 손을 모아 '8'을 만든다(손가락 굴곡은 C8 신경).

❻ 차표 한 장을 손가락에 끼운다(손가락 벌림/모음은 T1 신경).

❼ '위는 위, 아래는 아래'(경추 신경근은 추체의 위로부터, 요추 신경근은 추체의 아래로부터 나온다).

❽ 어깨 위쪽을 두드리며 '5! 6!'(C5 · C6 병변으로 인한 방사통), 등 위쪽을 두드리며 '7! 8!'(C7 · C8 병변으로 인한 방사통).

제2장

근골격 영상의 부위별 판독

경부

흉부 정면상에서도 관찰되는 경추 X-ray 소견

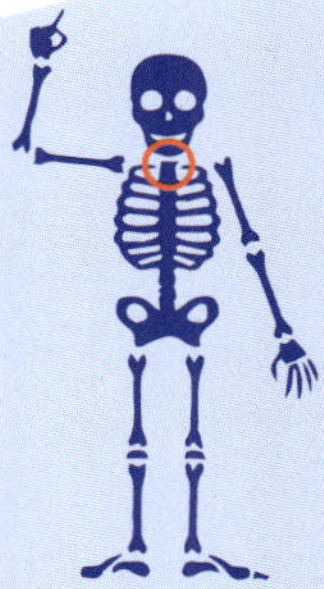

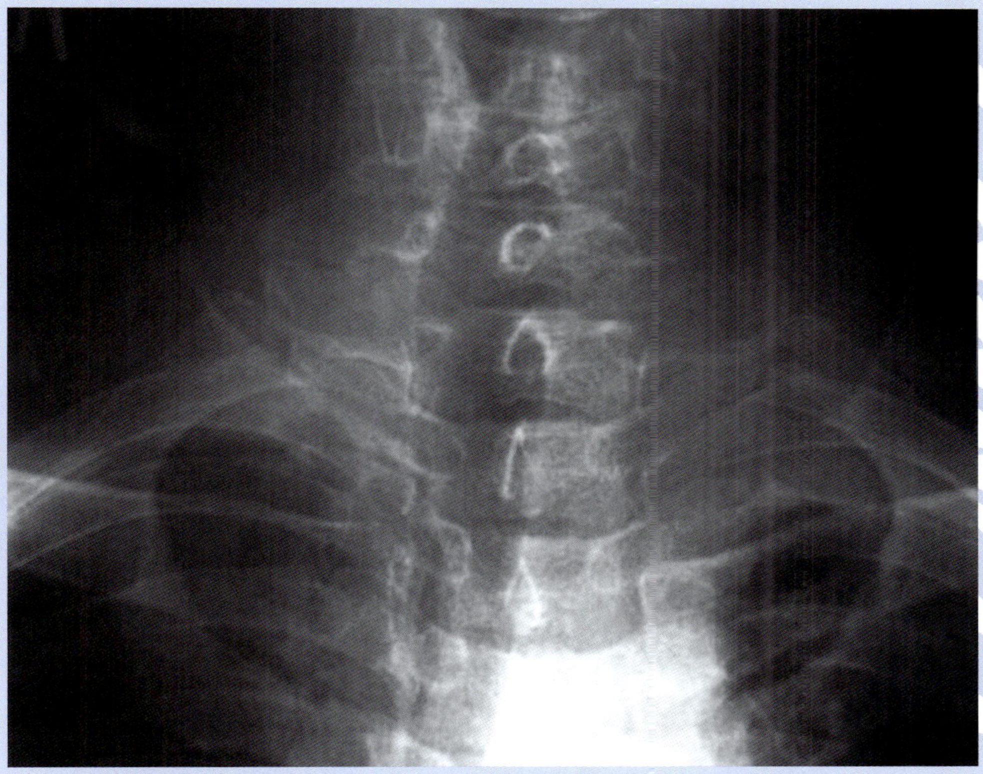

61세 · 남성. 왼쪽 견갑골 안쪽에 욱신거리는 통증과 왼쪽 중지 · 약지 · 소지에 저림 증상이 나타난다.

Q

이 경추 X-ray의 이상 소견은?

앞 페이지의 X-ray 사진은 왼손 저림을 호소하며 내과 외래 진료를 받은 환자의 경추 정면상이다.

Case

환자 : 61세, 남성.

주요 증상 : X년 3월부터 왼쪽 견갑골 안쪽에 욱신거리는 통증(✐ C7 · C8의 방사통을 의심). 초진 시(4월 말)에는 통증 증가, 야간 불면(✐ 안정 시 야간 통증은 염증이나 악성 종양을 의심), 왼쪽 중지 · 약지 · 소지의 저림(✐ 왼쪽 C7 · C8 병변)을 호소하였다.

신체 소견 : 왼쪽 주관절 신전 4/5(C7), 왼쪽 수관절 장굴 4/5(C7). 악력(C8)은 오른쪽 47kg, 왼쪽 8kg으로 왼쪽에서 근력이 크게 저하되었다.

위와 같은 소견으로 'C7, C8 모두에 병변이 있으며, 악력이 저하되어 있으므로 C8 병변으로 인한 장애가 더 크다' 고 판단하였다

병변 부위와 증상의 차이가 진단의 관건

그러나 경추 MRI 측면상을 확인하면, C5/6과 C6/7의 추간판이 살짝 돌출해 있을 뿐이었다. 이것으로는 C6 · C7 신경근의 병변이라고 설명이 되지 않는다.

이상하게 생각되어 경추 정면상을 다시 검토한 결과, 기관의 오른쪽으로의 편위와 좌폐첨의 apical cap이 증가한 것을 발견하였다. CT를 촬영한 결과, **좌폐첨의 Pancoast 종양**임이 밝혀졌다. 경추 X-ray를 촬영하면 촬영된 범위의 흉부도 꼭 확인하도록 한다.

본 증례와는 반대로 흉부 X-ray 정면상에는 경추 하방도 찍혀 있다. 내과 선생님들이 가장 자주 접하게 될 흉부 정면상에서 경추도 함께 평가하면 진단에 도움이 된다.

Pancoast 종양의 소견

앞(→p19) 페이지의 증례는 좌폐첨의 Pancoast 종양이었다. 기관의 오른쪽 편위와 왼쪽 제2 늑골 아래쪽의 폐첨에 연부 음영이 있으며, apical cap의 증대를 보인다(우폐첨과 비교해 본다). 또한, 흉부 CT 영상에서는 좌폐첨에 추체 파괴와 추체에 접한 종양이 확인된다(그림 1).

Pancoast 종양은 폐첨부터 상완신경총을 상부에서 침윤해 가드로 소지부터 저림이 나타나기 시작한다. 소지의 저림 증상을 보인다면 Pancoast 종양의 가능성을 염두에 둔다. 또한, 경추 정면상에서는 폐첨을 반드시 확인한다.

Abnormal apical cap

Apical cap은 폐첨의 가장자리를 따라 나타나는 임상적인 의미가 없는 음영이다. 제1 늑골하연에서 5mm 이내의 음영으로 종종 물결 모양(curved density)을 보이며, 인구의 10%에서 나타난다. 흉막하 폐의 비특이적 섬유성 반흔이다[1]. 단, 하연이 물결 모양이 아니거나(비대칭적이거나) 5mm 이상으로 두꺼워져 있으면 이상 소견이다.

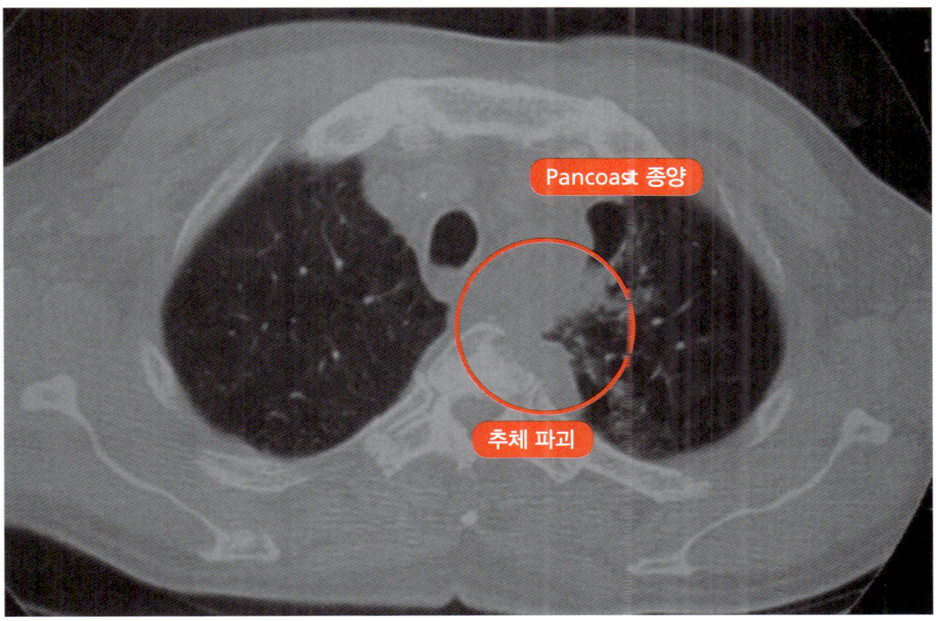

그림 1 흉부 CT 영상

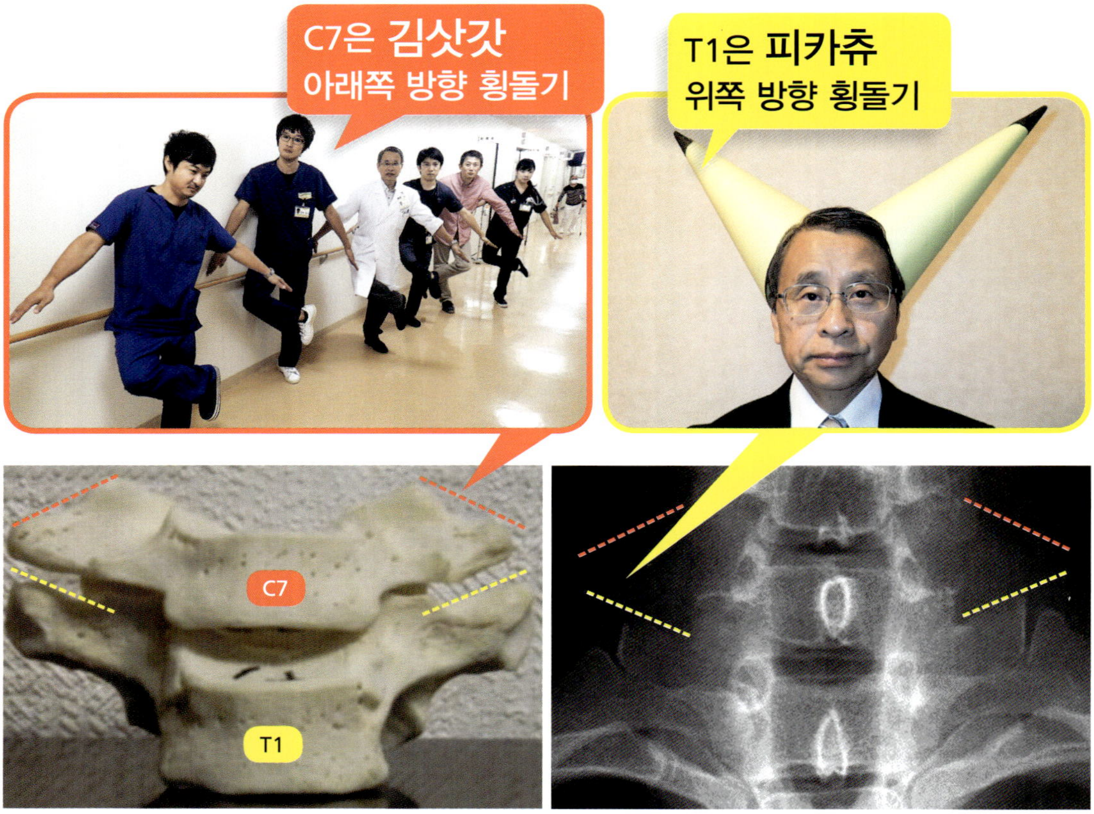

그림 2 횡돌기의 방향으로 경추(C7)/흉추(T1)를 판별한다.

흉부 X-ray에서 보이는 경추

경추의 하방은 흉부 X-ray 정면상에서도 보이며 경추도 확인해두면 일석이조!

횡돌기의 방향으로 경추(C7)와 흉추(T1)를 판별

경추인지, 흉추인지는 **횡돌기**의 방향으로 판단한다. C7의 횡돌기는 아래쪽 방향이며, T1은 위쪽 방향이다(그림 2). 보통은 T1부터 늑골이 나오나, 아래쪽 방향 횡돌기로부터 늑골이 나와있으면 **경늑골**(cervical rib)*이라고 판단한다(그림 3). 경늑골에 상완신경총이 압박되어 상지에 저림이 나타나는 경우가 있다.

***경늑골** : 제7 경추(C7, 드물게 C6 · C5에도)에 발생하는 늑골의 기형. 양측성으로 나타나는 경우가 많음.

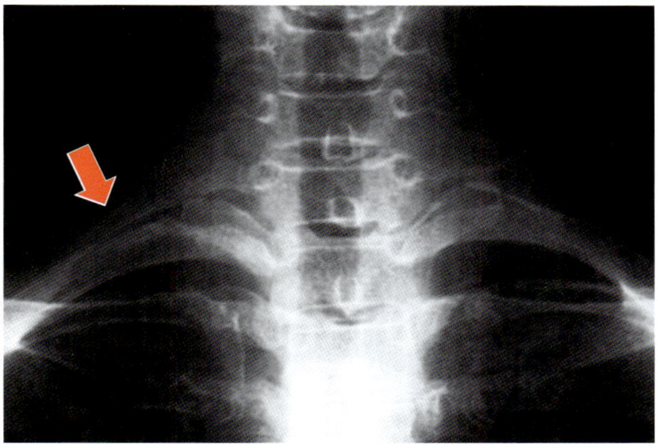

그림 3 경늑골(cervical rib)
아래쪽 방향의 경추 횡돌기로부터 늑골이 나와있으므로 이 늑골은 경늑골이다.

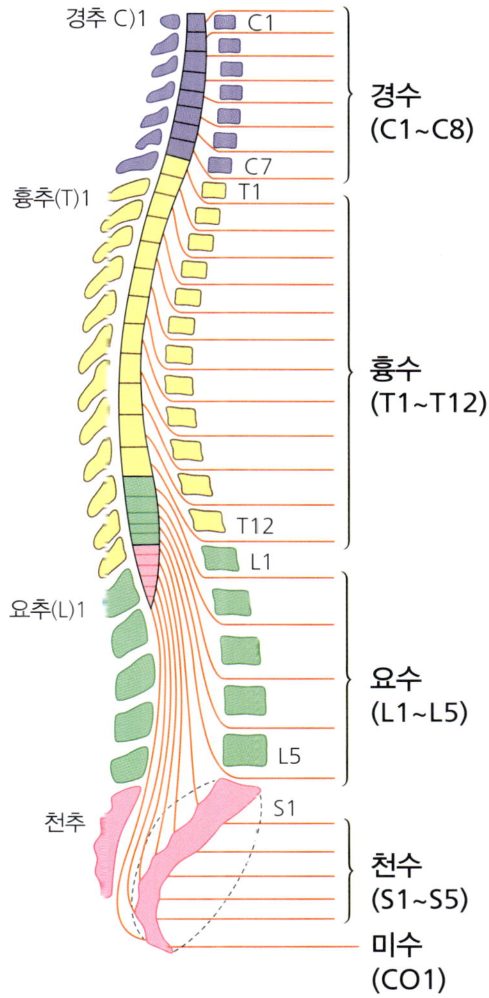

그림 4 추체와 신경근의 관계

손가락의 저림과 경추의 이상 부위

T1 추체의 위에는 C8 신경근이 나온다. C7 추체의 위에서는 C7 신경근, C6 추체의 위에서는 C6 신경근, 즉, 경추 추체 위에서 동일 신경근이 나오는 것이다(**그림 4**).

OK 사인으로 기억하기!

왼손으로 OK 사인을 만들면 '6'으로 보인다. 엄지와 검지의 감각은 C6 신경근이 지배한다. 엄지로부터 하나씩 건너뛰어 중지는 C7 신경근, 소지는 C8 신경근의 감각지배 영역이다.(➡ p13). 따라서 어느 손가락에 저림이 있는지는 경추의 이상 부위를 진단하는 지표로써 중요하다.

Luschka 관절의 골극과 저림

경추 정면상에서 체크해야 할 것은 추체 측방의 **Luschka 관절**(unconvertebral joint)이다(그림 5). 만약 여기에 골극이 있고, 외측 방향으로 돌출되어 있다면(그림 6) 추간공이 협착될 것이다.

추간공은 사위상(oblique view)으로 본다(그림 7). 예를 들어 무지에 저림이 있다면 C6 추체 위에서 나와있는 C6 신경근의 감각에 의한 것이므로(OK 사인), C6 추체의 Luschka 관절 골극 유무를 확인한다. C6 추체의 Luschka 관절 골극은 C5/6 추간공으로 돌출되어 C6 신경근을 압박한다.

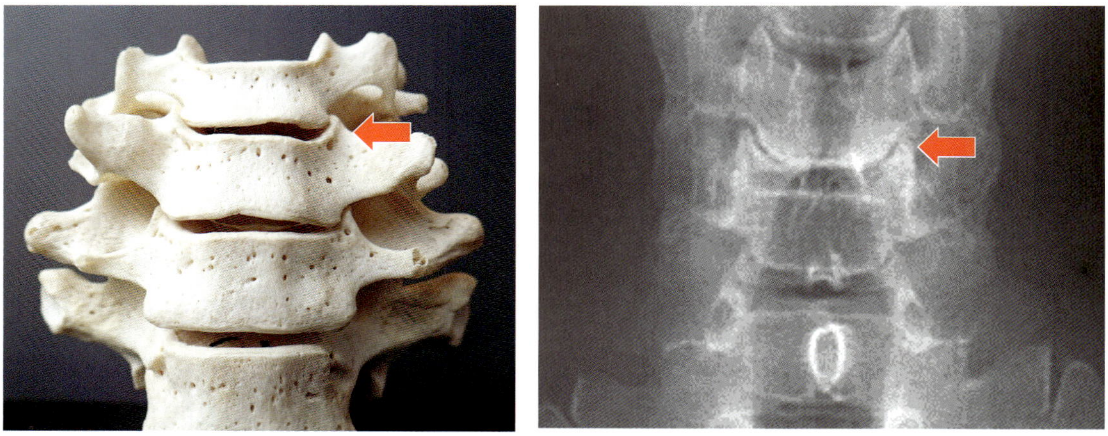

그림 5 Luschka 관절
경추 정면상에서는 Luschka 관절을 꼭 확인! 골극이 있다면 추간공 협착이 있을 것이다.

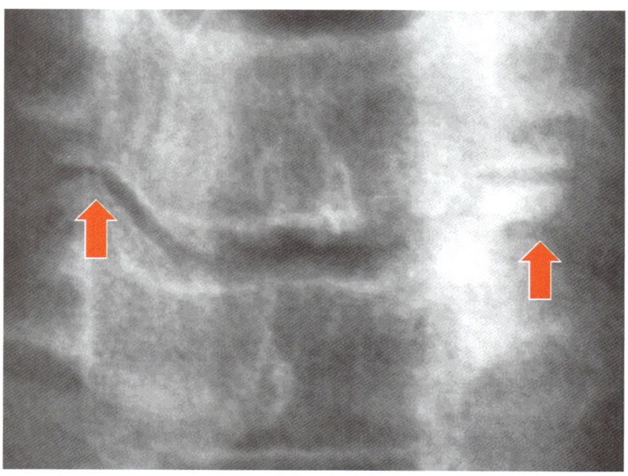

그림 6 Luschka 관절의 골극

경추 정면상의 극돌기

두갈래인가 한갈래인가

극돌기는 C5보다 위는 두갈래, C6은 두갈래 혹은 한갈래, C7은 대부분 한갈래이다(**그림 8**). 경추 X-ray 정면상으로 보면 C7 극돌기는 뚜렷한 타원형으로 보이지만(**그림 9**), 그보다 위에 있는 극돌기는 두갈래로 갈라지기 때문에 판별하기가 쉽지 않다. C6이나 C5보다 위가 두갈래인 것을 알고 있다면 몇 번 경추인지 판별할 수 있다.

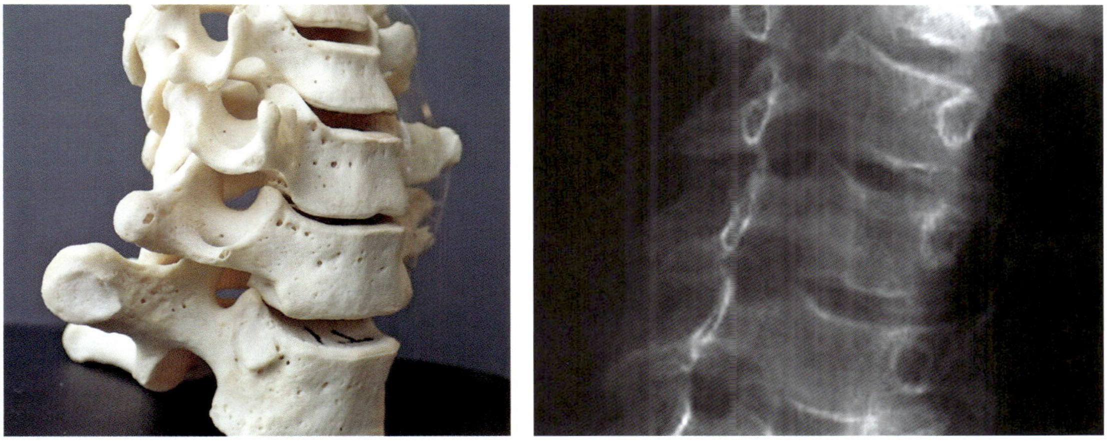

그림 7 **경추의 사위상(oblique view)**
추간공은 사위상에서 잘 관찰된다. Luschka 관절의 골극도 사위상에서 판단한다.

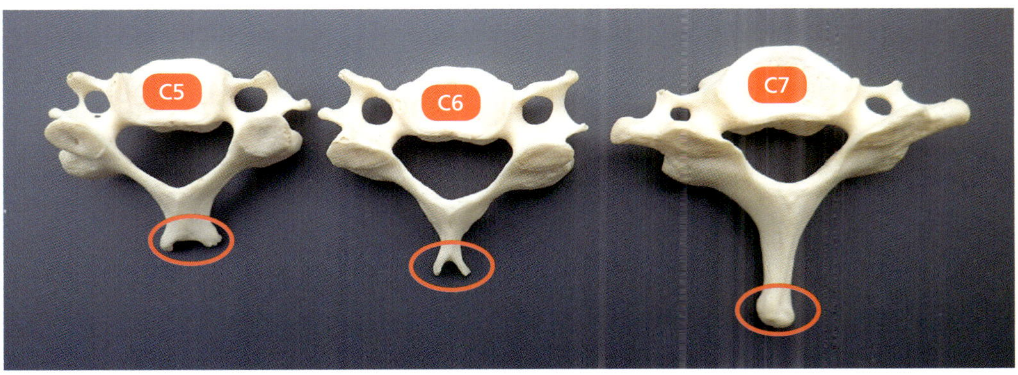

그림 8 **경추 극돌기의 모양**
C5보다 위는 두갈래, C6은 두갈래 또는 한갈래, C7은 대부분 한갈래이다.

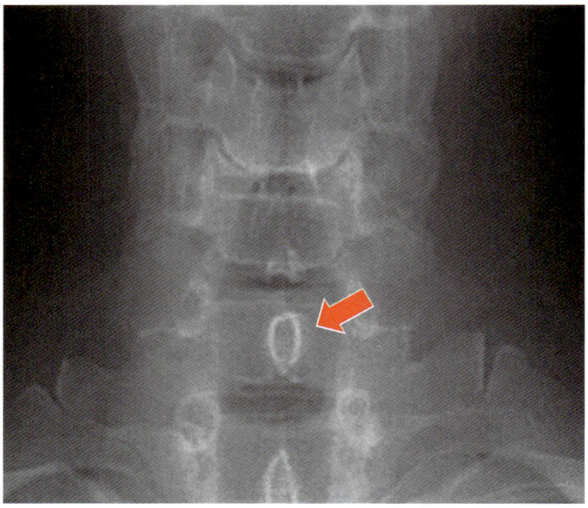

그림 9 **극돌기(spinous process)**
중심의 극돌기 모양에 주목! C7은 타원형으로 하나, C6 이상은 두갈래로 뚜렷이 보이지 않는다.

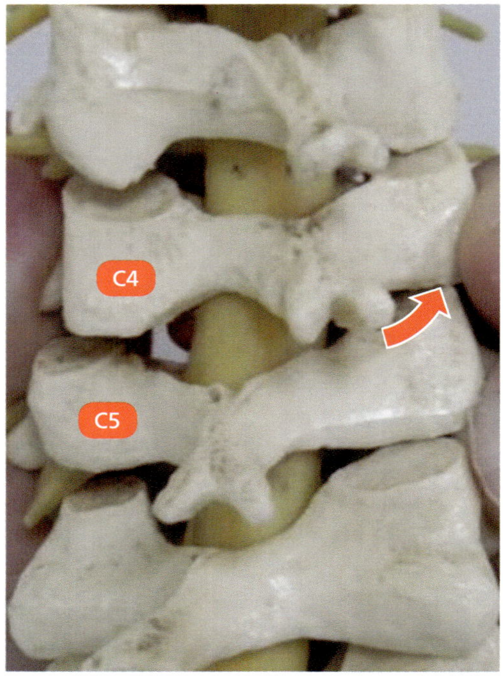

그림 10 **편측 탈구 (unilateral facet dislocation)**
C4/5 추간관절에서 편측 탈구하면 C4보다 위에 있는 극돌기가 옆으로 어긋난다.

일직선상에 있는가

경추 극돌기를 볼 때는 전체 극돌기가 일직선상에서 세로로 나열된 것을 확인한다. 만약 **탈구**가 있다면 옆으로 어긋난다(**그림 10**). 경추 외상은 전체 극돌기가 세로로 일직선상에 나열되어 있는지를 확인한다.

탈구가 있다면 경추 보조기를 착용하고 백보드에 고정 후 대학병원이나 3차병원 응급실로 이송한다.

*흉부 X-ray 정면상에서 가장 놓치기 쉬운 것은 횡경막 뒤와 심장 뒤쪽의 병변이다. 또한, 흉부 X-ray 정면상에서는 견관절도 보인다는 사실을 명심한다. 견관절의 극심한 변화를 흉부 X-ray로 알게 되는 경우도 많다. 상완골두와 견봉의 간격이 좁다면 회전근개 파열(rotator cuff tear)을 의심할 수 있다(➡ p58).

반복 학습

❶ 흉부 X-ray 정면상*에서 폐첨의 **apical cap 증대, 늑골 파괴** 소견에 주의.

❷ 경추 혹은 흉추는 횡돌기로 판단. **아래쪽 방향이 C7**(경추), **위쪽 방향이 T1**(흉추).

❸ 양쪽 팔에 저림이 있다면 **Luschka 관절의 골극** 유무를 확인. 있다면 추간공이 협소할 것이다.

❹ 무지(엄지)의 지각은 **C6** 신경근('OK 사인'으로 암기). 무지에서 하나씩 건너뛰며 중지는 **C7**, 소지는 **C8** 신경근.

❺ 무지의 저림은 C6 경추의 Luschka 관절의 골극을 확인한다. 중지의 저림은 C7, 소지의 저림은 C8 경추의 Luschka 관절을 확인한다.

❻ **극돌기**는 대부분 C6 이상은 두갈래, C7은 한갈래이다.

❼ 극돌기가 그 아래의 추체보다 옆으로 어긋나 있다면 **편측 탈구**

참고문헌

1. 大場覚：胸部X線写真の読み方，第2版．中外医学社，2001．

Q1 47세 · 여성. 목 통증을 호소하여 내원. 진단은?

초진 시

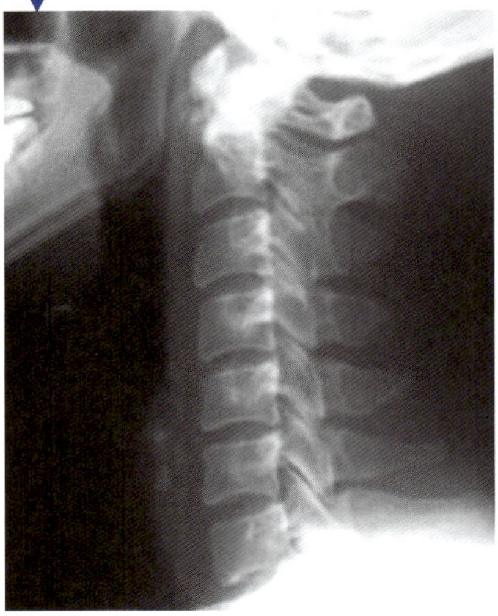

일주일 후

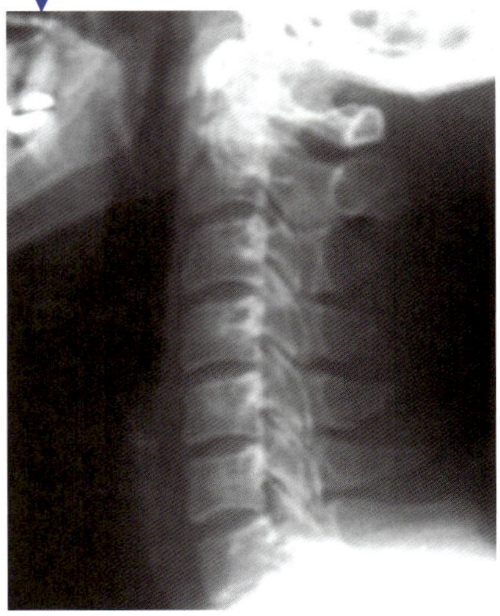

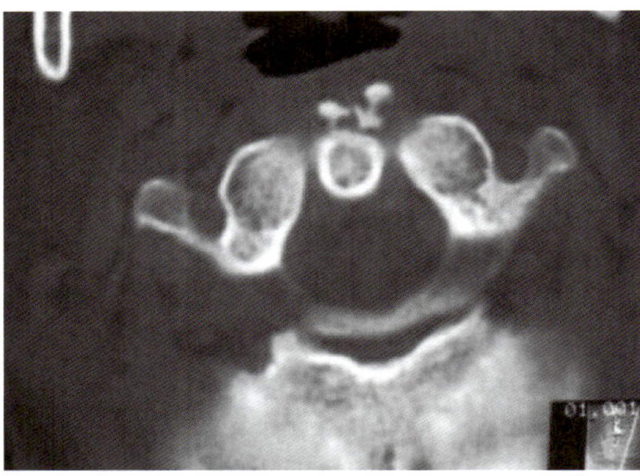

초진 시

해답은 p142

손 · 손가락

수부 X-ray에서 확인할 사항

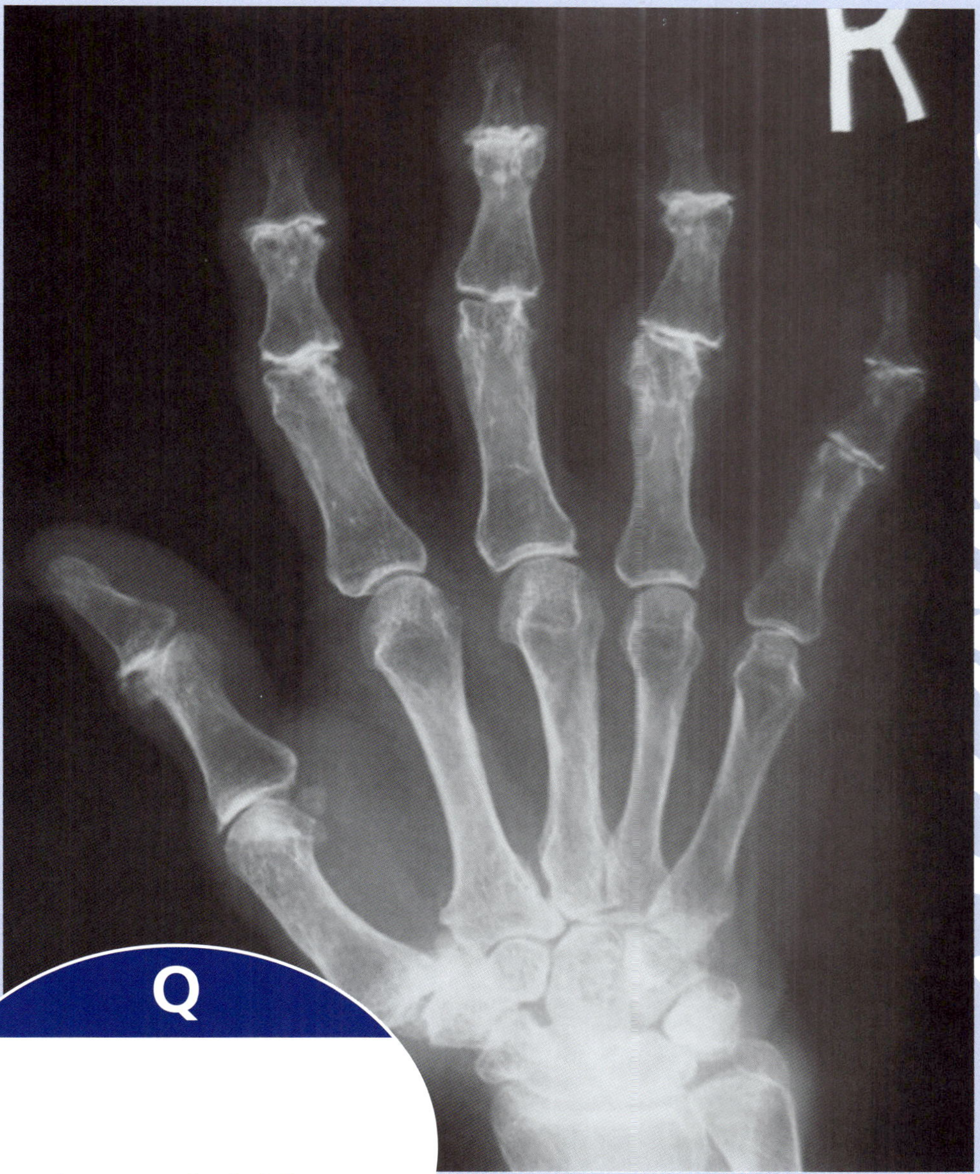

Q

이 X-ray의 진단은?

80세 · 여성. 농사.
과거에 숯을 만들고 소를 방목하였다. 현재 손의 통증은 경미하다.

여기에서는 손의 X-ray에 대해 공부해 보자. 특히 의원급에서 유용한 포인트를 정리하였다.

앞 페이지의 질문에 대한 답은 손의 **변형성 관절증**(osteoarthritis: OA)이다. 손의 OA에는 호발 부위가 있다. 이것을 알아두면 류마티스관절염(rheumatoid arthritis: RA)과의 감별 진단에 도움이 된다.

손의 변형성 관절증(OA, 퇴행성 관절증)

호발 부위는 DIP · PIP · 무지 CM!

앞 페이지의 X-ray에서는 ❶ **DIP관절**(distal interphalangeal joint. 말초에서 첫 번째 관절. 원위지절간관절), ❷ **PIP관절**(proximal interphalangeal joint. 말초에서 두 번째 관절. 근위지절간관절), ❸ **무지CM관절**(carpometacarpal joint. 무지 말초에서 세 번째 관절. 수근중수관절)에 관절 간격의 협소화와 변형이 있다. 손의 OA 호발 부위는 이 세 군데이다(그림 1). 육안 소견은 그림 2와 같다.

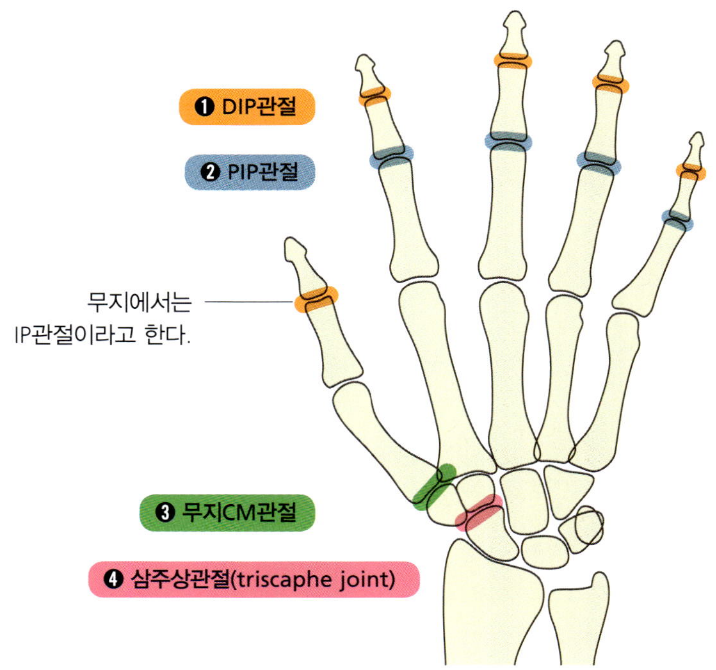

그림 1 손의 변형성(퇴행성) 관절증의 호발 부위

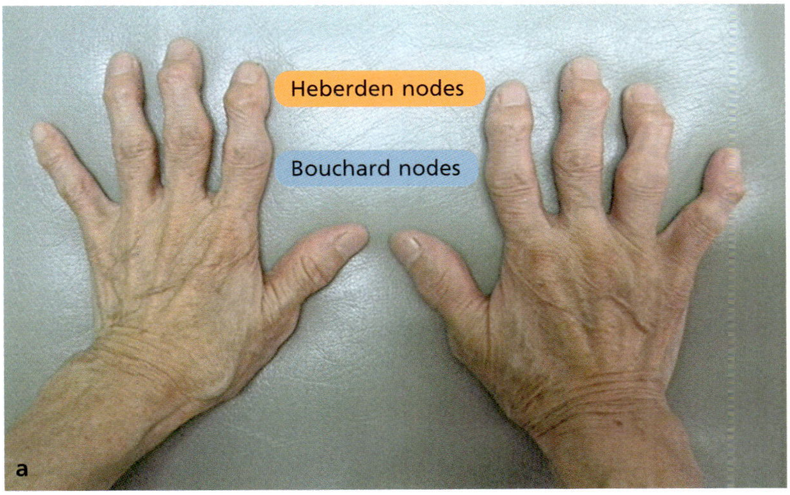

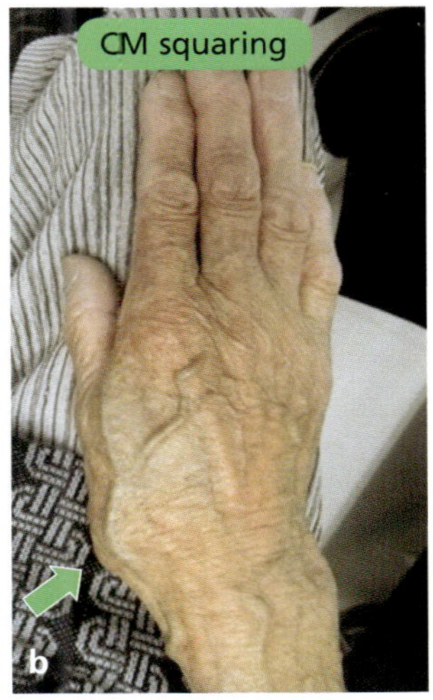

그림 2 손의 변형성 관절증의 시진

a : DIP가 부어 있다면 Heberden 결절, PIP가 부어 있다면 Bouchard 결절('부샤르'라고 발음).
b : 무지CM관절의 변화가 진행되면 위 그림과 같이 튀어나와 CM squaring이라고 한다.

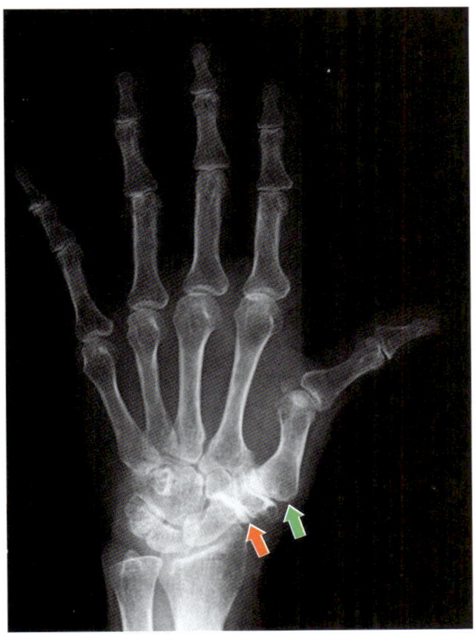

그림 3 삼주상관절의 변화를 수반하는 손의 변형성 관절증

무지CM관절(➡)과 삼주상관절(➡)의 변화에 주목!

수근골의 변화는 많지 않으나, 이전(➡ p29)의 증례와 같이 무지CM관절 부위의 ❹ **삼주상관절**에도 변화를 일으킬 수 있다(**그림 3**). 손의 OA는 대부분 이 네 부위에서 발생한다.

MP관절에는 변화가 없음!

OA에서는 MP관절(metacarpophalangeal joint. 제2~4지의 말초로부터 세 번째 관절. 중수지절관절)에는 변화가 없는 것에 주의한다(이전의 X-ray에서도 MP관절에는 변화가 없는 것을 확인한다). 이는 RA와의 큰 감별점이 된다. MP관절에 변화가 있는 경우, RA나 **가성통풍**[피로인산칼슘(CPP) 결정침착증]을 의심한다.

또한, 만약 RC관절(radiocarpal joint. 요골수근관절)에 국한된 변화가 있는 경우에는 역시 **가성통풍**(pseudogout)을 생각할 수 있다. RC관절의 단독 변화는 가성통풍에 특이적이기 때문이다(그림 4). OA의 경우, RC관절은 보통 침범하지 않는다. CM관절의 OA로 통증이 심할 때는 보조기를 제작하는 경우도 있다.

손의 류마티스관절염(RA)

호발 부위는 PIP · MP · 수근골 전체!

손의 RA는 특히 ❶ **PIP관절**, ❷ **MP관절**, ❸ **수근골 전체**의 변화가 많다(그림 5). DIP관절의 변

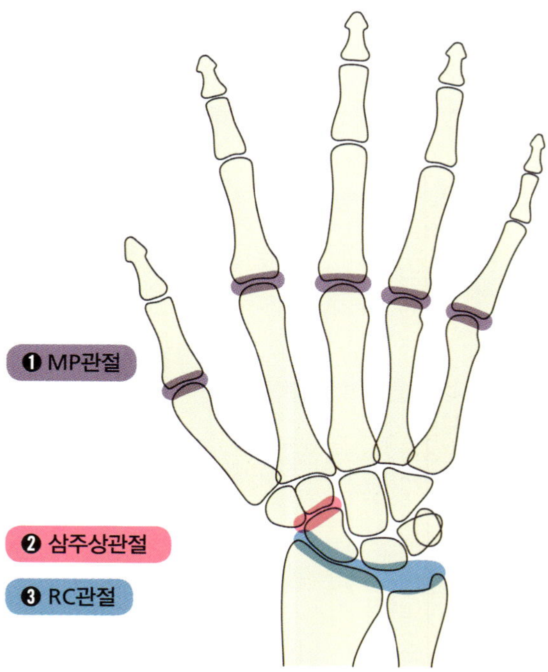

그림 4 손의 가성통풍 호발 부위

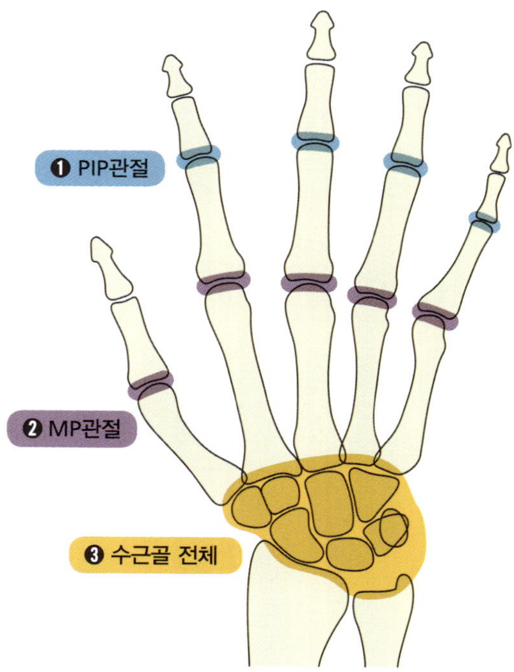

그림 5 손의 류마티스관절염 호발 부위

화는 RA에서는 적으나, 전혀 없는 것은 아니다(그림 6).

류마티스관절염 환자의 90% 이상에서 수근관절이 침범된다. RC관절, CM관절, 중수근관절(mid-carpal joint)을 모두 침범할 수 있으며, 병변이 진행되면 관절의 심각한 파괴 및 변형을 야기한다.(그림 7).

골파괴(osteoclasia)의 조기 발견을 위해서는

RA에서는 활막에 의한 골파괴가 일어난다. 손가락 관절에서는 그림 8과 같이 최초 연골에는 활막에 의한 파괴에 저항성이 있으며, 연골로 덮여 있지 않은 주변의 뼈 부분부터 파괴가 시작된다. 이를 **골미란**(marginal erosion)이라고 한다.

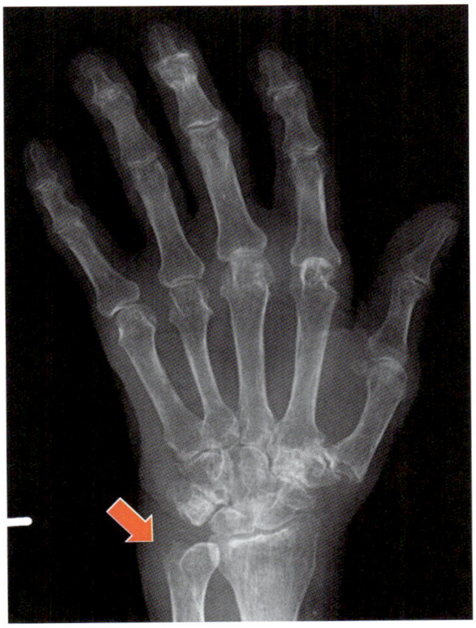

그림 6 손의 류마티스관절염

MP관절, 제1 · 2 중수골, 수근골 관절의 변화가 강하다. 척골 경상돌기의 골미란(➡)에 주의(호발 부위). 이 환자는 류마티스관절염이지만, DIP 관절에도 변화가 있다.

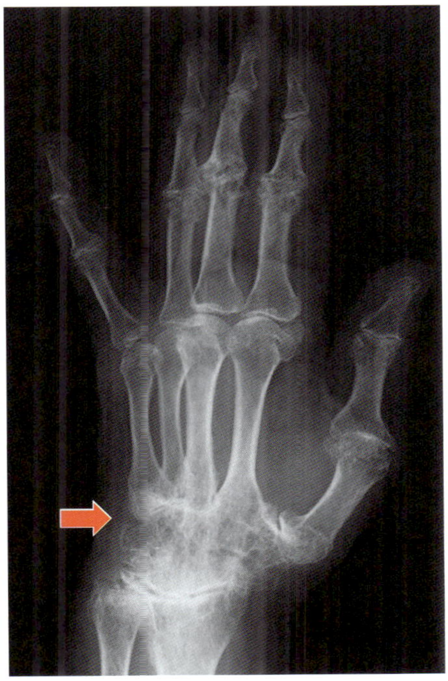

그림 7 수근골의 골강직

진행된 류마티스관절염에서 수근골의 유합이 관찰될 수 있다.

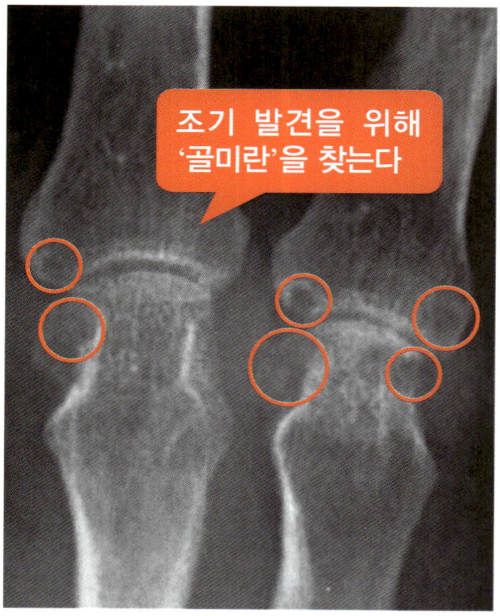

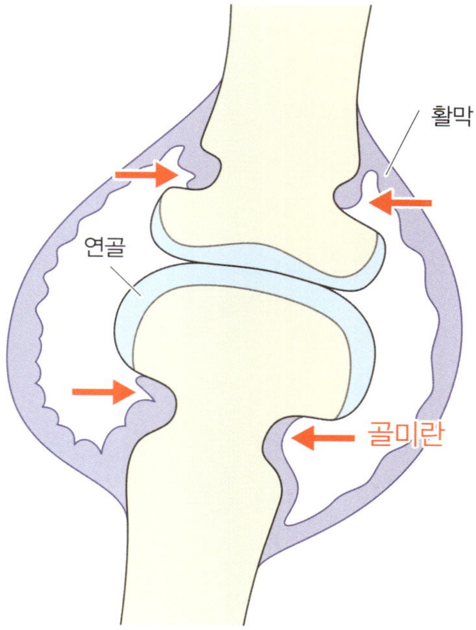

그림 8 **골미란**

류마티스관절염에 의한 골파괴는 주변의 연골이 없는 부분으로부터 시작하여 중심으로 향한다. 주변의 골파괴를 골미란(marginal erosion)이라고 한다.

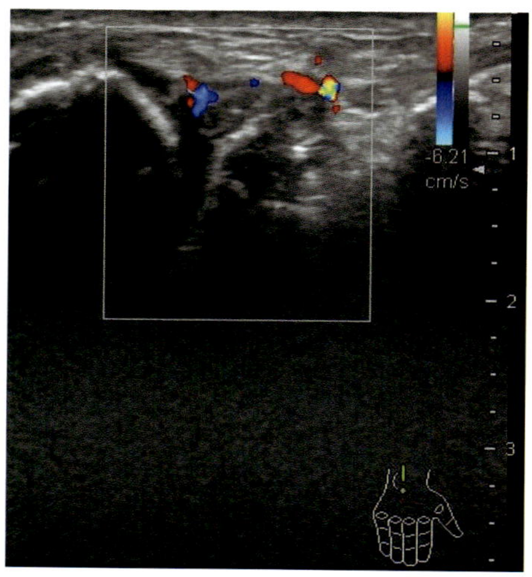

그림 9 **손의 류마티스관절염 초음파 소견 (컬러도플러검사)**

류마티스관절염에서는 활막 증식(검은색으로 보임)과 혈류 증가가 보인다.

일단 관절 주변이 파괴되면, 여기서부터 관절의 중심 쪽을 향해 뼈와 연골이 파괴된다. 그러므로 초기에 RA로 인한 골파괴를 발견하기 위해서는 관절 주변의 골기란을 찾는다.

다만 X-ray에서 골변화가 나타나는 데에는 연 단위의 시간이 걸린다. RA의 조기 변화 발견에는 컬러도플러검사(초음파)를 이용한 활막 증식 · 혈류 증가 검출이 유용하다(그림 9). 통증이 있고 부어 있는 부분에 초음파 검사를 시행해 본다.

최근에는 생물학적 제제의 발전으로 RA의 중증례도 감소하고 있다. 또한, 이전에는 산업 재해에 의한 손의 외상이 매우 많았지만 최근에는 위험한 작업은 기계로 교체되면서 환자가 급격히 줄어들었다. 무척 기쁜 일이지만, 한편으로 수부외과 술기의 계승은 점점 어려워지고 있다.

달인의 메모

그림 10은 **제5 중수골 단독의 단축**이다. 가족성 1형 당뇨병으로 이런 경우가 있다고 한다[1]. 주먹을 쥐어도 제5 중수골두의 돌출(knuckle)이 없다.

'핑퐁은 가르치기 어렵다'

가끔씩 제4 · 5지의 두 중수골이 단축되는 경우가 있다. 이런 경우, 주먹을 쥐면 제2 · 3 중수골두는 돌출되어 있으나(knuckle), 제4 · 5 중수골두는 돌출되지 않으며(dimple: 보조개) 이를 knuckle-knuckle-dimple-dimple sign이라고 한다.

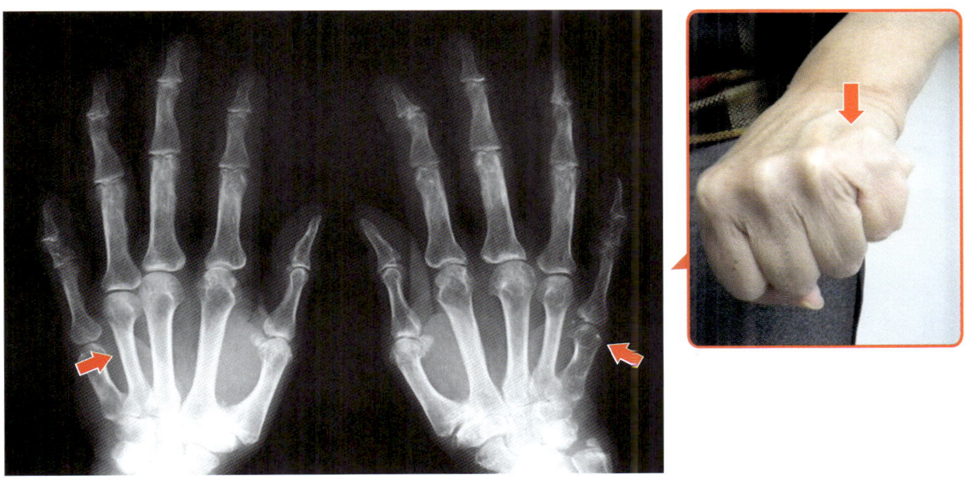

그림 10 가족성 1형 당뇨병에서 제5 중수골의 단축
주먹을 쥐어도 제5 중수골두의 돌출(knuckle)이 없다.

정상에서는 제4 · 5 중수골두 선단(앞쪽 끝)에 선을 긋고, 연장시키면 제3 중수골두 선단에 접한다. 이 선이 중수골두를 가로지르는 경우를 **중수골 징후**(metacarpal sign)라고 하며, 여러 질환에서 나타난다. 감별할 진단의 암기법으로는 'Ping Pong Is Tough To Teach(핑퐁은 가르치기 어렵다)'이다[2]. 즉, pseudo-hypoparathyroidism(가성부갑상선기능저하증), pseudopseudo-hypoparathyroidism(가성가성부갑상선기능저하증), idiopathic(특발성 질환), trauma(외상), Turner's syndrome(터너증후군), trisomy 13/18(13/18번 염색체 이상)이다.

예전에 본원을 방문한 인턴 선생이 대학 시절, 내분비학 수업 중 교수에게 이 얘기를 듣자 바로 뒷자리의 학생이 '앗 내 손이 그렇네!'라고 말해 검사한 결과가 가성부갑상선기능저하증이었다고 한다.

반복 학습

❶ 손의 **변형성 관절증**(OA) 호발 부위는 **DIP · PIP · 무지CM관절**(MP관절에는 변화 없음!). 드물게 삼주상관절에도.

❷ **MP관절**에 변화가 있다면 **류마티스관절염**(RA) 또는 **가성통풍**을 의심한다.

❸ 손의 RA 호발 부위는 **PIP · MP관절과 수근골 전체**.

❹ 수근골 중 **RC관절**(요골수근관절)에 국한된 변화가 있다면 **가성통풍**.

참고문헌

1. Patel VK, et al : Insulin resistance Type A and short 5th metacarpals. Diabet Med 20 (6) :500–504, 2003. PMID 12786688
2. Dähnert W : Radiology review manual. Williams and Wilkins, 1996.
3. Resnick D : Diagnosis of bone and joint disorders. Saunders, 1995.

Q2 수지 말단의 통증으로 내원. 진단은?

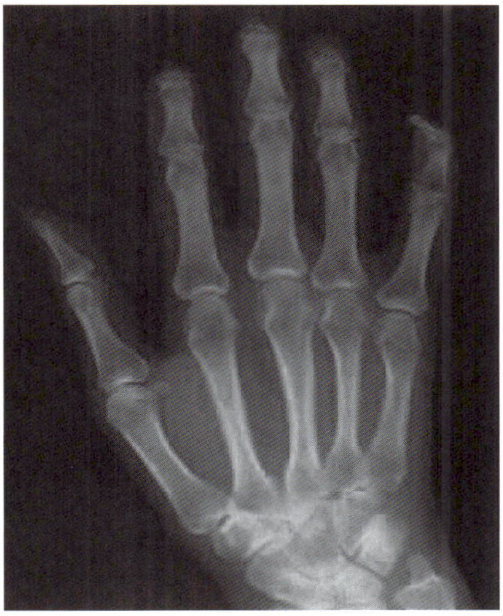

Q3 무지구의 통증으로 내원. 진단은?

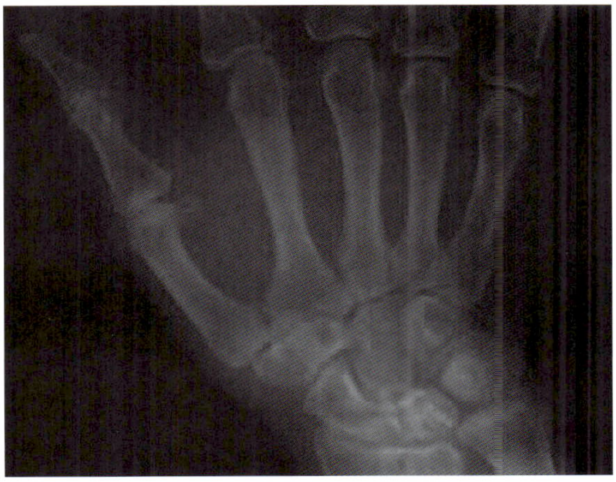

해답은 p142

Q4 스키 타던 중 낙상하여 내원. 진단은?

왼손

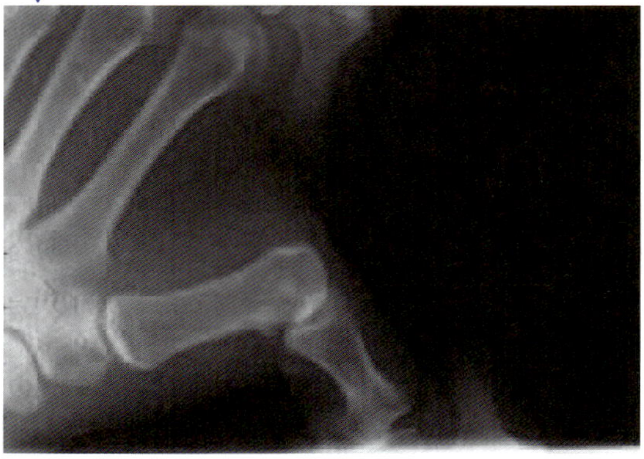

오른손

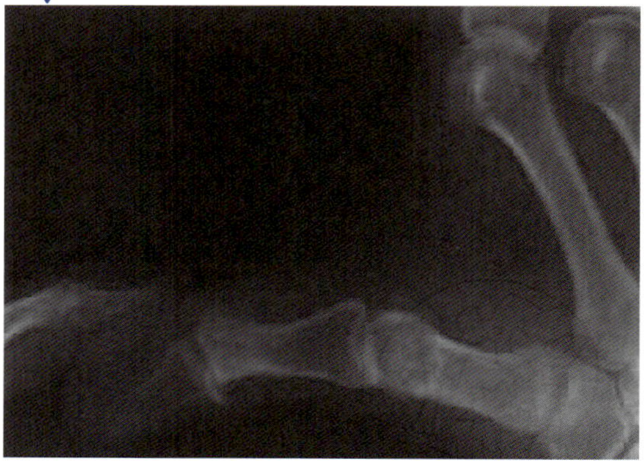

양측 모두 무지 외측에 부하를 주며 촬영하고 있다.

해답은 p142

손목 · 팔꿈치

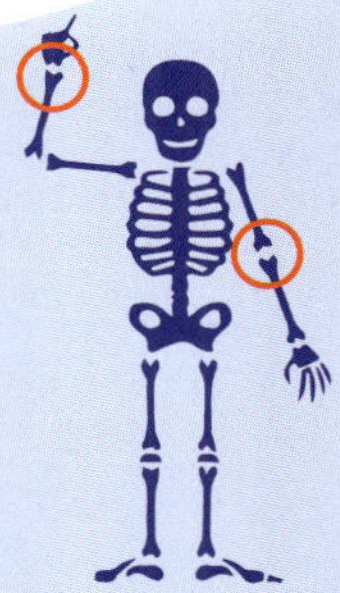

FOOSH!
손을 짚고 넘어졌을 때

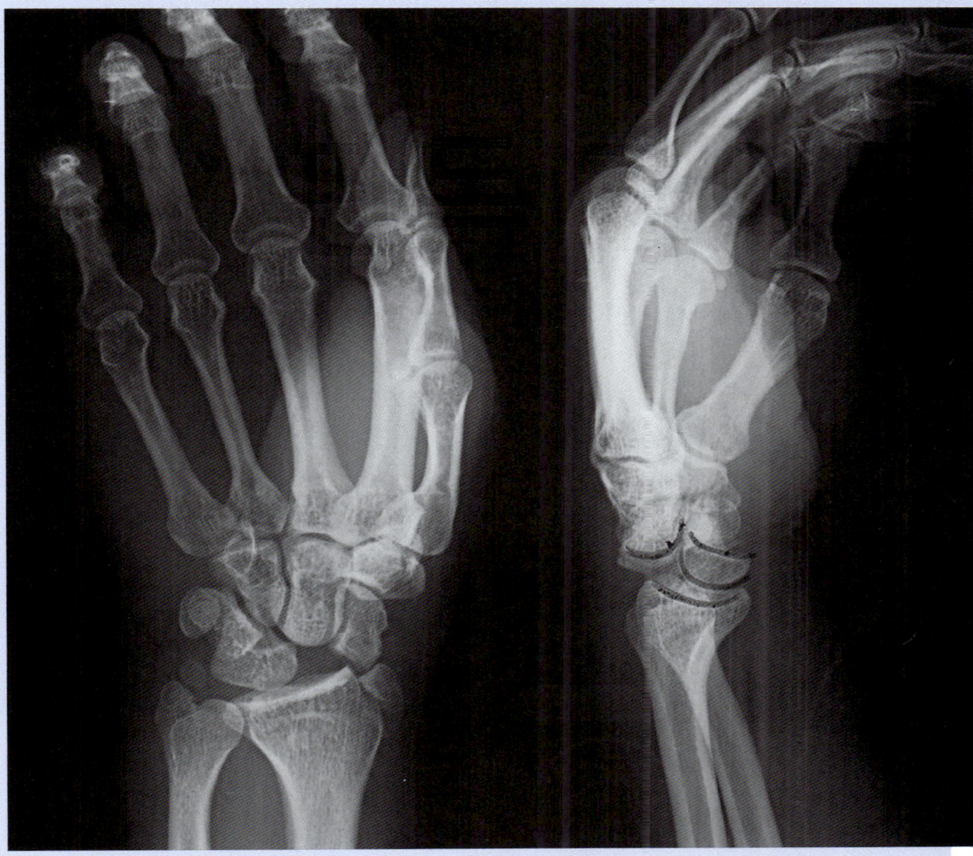

54세 · 남성

Q

왼손을 짚고 넘어진 후 발생한 왼손 관절통. 이 X-ray의 이상 소견은?

상지의 외상은 낙상 등에서 손을 땅에 짚으면서 발생하는 경우가 많으며, 이를 'FOOSH'라고 한다. 즉 'fall on an outstretched hand'이다.

앞 페이지의 X-ray는 왼손을 짚고 넘어진 후의 왼손 관절이다. 정면상으로 월상골과 주상골 사이가 분리(Terry Thomas sign, ➡ p46)되어 있는 것을 확인할 수 있다. 또한, 요골 경상돌기의 골절, 척골 경상돌기의 앞에 sesamoid bone(종자골)을 확인할 수 있다. 측면상에서는 요골 앞에 월상골이 있으나, 그 전방에 있어야 할 유두골이 배측으로 탈구되었다(월상골 주위탈구). 그림 1은 각 수근골의 명칭이다.

여기에서는 FOOSH에서 자주 발생하는 상지의 골절이나 탈구의 X-ray를 판독해 보자.

요골 원위단의 골절

Colles' fracture

강하게 손을 짚으면 요골 원위가 손등 쪽으로 전위된다. 수관절이 그림 2와 같이 손바닥 쪽으로 부풀어 오르는 것이 특징이다. 손등 쪽보다 손바닥 쪽에서 이 커브가 잘 관찰된다. 자신의 수관절과 비교해 보자. 정상에서는 절대로 이 커브가 생기지 않는다(그림 3). Colles 골절의 정복(reduction)

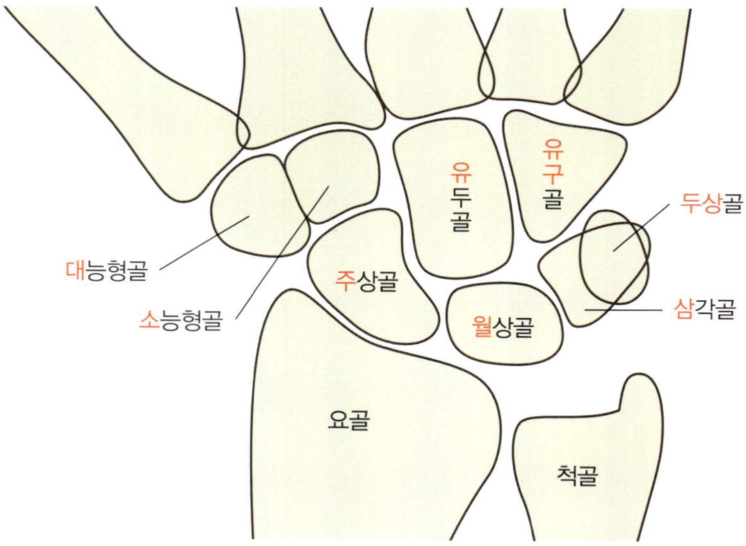

그림 1 수근골의 명칭

수근골의 암기법은 여러 가지가 있는데, 예를 들어 대능형골로부터 시계방향으로 '대소 유구에 두상 삼개월 월주상'이라고 기억한다.

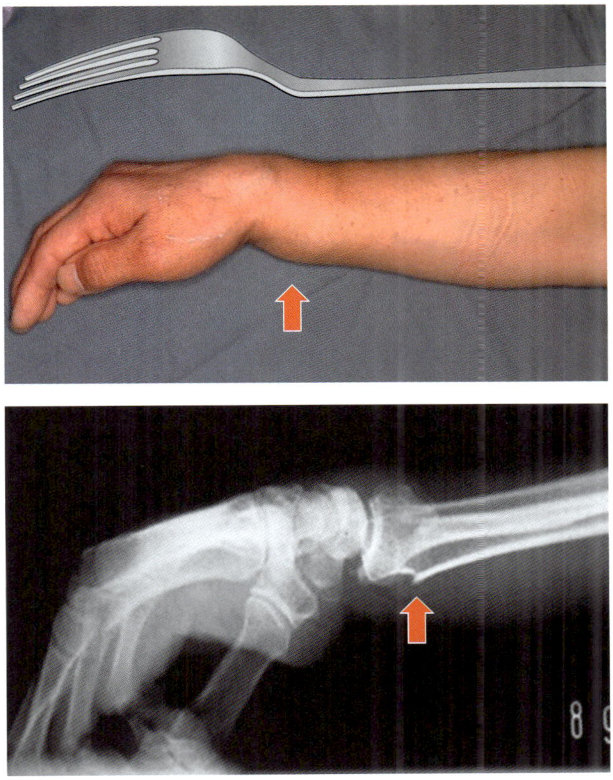

그림 2 Colles 골절의 포크 모양 변형
(dinner fork deformity)

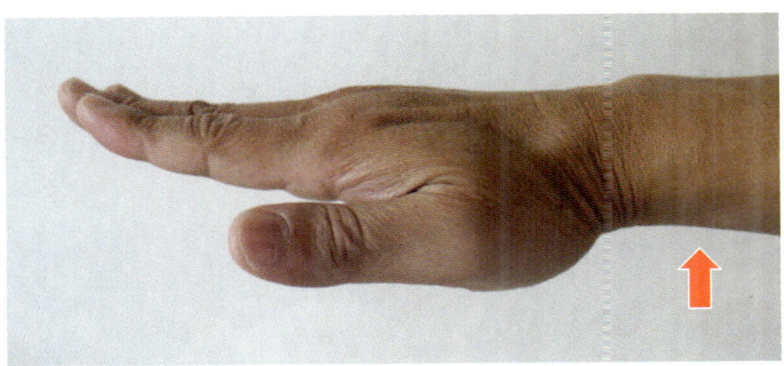

그림 3 정상 수관절
그림 2와 같은 커브는 없다.

은 원위(distal)로 견인하며 장굴 → 척굴시킨다.

손가락을 포크 날이라고 하면 마치 포크를 뒤집어 놓은 모양과 닮아 **포크 모양 변형**(dinner fork deformity)이라고 한다. 이 형태를 보이면 거의 **Colles 골절**이라고 단정할 수 있다.

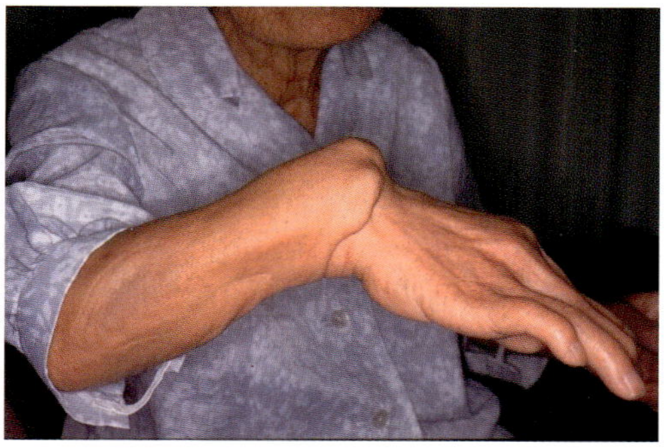

그림 4 Smith's fracture(old)
요골 원위단이 손바닥 쪽으로 전위되었다.

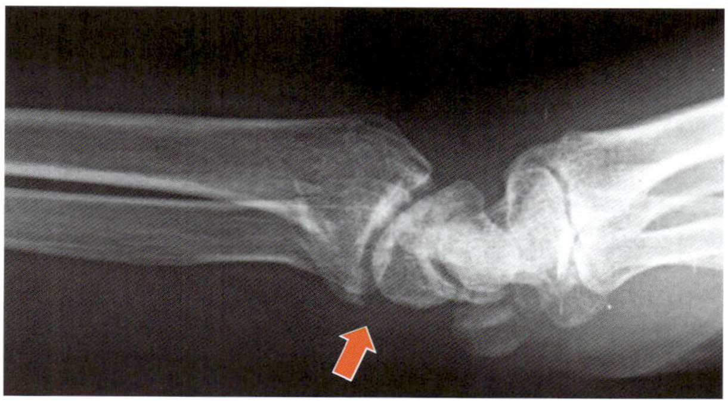

그림 5 Smith 골절
요골 원위단이 손바닥 쪽으로 전위되었다.

Smith's fracture

또한, 손바닥이 아닌 손등으로 짚으면 요골 원위 골절은 역으로 손바닥 쪽으로 전위되어 **Smith 골절**이 된다(**그림 4, 5**).

Barton's fracture

관절면을 침범하는 골절(intra-articular fracture)은 비교적 흔한 편이며, 골편이 손등 쪽으로 전위되는 것을 **배측 Barton 골절**, 손바닥 쪽으로 전위되는 것을 **장측 Barton 골절**(**그림 6**)이라고 한다. 관절면이 불규칙한(irregular) 경우에는 수술이 필요한 경우가 많다.

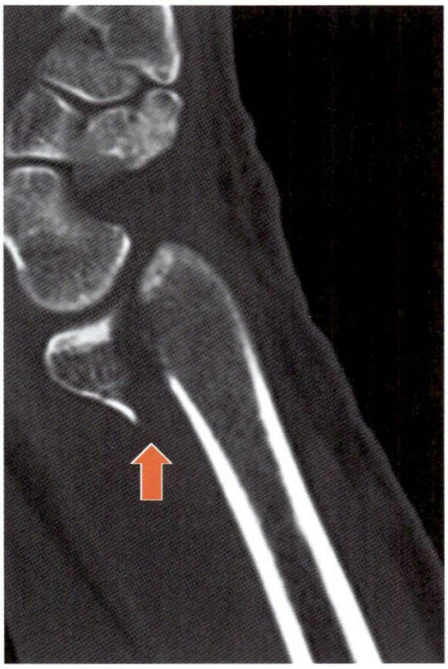

그림 6 volar Barton fracture
손바닥 쪽 골편이 손바닥 쪽으로 어긋남. 이 증례는 관절면이 불규칙해 수술이 필요하다.

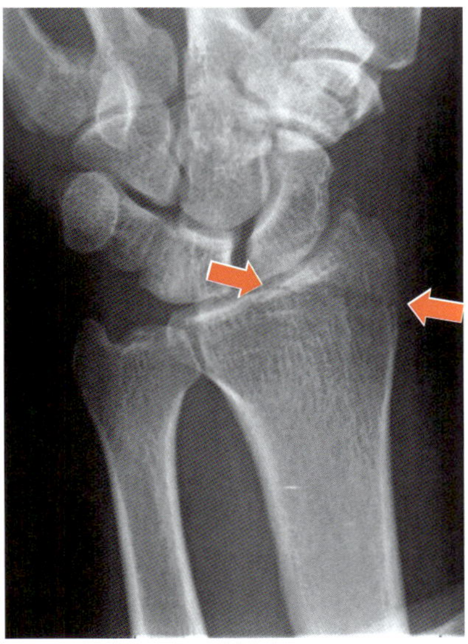

그림 7 Chauffeur's fracture
요골 경상돌기에 비스듬하게 골절선이 보인다. 야구에서 1루수가 글러브 바깥쪽으로 주자에게 터치를 시도하다 골절되었다.

Chauffeur's fracture

간혹 접하게 되는 것 중에 **Chauffeur 골절**이 있다. Chauffeur란 운전기사를 뜻한다. 예전에는 자동차의 시동을 걸 때 자동차의 앞쪽 구멍에 크랭크를 연결하고 회전을 시켰는데, 이때 엔진이 걸리면서 크랭크가 회전하고, 수관절의 외측에 부딪혀서 이 골절이 발생하였다. 요골 경상돌기에 경사골절이 발생한다.

그림 7은 야구 도중 글러브(수관절) 외측으로 주자를 터치하려다 발생한 골절이다.

요골 원위단 골절을 찾는 방법

pronator quadratus sign

요골 원위단 골절을 찾는데 유용한 **pronator quadratus**(방형회내근) **sign**(그림 8)이 있다. 요골의 장측에 부착하는 근육이며, 골절되면 이 근육이 종창하여 측면 X-ray에서도 확인된다. 이 사인이 보이면 요골 원위단 골절의 존재를 의심한다.

요골 관절면은 손바닥 쪽을 향해 10°~25° 기울어진다

또한, **요골 관절면**은 장측을 향해 10°~25° 기울어져 있으며, 배측을 향하지 않는다. 그림 8을 보면 요골 관절면이 손등 쪽을 향해 있으며, 이것만으로도 Colles 골절이 존재한다는 것을 알 수 있다.

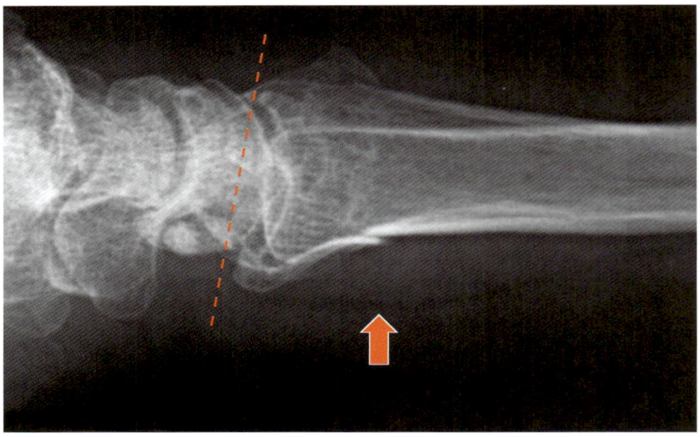

그림 8 요골 원위단 골절에서 보이는 pronator quadratus sign
방형회내근이 종창(swelling)되어 그 표면의 검은 지방층이 장측으로 돌출되었다. 또한, 점선은 요골 관절면으로 보통은 장측으로 10°~25° 기울어져 있다. 이 증례와 같이 배측을 향하는 경우에는 Colles 골절이다.

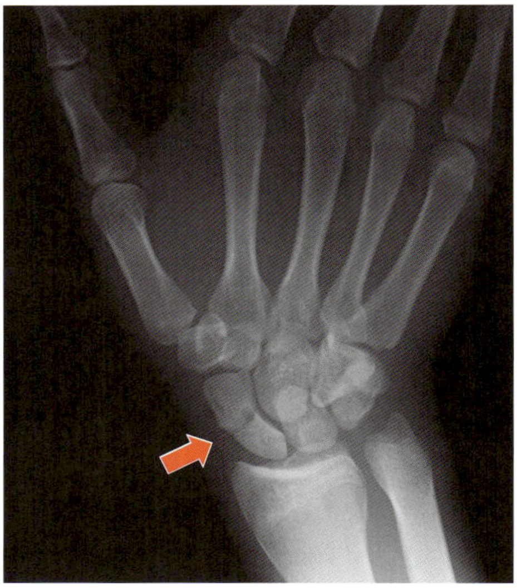

그림 9 주상골 골절
주상골은 앞으로 기울어(전경) 있으므로, AP view(전후)에서는 주상골이 단축되어 보인다. 따라서 주상골의 X-ray는 수관절 척굴위에서 경도 배굴하여 촬영한다.

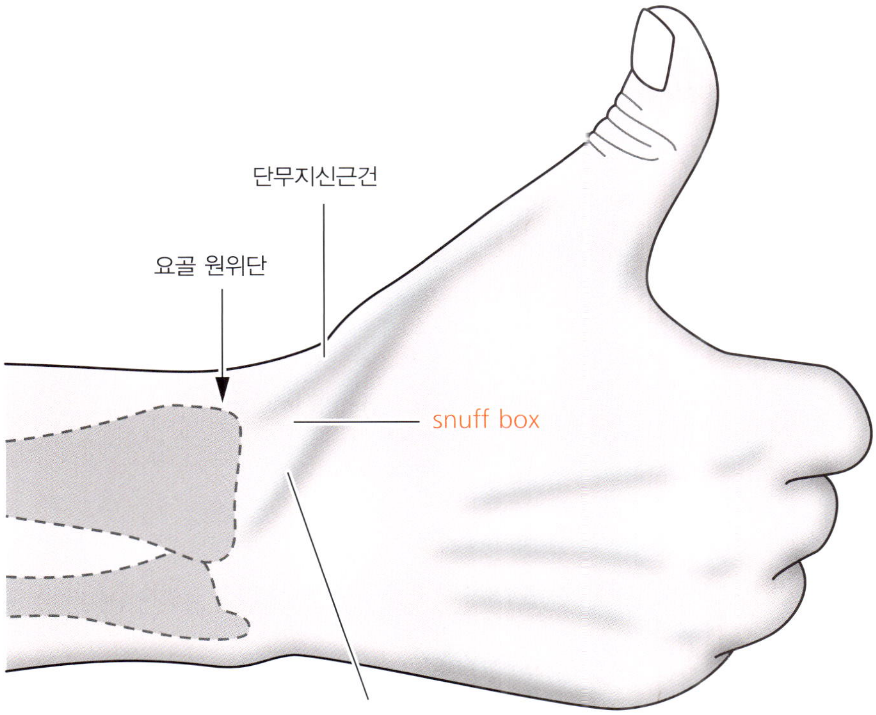

그림 10 Snuff box

주상골 골절

주상골 골절(scaphoid fracture, 그림 9)은 놓치기 쉬우므로 주의해야 한다.

Snuff box에 압통이 있다

무지를 젖히면(신전) '좋아요!(엄지척)'의 모양이 된다. 젖힌 상태에서 무지를 긴장시키면 그림 10과 같이 장무지신근건과 단무지신근건을 만질 수 있다. 이 사이에 움푹한 부분을 snuff box라고 한다. 코담배(snuff)는 이 움푹 패인 부분에 담배가루를 넣고 코로 가까이 들이마신다.

주상골 골절의 경우, 이 부분에 압통이 있다. snuff box는 골절이 있으면 부어올라 구분이 어려워지나, 엄지를 젖히면(좋아요!) 긴장한 2개의 건을 만져볼 수 있다. 이 2개의 건 사이를 만져 압통을 확인한다.

월상골 탈구, 월상골 주위 탈구

손을 짚어 월상골이 손바닥 쪽으로 탈구되거나, 그 원위의 수근골이 손등 쪽으로 탈구되는 것이다. 수관절 X-ray 정면상을 보는 경우, 그림 11과 같이 수근골의 배열이 평행한 것에 주의한다. 3개의 선이 잘 그려지지 않는 것은 이상 소견이다.

정면상은 Terry Thomas의 치아와 같은, 측면상은 쓰러진 찻잔 같은

앞 페이지(➡ p39)의 X-ray는 **월상골 주위탈구**(그림 12)이다. 정면상에서 수근골의 배열이 평행하지 않고 월상골과 주상골 사이에 틈이 있다. 이를 **Terry Thomas sign**이라고 한다(그림 13). Terry Thomas(1911~1990)라고 하는 영국 코미디언의 앞니 사이에 틈이 있었기 때문에 붙여진 이름이다.

또한, 정상적인 수근골의 X-ray 측면상은 받침(saucer) 위에 찻잔이 있고, 그 위에 사과가 있는 것처럼 보인다(그림 14). 그러나 이상이 생겨 이 위치가 무너지는 것을 **spilled tea cup sign**이라고 한

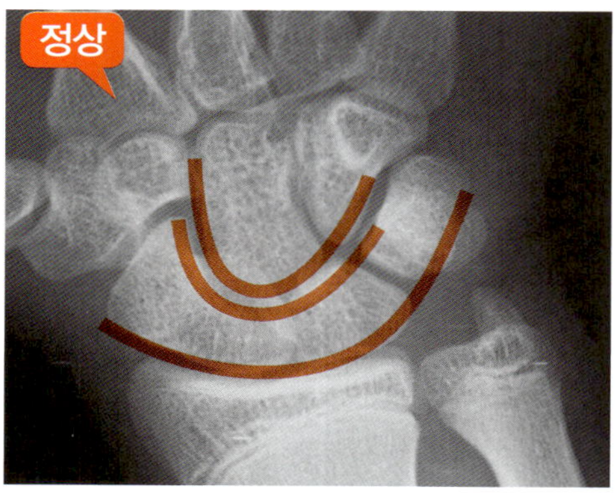

그림 11 정상적인 수관절(정면상, AP view)
3개의 선이 평행하다.

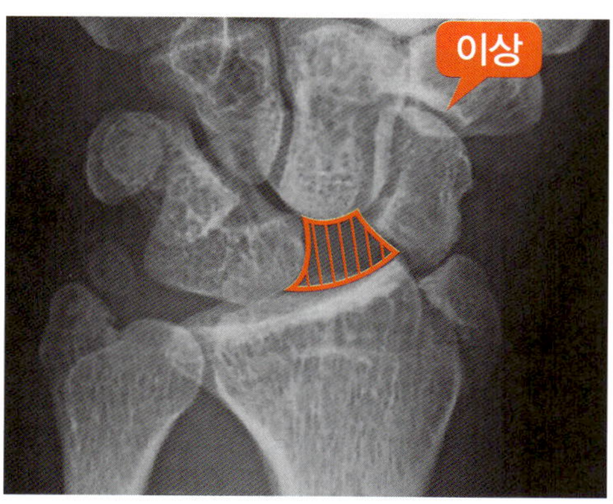

그림 12 월상골 주위탈구(Terry Thomas sign)
그림 11과 같은 3개의 선을 평행하게 그을 수 없으며 월상골과 주상골 사이에 틈이 있다[앞 페이지(➡ p39)의 X-ray 정면상].

다. 즉, 찻잔이 쓰러져 차가 쏟아지는 것이다. p39의 측면상이 이에 해당한다.

그림 13 Terry Thomas sign

영국 코미디언 Terry Thomas는 "벌어진 앞니"가 트레이드 마크였다.

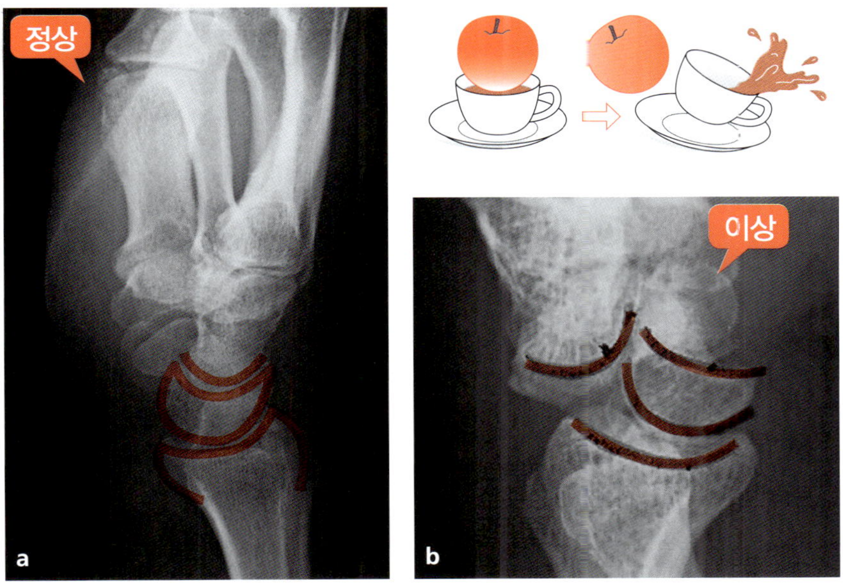

그림 14 수근골(측면상)

a : 요골의 원위에 월상골, 그 원위에 유두골이 배열된다.

b : spilled tea cup sign[앞 페이지(➡ p39)의 X-ray 측면상]

소아 주관절 판독의 비법

소아 주관절 X-ray 판독의 비법을 두 가지 소개한다.

우선, **상완골 전방 골피질에 그은 선**(anterior humeral line)**은 상완골 소두**의 중앙 1/3 지점을 지

a

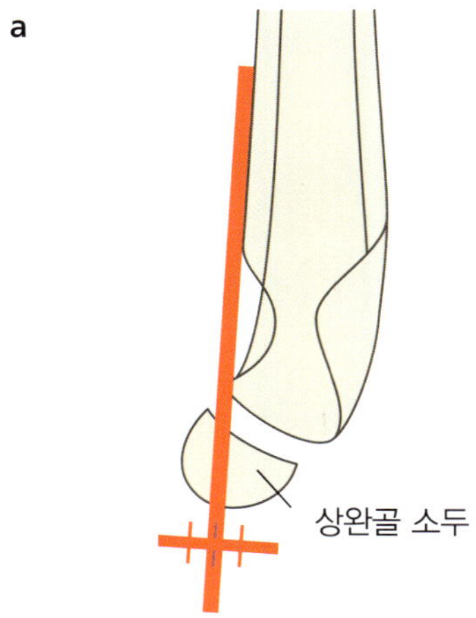

X-ray에서 상완골 전방 골피질에 그은 선(anterior humeral line)은 상완골 소두의 중앙 1/3 지점을 지난다.

c

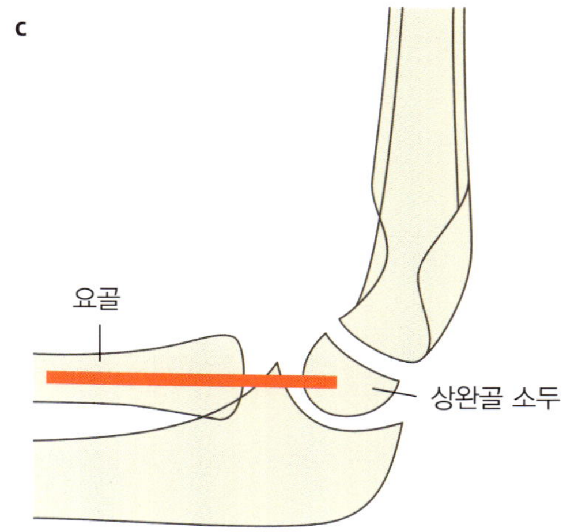

요골의 연장선 위에 반드시 상완골 소두가 있다(어떤 방향에서 찍어도).

b

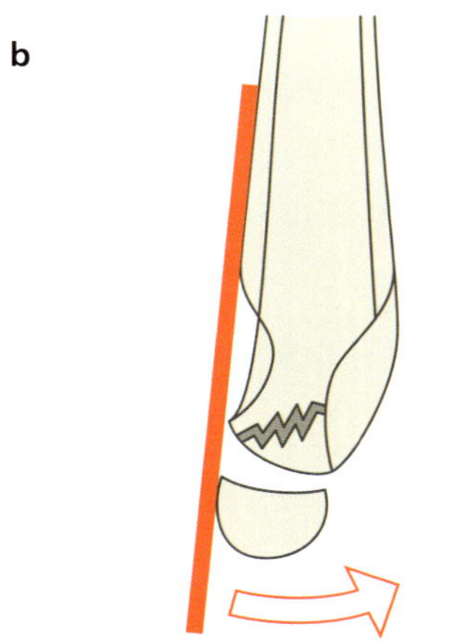

상완골 소두 중 1/3을 지나지 않는다면 골절로 인해 전위된 것으로 생각한다.

d

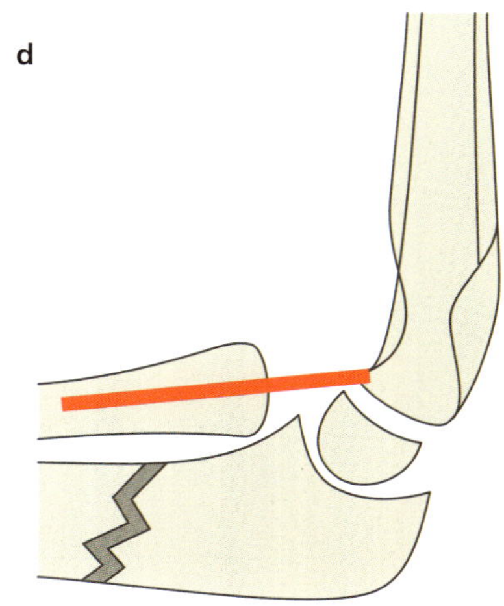

요골의 연장선 위에 상완골 소두가 없다면 요골의 탈구이다. 이 예는 몬테기아탈구골절(척골 골절 + 요골두 탈구).

그림 15 소아 주관절 판독의 비법

상완골 전방 골피질에 그은 선은 상완골 소두 중 1/3을 지난다. 요골의 연장선 위에는 항상 상완골 소두가 있다.

난다(그림 15a). 만약 이 선이 상완골 소두의 전방으로 어긋나는 경우, 상완골 과상골절(supracondylar fracture of humerus)에 의해 상완골 소두가 후방으로 전위되었을 가능성이 있다(그림 15b, 16).

다음으로, **요골 근위부의 연장선 위에는 항상 상완골 소두**가 있다(그림 15c). 만약 그렇지 않다면, 요골두가 탈구되었을 가능성이 있다(그림 15d).

몬테기아탈구골절(Monteggia fracture dislocation)은 척골 골절과 요골두의 탈구가 발생하는 것으로, 탈구를 놓치기 쉬우므로 반드시 확인한다(그림 17).

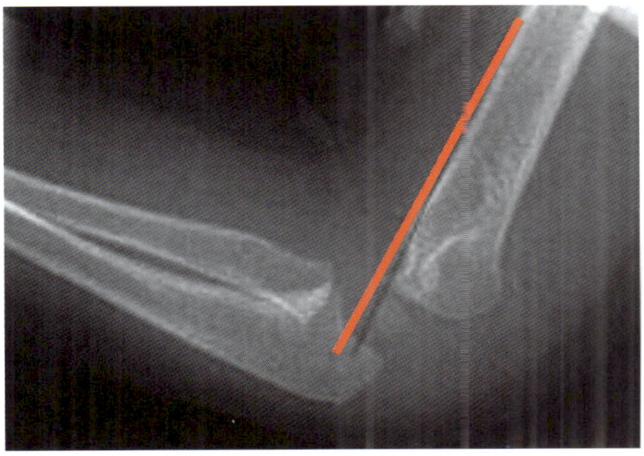

그림 16 상완골 과상골절
상완골 전방 피질골의 연장선이 상완골 소두의 전방으로 나왔다. 상완골 과상골절로 원위 골편이 후방 전위된 것을 의미한다.

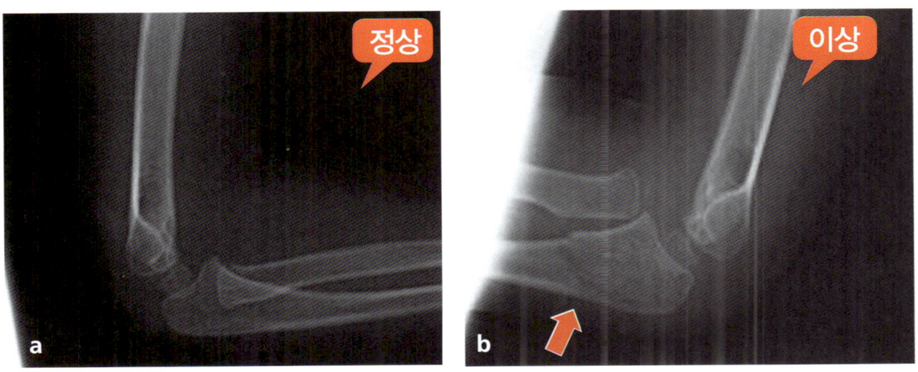

그림 17 정상 팔꿈치와 몬테기아탈구골절
a는 정상 팔꿈치. b는 요골두의 연장선 위에 상완골 소두가 없으며, 상방으로 요골이 탈구되었다. 또한, 척골 골절이 보이는, 몬테기아탈구골절이다.

요골두 / 요골 경부 골절

요골두 골절과 **요골 경부 골절** 역시 손을 짚어 팔꿈치가 신전될 때 발생하는 골절이다(그림 18, 19). 요골두 부근에 골절이 발생할 수 있다는 것을 알고 있지 않으면 놓치기 쉽다.

Fat pad sign을 확인

이러한 주관절 내의 골절로 출혈이 발생하면 **fat pad sign**이 관찰되며(그림 20), 진단에 도움이 되는 소견이다.

진단에 확신이 없을 때에는 초음파를 시행해 관절액을 확인한다. 관절 내 출혈은 가동범위를 제한하며, 주두 약간 후상방에서 이를 천자하면 회복된다.

요골 경부 부근의 병변에 의한 후골간신경마비

요골 경부 부근에 요골신경의 분지인 후골간신경이 있으며, 이 부근의 병변으로 인해 **후골간신경마비**(posterior interosseous nerve palsy)가 발생하는 경우가 있다. 그림 21, 그림 22는 요골 경부 부근의 암 전이에 의한 후골간신경마비이다. **pistol sign**이라고 하며 왼손은 견고하게 권총 모양을 만들 수 있으나 오른손의 엄지와 검지는 완전히 신전시킬 수가 없다(그림 21). 요골신경마비와 달리 수관절의 신전은 가능하다.

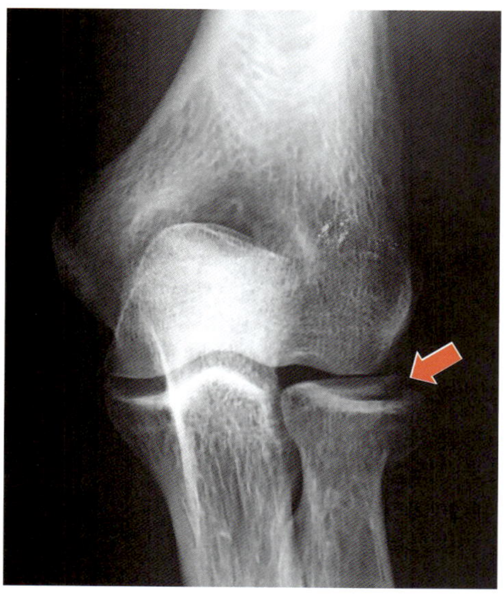

그림 18 요골두 골절

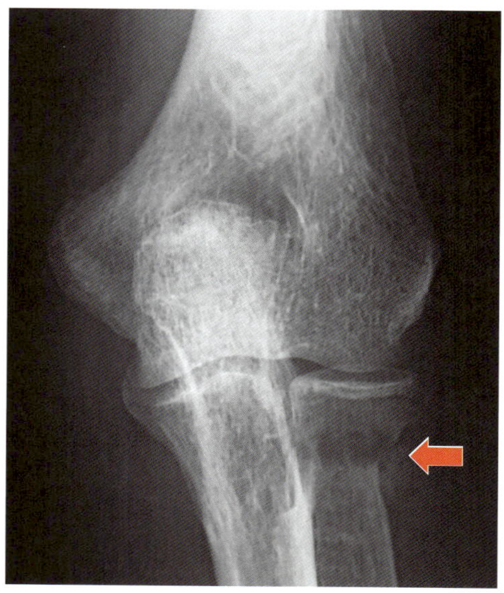

그림 19 요골 경부 골절

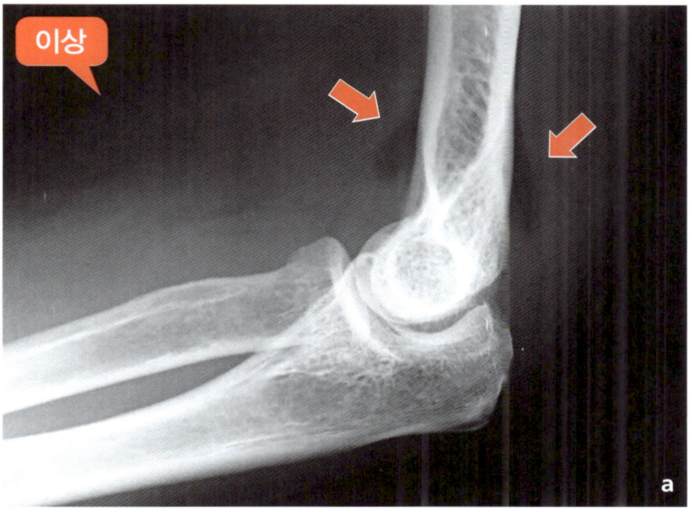

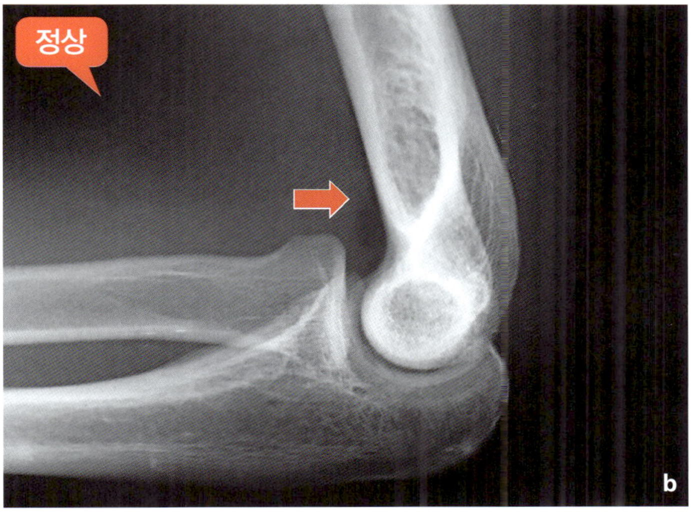

그림 20 주관절의 fat pad sign

a : 골절에 따른 출혈이 있으면, 八자 형태로 앞뒤에 저음영의 fat pad가 보인다.

b : 전방에 소량의 검은 지방 음영이 있으며, 후방의 fat pad는 정상에서는 보이지 않는다.

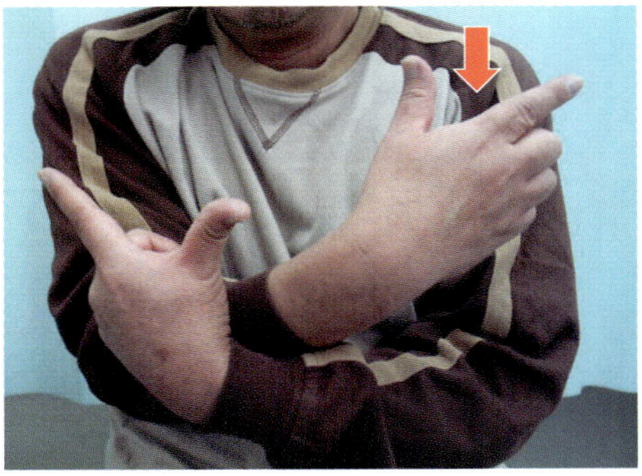

그림 21 pistol sign

오른손의 후골간신경마비로 인해 오른쪽 엄지와 검지의 완전한 신전이 되지 않아, 불완전한 권총 모양이 된다.

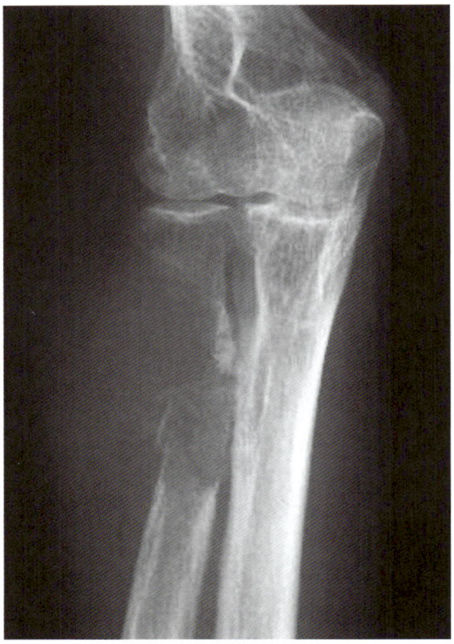

그림 22 **후골간신경마비**

암 전이에 의한 요골 경부에 용해(osteolysis)가 보이며, 이로 인해 후골간신경이 마비되었다.

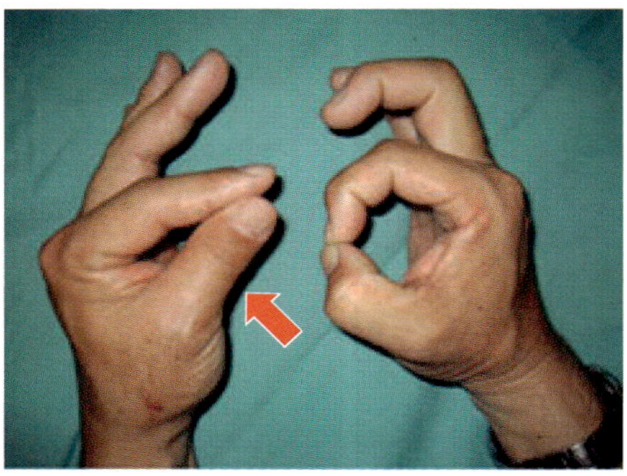

그림 23 **좌측 전골간신경마비로 인한 tear drop sign(perfect O를 만들지 못함)**

정중신경 분지(전골간신경)의 손상으로 좌측 장무지굴근건이 마비되어 무지의 굴곡이 불가능해져 손가락으로 OK와 완전한 원을 만들지 못하고, 눈물방울처럼 된다.

또한, pistol sign과 함께 **tear drop sign**도 기억해두자. 그림 23은 63세 · 남성으로 술에 취해 넘어져 전완 원위 내측을 테이블 모서리에 부딪혀 왼쪽 무지 굴곡이 불가능하며, 첫째와 둘째 손가락의 저림을 호소하였다. 이는 정중신경가지의 전골간신경 손상으로 장무지굴근의 마비이다. 손가락으로 OK를 만들면 완전한 원(perfect O)이 아닌 눈물방울(tear drop) 모양이 된다.

상완골 과상골절

상완골 과상골절(supracondylar fracture of humerus)(그림 24)도 손을 짚고 넘어졌을 때 발생하는 경우가 많다.

소아에서 발생하기 쉽다

손을 짚었는데 왜 팔꿈치가 골절되는지 의아할 것이다. 소아에서는 팔꿈치가 과신전하기 때문이다(그림 25). 손을 짚고 팔꿈치가 과신전되면 주두가 상완골 과상부에 충돌해 골절을 일으킨다.

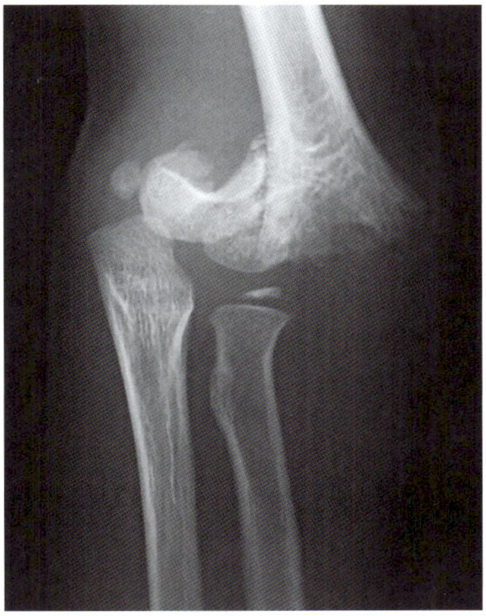

그림 24 상완골 과상골절

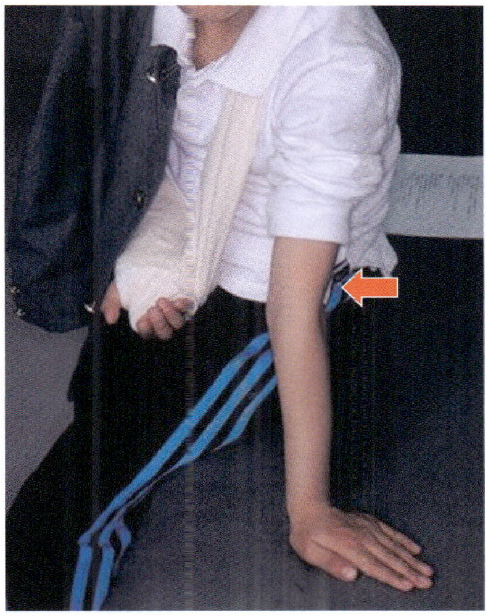

그림 25 팔꿈치의 과신전
소아는 팔꿈치가 과신전되므로, 손을 짚으면 주두가 상완골 과상부에 충돌해 상완골 과상골절이 발생한다.

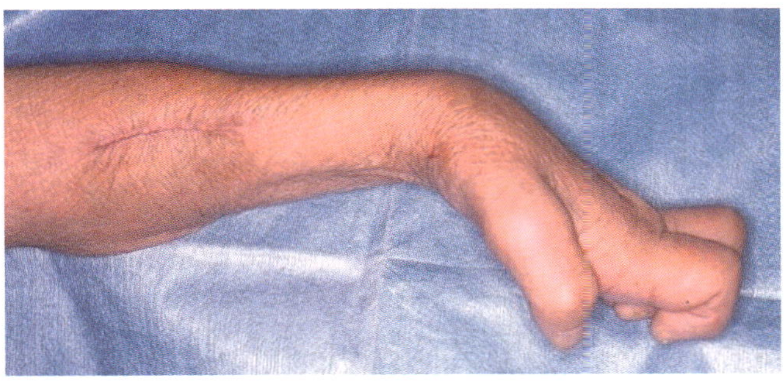

그림 26 Volkmann's contracture
이 증례는 상완골 과상골절이 아닌, 의식장애로 전완 위에 24시간 누워 있었던 고령환자에서 발생한 Volkmann 구축이다.

Volkmann 구축

상완골 과상부 골절의 가장 심각한 합병증으로 Volkmann 구축(그림 26)이라는 허혈성 손상이 발생할 수 있다. 정확한 원인은 밝혀지지 않았지만 골절 자체 혹은 무리한 정복, 잘못된 자세로 고정하거나 붕대를 너무 꽉 조이는 것 등이 유발인자로 추정된다.

'소아의 팔꿈치 골절은 매우 무섭다'는 것을 잊지 말자.

반복 학습

손을 짚고 넘어지면(FOOSH), 다음 다섯 가지의 외상을 집중적으로 찾아라!

❶ 주상골 골절

❷ 월상골 탈구, 월상골 주위탈구

❸ 요골 원위단 골절(Colles 골절, Smith 골절, Barton 골절, Chauffeur 골절)

❹ 요골두 / 요골 경부 골절

❺ 상완골 과상골절

Q5 손목(수근부) 통증으로 내원. 진단은?

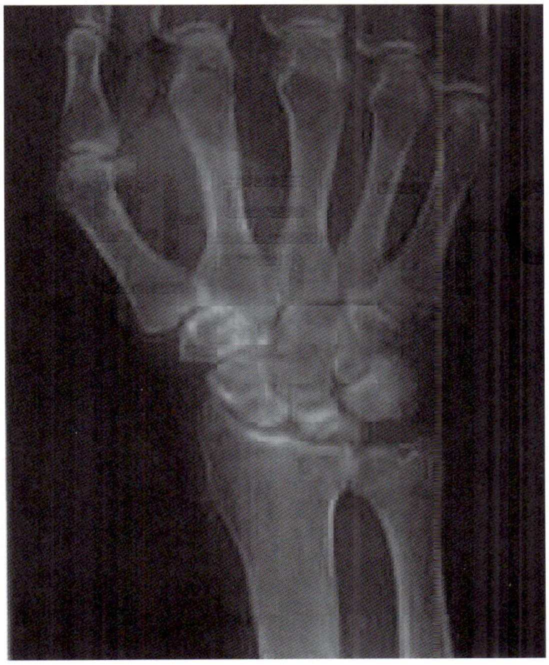

해답은 p143

Q6 류마티스관절염 환자. 갑자기 네 번째와 다섯 번째 손가락의 신전이 되지 않았다. 진단은?

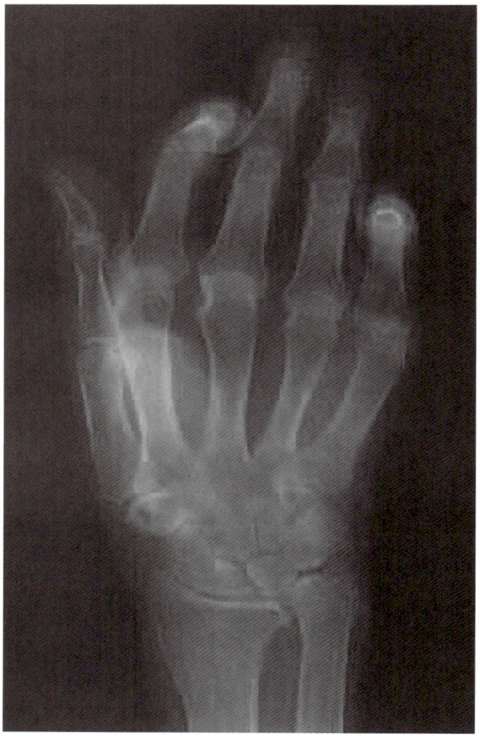

해답은 p143

어깨 질환의 X-ray 소견

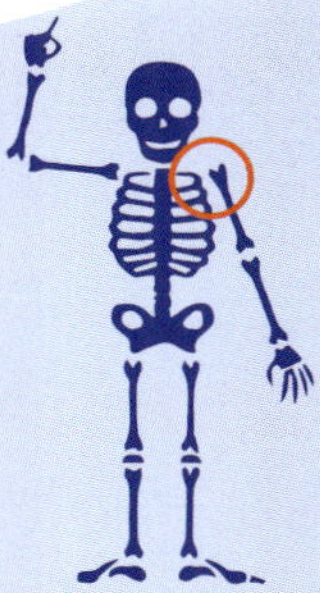

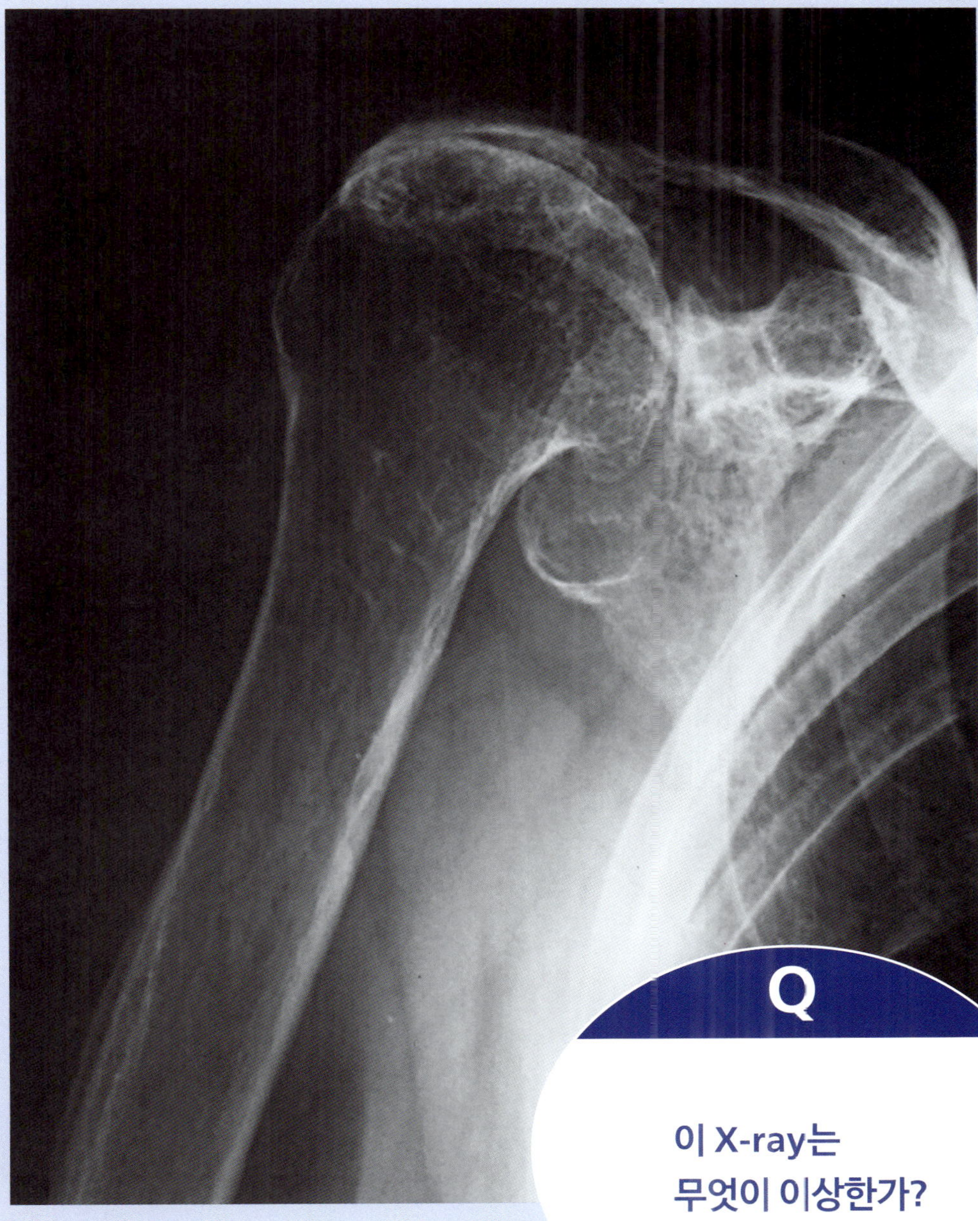

70세 · 남성

Q

이 X-ray는
무엇이 이상한가?
진단은?

앞 페이지의 단순 X-ray 진단은 **회전근개 파열**로 인한 관절염(cuff tear arthropathy)이다. 사실, 이것만 보아도 '회전근개(rotator cuff)가 파열되어 있다'고 바로 진단할 수 있다. 회전근개 파열은 손이나 팔꿈치를 짚고 넘어지면서 발생하기도 하지만 류마티스관절염으로 발생하기도 한다. 어깨에 대한 X-ray 진단법을 마스터해 두는 것이 중요하다.

또한, 초음파는 이제 견관절 진단에 필수적이다. 내과 의사들은 초음파를 다루는 데 익숙하므로 프로브를 어깨에 대는 것만으로도 많은 정보를 얻을 수 있을 것이다. 최근에는 류마티스성 다발근통(polymyalgia rheumatica)의 진단 기준에 어깨초음파도 포함되어 있다.

여기에서는 어깨 X-ray와 초음파의 판독 요령을 설명하려고 한다. 이 정도만 숙지한다면 견관절 영상진단은 큰 어려움이 없을 것이다.

어깨의 X-ray

고도의 회전근개 파열은 단순 X-ray 검사로 알 수 있다. 정상 견관절과 앞 페이지의 영상을 비교해 보자(**그림 1**).

고관절과의 차이점

고관절에 있는 ball and socket이라고 하는 대퇴골두는 비구로 둘러싸여 안정적이다. 그러나 견관절은 **그림 2**의 이미지처럼 관절와(glenoid)가 얕기 때문에 골두를 관절와로 당기는 벡터가 필요하다. 이 역할을 하고 있는 것이 **회전근개**이다[1].

회전근개는 4개의 건으로 이루어져 있으며, 'SITS'라고 기억한다. 즉, supraspinatus muscle(**극상근**), infraspinatus muscle(**극하근**), teres minor muscle(**소원근**), subscapularis muscle(**견갑하근**)이다(**그림 3**). 이 4개의 건(힘줄)이 엉키듯이 골두의 대결절·소결절에 붙어 있다.

힘줄로 당겨져 안정화

한편, **삼각근**은 견봉·쇄골로부터 기시하여 삼각근조면*에 부착한다(**그림 4**).

* 필자는 졸업 후 3년째에 덴류강 깊숙한 벽지의 작은 병원에 있을 때, 이 삼각근조면을 골막반응(periosteal reaction)으로 착각하여 환자를 편도 2시간 거리의 도시에 있는 병원에 의뢰한 적이 있다. 회신은 '이는 삼각근조면으로 정상 소견임'이었다.

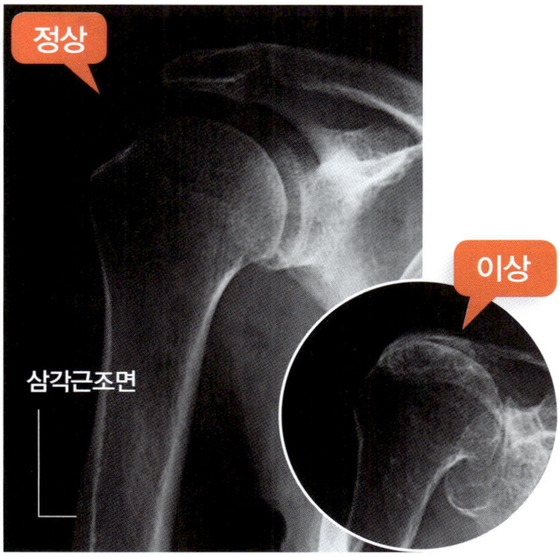

그림 1 정상 견관절

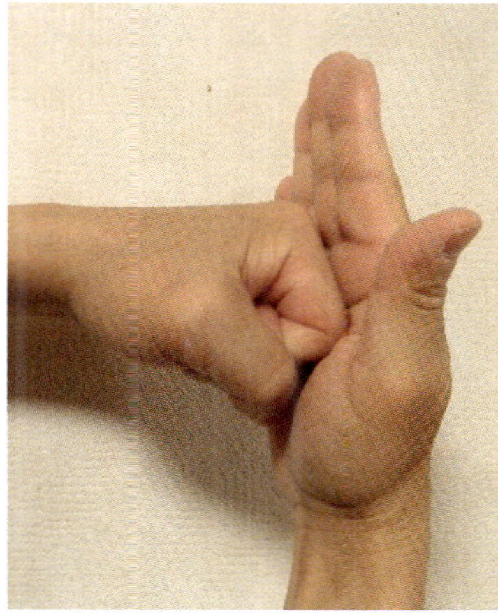

그림 2 견관절의 이미지

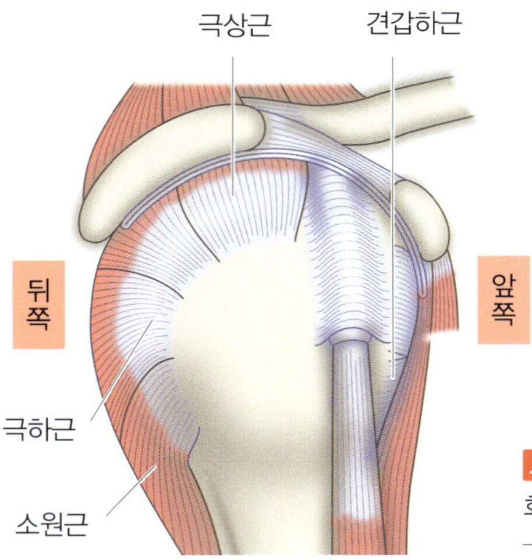

그림 3 회전근개(rotator cuff)

회전근개의 후방은 SIT라고 기억한다. **s**upraspinatus(극상근) →**i**nfraspinatus(극하근) →**t**eres(소원근) 순이다.

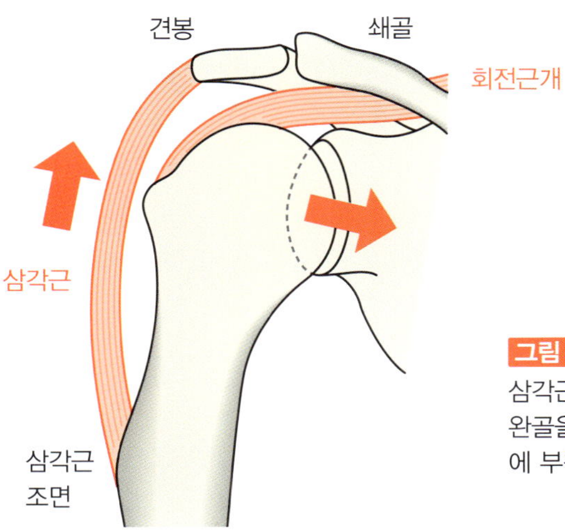

그림 4 회전근개와 삼각근의 벡터

삼각근은 견봉 · 쇄골로부터 기시하여 삼각근조면에 부착하고 상완골을 위쪽 방향으로 당겨 올린다. 회전근개는 대결절 · 소결절에 부착하여 골두를 관절와로 당긴다.

따라서, 그림 4와 같이 회전근개가 골두를 관절와로 당기면서 삼각근이 상완골을 거상하고 있다. 그 때문에 회전근개가 파열되면 관절와로 당기는 벡터가 소실되고, 골두는 삼각근에 의해 위쪽으로 당겨 올라가게 되며 앞 페이지(➡ p57)와 같은 X-ray 소견을 보인다.

그러므로 상완골두의 상방 전위 확인만으로 회전근개의 파열을 진단할 수 있다. 이를 X-ray에서 발견하는 경우도 있다(➡ p26). 흉부 영상에서도 양쪽 견관절을 잘 확인하도록 한다.

회전근개가 파열되어도, 상완이두근 장두건을 회전근개 대신 상완골두의 depressor로 사용하는 환자가 있으며, 정상적인 견관절 굴곡(상지 거상)이 가능한 경우가 있다. 거상이 불가할 경우, 회전근개 봉합술이 필요하다.

어깨초음파

초음파로 어깨를 확인해 보자!

프로브를 댈 곳은 두 부위이다(그림 5). 간단하지만 얻을 수 있는 정보가 매우 많다.

그림 6은 회전근개의 정상 소견이다. 일러스트(그림 7)와 비교해 보자. 어깨 표면부터 피부, 피하지방, 근막, 삼각근, peribursal fat(점액낭 주위 지방), 극상근건, 골두 순이다.

부위 ❶에서 진단할 수 있는 이상 소견

회전근개 파열은 그림 8과 같이 보인다. 회전근개가 위로 볼록하지 않고 평평하게 보이므로

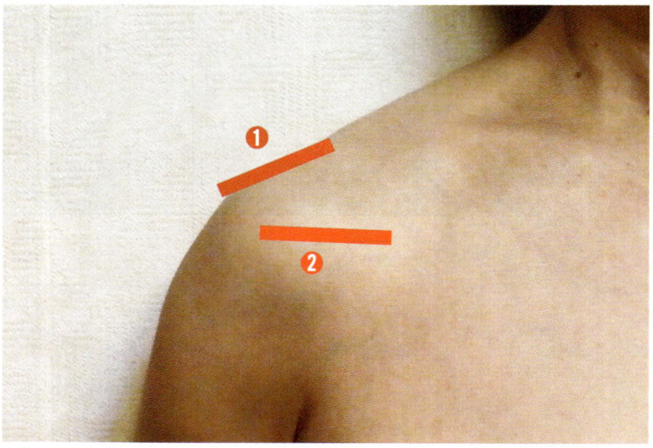

그림 5 어깨 초음파 검사 부위

프로브는 두 부위의 피부에 수직으로 댄다. ❶에서 회전근개를 확인하고, ❷에서 상완이두근 장두건을 본다.

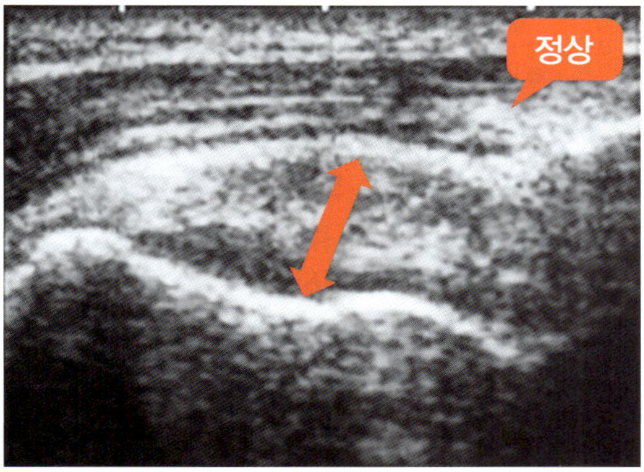

그림 6 정상적인 회전근개의 초음파 영상
극상근건의 두께(peribursal fat의 아래에서 골두까지)는 6mm 이내. 이보다 두꺼우면 충돌증후군을 의심한다.

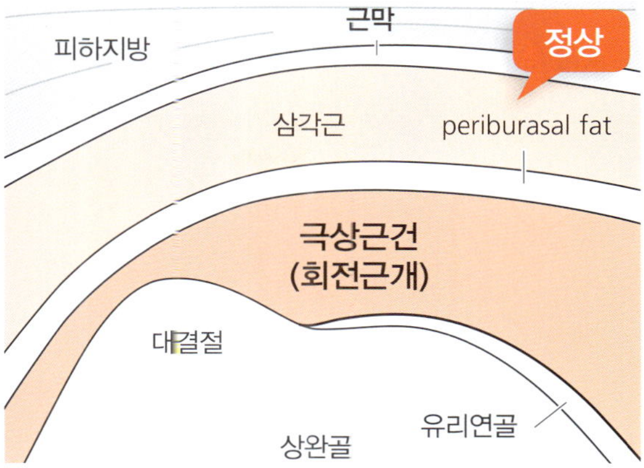

그림 7 정상적인 건판의 도식
위에서부터 피부, 피하지방, 근막, 삼각근(견봉에 부착), periburasal fat, 극상근건, 상완골의 순서이다.

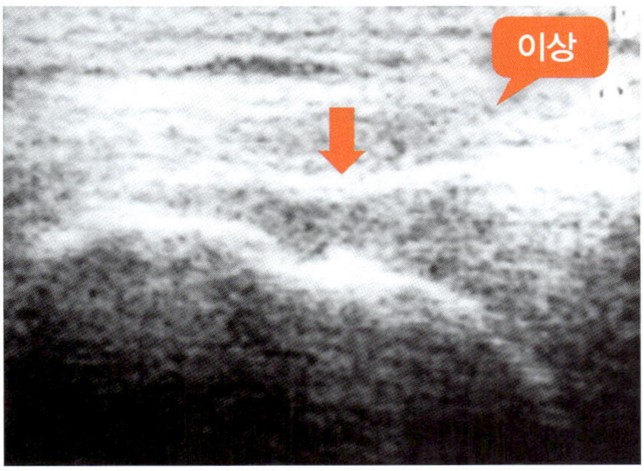

그림 8 회전근개 파열의 초음파 영상
극상근건이 파열되어 평평하게 보인다.

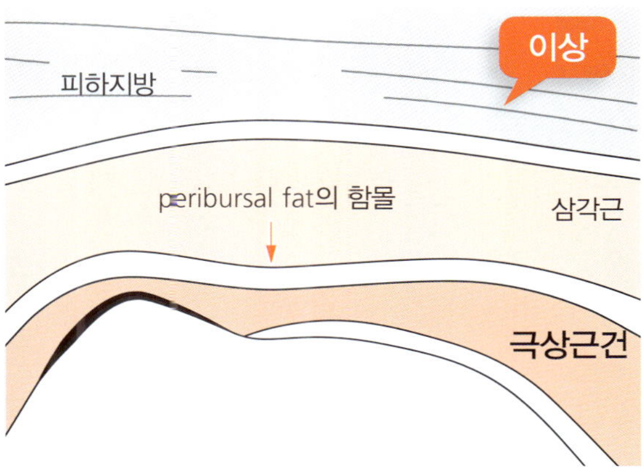

그림 9 회전근개 파열의 도식

(**그림 9**) 진단은 매우 쉽다.

극상근건(회전근개)의 두께는 6mm 이내이며, 위로 볼록하다. 근육과 달리 건은 비후(hypertrophy)되지 않으므로 연령, 성별에 의한 차이는 없다. 이것이 두꺼울 경우, **충돌증후군**(impingement syndrome)을 의심한다(**그림 10**). 충돌증후군이란 회전근개가 비후되어 어깨 굴곡(상지 거상) 시 회전근개가 골두와 견봉 사이에 끼여 통증이 발생하는 것이다. 또한, 점액낭(bursa)의 점액은 peribursal fat과 회전근개 사이에 저류된다(**그림 11**).

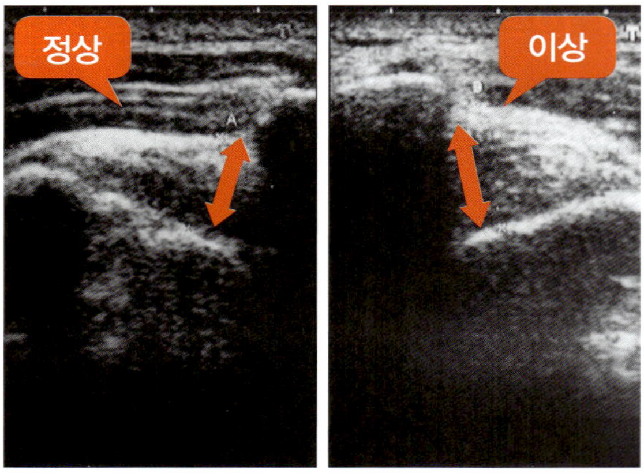

그림 10 충돌증후군의 초음파 영상

오른쪽 그림(왼쪽 어깨)은 극상근건이 6mm 이상으로 두꺼워져 있다(충돌증후군).

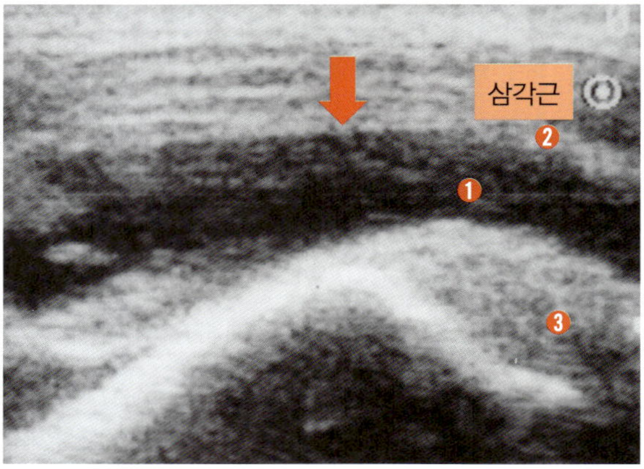

그림 11 Subacromial subdeltoid bursa

❶ 점액낭(bursa) 액체가 저류되어 있다. 점액낭은 ❷ peribursal fat과 ❸ 회전근개(극상극건) 사이에 있다. Subacromial subdeltoid bursa라고 한다.

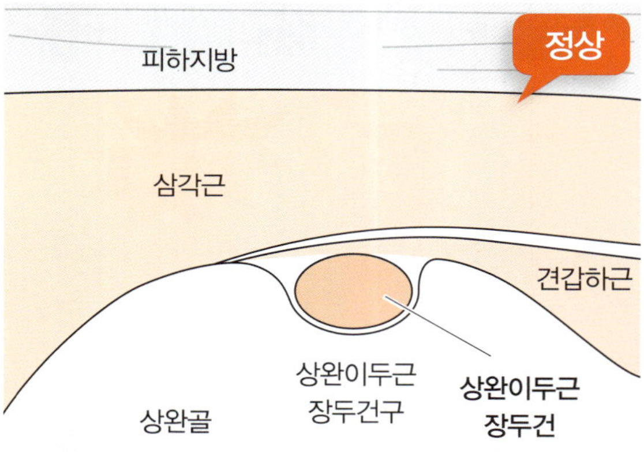

그림 12 정상적인 상완이두근 장두건의 그림

상완이두근 장두건은 결절간 고랑(bicipital groove) 속에 들어 있다. 고랑에서 돌출되었다면 장두건의 종창이다.

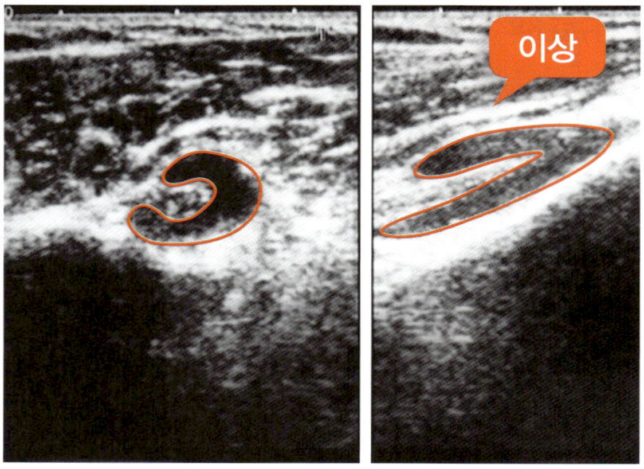

그림 13 상완이두근 장두건염의 초음파 영상

왼쪽은 단축 영상, 오른쪽은 장축 영상. 상완이두근 장두건 주위 삼출이 있어, 상완이두근 장두건염이다.

방법 ❷로 진단할 수 있는 이상 소견

한편, 상완이두근 장두건은 **그림 12**와 같이 보인다. 결절간 고랑(bicipital groove) 속에 장두건이 존재한다. 만약 고랑에서 전방으로 돌출되었거나, 주위에 삼출(effusion)이 있다면 **상완이두근 장두건염**이다(**그림 13**).

또한, **류마티스성 다발근통**(polymyalgia rheumatica, PMR)의 경우 점액낭의 액체 저류(fluid collection) · 혈류 증가, 상완이두근 장두건 주위의 삼출 · 혈류 증가를 확인할 수 있다(**그림 14**).

PMR의 어깨초음파 소견은 현재 '관절초음파에서 어깨 및 고관절의 점액낭염 또는 양쪽 어깨의 점액낭염'으로 진단 기준에도 포함되어 있다. 외래에서 간단히 PMR을 의심할 수 있다.

PMR 진단에는 양쪽 어깨의 통증과 ESR/CRP 수치가 필수이다. 여기에 점액낭염 초음파 소견이 추가되면 민감도가 상승한다. 다만 PMR의 20%는 최초의 ESR이 40mm/h 미만이다. 또한, PMR의 대부분은 프레드니솔론 12.5~25.0mg/day로 급속히 개선된다.

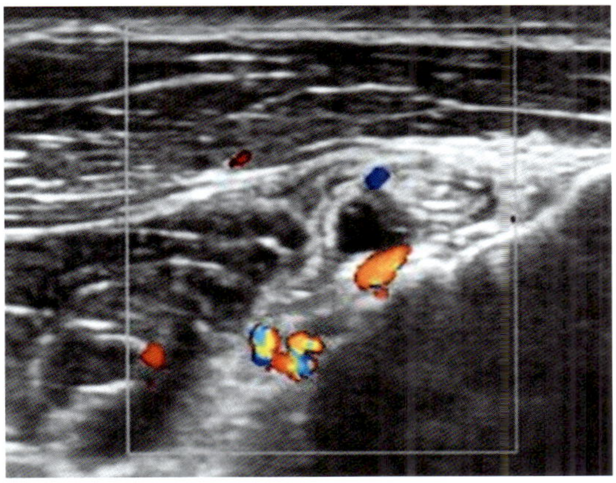

그림 14 **류마티스성 다발근통(PMR)의 초음파 영상**

컬러도플러검사. 상완이두근 장두건 주위에 삼출 및 혈류 증가가 나타난다.

견봉의 골극에도 주의하자

어깨 X-ray에서 견봉 아래에 **골극**이 보이는 경우가 있다(그림 15). 이를 미리 염두에 두지 않으면 골극을 발견하기 어렵다.

이러한 골극이 있으면 충돌증후군을 일으킬 수 있다고 한다. 또한, 골극이 없어도 사위상(oblique view)에서 봤을 때 견봉의 전방이 아래쪽으로 구부러져 있으면 충돌증후군이 발생할 수 있다.

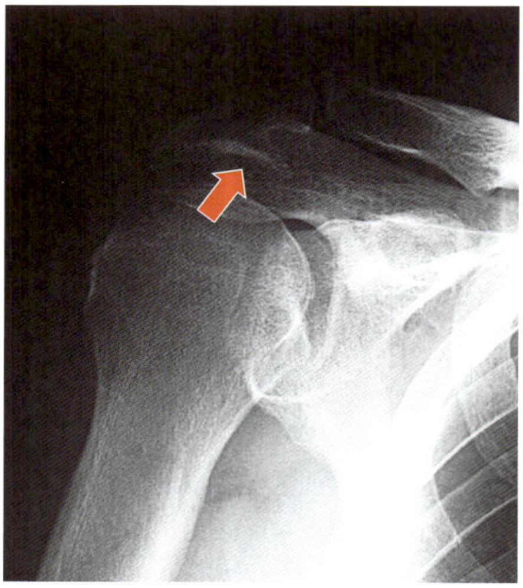

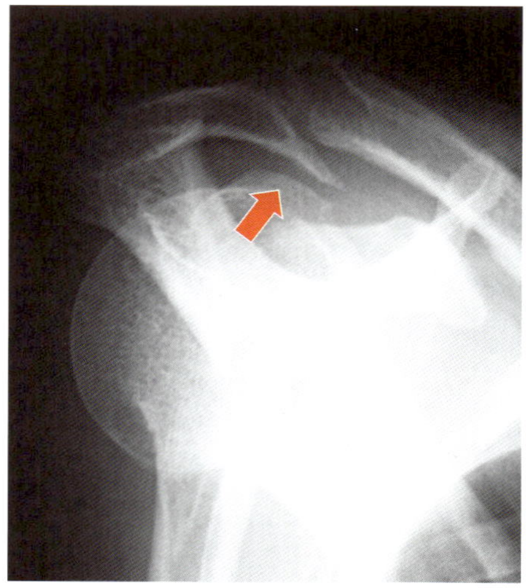

그림 15 견봉의 골극

견봉의 아래 골극에 주의. 오른쪽 그림과 같이 사위상(oblique view)에서 잘 관찰된다. 주의하지 않으면 발견하기 어렵다.

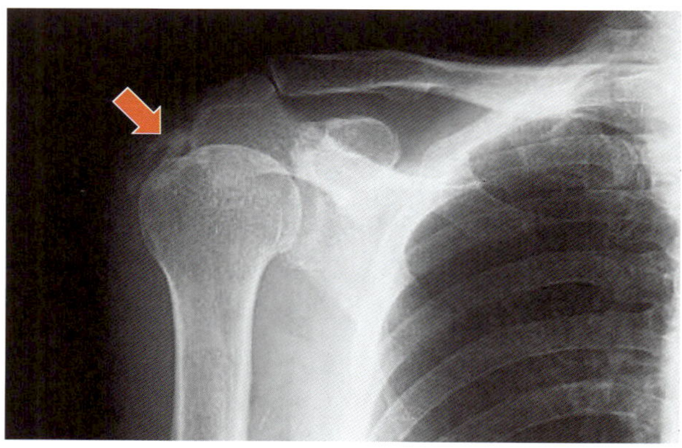

그림 16 석회침착성 점액낭염

특별한 원인없이 발생한 갑작스러운 어깨 통증으로 내원하였다.

석회침착성 점액낭염

석회침착성 점액낭염에서는 특별한 원인없이 갑작스러운 어깨 통증이 발생한다. 빈도가 매우 높기 때문에 중요하다. X-ray로 석회화를 확인할 수 있다(그림 16). 스테로이드와 국소마취제를 혼합한 주사가 효과적이다. 스테로이드는 반드시 국소마취제와 함께 주사해야 한다. 스테로이드 단독으로 주사하면 극심한 고통을 호소한다.

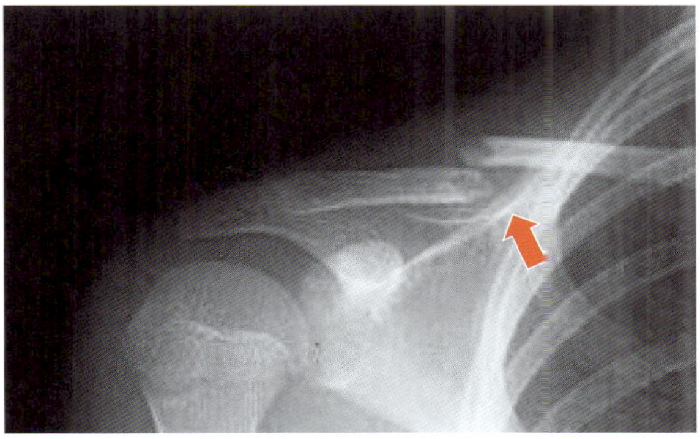

그림 17 clavicle fracture
쇄골의 중간 1/3에서 골절되는 경우가 많다. 쇄골 근위는 흉쇄유돌근에 이끌려 위쪽으로, 쇄골 원위는 팔의 무게로 인해 아래쪽으로 전위한다.

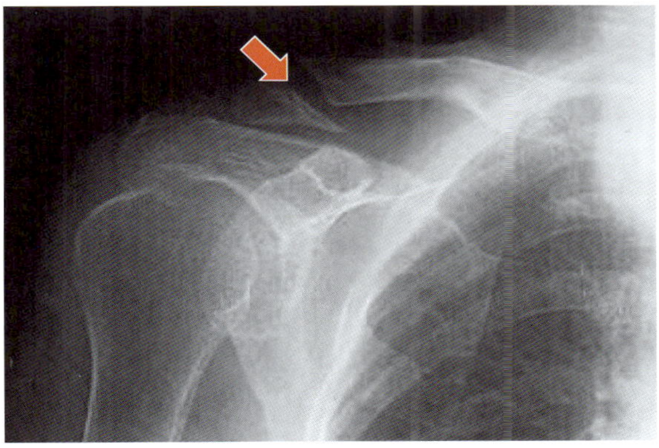

그림 18 distal clavicle fracture
불유합 혹은 가성관절(pseudarthrosis)이 되기 쉽다. 오래된 골절은 골절단이 경화되어 있는 경우가 많다. 경화상(sclerosis)이 있다면 오래된 골절!

쇄골 골절

쇄골 골절은 쇄골 중간 1/3에서 발생하는 경우가 흔하며, 대부분 근위 골편은 흉쇄유돌근에 이끌려 위쪽으로, 원위 골편은 상지의 무게 때문에 아래쪽으로 전위된다(**그림 17**). **쇄골 외측단 골절**(**그림 18**)은 불유합 혹은 가성관절이 되기 쉽다.

또한, 골절이 최근의 골절인지, 오래된 골절인지는 골절단을 보면 알 수 있다. **오래된 골절**은 골절단의 경화상(sclerosis)이 있는 경우가 많다.

견관절 탈구

견관절 탈구에는 **전방 탈구**(그림 19), **하방 탈구**(그림 20), **수직 탈구**(그림 21, 22), **후방 탈구** 등이 있다.

전방 탈구, 하방 탈구에서는 상완골두가 탈구해 견봉이 눈에 띄며, 이를 **epaulet sign**이라고 한다. 군인이나 경찰이 어깨에 달고 있는 것이 epaulet(견장)이다.

또한, 상완의 축에 주의한다. 그림 23에서 오른쪽 상완의 축이 왼쪽에 비해 안쪽으로 치우쳐 있는

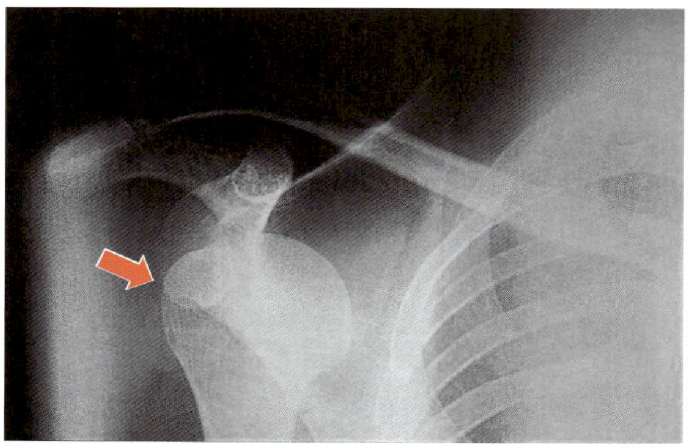

그림 19 전방 탈구
가장 흔히 볼 수 있다.

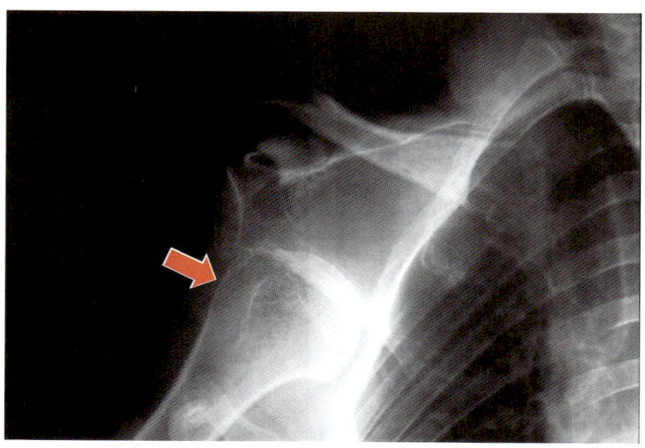

그림 20 하방 탈구

것을 알 수 있다. 이것만으로도 탈구라는 것을 알 수 있다.

후방 탈구(그림 24~26)는 **뇌전증 발작**(seizure)의 후궁반장(opisthotonus)에서 일어나는 경우가 있다. 그림 24에서는 명백한 이상 소견이 관찰되지만 환자가 비만이라면 알기 어려울 수 있다. 또한, 정면상 X-ray만으로는 놓칠 수 있다(그림 25). 축상(axial view, 그림 26)에서는 명확하지만 판독이 어려울 수도 있다. 뇌전증 발작 후의 어깨 통증에는 후방 탈구를 염두에 두어야 한다.

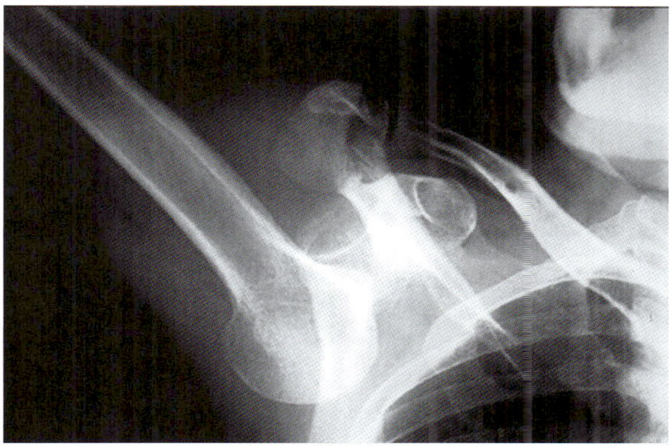

그림 21 **수직 탈구**

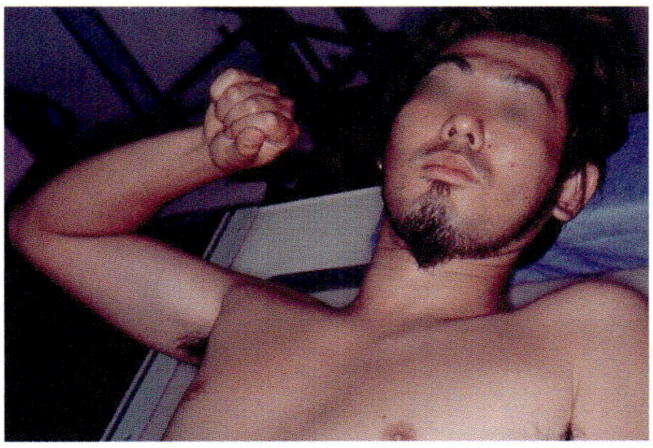

그림 22 **수직 탈구**

맨홀에 빠져 부상을 입었다. 건장한 남성이 이런 모습으로 내원하였다.

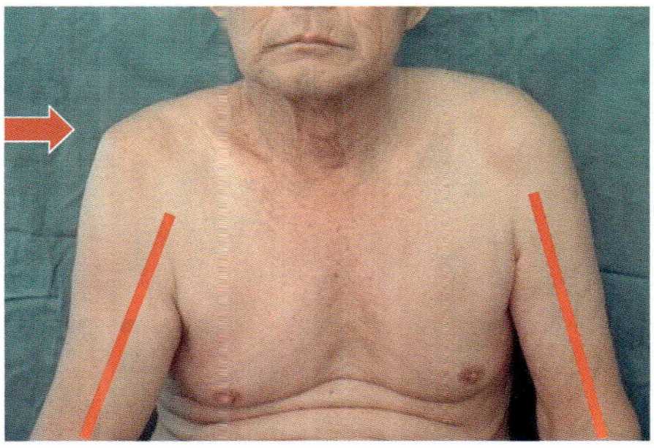

그림 23 **오른쪽 견관절 탈구**

오른쪽 어깨가 각져 있는 것에 주의한다(➡). epaulet sign이다. 또한, 오른쪽 상완의 축이 왼쪽에 비해 안쪽으로 치우쳐 있는 것에 주의.

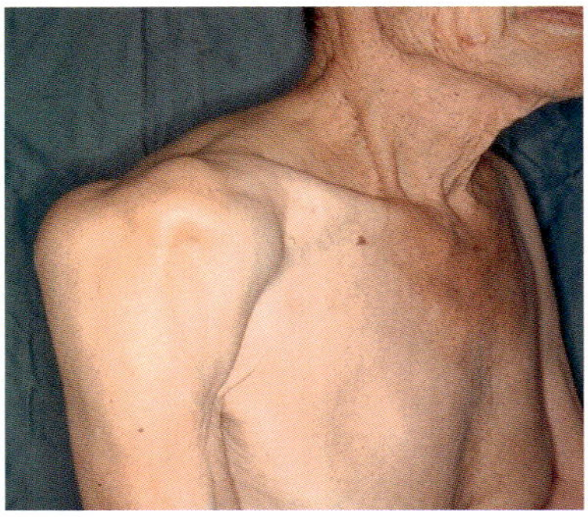

그림 24 **후방 탈구**

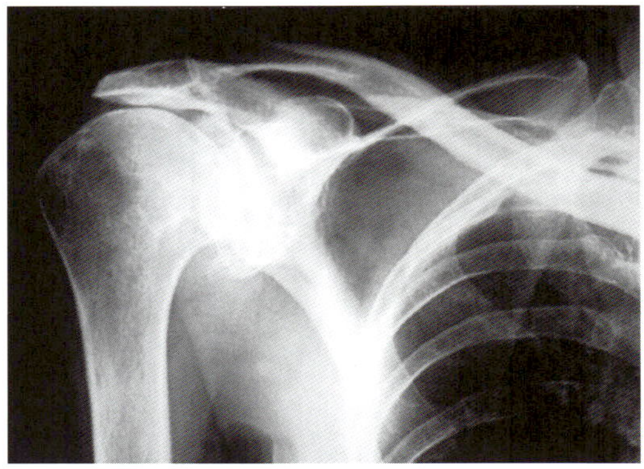

그림 25 **후방 탈구 X-ray**
정면상에서는 알 수 없다.

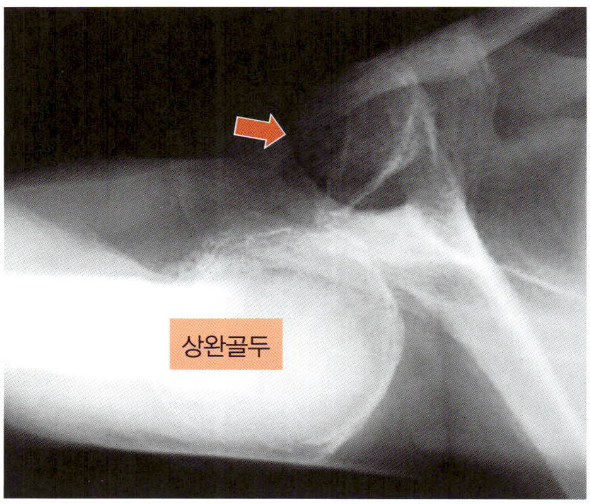

그림 26 **축상(axial view)으로 알 수 있는 후방 탈구**
상완골두가 관절와(➡)의 후방에 있다.

또한, 견관절 탈구로 상완골두가 관절와를 벗어날 때, **골두의 함몰 골절**이 일어날 수 있으며 이를 **Hill-Sachs lesion(**그림 27~29)이라고 한다. 이것이 있다면 **습관성 탈구**가 발생하기 쉽다.

더불어 **Bankart lesion(**그림 30)이라고 하여 전방 탈구 시 구개 하방 **관절와순의 박리** 및 **견열**(avulsion) **골절**을 일으키는 경우도 있다. 이는 Hill-Sachs lesion과 합병되는 일이 많다. 견관절 탈구를 확인한 경우, Hill-Sachs lesion과 Bankart lesion의 존재에 주의한다.

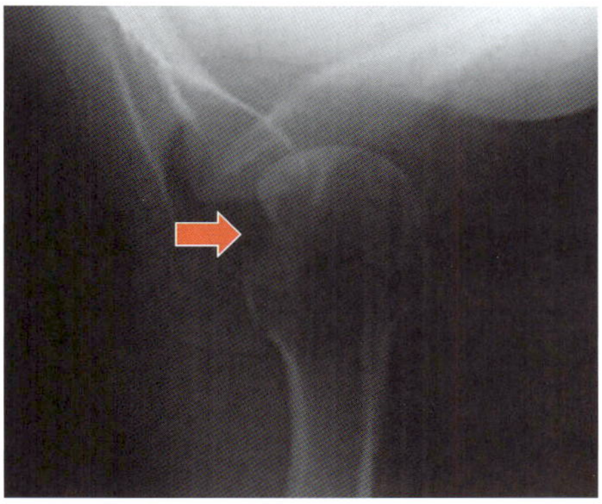

그림 27 상완골두 후방의 함몰 골절 (Hill-Sachs lesion)

이것이 있다면 습관성 탈구가 생기기 쉽다.

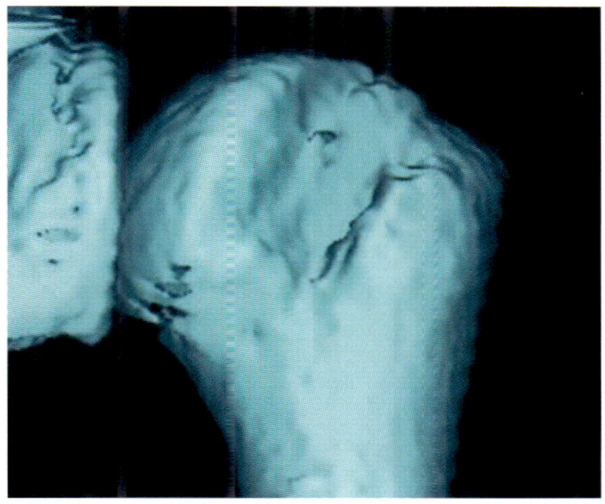

그림 28 상완골두 후방의 함몰 골절 (Hill-Sachs lesion)

3차원 CT 영상

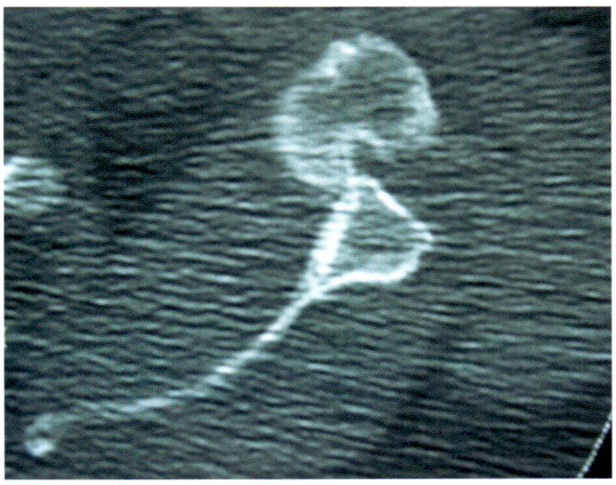

그림 29 Hill-Sachs lesion에 의해 상완골두가 관절와를 벗어나는 순간

Hill-Sachs lesion이 있으면 습관성 탈구가 발생하기 쉽다. CT 영상.

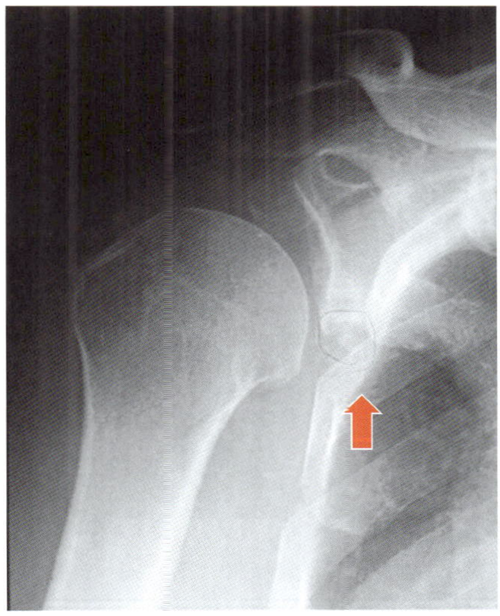

그림 30 Bankart lesion

견쇄관절 탈구

견쇄관절 탈구는 주로 외부로부터 직접적인 힘이 가해져 발생하며, 추락하거나 넘어지면서 어깨를 지면에 부딪히며 손상되는 경우가 흔하다. 쇄골 외측단이 상방으로 튀어나온다(그림 31, 32). 실제로는 쇄골이 위로 튀어나오는 것이 아니라, 견봉이 상완의 중력에 의해 내려가는 것이다. 쇄골을 손가락으로 누르면 피아노 키처럼 내려가서 **piano key sign**이라고 한다(그림 33).

정상적인 쇄골 외측단은 견봉보다 약간 튀어나와 있다(그림 34, ➡). 따라서 손가락으로 만지면 견쇄관절은 반드시 식별 가능하다. 자신의 견쇄관절을 촉진해 보자.

단, 쇄골 하단과 견봉 하단은 동일한 선상(붉은 선)에 있는 것에 유의한다. 그림 34는 정상 소견이다.

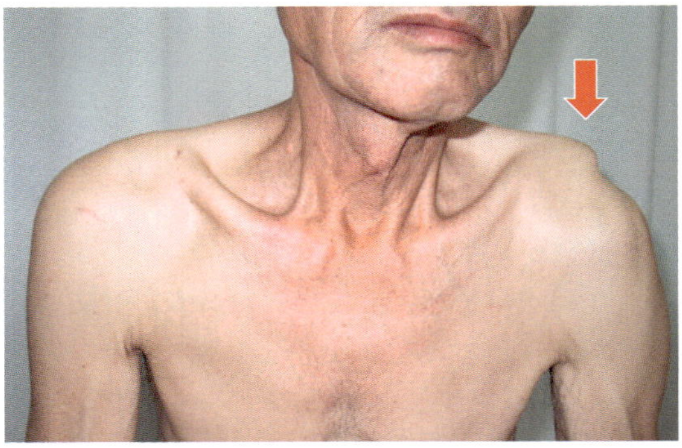

그림 31 견쇄관절 탈구
쇄골이 위로 튀어나온다.

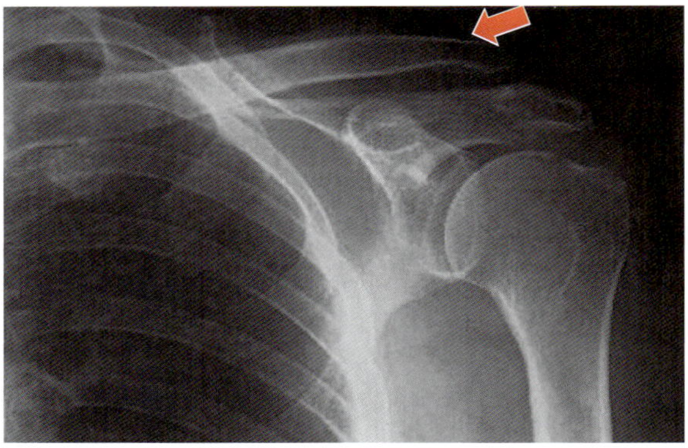

그림 32 견쇄관절 탈구

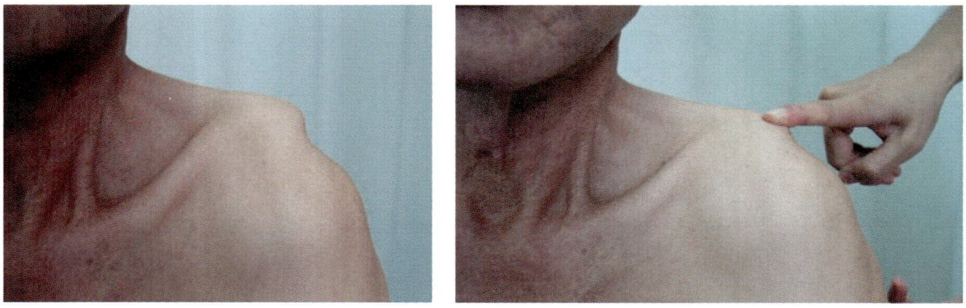

그림 33 견쇄관절 탈구와 piano key sign
손가락으로 누르면 내려간다. piano key sign이라고 한다.

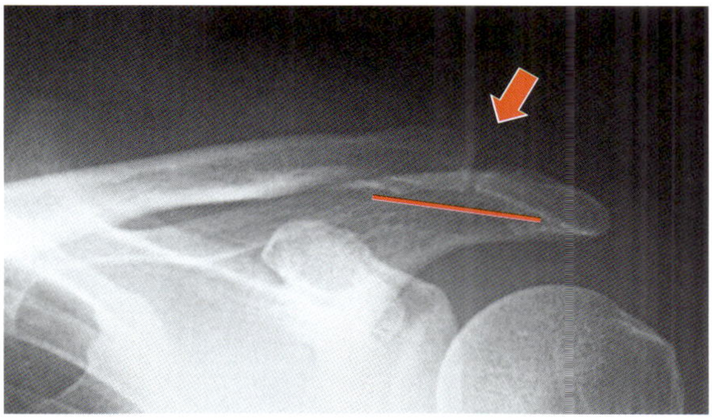

그림 34 견쇄관절의 정상 소견

상완골 근위부 골절

상완골 근위부 골절(proximal humerus fracture)은 고령자에서 매우 흔한 골절이다. 고령자에서흔한 골절은 다음과 같다.

① 척추압박골절(➡ p80, 83)

② 대퇴골 근위부 골절(➡ p92)

③ 상완골 근위부 골절

④ 요골 원위단 골절(➡ p40)

그림 35는 동네에서 열린 '낙상 예방교실'에서 계단을 오르다가 넘어져 좌측 상완골 근위부 골절이 발생한 것으로, 낙상 예방교실이 '낙상 촉진교실'이 되어버린 사례이다.

'**근위부**'의 골절은 고령자에서 흔히 발생하는 외상이다(그림 36).

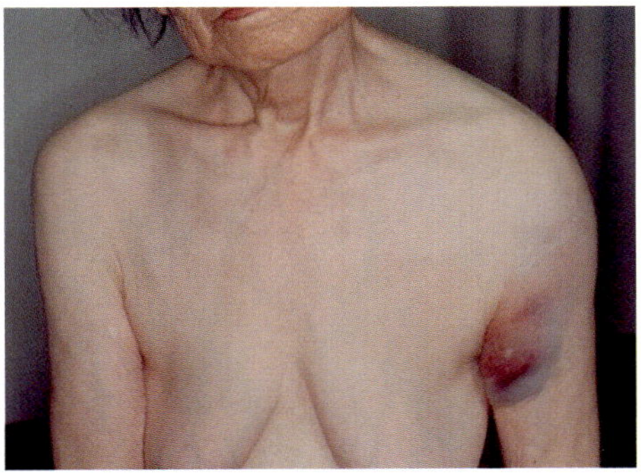

그림 35 좌측 상완골 근위부 골절

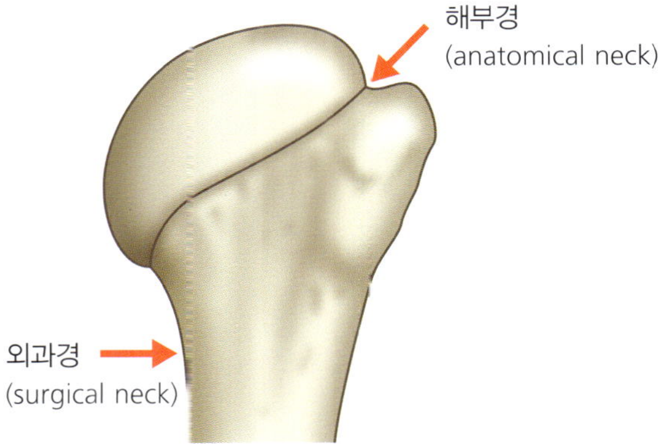

그림 36 외과경에서 골절이 발생하기 쉽다.

오구돌기 골절

놓치기 쉬운 골절 중 드물지만 **오구돌기**(coracoid process) **골절**이 있다. 오구돌기(그림 37, 38)를 직접 만져 본다. 견쇄관절 바로 앞 아래쪽에 있는 돌기이다.

여기에 직접적인 충격이 가해진 경우, 예를 들어 클레이 사격의 반동 등으로 인해 발생한다. 축상(axial view)을 확인하지 않으면 알 수 없다(그림 39). 어깨 외상은 정면, 축영상, 사위(scapular Y)의 세 방향에서 X-ray를 촬영한다.

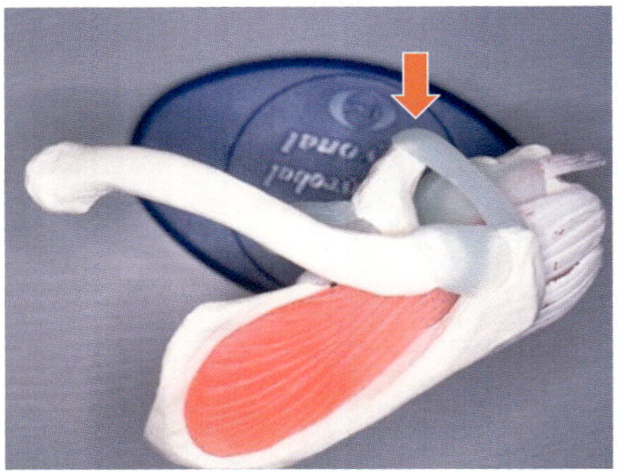

그림 37 오구돌기

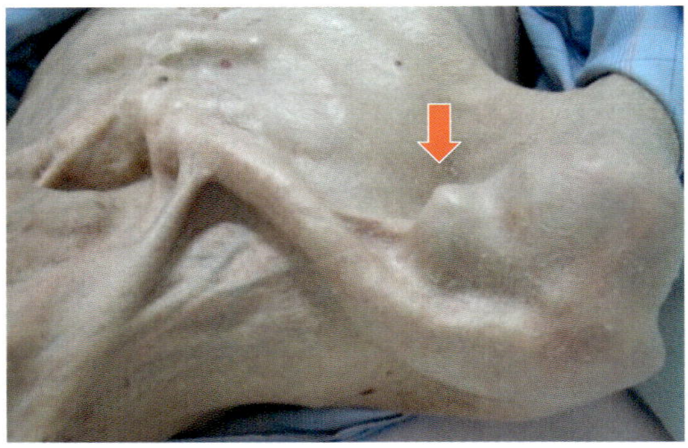

그림 38 오구돌기
매우 마른 사람으로 외부에서도 오구돌기(➡)를 확인할 수 있다.

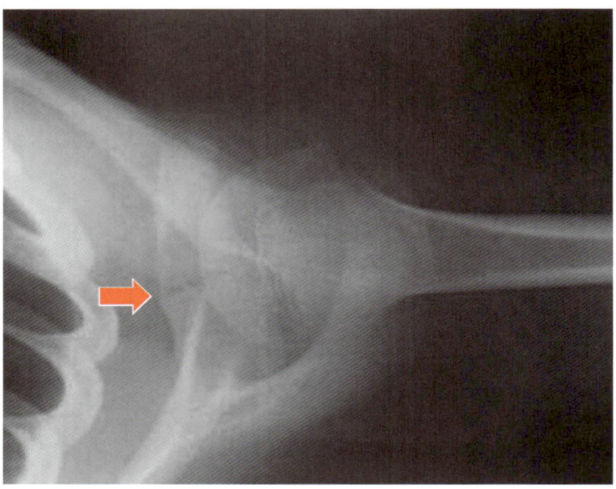

그림 39 오구돌기 골절

반복 학습

❶ 어깨 X-ray에서 상완골 골두의 상방 전위를 보이면 **회전근개 파열**. 어깨초음파에서는 회전근개가 위쪽으로 볼록하지 않고 평평하게 보인다.

❷ 어깨초음파에서 회전근개가 **6mm 이상**이면 **충돌증후군**. 이 경우엔 종종 어깨 X-ray에서 **골극**이 보이는 경우가 있다.

❸ 어깨초음파에서 상완이두근 장두건이 결절간 고랑(bicipital groove)에서 돌출되었거나, 주위에 삼출이 있다면 **상완이두근 장두건염**. **류마티스성 다발근통**에서는 점액낭(bursa)이나 상완이두근 장두건 주위에 삼출 및 혈류 증가를 확인할 수 있다(컬러도플러검사).

❹ 어깨의 갑작스러운 극심한 통증은 석회침착성 점액낭염을 의심한다.

❺ 쇄골 골절은 근위는 위로, 원위는 아래로 전위한다.

❻ 견관절 탈구는 Hill-Sachs lesion, Bankart lesion에 주의한다.

❼ 견쇄관절 탈구에서는 piano key sign이 있다.

❽ 고령자에게 흔한 4가지 골절 : ① 척추압박골절, ② 대퇴골 근위부 골절, ③ 상완골 근위부 골절, ④ 요골 원위단 골절

❾ 오구돌기 골절은 어깨 축상(axial view)을 확인하지 않으면 알 수 없다.

참고문헌

1. Rockwood CA, et al : Rockwood and Matsen's the shoulder, 4th ed. Sounders, 2009.

COLUMN

한 장의 X-ray 사진에 얽힌 불행한 역사적 과거

이 X-ray(그림)는 외래에 내원한 노인의 어깨 사진이다. 어깨 통증을 호소하여 X-ray를 촬영해보니, 상완골두가 변형되어 변형성(퇴행성) 견관절증이 발생해 있었다. 대체 어떤 수상 기전이었는지 물어본 결과 놀랍게도 태평양전쟁 중 미드웨이해전의 생존자였으며, 항공모함 '소류(蒼龍)'의 통신병이었다.

*

1942년 6월, 제2차 세계대전 중 일본 해군은 거의 모든 병력으로 미드웨이 섬을 공격, 미 해군 항공모함 부대를 유인하여 섬멸을 하고자 하였다. 일본 쪽 항공모함은 '아카기', '카가', '소류', '히류'의 4척이 투입되었다. 먼저 1차 공격대가 미드웨이 비행장을 폭격한다. 일본군은 미드웨이 주변에 미군 항공모함이 있다고 생각했다.

일본 쪽 항공모함에 대기하고 있던 2차 공격대는 미군 항공모함 격침을 위해 어뢰를 탑재하고 있었다. 그러나 미군 항공모함은 보이지 않았으며, 이로 인해 지상 공격용의 폭탄으로 변경하게 된다. 하지만 폭탄으로 바꾸자마자, 정찰기로부터 미군 항공모함을 발견했다는 무전이 들어온다. 일본군의 위치도 미군에게 이미 노출되었을 가능성이 있어, 야마구치 다몬 소령은 보통 폭탄으로 즉시 발함할 것을 나구모 츄이치 사령장관에게 전한다.

그러나 항공모함을 격침하기에 보통 폭탄은 어뢰에 비해 너무 약했다. 나구모 사령관은 다시 폭탄에서 어뢰로의 변경을 명령하였고 변경 작업이 끝나갈 무렵, 미군의 항공모함 함재기가 일본군을 공격하였다. 마침 귀환한 1차 공격대를 수용하고 있던 일본군은 고도 5,000m에서 급강하해온 미군 항공모함 함재기를 알아채지 못하였다.

이 전투로 일본군은 항공모함 4척, 항공기 300기, 그리고 수많은 병력을 한 순간에 잃었으며 이것은 태평양 전쟁의 전환점이 되었다.

*

이 항공모함 '소류'의 통신병이었던 환자는 폭탄에 의해 오른쪽 어깨에 큰 부상을 입었다.

'소류'는 가라앉기 시작했고 환자는 해면으로 뛰어들어 구축함에 의해 구출되었다. 그 후, 해군병원에서 어깨 수술을 받았다고 한다.

*

1장의 X-ray 사진에 얽힌 어두운 역사적 사실과 환자의 힘들었던 과거를 상상하며 깊이 감동하였다.

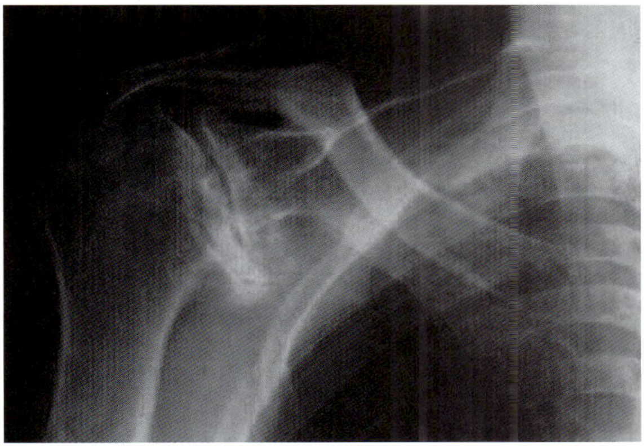

그림 미드웨이 해전 생존자의 오른쪽 어깨(변형성 견관절증)

척추 · 허리

요추 X-ray 판독

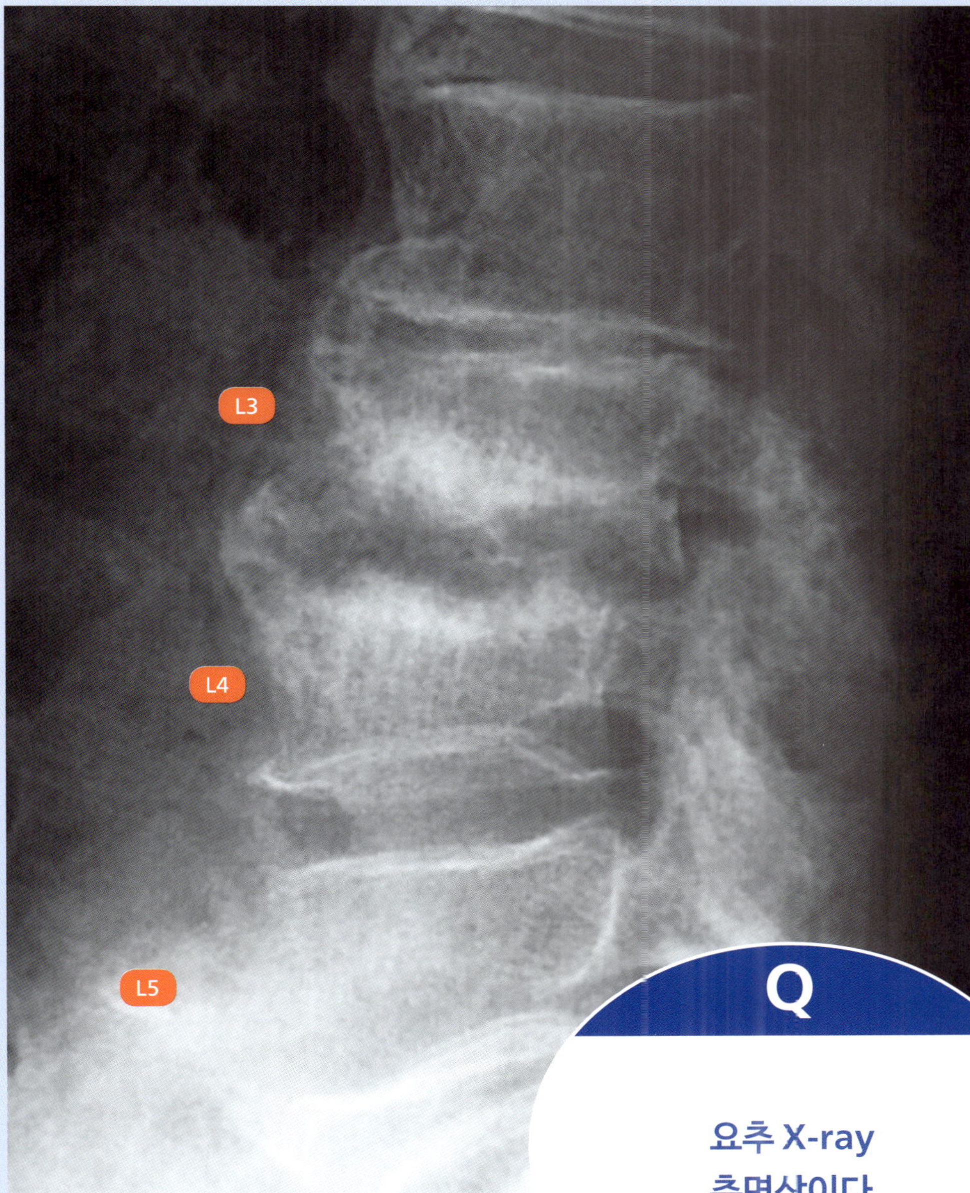

79세 · 남성.
39℃ 발열, 요통.

Q

요추 X-ray
측면상이다.
진단은?

앞 페이지의 X-ray 진단은 **화농성 척추염**이다. 먼저 L3/4 추간판과 L3와 L4의 추체 변연이 파괴된 것에 주목한다.

'허리가 아프다'고 호소하는 환자는 내과에서도 적지 않을 것이다. 여기에서는 내과에서 유용한 척추 X-ray 판독으로 화농성 척추염과 전이성 척추 종양, 변형성 척추증과 vacuum phenomenon(수핵의 변성)의 구별과 골다골증의 판정에 대한 착안점을 알아보자.

화농성 척추염과 전이성 척추 종양의 차이

화농성 척추염(septic spondylitis)의 감염균은 *Staphylococcus*와 *Escherichia coli*가 흔하며 세균은 추체 후방의 Hahn cleft(**그림 1**)에 있는 동맥을 경유해 추체로 침입한다. Hahn cleft는 MRI에서 확인되지만 때로는 단순 X-ray에서도 관찰 가능하다.

세균은 추간판도 파괴한다

추체 내에 들어간 감염균은 종말동맥으로 들어가 추체 전방의 변연에 이르면 증식을 시작한다(**그림 2**). 균은 단백질 분해효소(프로테아제)를 가지고 있기 때문에 추체 변연에서 증식을 시작하면

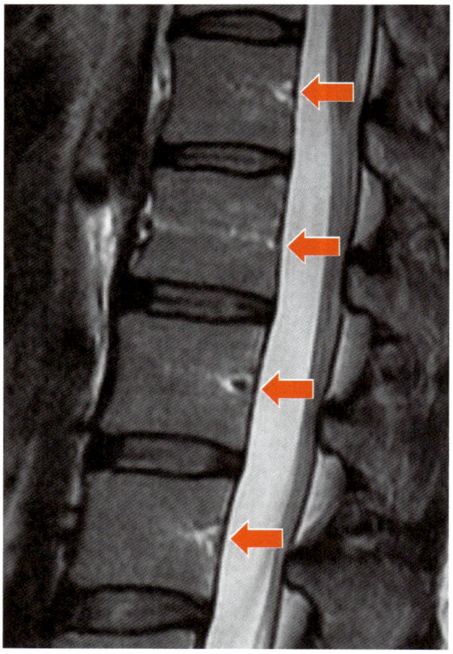

그림 1 Hahn cleft의 MRI 영상
추체 중심의 선상 고신호가 Hahn cleft. 이곳에 동맥과 정맥이 있으며 혈류를 통해 감염균이 후방에서 추체 내로 진입한다.

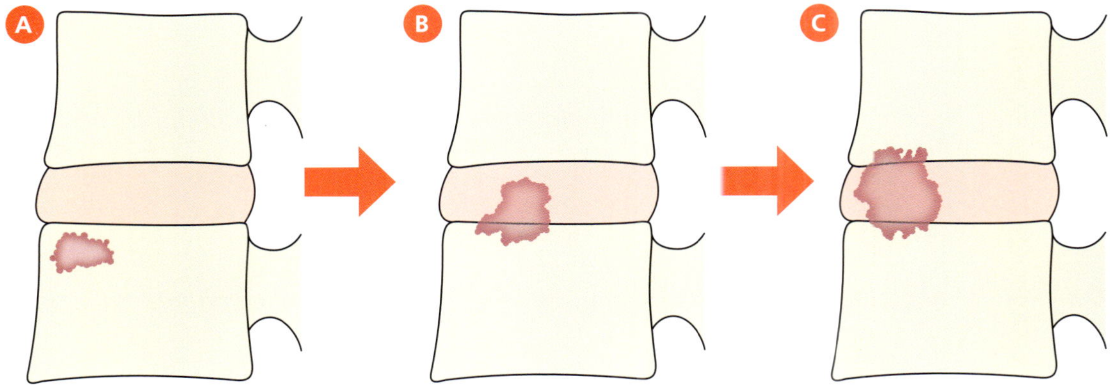

그림 2 **화농성 척추염의 기전**
세균은 추체의 종말동맥으로 들어가 추체 전방의 변연에서 멈추며, 여기에서 증식을 시작한다(A).
단백질 분해효소로 추간판 내에 침입해(B), 추간판을 파괴해 간다(C).

바로 추간판 내로 뚫고 들어가 추간판이 파괴되기 시작한다. 따라서, 화농성 척추염 영상의 특징은 '추간판과 그 주변의 추체가 파괴되는 것'이다.[1]

MRI로 보면 그림 3과 같다. 화농성 척추염의 영상 검사는 MRI의 민감도가 가장 높아 진단에 도움이 된다. MRI에서는 특히 경막외 농양, 척주 주변 농양, 추간판 농양에 주의한다. 심한 통증이 느껴지면 **경막외 농양**을 의심한다. 그림 3에서는 추간판 내부와 L4 추체 전방에 **농양**이 있다는 사실에 주의한다.

또한, **결핵성 척추염**(tuberculous spondylitis)의 경우는 추간판을 침범하지 않는다. 추체의 전 · 후방으로 배농이 많고 또한, 척추 세 레벨 이상 퍼지는 경우가 많다. 네팔 등에서는 아직도 흔한 질환이다.

악성 종양은 추간판을 파괴할 수 없다

한편, **전이성 척추 종양**의 경우, 악성 종양은 추체 내에서 증식하지만 추간판을 파괴하는 경우는 없다(그림 4). 추간판에는 혈류가 거의 없으며 악성 종양세포의 증식인자(IGF, TGF-β) 등이 거의 없는 '불모지'이기 때문에 추간판에서는 증식할 수 없는 것이다. 다시 말해 '추간판이 파괴되는 것이 화농성 척추염, 추간판이 파괴되지 않는 것이 전이성 척추 종양'이라고 기억한다.

또한, **척추압박골절**은 보통 MRI에서의 신호 변화가 극돌기에까지 미치지 않는다(체간의 굴곡 손상에 의한 Chance fracture는 제외). 만약 극돌기에도 신호 변화가 있는 경우는 전이성 척추 종양을 의심한다.

전이성 척추 종양은 추체 후방에서 많이 전이되며 후방으로 더욱 진전된 경우 의심할 수 있다. 이것은 골반 내 장기로부터의 전이는 척추관 내의 Baston venous plexus(with no valves)를 통한 경우

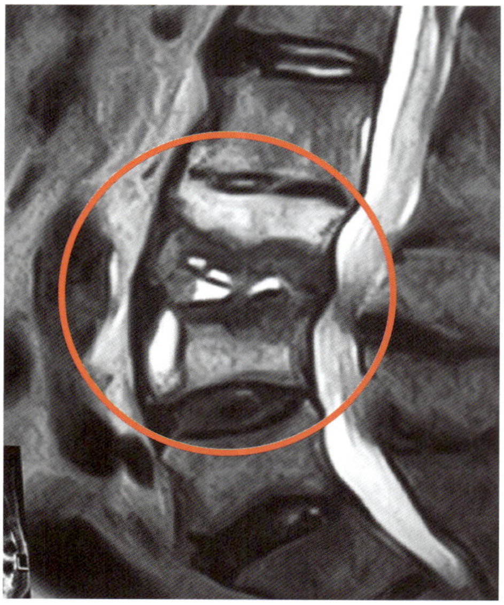

그림 3 화농성 척추염의 MRI 영상 (T2 강조)

추간판과 그 주변의 추체 파괴, 고신호의 농양도 확인된다. 추간판 파괴는 필연적이다.

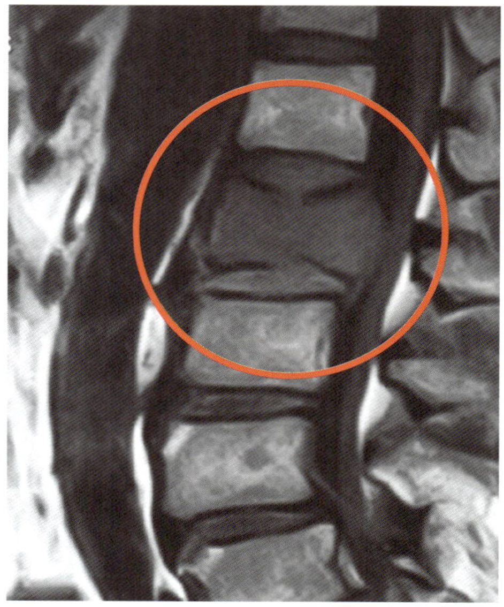

그림 4 전이성 척추 종양의 MRI 영상 (T1 강조)

제2 요추의 식도암 전이. 추간판은 침범당하지 않는다. 추체가 후방으로 부풀어 있는 것에 주목한다.

가 많은데 추체정맥은 추체 후방에서 풍부하기 때문이다. 또한, **그림 4**와 같이 추체가 후방으로 팽창된 경우에도 전이가 의심된다.

MRI 영상에서의 전이성 척추 종양은 T1에서 저신호인 경우가 많고, T2에서는 다양하다. STIR와 T1에서의 Gd(가돌리늄) 조영은 고신호를 보이는 경우가 많다.

변형성(퇴행성) 척추증과 진공 현상의 차이

그림 5는 전형적인 **변형성 척추증**(spondylosis deformans)의 X-ray이다. 추간판의 두께가 유지되고 또한, 전방에 **골극**이 생긴 것에 주목한다. 이것이 변형성 척추증의 특징이다.

추간판은 내부에 수핵이 있고 그 외측에 섬유륜이 있다. 외측의 섬유륜은 추체와 샤피섬유(Sharpey fibers, 섬유륜의 가장 외측)로 견고하게 결합되어 있다(**그림 6**). 추체와 섬유륜은 같은 중배엽에서 유래된 반면 수핵은 내배엽에서 유래한다.

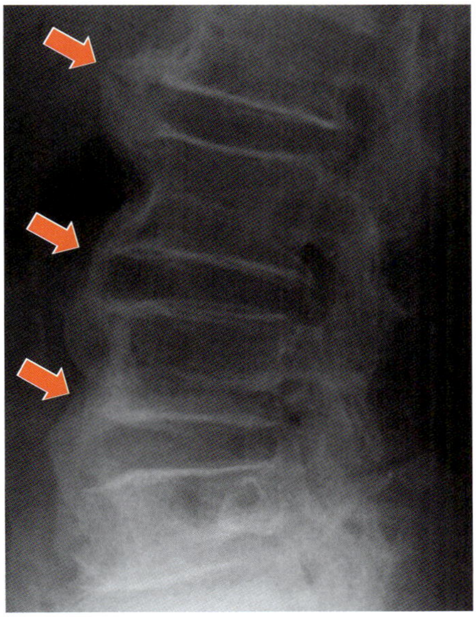

그림 5 **변형성 척추증의 X-ray 측면상**
추간판의 두께가 유지되고(수핵이 변성되지 않음), 전방에 골극이 있다. 수핵의 수압으로 전종인대가 전방으로 밀려난다. 전종인대(ALL)는 추간판에서 수 mm 떨어진 곳에서 추체에 부착하므로, 추체를 견인해 골극이 생긴다.

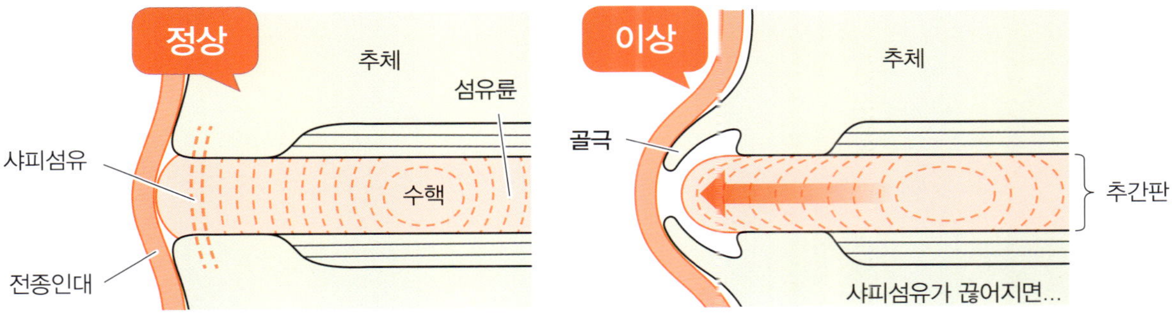

그림 6 **변형성 척추증의 기전**
❶ 먼저 섬유륜 주변 샤피섬유가 끊어지면, ❷ 수핵의 수압에 의해 추간판이 전방으로 돌출되고 전종인대도 전방으로 나온다. ❸ 전종인대는 추간판으로부터 수 mm 떨어진 추체에 부착하므로 이 부분의 뼈를 견인하여 '골극'이 생긴다

수핵의 수압으로 전방에 골극이

변형성 척추증은 샤피섬유가 먼저 끊어지는 것으로 시작한다 이때 추간판의 수핵이 유지되면 수핵은 수분이 풍부하며 수압을 가지고 있기 때문에 추간판은 전방으로 돌출된다(그림 6). 추체 전방에는 전종인대가 있지만 이 인대는 추체 변연에서 수 mm 떨어진 추체 전방에 부착되어 있다. 추간판이 전방으로 나오면 전종인대도 전방으로 끌려가고 이로 인해 전종인대가 부착되어 있는 추체가 견인되어 골극이 생긴다. 즉, 변형성 척추증에서는 추간판 수핵의 수압에 의해 골극이 발생하는 것이다.

따라서 '변형성 척추증은 추간판의 두께가 유지되고 또한, 전방에 골극이 생기는 것이 특징'이다. 한편, 후종인대는 추체와 단단히 결합되지 않으므로, 추체 후방에는 골극이 생기지 않는다.

이러한 사실을 알고 나면 그림 5가 새롭게 보일 것이다.

만약 수핵이 변성되면....

그렇다면 그림 7은 어떤가? 추간판에는 가스(N_2가 많음)가 확인된다. 이를 **진공 현상**(vacuum phenomenon)이라고 한다. 이것은 추간판의 수핵이 변성된 것이다.

수핵은 수분이 풍부하고 수압이 있다. 이것이 변성되면 수압이 소실되고, 추간판의 두께는 매우 얇아진다. 수압이 소실되므로, 추간판이 전종인대를 밀어내지 못해 골극이 생기지 않는다.

그리고 기지개를 켜면 추간판 내부가 음압이 되어 주위 조직으로부터 질소가 나와 그림 7과 같은 X-ray 소견을 보인다. 이 상태를 **추간골연골증**(intervertebral osteochondrosis)이라고 한다.

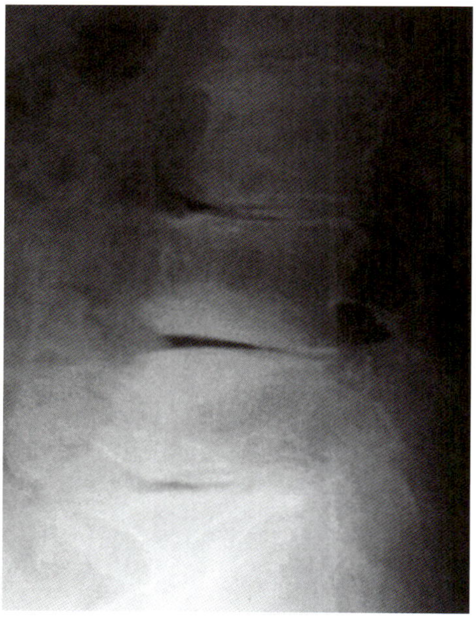

그림 7 진공 현상의 X-ray 측면상
수핵의 변성. 추간판은 좁아지고, 내부에 가스가 있다. 수핵에 의해 전종인대가 전방으로 밀려나지 않고, 골극은 관찰되지 않는다. 이런 상태를 추간골연골증(intervertebral osteochondrosis)이라고 한다.

독자분들도 손가락관절 마디를 꺾어서 소리를 내 보라. 소리를 낸 직후에 손의 X-ray를 찍으면 관절 내 위와 같은 가스를 확인할 수 있다. 소리를 낸 후 15~20분 동안은 소리를 낼 수가 없고, 가스는 서서히 주변에 흡수된다. 완전히 가스가 흡수된 후에는 다시 소리를 낼 수 있게 된다.

골다공증의 판정

추체에는 가로와 세로 골량이 있다. **골다공증**(osteoporosis)이 진행되면 가로 골량이 소실된다. 세로 골량은 체중을 지탱하는 데 중요하기 때문에 남아 있지만 골 감소가 계속 진행되면 세로 골량도 수가 줄고, 대신 하나하나의 세로 골량이 굵어진다. 따라서 그림 8과 같이 세로 골량이 두드러지면 골다공증의 진행을 의심한다. 골다공증의 치료는 골밀도 수치와 WHO의 FRAX 점수에 따라 결정한다.

척추압박골절

흉추, 요추는 위에서 아래로 갈수록 점차적으로 커진다. 그러므로 추체가 위에 비해 작은 경우, **척추압박골절**의 존재를 의심한다. 다만 제5 요추는 제4 요추에 비해 약간 작은 경우가 많다.

또한, 척주의 전연(anterior margin)이 부정확한 경우에는 **급성 골절(acute fracture)**을 의심한다(그림 9). **만성 골절(chronic fracture)**의 경우 remodeling되어 매끄러운 경우가 많다(그림 10).

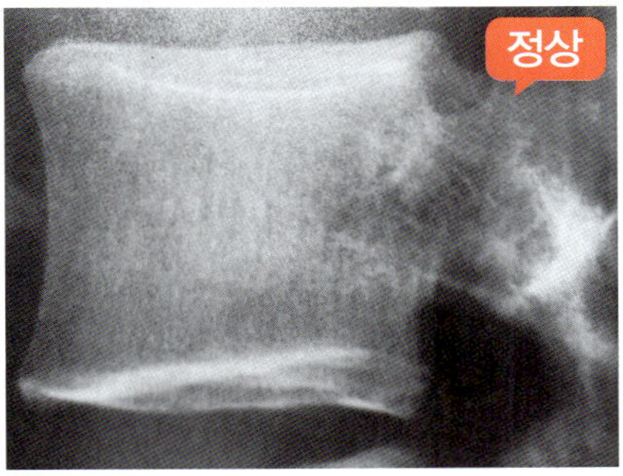

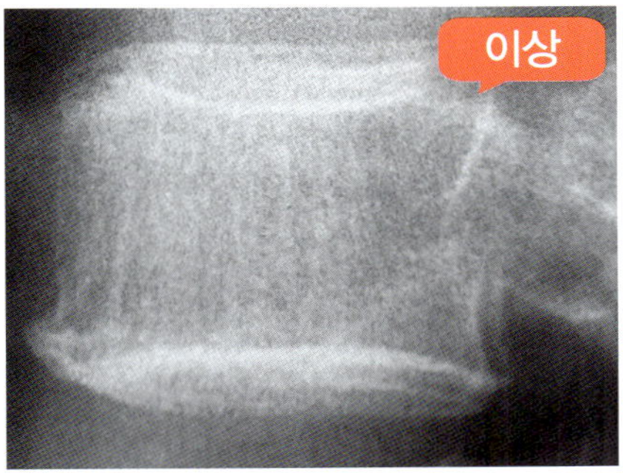

그림 8 정상과 골다공증의 추체
골다공증이 진행되면 가로 골량이 줄어든다. 세로 골량은 감소하지만 뼈가 더해져서 그 폭이 넓어지고 이상 영상처럼 세로 골량이 두드러지게된다. 즉, 구조 유지에 중요한 골량은 끝까지 남는다. 추체에서 세로 골량이 뚜렷하다면 골다공증을 의심한다.

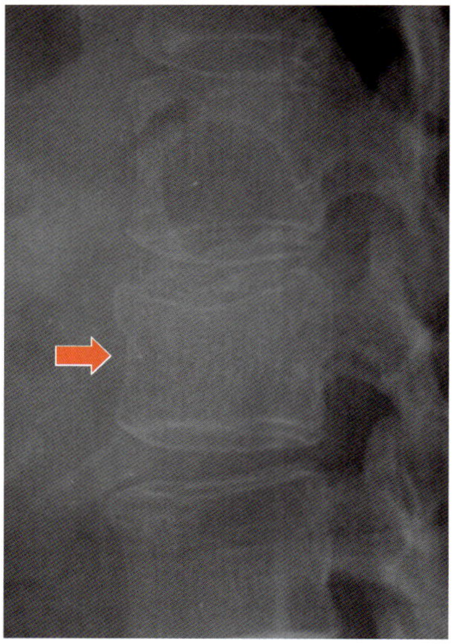

그림 9 **척추의 급성 골절**

추체 전연이 불규칙(irregular)한 경우, 급성 골절인 경우가 많다.

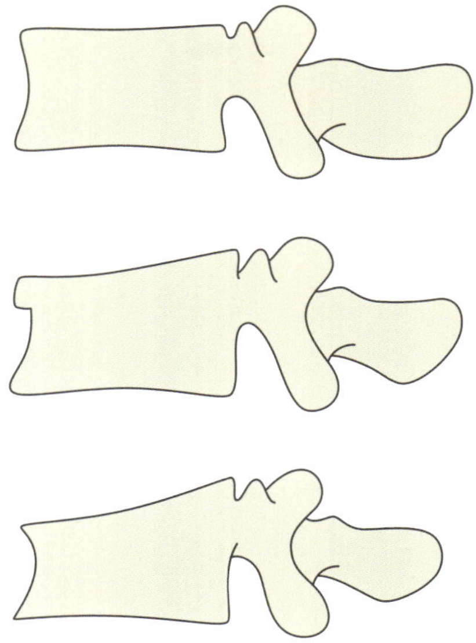

그림 10 **정상, 급성 골절, 만성 골절 추체**

MRI로는 급성과 만성을 감별할 수 있다

추체가 확실히 급성 골절인지 아닌지는 MRI를 사용하지 않으면 알 수 없다.

MRI는 H^+(프로톤)의 농도를 본다. H^+가 많은 것은 물(H_2O)과 지방(CH_3^-)이다. MRI로 보면 물은 T1에서 검게(저신호강도) 보인다. 수액은 물이므로 수액이 검게 찍히면 T1 강조 영상임을 알 수 있다. T2에서 수액은 반대로 희게(고신호강도) 보인다.

MRI에서 최소한 기억해야 할 것은 '병변은 보통 T2에서 고신호강도'가 된다는 것, '근골격계에서 자주 사용하는 STIR는 물과 지방은 비슷하기 때문에 지방을 제거'하는 것, '뇌 MRI에서 사용하는 FLAIR는 물만 검은색으로 하는 것' 정도 되겠다.

그림 11을 참조한다. 골절되면 추체에는 수분이 증가하므로 왼쪽의 T1 영상(뇌척수액이 검다)에서 추체는 검게 된다. 반대로 오른쪽 T2 영상(뇌척수액이 하얗다)에서는 하얗게 된다. 또한, STIR 영상(지방 억제)에서 추체골절은 더 하얗게 찍힌다.

만약 추체가 골절되었다고 해도 신호강도가 주변 추체와 같다면 만성 골절이다. 고령자의 경우 추체는 황색골수(fatty marrow)이기 때문에 지방 농도에 가깝다.

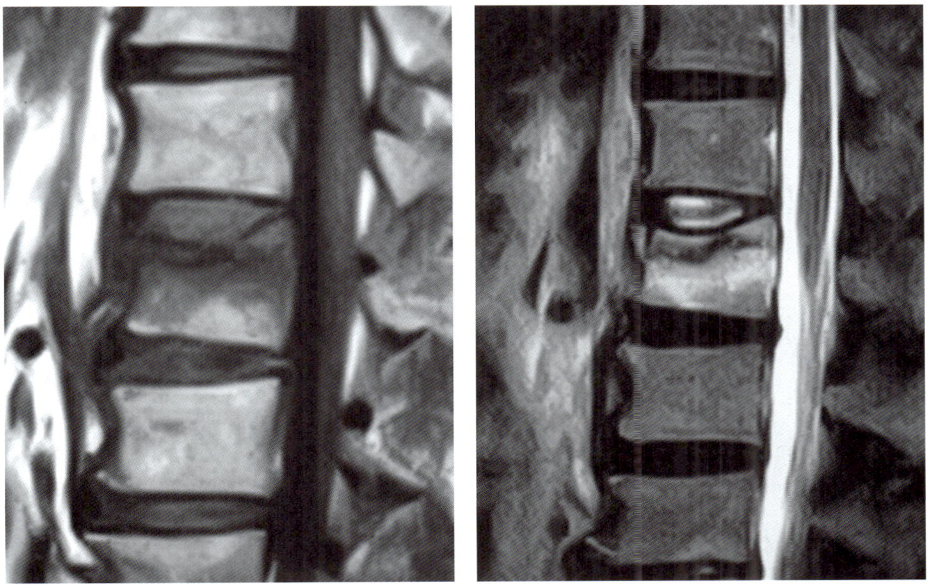

그림 11 압박골절의 MRI 소견

왼쪽은 T1(뇌척수액이 검은색), 골절되면 뼈는 수분이 증가해 T1에서 저신호강도를 보인다. 오른쪽은 T2(뇌척수액이 하얀색), 골절은 고신호강도를 보인다.

반복 학습

❶ 추간판이 파괴되는 것은 **화농성 척추염**, 파괴되지 않는 것은 **전이성 척추 종양.**

❷ **변형성 척추증**(섬유륜의 변성)은 추간판의 두께가 유지되며 또한, 전방으로 **골극**이 생기는 것이 특징. 한편, **진공 현상**(수핵의 변성)에서는 수핵의 수압이 소실되므로 추간판의 두께가 매우 얇아져 전종인대를 밀어내지 못하고 골극도 생기지 않는다.

❸ 추체의 X-ray에서 세로 골량이 뚜렷하면 **골다공증**의 진행을 의심한다.

❹ 추체 전연이 불규칙(irregular)한 경우, 급성 골절을 의심한다. 만성 골절은 전연이 매끄러운 경우가 많다.

참고문헌

1. Resnick D, Niwayama G : Diagnosis of bone and joint disorders. Saunders, 1987.

요추 천자 요령

수천 번이나 요추 천자를 하다 보면 '실수하지 않는 중요 체크 포인트'를 알게 된다. 방법이 해부학적으로 적절하다면 천자는 성공할 수 있다.

❶ 몸은 동그랗게 말고, 허리와 견갑골 부위는 모두 바닥에 수직으로!

우선 무엇보다 중요한 것은 자세이다. 환자를 옆으로 눕히고, 고양이처럼 동그랗게 구부리게 한다(그림 1). 그러면 극돌기간이 열린다.

그림 2는 천자에 매우 고생한 사례이다. 왜 고생했는지 궁금해서 수술 후, 요추 측면 X-ray를 찍어보니 이 환자는 극돌기가 매우 크고, 극돌기간이 매우 좁다는 것을 알게 되었다. 극돌기의 크기는 개인차가 크다. 따라서, 최대한 몸을 둥글게 말아 극돌기 사이를 벌리는 것이 무엇보다 중요하다.

그리고 또 하나 중요한 포인트는 허리와 견갑골 부위 모두 바닥에 수직으로 하는 것이다(그림 3). 흔히 허리만 수직이고 견갑골 부위는 전방에 있는 경우가 있다(그림 4). 이렇게 되면 척추가 회전되어 실패할 확률이 높아진다.

이 두 가지(몸을 동그랗게 말고, 허리와 견갑골 부위는 모두 바닥에 수직으로)는 반드시 지키도록 한다!

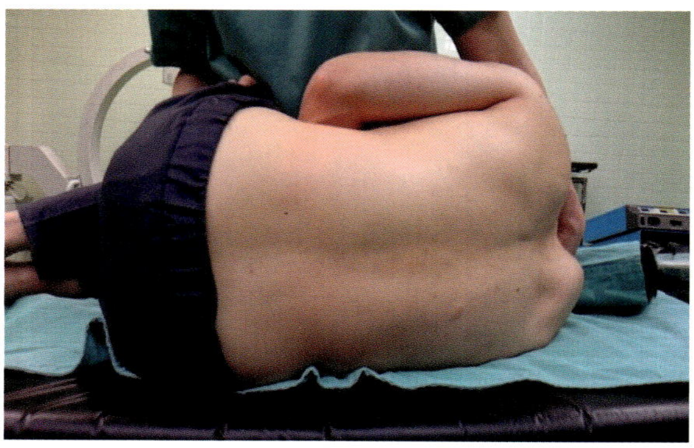

그림 1 요추 천자 자세
고양이처럼 최대한 둥글게 만든다.

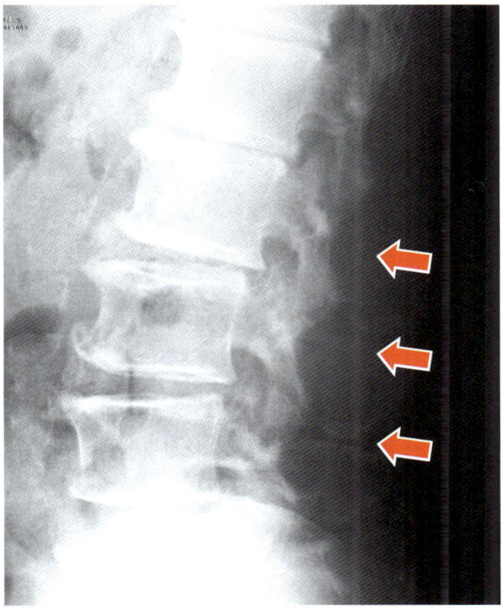

그림 2 **요추 마취가 매우 어려웠던 사례**

왜 힘들었는지 궁금해서 수술 후, 요추 측면 X선을 찍어보니 극돌기는 크고 극돌기 사이가 매우 좁았다. 극돌기의 크기는 개인차가 크다. 따라서 자세를 최대한 동그랗게 하여 극돌기 사이를 벌려야 한다.

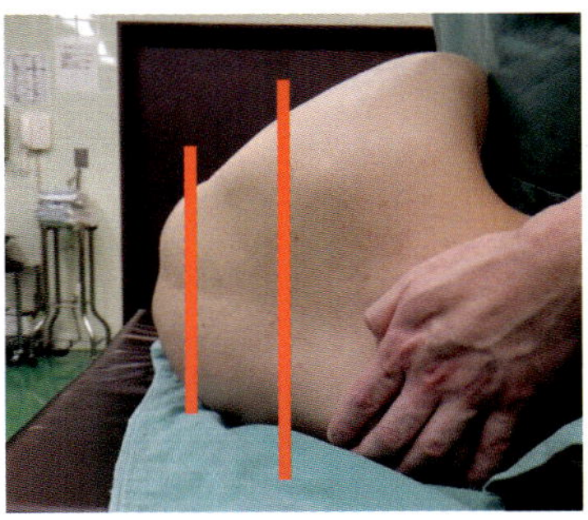

그림 3 **올바른 자세**

허리와 견갑골 부위 모두 바닥과 수직이 되게 한다.

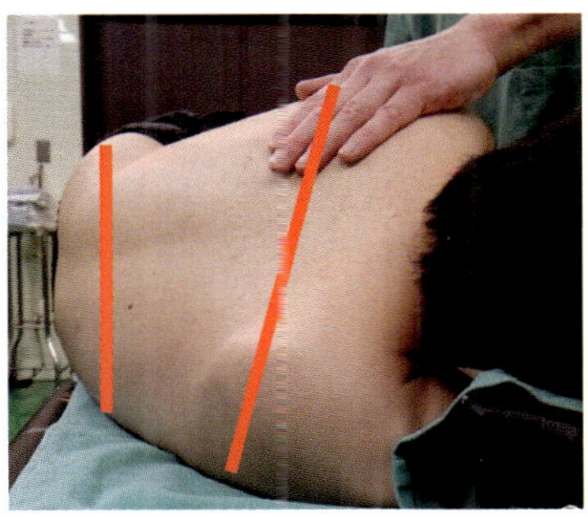

그림 4 **잘못된 자세**

그렇지 않으면 척추가 옆으로 회전된다.

❷ 극돌기를 확실하게 엄지로 잡고, 엄지손가락 한 가운데에 바늘을 찔러 바닥에 수평, 머리쪽으로 약간 기울인다.

다음으로 중요한 것은 극돌기를 확실하게 손가락으로 짚는 것이다(그림 5a). 극돌기를 확실하게 짚지 않는 한 천자는 성공할 수 없다.

비만 환자는 극돌기를 만지기 어려우며, 이런 경우에는 자신의 엄지를 상하(천장, 바닥) 방향으로 움직여 지방을 밀어내면, 극돌기의 대략적인 폭을 손가락으로 느낄 수 있다(그림 5b).

극돌기의 폭을 확인하면, 엄지손가락 중심에 극돌기를 위치시키고(그림 5c), 이 엄지의 중간을 지표로 바늘을 찌른다(그림 5d).

극돌기는 두미(cephalo-caudal) 방향으로 기울어지므로(그림 5e), 바늘은 약간 머리쪽을 향해 찌른다(그림 5d). 또한, 눈의 위치는 바늘과 같은 높이로 한다(그림 5f). 바늘을 위에서 내려다보면, 바늘이 바닥과 수평이 되어 있는지 알 수 없다.

또한, 추궁간이 가장 넓은 곳은 L5/S1로 가장 자입하기 쉬우나, 고령으로 척추관 협착증이 있으면 dry tap(수액 흡인 불능)인 경우도 많다. 이는 척추관 협착증이 요추 하위에서 많기 때문이다.

● 응용 1: 변형성 척추증 lateral approach

여기서 문제는 극돌기 사이의 극간인대가 골화되었거나, 추간판 변성으로 극돌기 사이 공간이 없을 때이다. 이런 경우 극돌기 사이로 자입하는 것은 포기하고, lateral approach를 실행한다. 극돌기 중심으로부터 3~5mm 떨어진 곳이면 충분하며(1cm 이상 벌어지면 안된다), 중심을 향해 비스듬히 넣는다. 극돌기 측면을 스치듯이, 천장 방향으로 15° 정도 비스듬히 넣으면 된다.

● 응용 2: 측만증 극돌기는 돌출 쪽과 반대쪽으로 기운다.

측만증이 있는 경우, 요추 정면 X-ray를 잘 확인해 둔다. 척추가 돌출된 쪽에 rib hump 또는 lumbar hump가 있지만, 돌출 쪽과 반대쪽으로 극돌기가 기울어진다(그림 6). 측만에서는 추체도 회전되기 때문이다. 따라서, 극돌기를 짚으면 척추가 돌출된 쪽으로 바늘을 약간 기울이면 진입하기 쉽다.

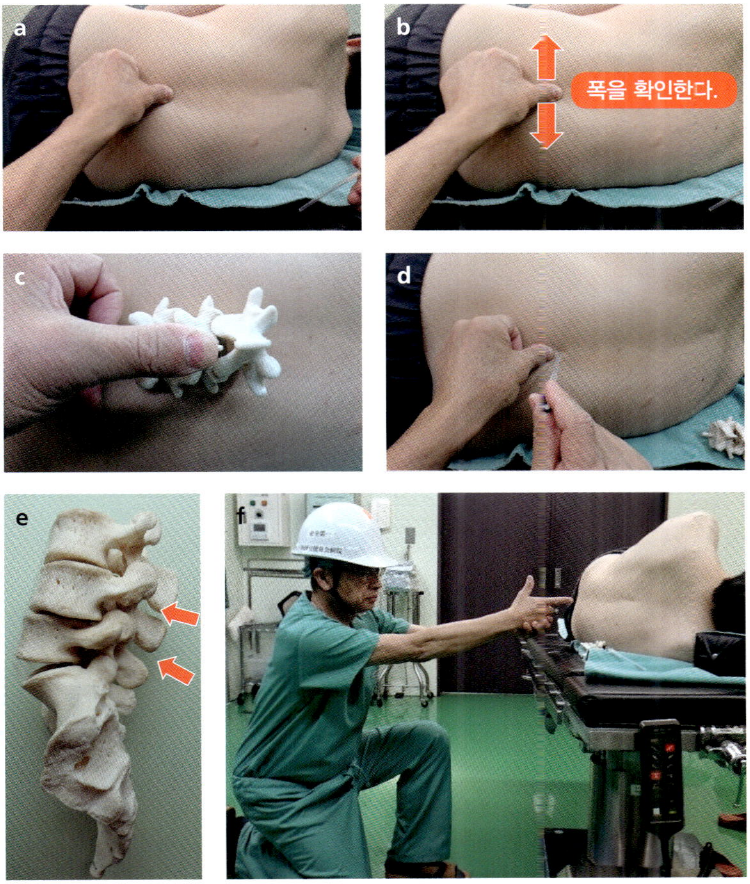

그림 5 요추 천자의 포인트

a : 극돌기를 확실하게 엄지로 짚는다.

b : 비만 환자의 경우 엄지를 상하(천장/바닥) 방향으로 움직여, 극돌기의 폭을 손가락으로 확인한다.

c : 극돌기의 폭을 확인 후 엄지의 중간에 위치시킨다. 이후, 절대로 이 엄지를 떼지 말아야 한다. 이 엄지 끝의 중심이 자입점의 지표이다. 여기서 1, 2mm라도 어긋나면 넣기 어려워진다.

d : 엄지손가락 중간이 바늘 자입점이다. 또한, 극돌기는 두미 방향으로 기울어 있어, 약간 두측을 향하게 하는 것이 좋다.

e : 극돌기는 두미 방향으로 기울어지므로, 바늘은 약간 두측으로 기울여 자입한다.

f : 눈은 바늘과 같은 높이로 한다. 바늘을 위에서 내려다보면 바늘이 바닥에 수평으로 들어가는지 알 수 없다(단, 실제 수술 시 헬멧은 불필요).

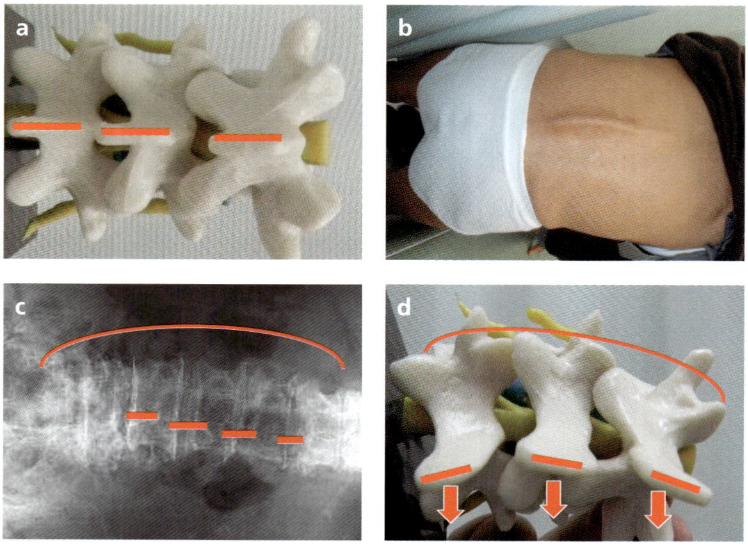

그림 6 **측만증의 요추 천자 포인트**

a : 정상적인 극돌기는 정중앙에 있다.
b : 측만이 있으면 극돌기는 척추의 돌출 쪽과 반대쪽으로 기울어진다.
c : 위로 돌출한 측만이 있는 경우, 극돌기의 위치는 아래로 어긋나 있다. 이는 d처럼 돌출 쪽과 반대쪽으로 추체가 회전하고 있다는 것을 의미한다. 즉, 바늘은 돌출 쪽으로 약간 기울이는 것이 경막 안으로 진입하기 쉽다.
d : 측만이 있으면 척추의 돌출 쪽과 반대로 극돌기는 기울어진다. 그러므로 바늘을 돌출 쪽으로 기울여야 진입하기 쉽다.

요추 천자의 요령

❶ 몸은 최대한 둥글게 하고, 허리와 견갑골 부위는 모두 바닥에 수직.

❷ 극돌기를 반드시 엄지로 확실하게 짚고, 엄지손가락 중심에 위치시킨다.

❸ 엄지손가락 중심에서 바닥과 수평으로 바늘을 자입, 바늘은 두측으로 약간 기울인다.

❹ 측만이 있을 경우 바늘을 돌출 쪽으로 약간 기울인다.

고관절 ❶ 골절편

대퇴골 골절의 X-ray 소견

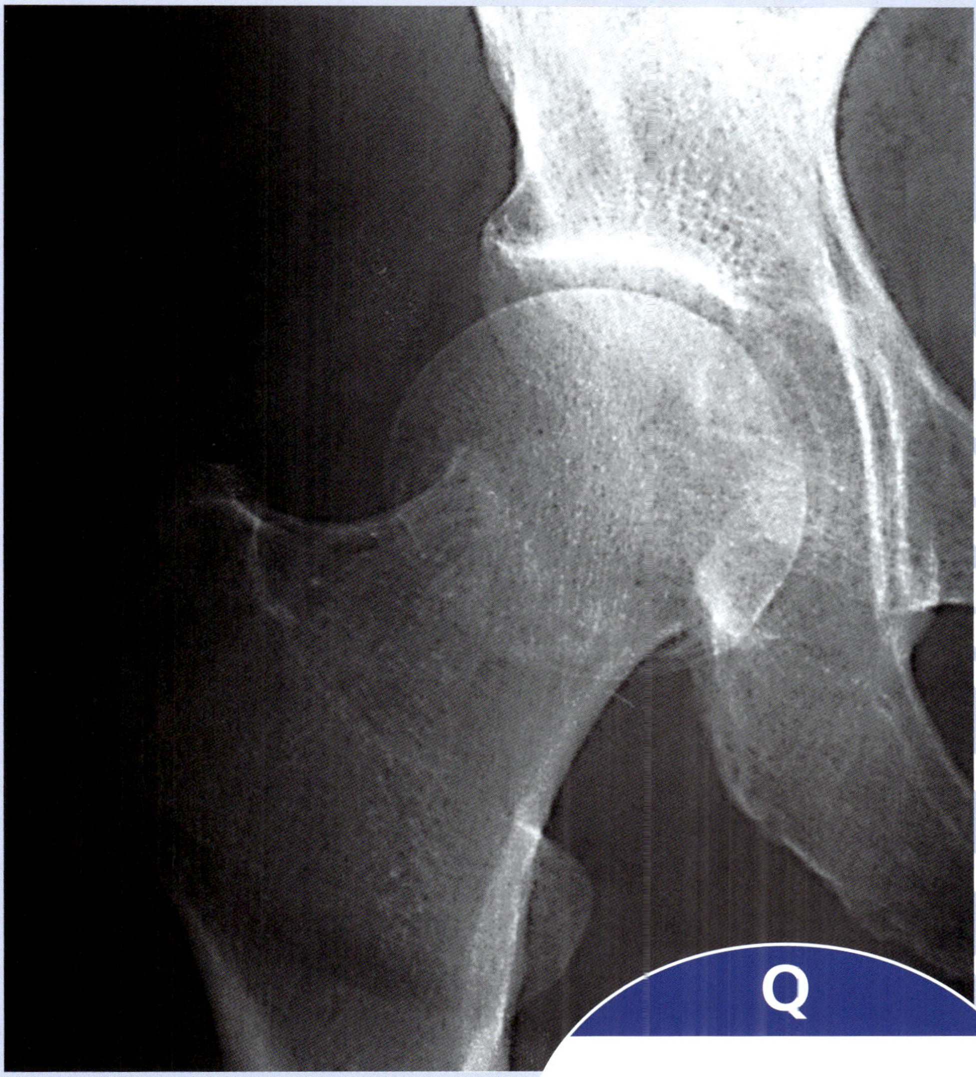

75세 · 여성

Q

낙상 후의 오른쪽 고관절 통증. 보행은 가능. 진단은?

앞 페이지 X-ray의 진단은 **대퇴골 경부 골절**(Garden 1형)이며 흔히 간과되는 골절이다. 골절선이 잘 보이지 않으며 전위가 작아 정상이라고 착각하기 쉽다.

대퇴골 근위부 골절은 특히 언어 소통이 어려운 고령자들에게서 간과되기 쉽다. 와병 중인 고령자에게 갑자기 38℃ 정도의 발열이 2~3일 발생하면 대퇴골 근위부 골절의 가능성이 있다. 기저귀를 갈 때 고관절을 벌리는 정도 외력으로도 골절을 입을 수 있다. 이 정도의 외력으로 골절이 발생할 것이라고 생각하지 않기 때문에 대퇴골 근위부 골절 등을 떠올리지 못하는 것이다. 필자 또한 일주일 정도 지나서야 진단할 수 있었던 적이 여러 번 있었다. 따라서 여기에서는 고관절의 골절에 관한 X-ray 판독법을 알아보자.

대퇴골 골절

'대퇴골 골절 자세'

대퇴골 골절이 발생하면 그림 1과 같이 하지의 외회전 · 단축이 일어나는 경우가 많다.

독자분들도 그림 2의 자세를 취해보라. 이것을 '대퇴골 골절 자세'라고 한다[*1]. '대퇴골 골절은 외회전 · 단축!'이라고 몸으로 기억하자.

방문 진료나 왕진 시 서혜부 통증을 호소하는 노인이 누워 있다면 외회전 · 단축을 확인한다.

청진으로도 진단할 수 있다

또한, 청진을 통해서 대퇴골 골절을 진단할 수도 있다. 청진기를 치골결합에 대고 슬개골을 손가락으로 두드리면, 골절된 쪽의 소리가 작게 들린다. 같은 방법으로 요폐(urinary retention)도 알 수 있다. 치골결합에 청진기를 대고 손가락으로 배를 아래로 두드리면 방광 확대부에서 소리가 바뀐다.

대퇴골 근위부 골절

경부인지, 전자간인지

대퇴골 근위부 골절은 그림 3과 같이 대퇴골 경부 골절과 대퇴골 전자부 골절로 나눌 수 있다.

골두 혈류는 외측/내측 대퇴회전동맥(median and lateral femoral circumflex arteries)로부터 대퇴골 경부로 들어가 골두에 이른다. 따라서 그림 3에서도 알 수 있듯이 **대퇴골 전자간 골절**에서는 골

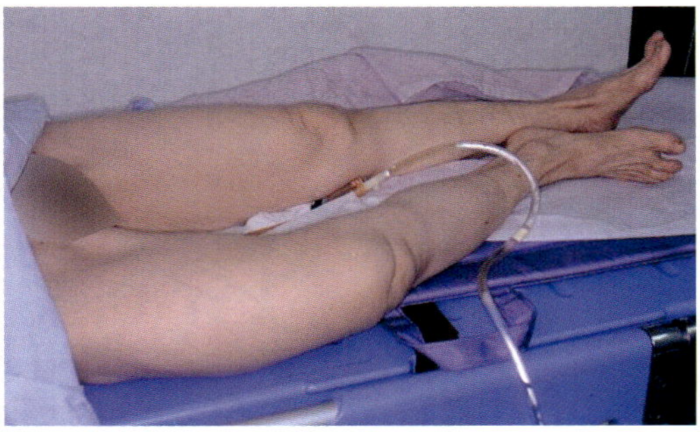

그림 1 우측 대퇴골 골간부 골절
오른쪽 다리가 외회전되어 발꿈치의 위치를 보면 왼쪽에 비해 단축되어 있다. 이와같이 대퇴골 골절은 외회전 · 단축을 일으킨다.

그림 2 대퇴골 골절 자세
우측 대퇴골 골절에서는 으른쪽 다리가 외회전 · 단축된다.

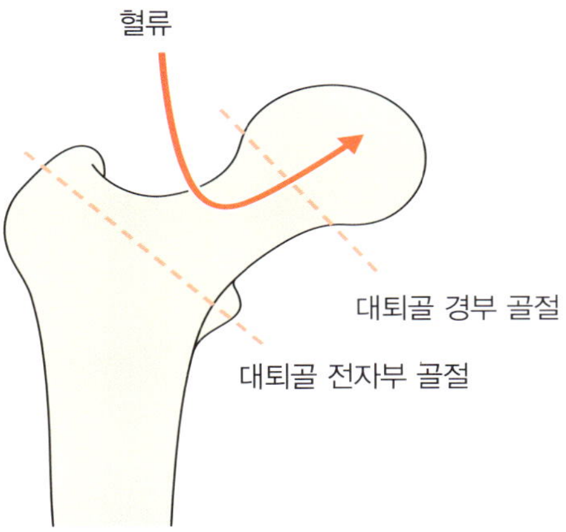

그림 3 골두 혈류와 대퇴골 근위부 골절
골두 혈류는 경부를 통해 들어가기 때문에 대퇴골 전자간 골절에서는 혈류가 유지되지만, 대퇴골 경부 골절로 골두가 전위되면 골두로의 혈류는 없다.

두의 혈류가 유지되며 수술에서는 그대로 뼈를 접합하면 된다.

한편, **대퇴골 경부 골절**의 경우, 골두가 전위되어 있다면 골두로의 혈류가 없기 때문에 골두를 인공 골두로 교체하는 경우도 있다.

*1 고관절 탈구에서는 반대로 고관절의 굴곡 · 내전이 나타나며 이것을 '고관절 탈구 자세'르 기억한다.

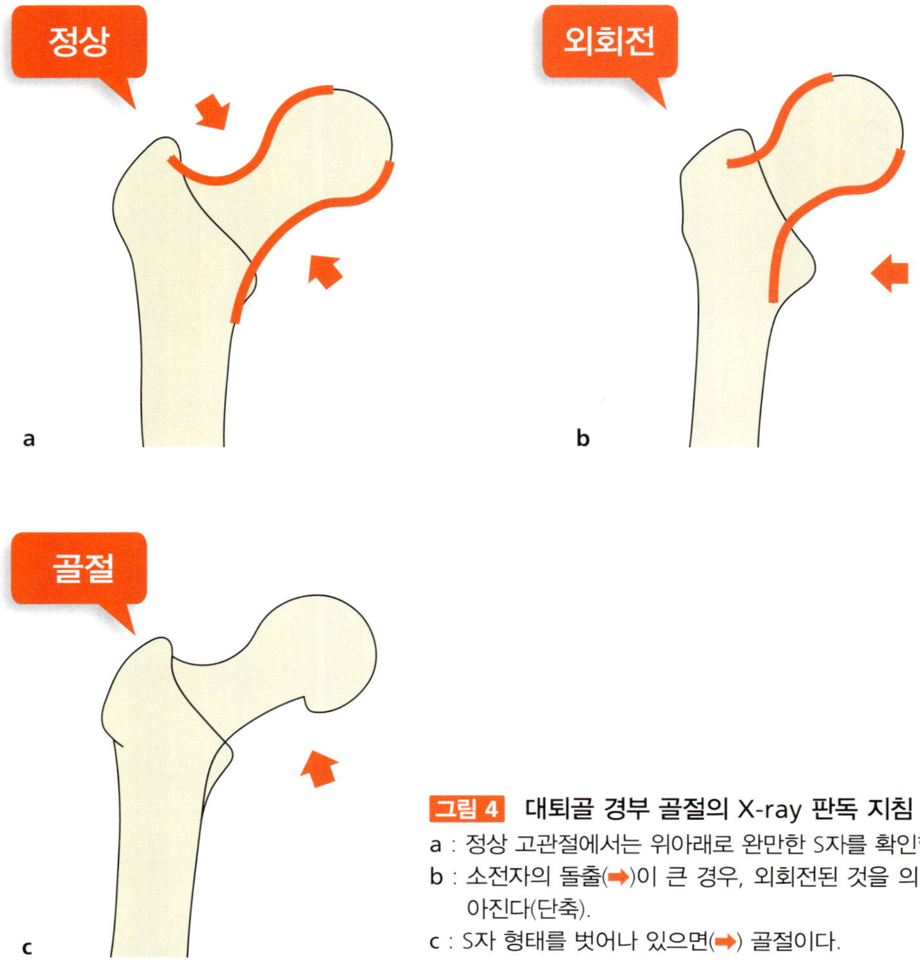

그림 4 대퇴골 경부 골절의 X-ray 판독 지침
a : 정상 고관절에서는 위아래로 완만한 S자를 확인할 수 있다(➡).
b : 소전자의 돌출(➡)이 큰 경우, 외회전된 것을 의미한다. 위쪽의 'S'는 짧아진다(단축).
c : S자 형태를 벗어나 있으면(➡) 골절이다.

대퇴골 경부 골절(fracture of the femoral neck)

X-ray에서 골절 진단은 간단하다. 뼈의 **피질**을 따라가면 된다. 피질이 끊긴 곳이 골절이다. 그러나 대퇴골 경부 골절에서는 이를 알기 어려운 경우도 많다.

정상적인 대퇴골 골두에서는 골두에서 경부에 걸쳐 위아래 모두 완만한 'S자'가 된다(**그림 4, 5**). 이 S자 형태가 유지되지 않으면 골절을 생각한다(**그림 4**, p91의 X-ray를 참고). 대퇴골이 골절되면 하지는 외회전 되는 경우가 많으며 이때 위의 S자는 짧아진다(**그림 4, 6**).

대퇴골 경부 골절에는 **Garden 분류**가 있으며, **그림 7**과 같다. 1형 · 2형에서는 환자의 골절이 경미하여 통증이 있어도 걸을 수 있다. 그러나 걷다 보면 3형 · 4형이 되어 걸을 수 없게 된다.

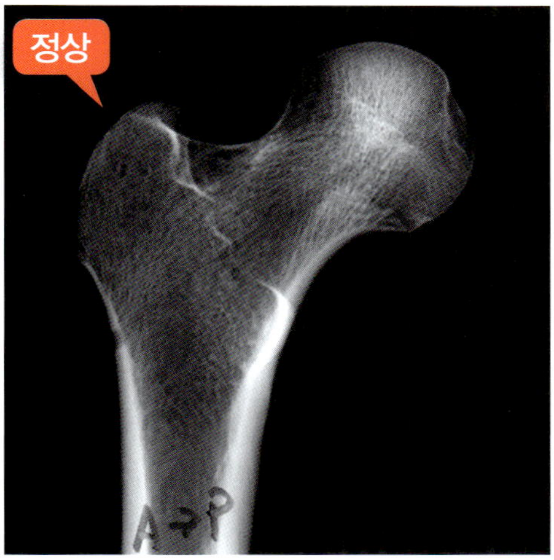

그림 5 정상 대퇴골 골두 (대퇴골 표본)

골두에서 경부에 걸쳐 위아래 모두 완만한 S자라는 것에 주목. 소전자는 돌출되어 있지 않다.

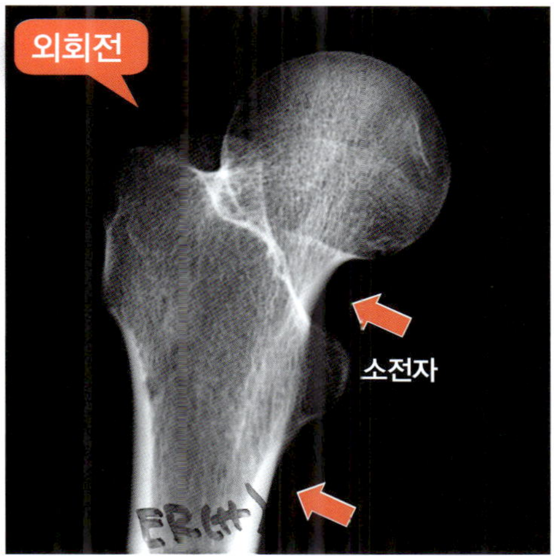

그림 6 정상 대퇴골 골두의 외회전 상태 (대퇴골 표본)

하지가 강하게 외회전하면 위의 'S'는 짧아진다. 소전자가 튀어나와 있는 것에 주의. 내측 피질골(➡)은 외회전하면 소전자 부분에서 끊기지만 같은 연장선상에 있다.

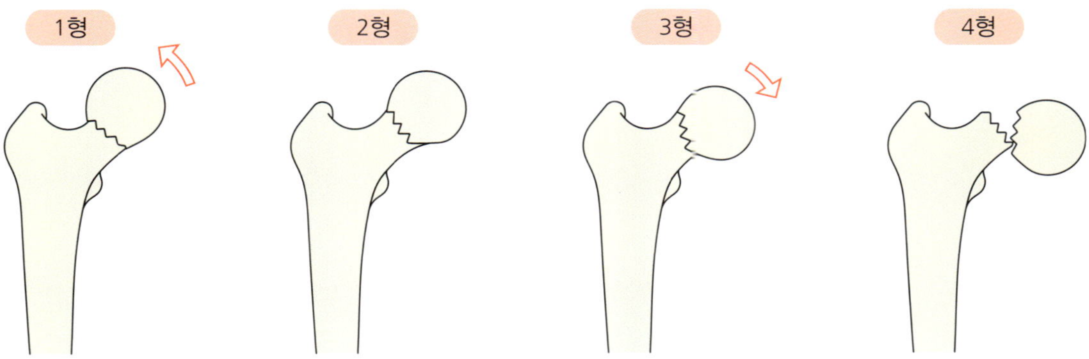

골두가 위로 젖혀져 있다 (valgus, impacted in-complete)

골두는 그대로 (non-displaced, complete)

골두가 아래를 향함 (varus, partially displaced, complete)

골두가 벗어나 있다 (fully displaced, complete)

그림 7 대퇴골 경부 골절의 Garden classification

대퇴골 전자간 골절(peritrochanteric fracture of femur)

한편, **그림 8**은 대퇴골 전자간 골절이다. 어디가 골절인지 알 수 있는가?

그림 9를 보자. 정상적인 대퇴골 내측 피질골은 경부와 골간부에서 **동일선상**에 있다. 고관절이 외회전하면 소전자 부분에서 피질골이 끊기지만 동일한 연장선상에 있다.

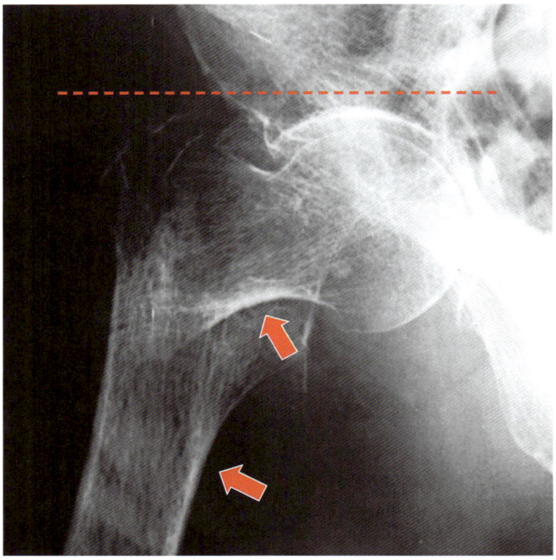

그림 8 **대퇴골 전자간 골절의 X-ray 정면상**
내측 피질골이 근위와 원위에서 동일한 연장선상에 없다 (➡)는 것에 주목. 또한, 대전자와 골두의 높이에 차이가 없는 것에 주의한다.

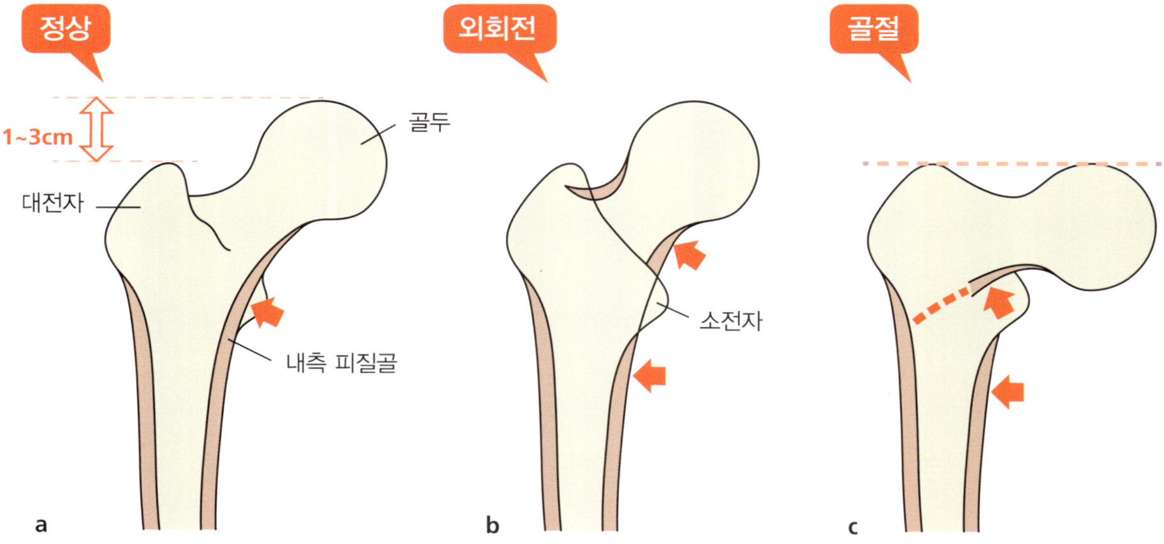

그림 9 **대퇴골 전자간 골절의 X-ray 진단 가이드**
a : 정상에서 골두와 대전자의 높이에는 1~3cm 차이가 있다. 내측 피질골은 연속된다.
b : 하지가 외회전하면 내측 피질골은 소전자 부분에서 끊기지만 동일한 연장선상에 있다.
c : 대퇴골 전자간 골절에서는 내측 피질골이 동일선상에 없다. 또한, 골두와 대전자의 높이에 차이가 없다.

만약, 내측 피질골이 동일한 연장선상에 없다면, 대퇴골 전자간 골절을 의심한다. 또한, 골두와 대전자의 높이에는 통상 1~3cm의 차이가 있다. 대전자와 골두의 높이에 차이가 없다면, 역시 대퇴골 전자간 골절을 의심한다.

반복 학습

❶ 대퇴골 골절은 하지의 **외회전 · 단축**을 유발한다.

❷ 대퇴골 골두에서 경부에 걸쳐 위아래 모두 완만한 **S자**인 것을 확인한다. S자 형태를 벗어나 있다면, **대퇴골 경부 골절**이다.

❸ 대퇴골 경부에서 골간부까지 내측 피질골이 **동일선상**에 있는 것을 확인한다. 동일한 연장선상에 없다면 **대퇴골 전자간 골절**이다.

❹ 와상 상태의 고령자에서 알 수 없는 고열이 발생하면 **대퇴골 근위부 골절**도 의심한다.

❺ 청진기로도 대퇴골 골절을 알 수 있다.

Q7 오토바이에서 낙상하여 내원. 진단은?

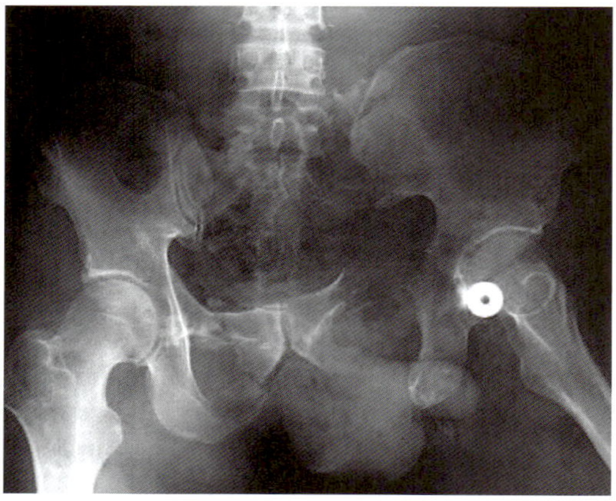

Q8 고관절의 통증으로 내원. 진단은?

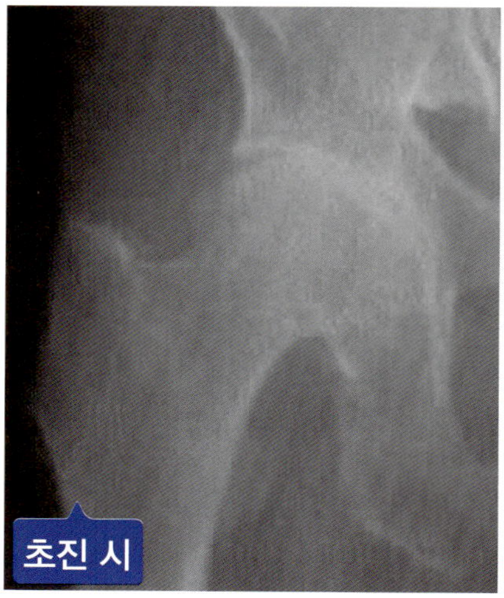

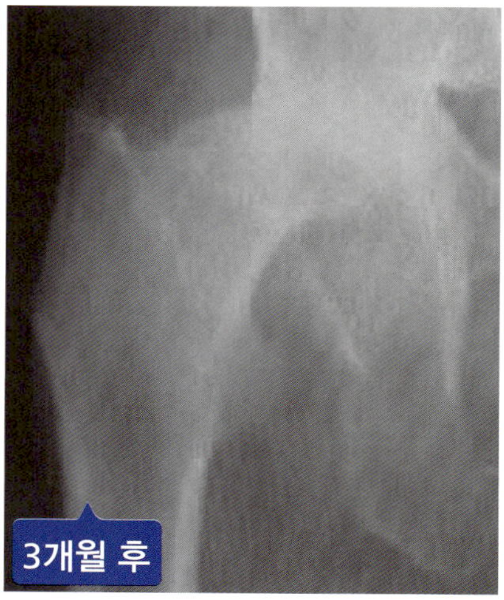

해답은 p143

고관절 질환의 X-ray 소견

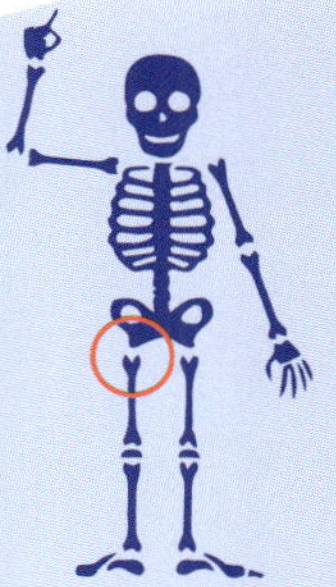

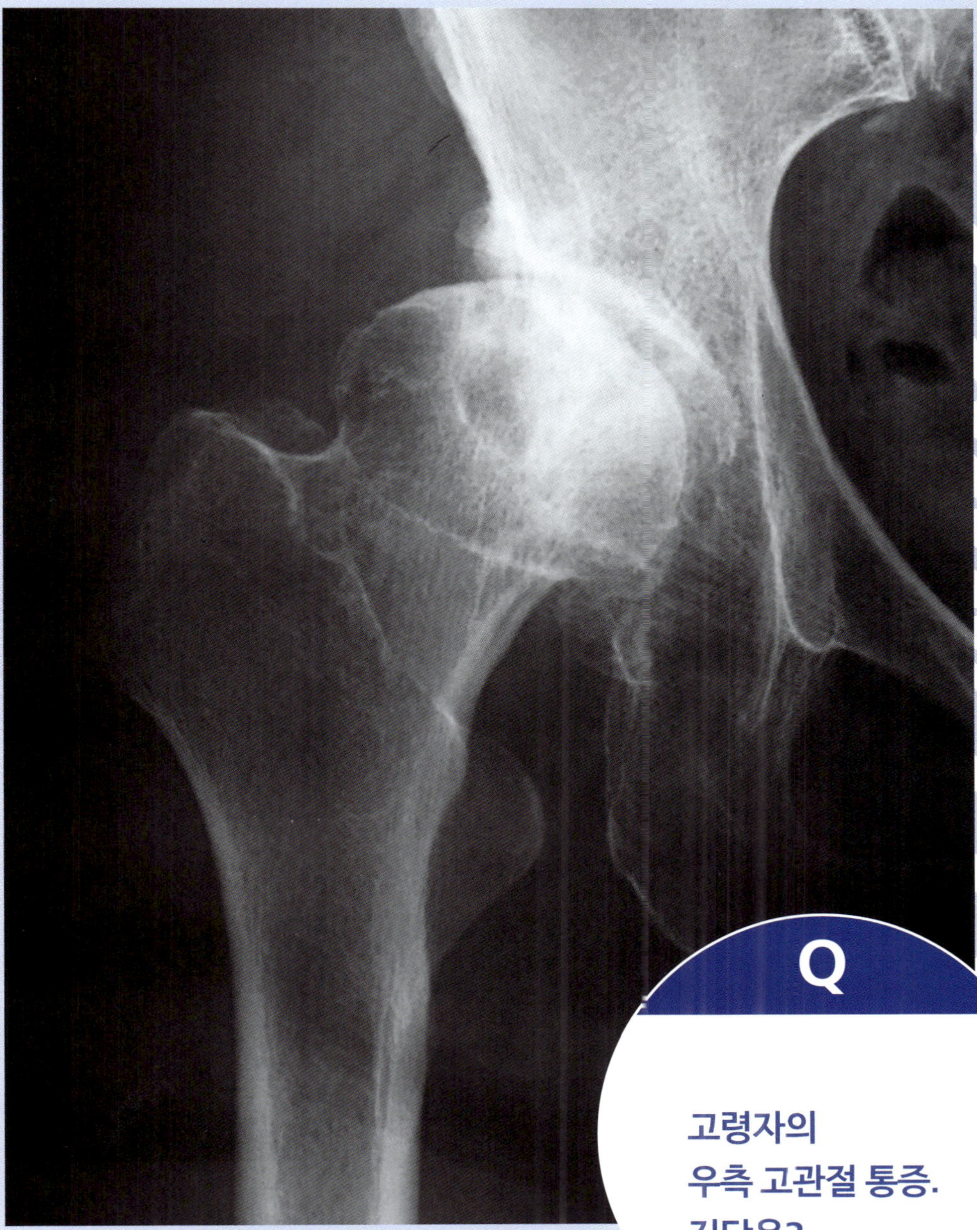

70세 · 여성

Q

고령자의
우측 고관절 통증.
진단은?

앞 장에서는 고관절 X-ray 판독법 중 골절을 다루었다. 고관절 X-ray에서 확인할 수 있는 다른 병변들이 많다. 여기에서는 변형성 고관절증, 류마티스관절염, 고관절액의 저류, 대퇴골두 괴사, 골다공증의 X-ray 판독에 있어 주목할 점을 설명할 것이다. 적은 지식만으로도 상당히 많은 것을 알게 될 것이다.

변형성 고관절증(OA)과 류마티스관절염(RA)

앞 페이지의 X-ray 진단은 **변형성 고관절증**(osteoarthritis : OA) 또는 **비구형성부전**[acetabular dysplasia, 골두에 대해 비구(지붕)의 '처마'가 부족하다]이다(**그림 1**).

OA는 하중 부위의 간격이 좁아지고, 골증식성 변화를 보인다

이처럼 변형성(퇴행성) 고관절증의 특징은 하중 부위(상방 외측)의 관절 간격 협소화와 골증식성 변화, 즉, 골경화상(하얗게 됨)과 골극 등이 있다. 특히 골두에 대한 비구(acetabulum)의 피복, 즉,

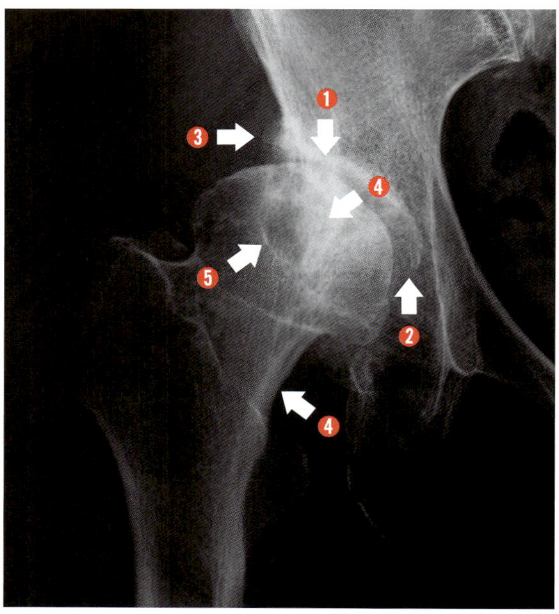

그림 1 **변형성 고관절증(앞 페이지 X-ray)**
❶ 골두 위쪽(하중 부위)만 관절 간격이 좁아지고, ❷ 내측 관절 간격은 유지된다. ❸ 비구(처마)가 부족하다. 골두 내 및 경부 내측에 ❹ 골경화상, 골두 내에 ❺ 골낭종이 있음

비구(지붕)의 '처마'가 작은 경우(비구형성부전), 단위 면적당 하중량이 증가한다. 또한, 앞(➡ p99)의 증례에서는 골두 내 낭종(cyst)도 형성되어 있다. 관절 내압 상승으로 인해 관절액이 골두 내부로 들어가게 된다. 체중이 실리지 않는 내측 관절 간격이 유지되고 있다는 점에 유의한다.

RA는 관절 간격이 균일하게 좁고, 골증식성 변화가 없다

이어서 **그림 2**를 보면, 이것은 **류마티스관절염**(rheumatoid arthritis : RA)이 고도로 진행된 것이다. 대퇴골두의 비구를 향한 **중심성 탈구**(acetabular protrusion)를 볼 수 있다. 대퇴골두와 매우 얇아진 비구(골두 위의 지붕)가 모두 골반 안으로 들어가 있다.*

① **관절 간격이 균일하게 좁고**, ② **골증식성 변화**(골극 · 골경화상)**가 없으며**, ③ **osteoporotic**(뼈가 얇다)한 것을 알 수 있다. 변형성 고관절증과 달리, 류마티스관절염의 경우 관절 간격이 균일하게 좁아지는 경우가 많다. 이를 **concentric narrowing**이라고 한다.

또한, 류마티스관절염에서는 활막의 염증에 의한 혈류 증가로 인해 탈회(demineralization)가 진행되어 osteoporotic하며, 골증식성 변화(골극 · 골경화상)는 원칙적으로 없다.

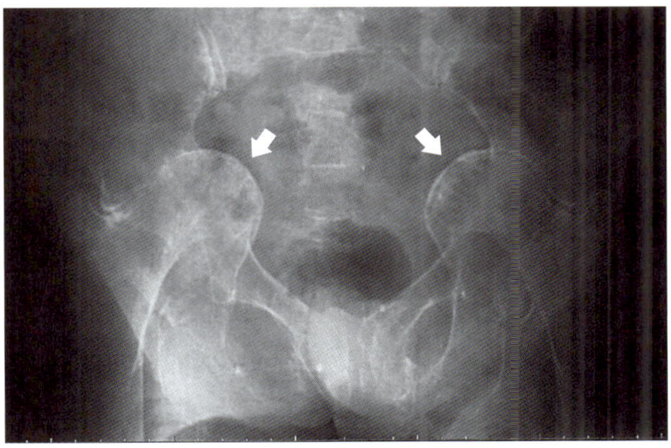

그림 2 류마티스관절염의 중심성 탈구
대퇴골두와 매우 얇아진 비구가 모두 골반 내로 들어가 있다(⇨). 비구와 대퇴골두 사이의 관절 간격이 균일하게 좁고(concentric narrowing), 골극이 없으며 osteoporotic하여 골경화 등의 변화가 없다(정상 좌측 고관절 X-ray인 **그림 3**과 비교해 보자).

* 최근에는 생물학적 제제도 사용하고 있어 이처럼 심한 류마티스관절염은 드물다.

표 1 변형성(퇴행성) 고관절증과 류마티스관절염의 차이

	관절 간격	골극, 골경화상	골다공증(뼈가 얇음)
변형성 고관절증	하중 부위만 협소화	있음	없음
류마티스관절염	전체적으로 좁음	없음	있음

OA와 RA의 차이

정리하자면 변형성 고관절증에서는 고관절 상방의 하중 부위가 좁아지고 골증식성 변화가 있다. 한편, 류마티스관절염에서는 고관절 간격이 균일하게 전체적으로 좁아지고 골극이 없으며 osteoporotic한 것이 감별 포인트이다(**표 1**).

고관절액 저류(삼출)

X-ray로 **고관절액 저류(삼출)**도 알 수 있다. **그림 3**은 고관절에 삼출(effusion)이 발생한 것이다.

이 이상 소견은 뼈만 봐서는 좀처럼 알기 어렵다. X-ray를 볼 때, 뼈뿐 아니라 **연부조직**에도 주목해야 한다.

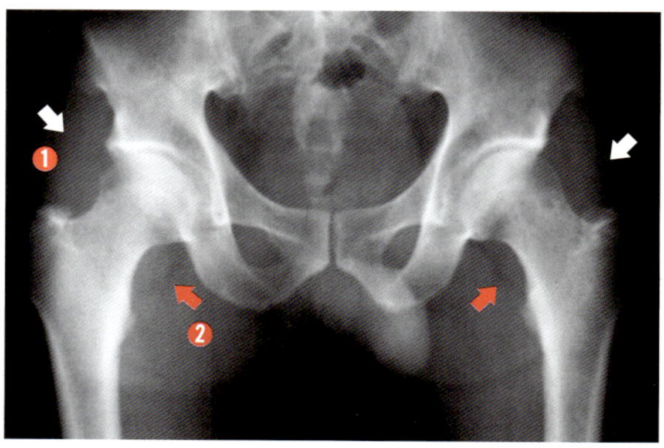

그림 3 오른쪽 고관절액의 저류

➡는 장요근, ⇨는 중둔근. 오른쪽은 ❶ iliopsoas sign과 ❷ gluteus medius sign이 보이며, 관절액의 저류를 확인할 수 있다.

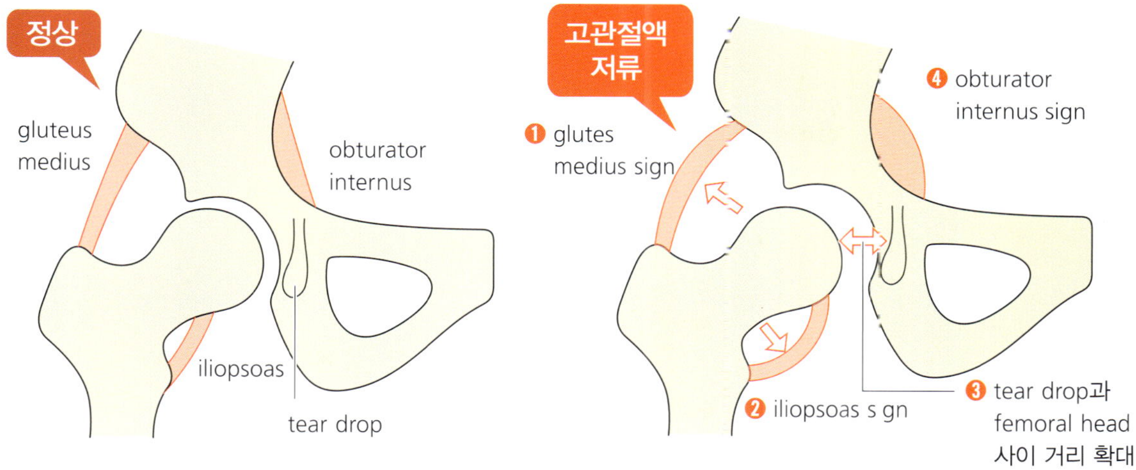

그림 4 고관절액 저류와 장요근/중둔근 사인

고관절액이 저류되면, 중둔근은 외측으로(❶ gluteus medius sign), 장요근은 내측으로(❷ iliopsoas sign), tear drop과 femoral head 사이 거리는 확대된다(❸). 염증이 있다면 골반 내의 내폐쇄근이 팽창한다(❹ obturator internus sign).

장요근과 중둔근의 폭

양쪽 대퇴골 경부의 내측에 보이는 **장요근의 폭**에 주목한다(그림 3, 4). 그림 3 오른쪽 장요근 폭이 넓은 것을 확인할 수 있다. 이것은 관절액 저류로 인해 장요근이 내측으로 밀려난 것이다. 한편, 대전자에 부착하는 **중둔근**은 외측으로 전위되어 있다. 이것도 관절액 때문이다.

관절액의 확인은 초음파로 한다. 관절 연골도 물처럼 검게 보이지만 물은 프로브로 압박할 때 변형되므로 감별할 수 있다.

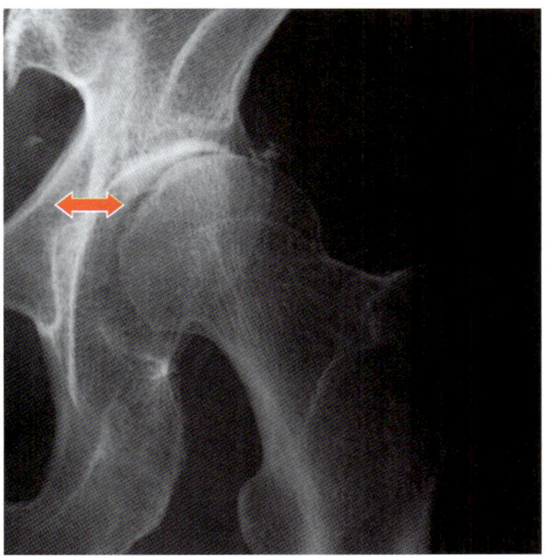

그림 5 고관절액 저류 (tear drop과 femoral head 사이 거리 확대)

이 증례에서는 고관절에 25mL의 삼출이 있었다.

tear drop과 femoral head 사이 거리

그림 5는 왼쪽 고관절 탈구 정복 후에 관절액이 저류된 것이다. 골두 내측 비구에는 '눈물'처럼 보이는 부분이 있으며, 이를 **tear drop**이라고 한다. 이 tear drop과 femoral head 사이 거리의 확대도 관절액 저류의 소견이다.

관절액의 감별이 필요할 때는 초음파 유도하에 천자한다.

대퇴골두 괴사

대퇴골두 괴사는 골두로의 혈류 감소로 인해 골두가 파괴되는 것을 말한다. 과음이나 스테로이드제가 계기가 되는 경우가 있다.

초기에 골두 바로 아래의 빈틈을 꼼꼼히 찾아야

대퇴골두 괴사는 그림 6과 같이 골두 아래의 작고 검은 공간에서 시작될 수 있다. 그러나 이 때는 괴사가 이미 상당히 진행된 상태이다. 고관절 통증이 있는 경우에는 골두 바로 아래를 꼼꼼히 찾아본다. 그림 7과 같이 골두의 파괴가 진행되면 한눈에 보아도 명백하게 보인다. 치료는 절골술, 인공골두치환술 등이 있다.

소아에게 발생하는 대퇴골두 괴사를 **Perthes병**(Legg-Calvé-Perthes disease)이라고 한다. Perthes

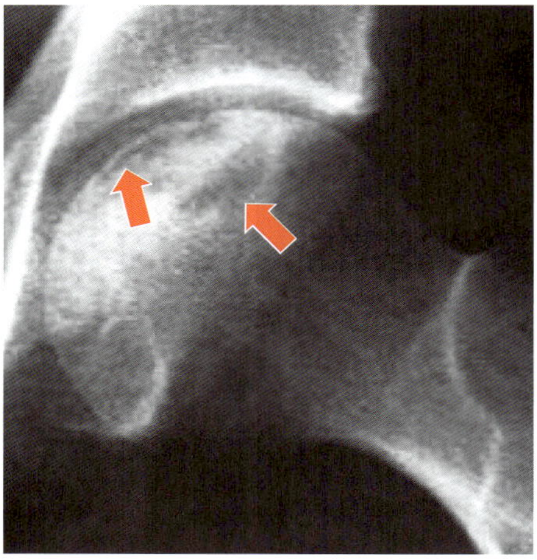

그림 6 대퇴골두 괴사
골두 바로 아래의 검은 공간에 주의. 비구 쪽의 변화는 없다. 이 시기(초기)에는 놓치기 쉽다.

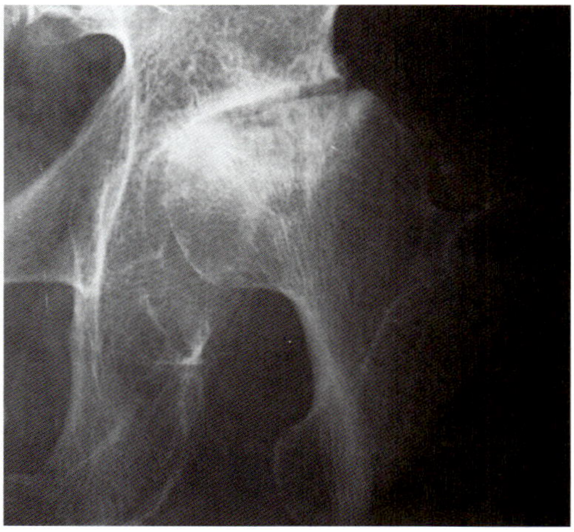

그림 7 대퇴골두 괴사의 진행
골두의 파괴·함몰, 관절 간격의 협소화를 볼 수 있다.

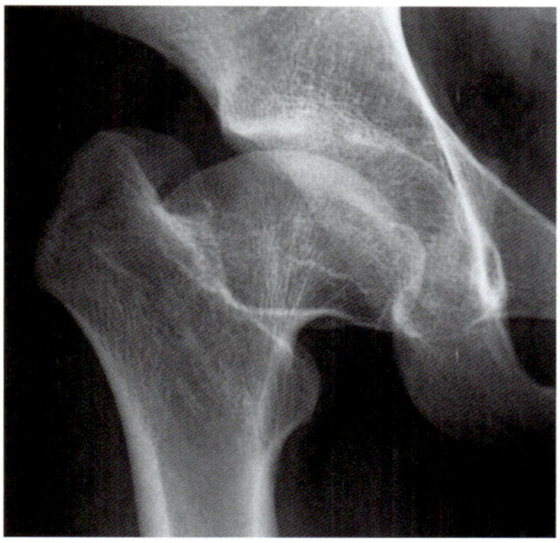

그림 8 소아기의 Perthes병(골두 괴사)에 의한 편평 골두

병의 경우, 괴사된 뼈가 흡수되어 리모델링이 진행되면 그림 8과 같은 **편평 골두**(coxa plane, mushroom deformity)가 될 수 있다. 일시적으로 염증을 일으켜 통증이 심할 때는 입원하여 하지를 견인하기도 한다. 어느 정도 성장한 후 절골술을 할 수도 있다.

골다공증의 정도

대퇴골두 내에는 골량이 있으며, 이를 관찰하면 **골다공증**의 진행 상태를 어느 정도 알 수 있다.

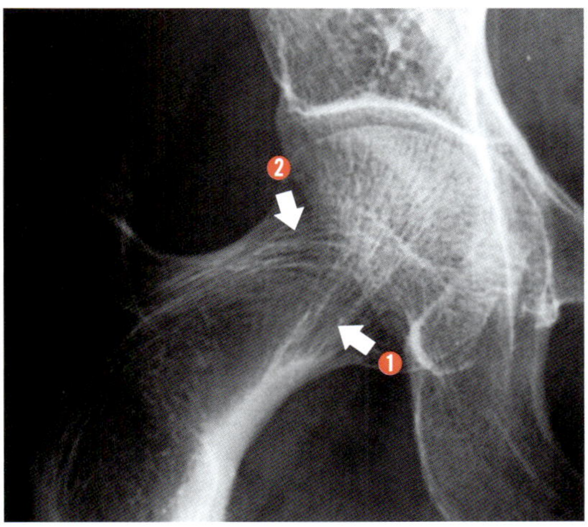

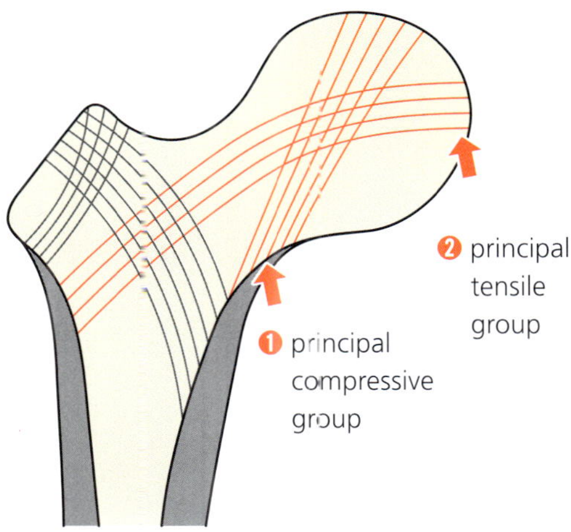

그림 9 골량(trabeculae)
골량에는 경부 내측부터 골두 상방을 향하는 ❶ principal compressive group과 대전자에서 골두 내측을 향하는 ❷ principal tensile group이 있다. 골다공증이 진행되면 ❷가 소실되며, ❶은 남지만 그 수는 감소한다.

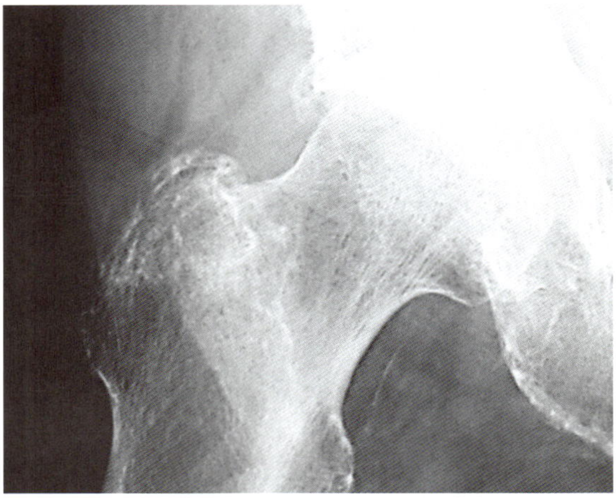

그림 10 **진행된 골다공증**
Principal tensile group의 골량이 거의 소실되고, principal compressive group만 남아 있다. 골다공증이 상당히 진행되었음을 알 수 있다.

골두의 골량 수에 주목하라

골량에는 ❶ 경부 내측에서 골두를 향하는 principal compressive group과 ❷ 대전자에서 골두 내측을 향하는 principal tensile group이 있다(**그림 9**).

골다공증이 진행되면, 우선 principal tensile group이 소실되기 시작하고, 보다 수직으로 중력에 저항하는 principal compressive group은 마지막까지 남지만 그 골량의 수는 점점 줄어든다.

따라서, 이들의 골량에 주목하면 골다공증의 정도를 알 수 있다. **그림 10**에서는 골다공증이 진행되어 principal compressive group만 남아 있다.

반복 학습

❶ **변형성 고관절증**은 고관절 간격 상방이 좁아지며, 골증식성 변화(골극, 골경화상)가 있다.

❷ **류마티스관절염**은 고관절 간격이 균일하게(전체적으로) 좁아지며, 골증식성 변화가 없고, osteoporotic하다.

❸ **대퇴골두 괴사** 초기에는 골두에서 작은 빈틈을 찾아라!

❹ **고관절액 저류(삼출)**는 연부조직을 주목하면 X-ray로 알 수 있다.

❺ 골두 내의 골량을 보면 **골다공증**의 정도를 알 수 있다.

무릎

무릎 X-ray 판독을 위한 기본지식

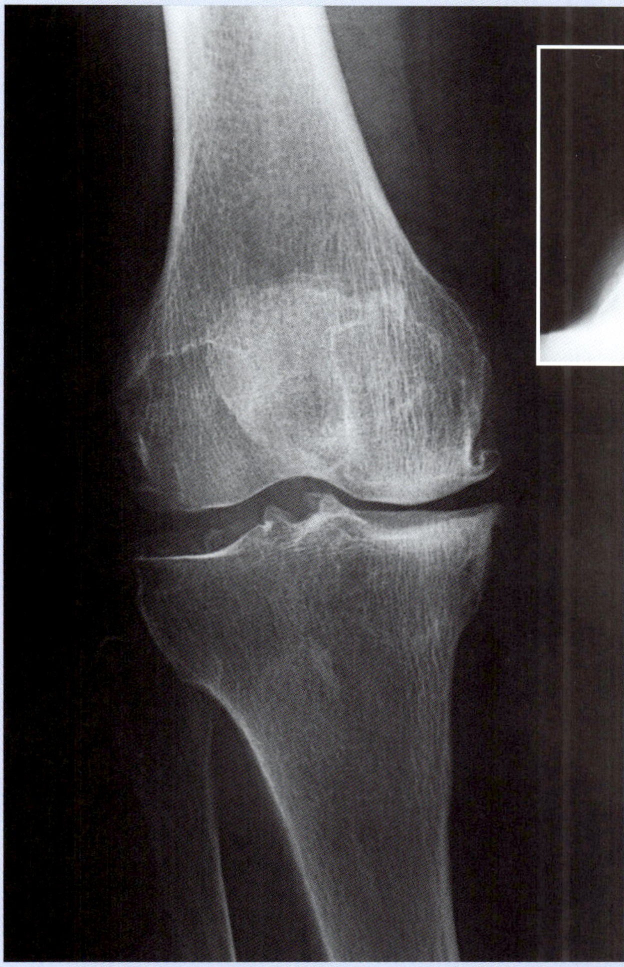

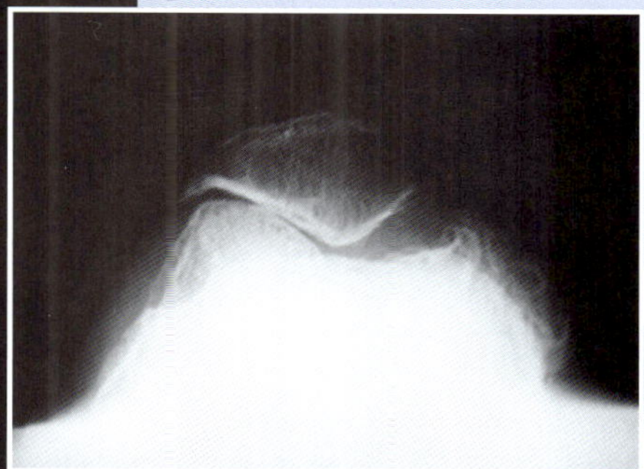

70세 · 여성

Q

보행 시 우측 무릎 안쪽의 통증. 진단은?

'무릎이 아프다'고 호소하는 고령 환자는 내과 외래에서도 적지 않다. 진단의 대부분은 변형성(퇴행성) 슬관절증, 류마티스관절염, 가성통풍, 대퇴골 괴사 등이며 내과 의사는 이러한 질환을 구분할 수만 있어도 무방하다. 또한, 슬관절액 저류(삼출)도 X-ray로 알 수 있다. 여기에서는 놓치기 쉬운 Segond fracture를 비롯한 무릎 X-ray의 핵심을 알아보자.

변형성(퇴행성) 슬관절증

앞 페이지의 X-ray 진단은 전형적인 **변형성 슬관절증**(osteoarthritis : OA)이다. 또한, 무릎 X-ray에서 비골이 있는 쪽이 '외측'이다(의외로 이것을 모르는 의사가 많으므로 주의).

무릎 내측 관절 간격의 변화

한발로 서 있을 때, 체중은 보통 무릎의 중심에 실린다. 그러나 체중이 증가하면, 무게 중심은 무릎의 **내측**으로 이동한다. 따라서 변형성 슬관절증은 대부분 내측 관절 간격의 협소화를 일으켜, **내반슬(genu varum)**이 되는 경우가 많다(그림 1).

또한, 내측에 **골극**이나 **골경화상**이 있는 것에 주의한다(그림 2a). 이런 골증식성 변화가 있는 것이 변형성 관절증의 특징이다.

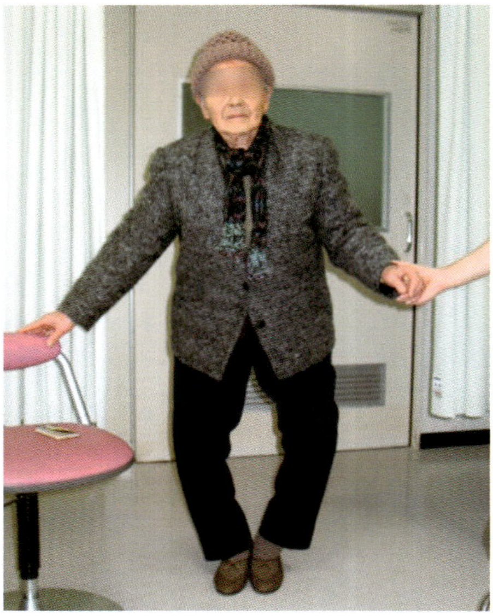

그림 1 변형성 슬관절증에 의한 내반슬
변형성 슬관절증은 내측 관절 간격이 협소해지고, 외측은 유지되므로 이렇게 내반슬이 되는 경우가 많다. 내반슬을 보이면, 진찰할 것도 없이 변형성 슬관절증이다!

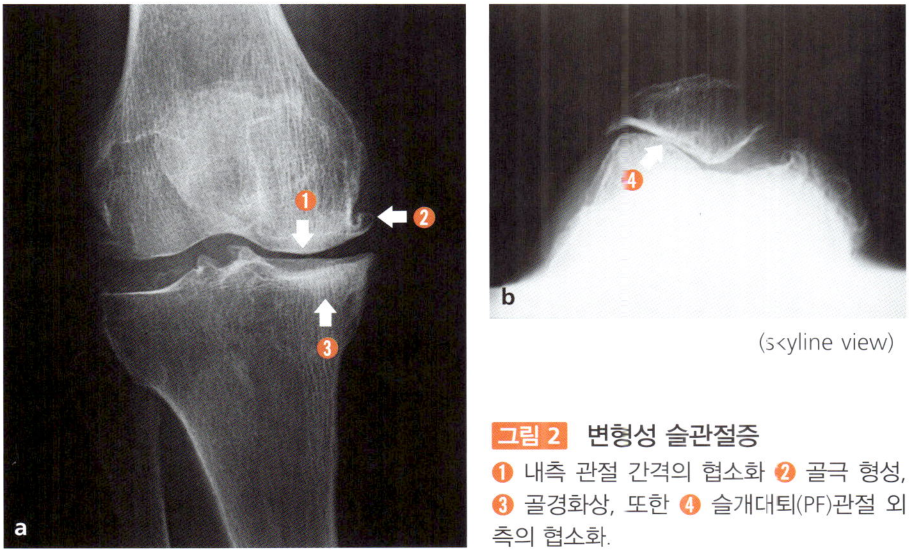

(s<yline view)

그림 2 변형성 슬관절증
❶ 내측 관절 간격의 협소화 ❷ 골극 형성, ❸ 골경화상, 또한 ❹ 슬개대퇴(PF)관절 외측의 협소화.

슬개대퇴관절의 변화

슬개대퇴관절(patellofemoral joint : PF관절. 슬개골 뒷면) 또한, 변화가 발생하기 쉽다.

변형성 슬관절증에서는 특히 PF관절의 **외측**에서 변화가 시작되는 경우가 많다(그림 2b). 이는 대퇴골 골축과 하퇴골 골축이 일직선상에 있는 것이 아니라 하퇴골이 10°~15° 외반(외반슬)되어 있기 때문이다. 그러므로 대퇴사두근이 수축하면, 슬개골에 외측으로 이동하려는 벡터의 힘이 작용한다. 따라서 PF관절 외측에 변화가 나타나기 쉽다. 그림 2b에서 PF관절 외측이 좁아지는 것에 주의한다.

즉, 변형성 슬관절증은 ① **내측 관절 간격**과 ② **PF관절**의 변화가 특징이다.

무릎은 체중의 85%를 지탱하기 때문에 변형성 슬관절증의 치료에서는 감량이 중요하다. 그러나 이를 대수롭지 않게 생각하는 경우가 흔하다.

보존적 치료에는 지팡이 사용, 대퇴사두근 훈련, NSAID가 있다. 국소마취제와 스테로이드를 혼합해 관절 내에 주사하는 것은 단기 통증 조절에 효과적이다. 히알루론산 주사의 효과는 '좋은 경우 그럭저럭 효과가 있고, 나쁜 경우 생리식염수 주입과 차이가 없다' 정도이다.

류마티스관절염

3곳의 모든 관절 간격이 협소화

한편, 그림 3은 **류마티스관절염**이다. 슬관절의 **내측**과 **외측**, **PF관절** 3곳의 모든 관절면이 좁고, **방사선 투과성이 높은**(osteoporotic) 것에도 주의한다. 또한, 류마티스관절염은 피부가 발적 되는 일

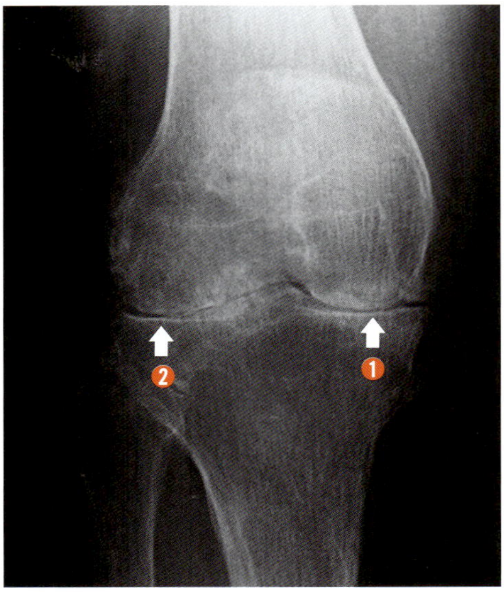

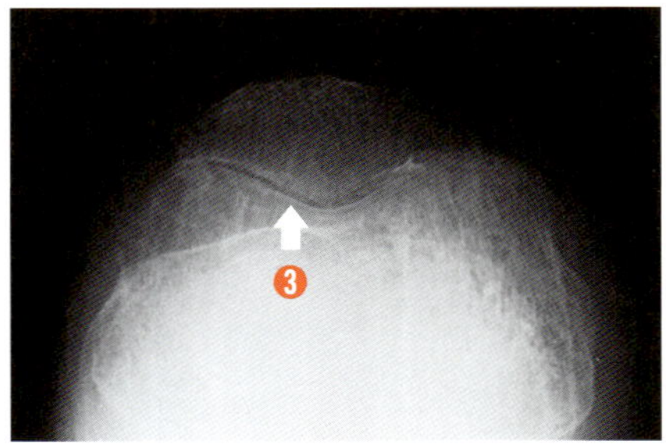

(skyline view)

그림 3 류마티스관절염

❶ 내측과 ❷ 외측의 관절 간격 그리고 ❸ 슬개대퇴(PF)관절 간격, 3곳 모두 좁아져 있다. 방사선 투과성이 높고(osteoporotic), 골증식성 변화(골극, 골경화상)가 없는 것에도 주의!

표 1 변형성 슬관절증과 무릎의 류마티스관절염과의 차이

	호발 부위	골극, 골경화상	골다공증
변형성 슬관절증	내측, 슬개대퇴(PF)관절	있음	없음
류마티스관절염	내측, 외측, 슬개대퇴(PF)관절	없음	있음

은 거의 없다.

골극이나 골경화상은 없다

또한, 변형성 관절증과 같은 골증식성 변화(골극, 골경화상)가 없는 것에도 주의한다. 류마티스관절염은 활막 증식에 의한 변화로 혈류가 풍부하기 때문에 탈회(demineralization) 흡수가 진행되어 **그림 3**과 같이 osteoporotic 해진다.

류마티스관절염과 변형성 슬관절증의 차이는 **표 1**과 같다. 또한, 변형성 슬관절증과 골다공증은 전혀 별개로, 골다공증이 없는 쪽이 변형성 슬관절증을 일으키기 쉽다.

가성통풍(CPPD disease)

고령자는 슬관절에 발생하는 가성통풍 발작이 매우 흔하며, '원인이 없고, 열감이 있는 무릎 통증'인 경우 가성통풍 발작을 강하게 의심한다. 변형성 관절증은 보통 열감이 없다. 양손으로 양쪽 무릎을 각각 만져보고 온도차가 있다면 **가성통풍이나 화농성 슬관절염, 류마티스관절염**을 의심한다.

특히 고령자의 발열에서 족관절의 가성통풍을 놓치기 쉬우므로, 내과 의사들은 신체 검사(physical exam)의 일환으로 양쪽 족관절의 온도를 손으로 만져 확인하도록 한다.

3곳의 관절 간격 중 비대칭적으로 발생할 수 있다

그림 4에서는 반월판에 CPP 결정(calcium pyrophosphate crystal : 피로인산칼슘 결정)의 침착을 확인할 수 있다. 이 결정이 침착하는 모든 병태를 가성통풍(피로인산칼슘 결정침착증 : calcium pyrophosphate crystal deposition disease = **CPPD disease**)이라고 한다. CPP 결정이 연골 변성을 일으키는 것은 확실하다.

가성통풍은 류마티스관절염과 달리 좌우가 대칭적이지 않다. 무릎의 경우 내측과 외측, PF관절의 어떤 관절 간격에서도 발생할 수 있다. 특히, **외측 또는 PF관절 단독**의 변형성 관절증을 보이는 경우, 가성통풍을 의심한다(그림 5).

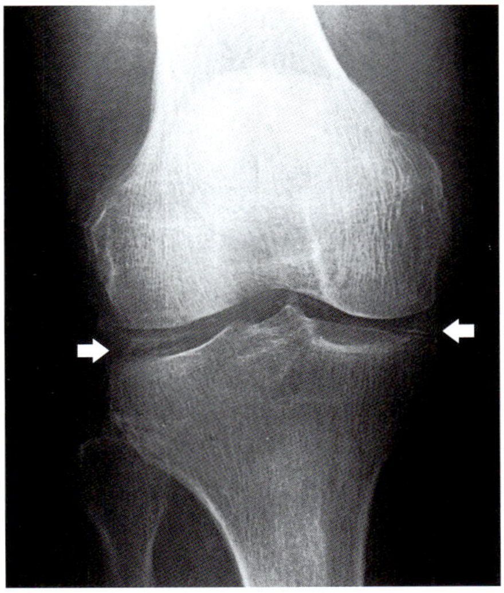

그림 4 **가성통풍(정면상)**
반월판에 석회화, CPP 결정이 보인다.

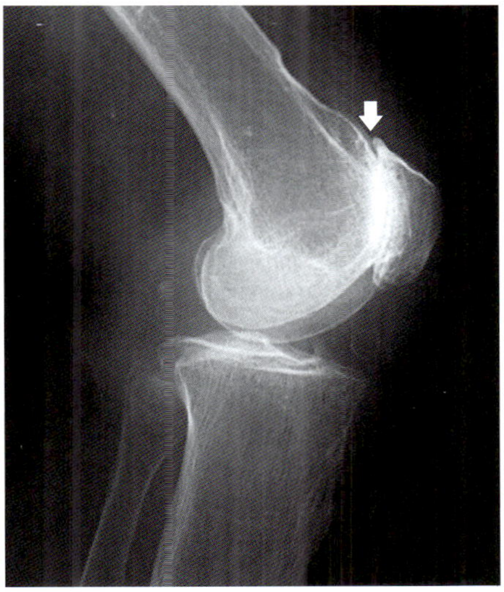

그림 5 **가성통풍(측면상)**
슬개대퇴(PF)관절의 단독 변화는 가성통풍을 의심한다. 본 증례에서는 정면 X-ray의 내·외측 모두 정상이었다.

무릎 · 치골결합 · 수관절의 X-ray 촬영을 통한 선별검사

또한, 가성통풍은 어깨 · 수관절 · 중수지절(MP)관절 등 변형성 관절증이 일어나지 않을 것 같은 관절에도 발생하는 것이 특징이다[1]. 가성통풍(CPPD disease)을 처음 제창한 McCarty에 따르면 **무릎**, **치골결합**, **수관절**의 X-ray 촬영은 가성통풍의 perfect screening이라고 하며, 이 3곳에 CPP 결정이 없다면 더 이상 검사를 진행할 필요가 없다고 한다[2].

검사와 확진

가성통풍은 기본적으로 노인성 질환이며 만약 60세 미만의 환자에서 확인된 경우, 가족력이나 저ALP혈증, 부갑상선기능항진증, 혈색소증(hemochromatosis), 저마그네슘혈증 등도 의심한다. 혈액검사 시 Fe, transferrin, ferritin, Ca, Mg, ALP, PTH 등도 검사한다[1].

확진은 관절액의 현미경 검사이다. 필자의 병원에서는 결정의 확인, 그람 염색 및 백혈구 수를 검사한다. 요산은 바늘 모양, CPP 결정은 막대 모양, 마름모 모양이다. 백혈구 수도 도움이 된다. 특히 50,000/μL를 넘는다면 **화농성 관절염**도 의심한다. 이를 '백혈구가 오만(50,000/μL)이 넘으면 감염이다!'라고 기억한다(참고로, μL=mm^3이다). 편광현미경이 있다면 CPP 결정과 요산 결정은 쉽게 구별할 수 있다.

가성통풍의 치료에는 NSAID, prednisolone, 스테로이드 관절주사, colchicine 등이 있다.

대퇴골 괴사

한편, 그림 6은 **대퇴골 괴사**이다. X-ray 및 MRI상으로 **골결손(bony defect)**이 있으며, 그 주위에

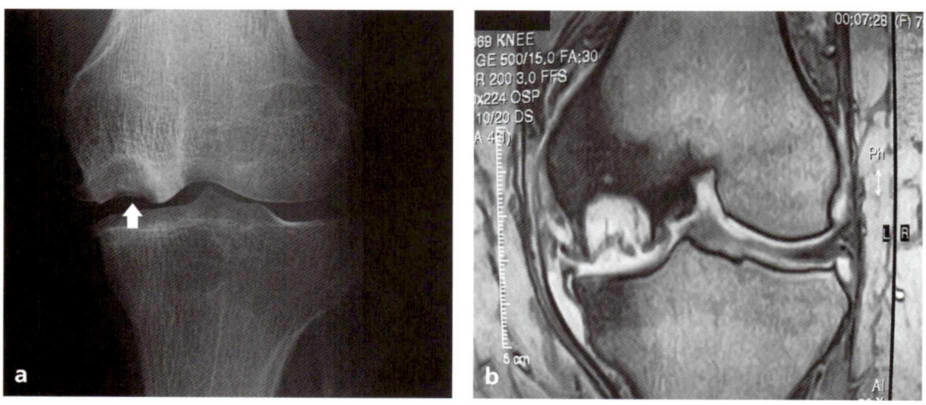

그림 6 대퇴골 괴사

X-ray(a) · MRI(b) 모두 대퇴골 내과(femoral condyle)에 골결손이 있으며, 그 주위에 골경화상이 있다. 대퇴골 내과에 흔하며, 변형성 슬관절증으로 오인된다.

골경화상이 있다. 초기에는 MRI에서 **골부종**이 관찰된다. 진행되면 **압괴**(collapse)가 발생한다.

변형성 슬관절증으로 오인하지 않아야

특히 무릎의 골괴사는 대퇴골 내과에 많고, 변형성 슬관절증으로 착각하기 쉽다. 원인은 외상이나 스테로이드 등으로 알려져 있다. 변형성 슬관절증으로 착각하게 되면, 스테로이드 주사를 반복하게 되므로 주의가 필요하다.

대퇴골 괴사가 심할 경우, 인공관절치환술을 실시한다.

Segond fracture

드물긴 하지만 응급 상황에서 매우 놓치기 쉬운 골절로 **Segond 골절**이 있다. 그림 7을 보면 외측 경골 고원(lateral tibial plateau)에 미세한 견열 골절이 있다. 이를 **lateral capsular sign**이라고도 한다.

전방십자인대의 손상이 동반되는 경우가 많다

보통 전방십자인대 손상은 럭비 등으로 무릎 바깥쪽에서 태클을 당해 무릎이 외반(valgus)되며 발

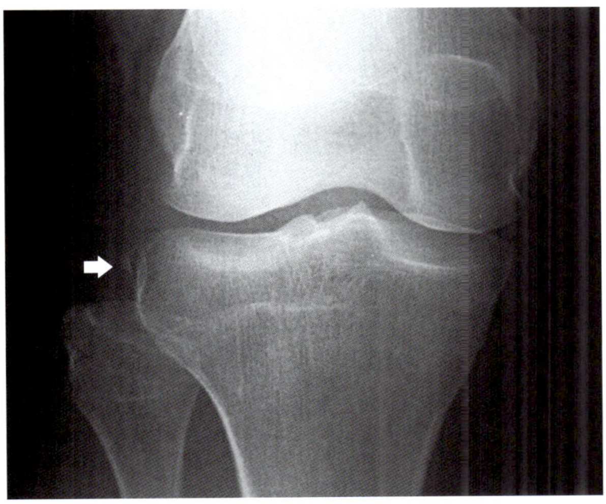

그림 7 Segond 골절
외측 경골 고원의 미세한 견열 골절에 주의한다. 흔히 전방십자인대 손상이 합병된다. 미세한 골편으로 여겨, 간과하지 않도록 한다.

생한다.

한편, Segond 골절의 경우, 경골의 내반·내회전에 의해 경골 외측 관절낭 부착부의 견열 골절이 일어난다. 이 미세한 견열 골절이 있으면, **전방십자인대 손상**도 75~100% 존재한다고 한다. 또한, 내측/외측 반월판 손상의 합병도 많다.

Segond 골절을 보면 반드시 정형외과에 의뢰하여 MRI를 촬영해야 한다.

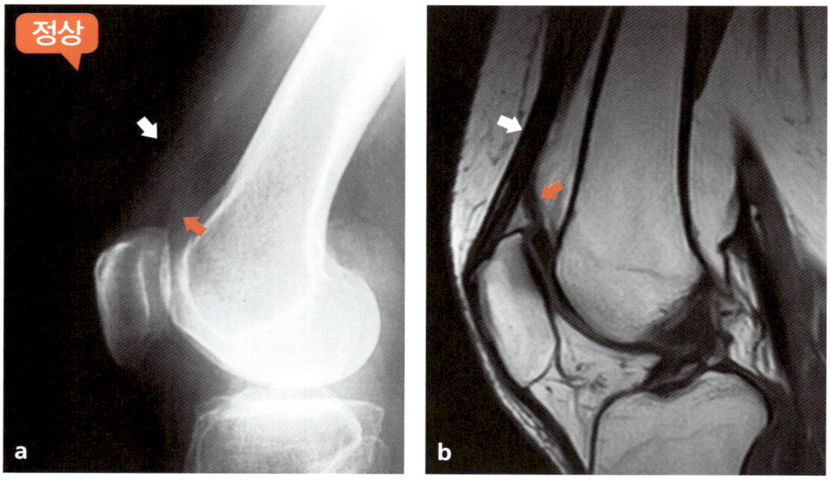

그림 8 **관절액 저류(삼출)가 없는 정상 무릎**
X-ray(a)·MRI(b) 모두 슬개골 상방에서 대퇴사두근(⇨)을 향해 비스듬히 슬개상낭(➡)이 있다. 슬개상낭의 전방과 후방에는 지방(fat)이 있다.

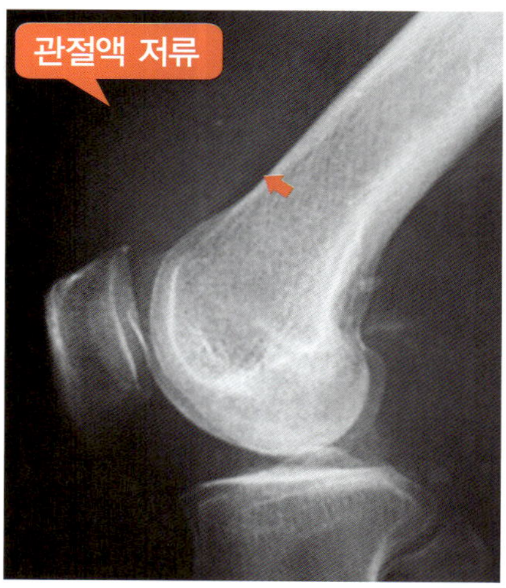

그림 9 **슬개상낭에 관절액 저류가 있는 경우**
슬개상낭의 면적이 넓어진다.

슬관절액 저류

슬관절액 저류는 X-ray로도 알 수 있다.

슬개상낭의 면적이 증가한다

먼저, 정상 무릎의 X-ray(그림 8a)와 MRI(그림 8b)를 보라. MRI에서는 대퇴사두근을 향해 비스듬히 슬개상낭(suprapatellar bursa)이 있으며, 그 전후에 지방이 있다. X-ray에서는 대퇴사두근과 슬개상낭은 하얗게, 지방은 검게 보인다.

슬관절액은 슬개상낭에 저류된다. 삼출(effusion)이 있으면, 그림 9와 같이 된다. 슬개상낭의 면적이 증가한 것을 확인할 수 있다. 삼출이 있을 경우 천자(흡인)하여 검사하지 않으면, 원인을 진단할 수 없다.

반복 학습

❶ **변형성 슬관절증**은 무릎의 2곳(내측, 슬개대퇴) 관절 간격에 변화. 골극, 골경화상이 있다.

❷ **류마티스관절염**은 무릎의 3곳 모두(내측, 외측, 슬개대퇴관절) 관절 간격이 협소화. 골극, 골경화상은 없다!

❸ 외측 또는 슬개대퇴관절에 국한된 변형성 슬관절증, 열감이 있다면 **가성통풍**(CPPD disease).

❹ **대퇴골 괴사**는 골결손이 있으며, 주위에 골경화상. 대퇴골 내과에 흔하며 변형성 슬관절증으로 오인하지 않도록!

❺ 경골 외측 관절낭 부착부의 미세한 견열 골절, **Segond 골절**에 주의한다! 전방십자인대의 손상이 동반되는 경우가 많다.

❻ **슬관절액 저류**는 X-ray로도 알 수 있다! 슬개상낭의 면적이 넓어지는 것에 주목한다.

참고문헌

1. Rosenthal AK, et al : Calcium pyrophosphate deposition disease, review article. N Engl J Med 374 (26):2575–2584, 2016. PMID 27355536
2. Hollander JL, et al : Arthritis and allied conditions ; Textbook of rheumatology. Lippincott Williams and Wilkins, 1989.

Q9 인대 손상 후, 대퇴부 통증을 호소하여 내원. 진단은?

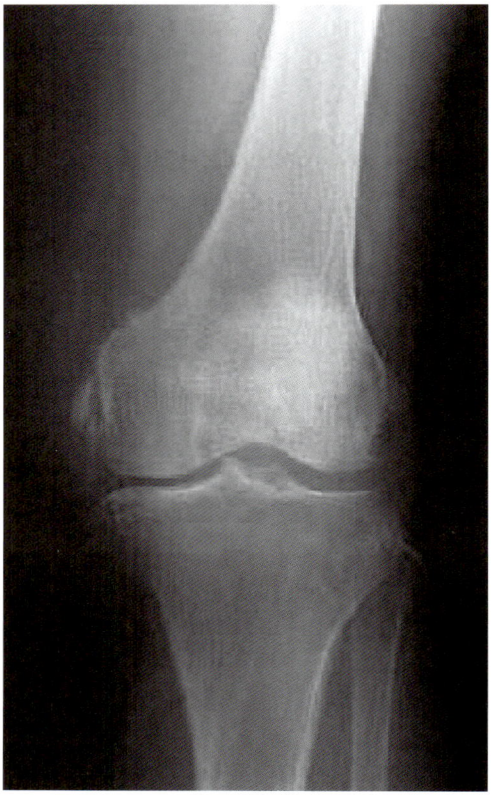

해답은 p144

Q10 무릎 통증으로 내원. 진단은?

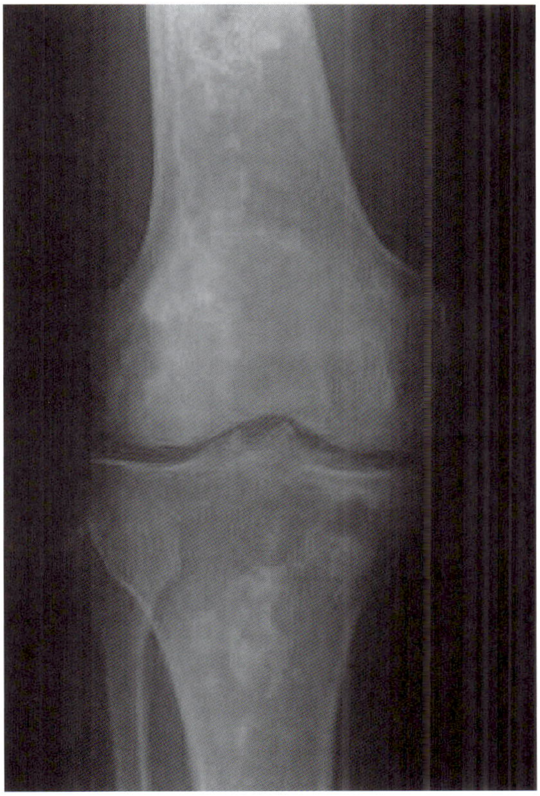

해답은 p144

하퇴 · 족관절 · 발가락

대표적인 족부 질환의 X-ray 소견

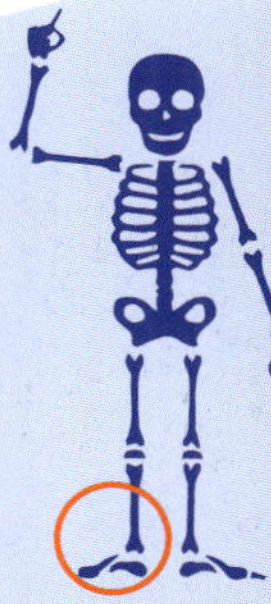

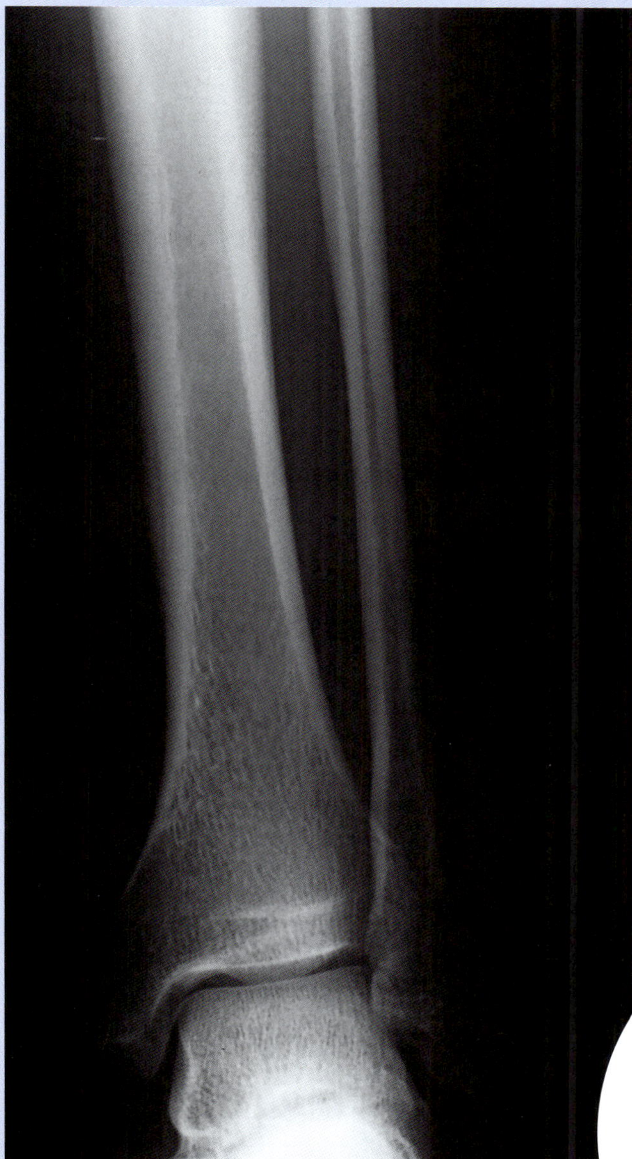

15세 · 중학생 남성.
육상 단거리 연습 중.

Q

보행 시 좌측 하퇴 · 경골 하방 내측 후방의 통증. 같은 부위에 압통도 존재. 진단은?

여기에서는 무릎 이하, 즉 하퇴~족관절 · 발가락의 대표적 질환에 대해 알아보자. 무릎 이하의 병변은 고령자뿐만 아니라, 과도한 운동을 하는 경우 등 젊은 연령층에서도 많이 발생한다.

신스프린트(shin splints)

앞 페이지 X-ray의 진단은 **신스프린트**이다. 하퇴삼두근은 내 · 외측비복근과 가자미근으로 이루어지며, 가자미근 근막은 경골 하방 내측에 부착한다. 특히 발이 외반(valgus, 발바닥이 외측으로 젖혀지는 동작)할 때, 이 부위가 가자미근에 의해 견인되며 통증이 발생한다. 이를 신스프린트라고 한다.

경골 하방 내측 후방에 압통이 있다.

압통점(그림 1)이 특이적이므로 진단이 용이하다. 심해지면 이 증례와 같이 **골막반응**(periosteal reaction, 새로운 뼈가 형성되는 것)이 발생한다(그림 2).

치료에는 운동 제한, NSAID 등이 있다.

발가락의 피로 골절

중족골(metatarsal bone)

다음으로 그림 3을 보자. 14세 · 여성이 마라톤 연습 중 왼쪽 발바닥에 통증을 느끼게 되었다.

발바닥의 하중은 발꿈치에 50%, 무지구에 30%, 소지구에 20%가 가해진다. 횡아치가 있어 보통 제 2~4 중족골에는 체중이 거의 실리지 않는다. 그러나 과도한 운동으로 횡아치가 느슨해지면, 이 중족골에도 체중이 실리게 되어 **피로 골절**이 발생한다.

초진 시의 X-ray(그림 3)에서는 제3 중족골 골간부에서 **가골**(callus) 형성을 볼 수 있다. 한 달 후의 X-ray(그림 4)에는 이 가골이 더욱 선명하다. 초진 시 X-ray에서는 압통이 있는 부위에 가골이 확인이 안되는 경우도 많으며 2~3주가 지나서야 비로서 가골이 확인되기 시작한다. 따라서 초진 시 이상이 없다고 단정 지으면 안 된다! 수주 간은 주의깊게 관찰하자.

피로 골절의 치료는 통증이 있다면 하중을 줄이거나 NSAID를 처방한다.

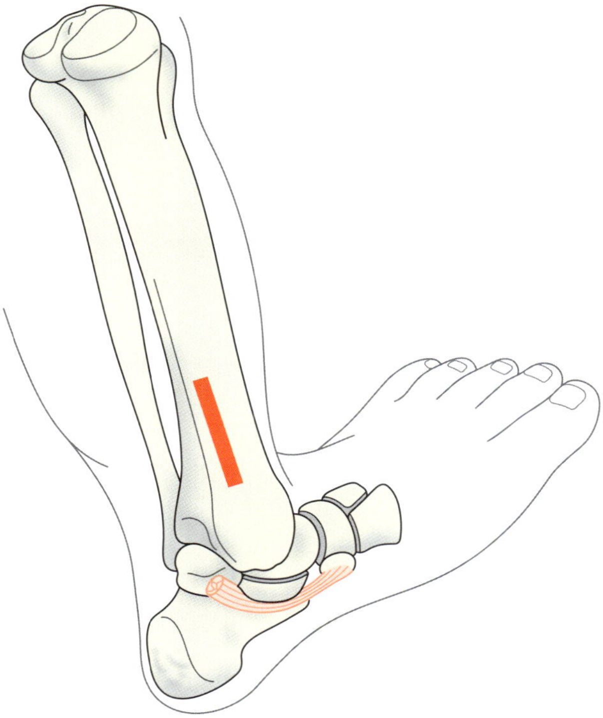

그림 1 **신스프린트의 압통점**

경골 하방 내측 후방(▬ 의 부위)에 압통이 있다.

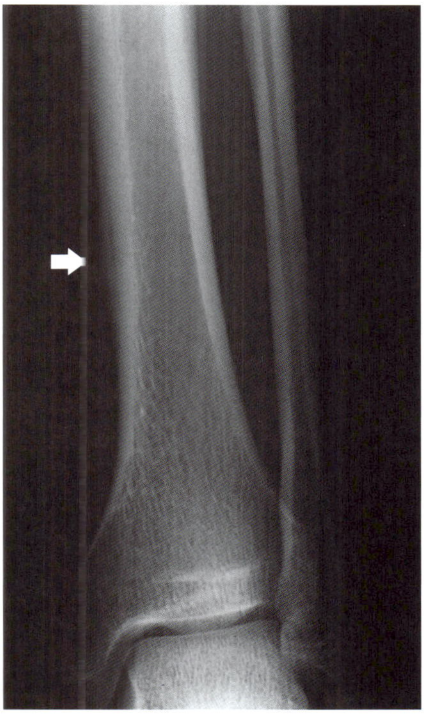

그림 2 **신스프린트의 골막반응**

신스프린트가 심해지면, 경골 내측에 골막반응이 발생한다.

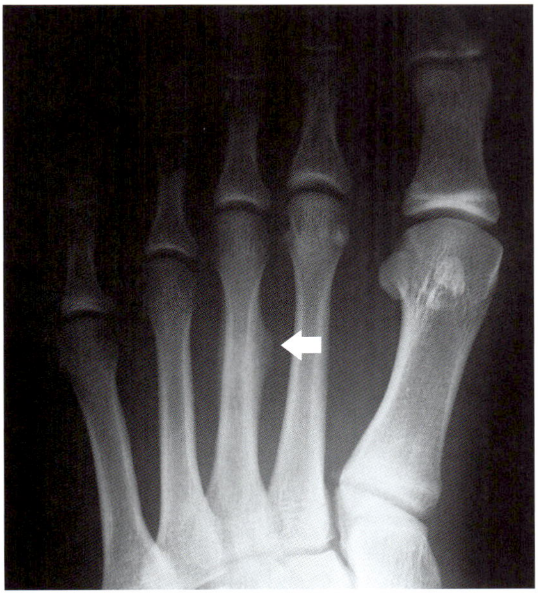

그림 3 **제3 중족골 피로 골절(초진 시)**

14세 · 여성, 왼쪽 발. 제3 중족골에 경도의 가골 형성.

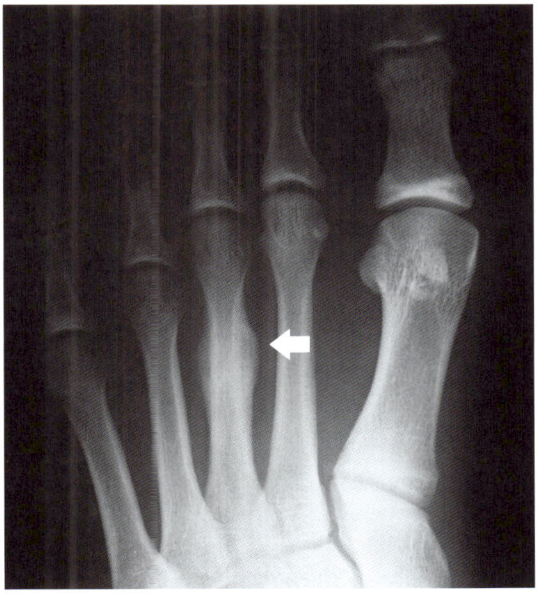

그림 4 **제3 중족골 피로 골절(초진 1개월 후)**

제3 중족골의 가골이 뚜렷해졌다.

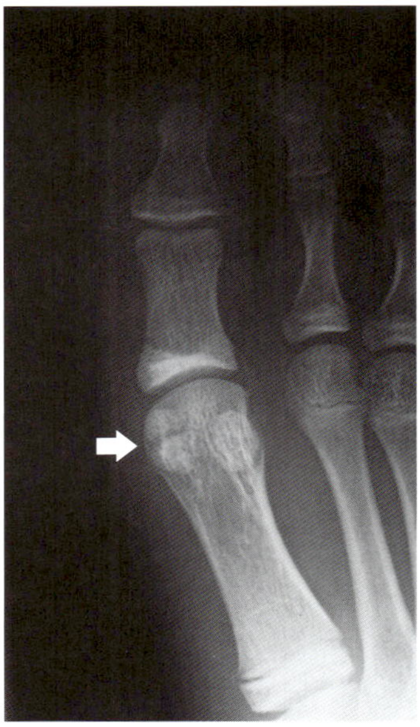

그림 5 이분 종자골
15세 · 남성. 마라톤 연습 중 발바닥 통증. 무지 MTP(중족지절)관절의 종자골 중 하나(tibial sesamoid)가 두 개로 갈라져 통증을 일으키고 있다.

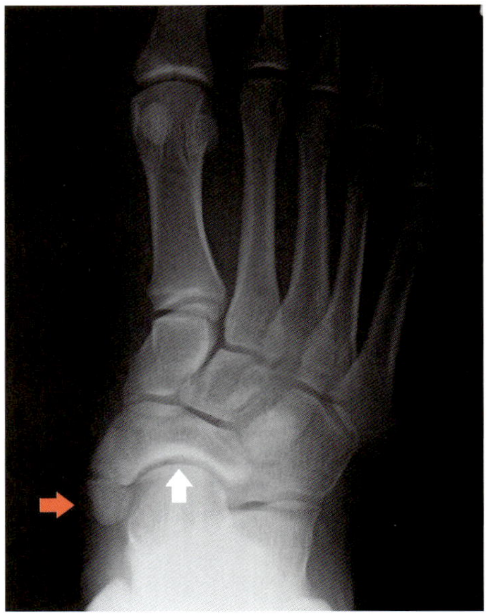

그림 6 부주상골
⇨는 주상골, ➡가 부주상골. 후경골근은 보통 주상골에 부착되지만, 부주상골이 있는 경우, 이 뼈에 부착된다. Overuse로 국소적 통증을 일으킨다.

이분 종자골(bipartite sesamoid)

발바닥 통증의 원인으로 **이분 종자골**도 흔히 볼 수 있다. 무지 MTP(중족지절)관절 부근의 굴근건 중에 2개의 종자골이 있다. 내측의 **tibial sesamoid**와 외측의 **fibular sesamoid**이다. 마라톤 등으로 피로 골절을 일으킨 것이 이분 종자골이다.

그림 5는 내측 종자골(tibial sesamoid)의 이분 종자골이다. 발바닥의 뼈와 일치하며 압통이 있기 때문에 진단은 용이하다.

부주상골(accessory navicular or os tibiale externum) 통증

사춘기에는 발 내측에 생기는 과잉골에 의한 **부주상골 통증**도 흔하다.

통상 존재하지 않는 골성 돌출 부위에 통증이 있다면

부주상골(그림 6)이란 주상골 내측에 생기는 과잉골이다. 후경골근(발을 저굴 내반함)은 보통 주상골에 부착하지만 부주상골이 존재하는 경우에는 이 곳에 부착된다. 그리고 overuse로 인해 해당 부위에 통증이 발생한다. 손으로 만져보면 부주상골의 골성 돌출이 있어 진단이 용이하다.

치료에는 운동 제한, NSAID가 있다.

통풍(gout)

'절벽에 튀어나온 바위'가

그림 7은 전형적인 **통풍**의 X-ray이다. 골 내에 공동이 있으며 요산 결정이 침착한다. 이를 **overhang lesion**이라고 한다. overhang이란 암벽등반 용어로 '절벽에 튀어나온 바위'를 가리킨다.

또한, 통풍은 항상 염증이 있는 것은 아니므로 류마티스관절염과 같이 골밀도가 감소하지 않는다. 즉, osteoporotic 하지는 않다. 또한 MTP관절 간격도 말기까지 유지되는 경우가 흔하다.

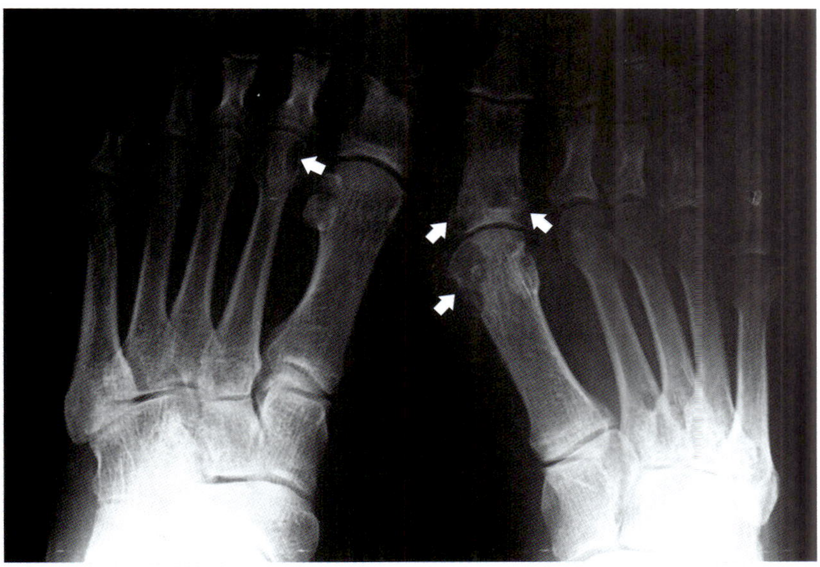

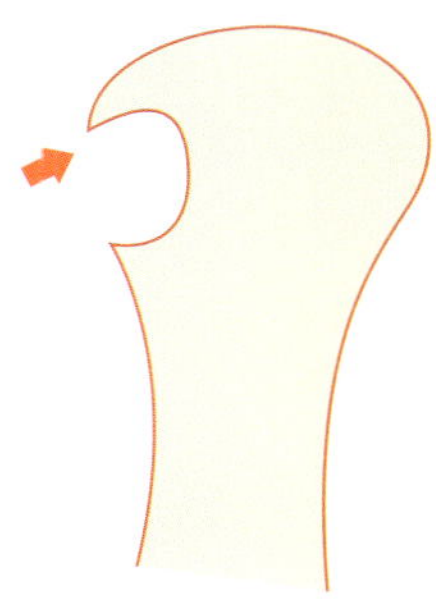

그림 7 통풍(overhang lesion)
80세 · 남성. 요산 결정이 침착하여 overhang lesion을 형성한다.

외반무지(hallux valgus)

외반무지각≧20°

외반무지란 무지 중족골과 기절골(근위지골의 장축)이 이루는 각도가 20° 이상인 경우를 가리킨다(그림 8). 정상은 15° 이하이다. 연필 끝이 15° 정도라고 하니, 연필을 대보면 좋다.

외반무지에서는 무지 내측의 돌출된 부분에 건막류(bunion)가 있으며 여기에 **점액낭염**을 일으킨다. 따라서 외반무지로 인한 통증은 무지의 내측에 있다.

외반무지는 초기라면 보조기를, 진행된 경우는 절골술을 시행하기도 한다.

족관절 측면은 연부조직도 잘 살펴보자!

족관절 측면의 X-ray에서는 **연부조직**도 주의깊게 관찰한다.

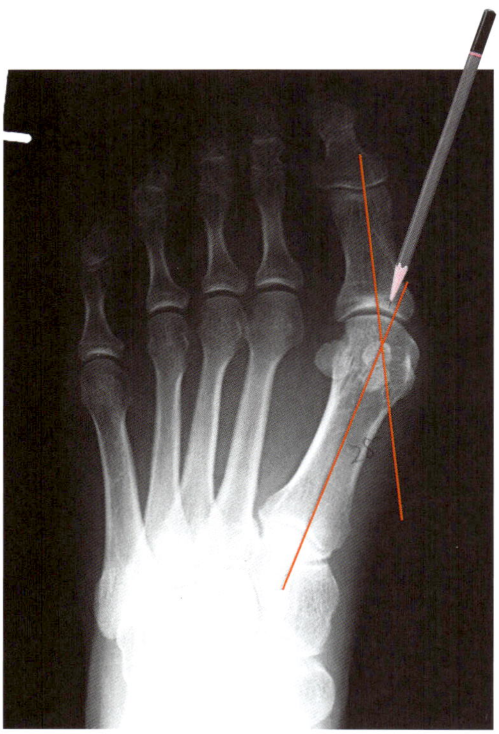

그림 8 외반무지
무지 중족골과 기절골(근위지골의 장축)이 이루는 각을 외반무지각이라 하며, 정상은 15° 이하(연필 끝이 약 15°). 20° 이상은 외반무지이다. 이 증례는 28°.

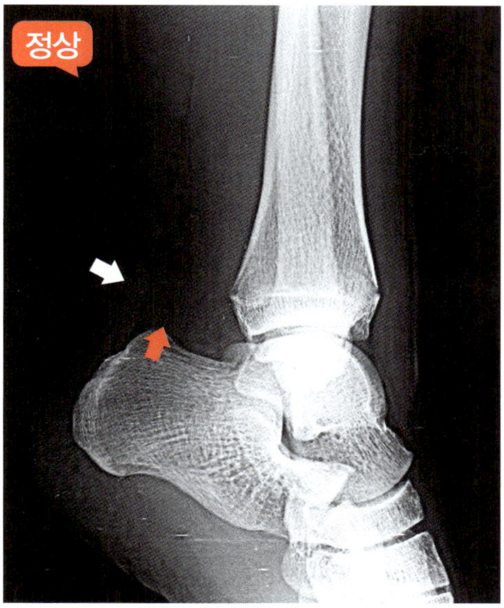

그림 9 검은 지방 음영
아킬레스건(⇨) 앞에 삼각형의 검은 지방 음영이 있다(➡). 이곳은 반드시 확인한다.

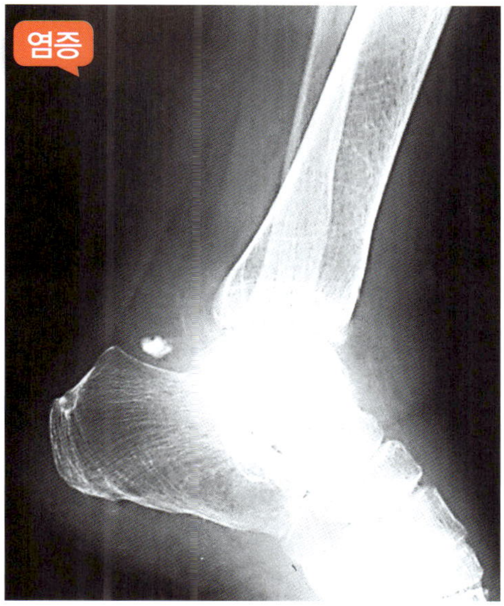

그림 10 하얀 음영(가성통풍)
삼각형의 검은 지방 음영이 CPPD(석회 음영이 관찰됨)에 의한 가성통풍으로 하얗게(수분 음영) 변화되었다.

염증은 '하얗게 음영이 증가'

그림 9에서는 아킬레스건 앞에 삼각형의 검은 지방 음영을 볼 수 있다. 족관절염이나 아킬레스건 주위에 **점액낭염** 등을 일으키면 이 검은 지방 음영(fat density)이 하얀 수분 음영(water density)으로 변한다. 이를 이용해 주변의 염증 존재를 추정할 수 있다.

그림 10은 이 부분의 CPPD(calcium pyrophosphate crystal deposition : 피로인산칼슘 결정침착)에 의한 **가성통풍**으로 하얗게 음영이 증가한 것이다.

관절액 저류(삼출)

또한, 족관절의 **관절액 저류**도 측면 X-ray로 어느 정도 알 수 있다.

그림 11을 보면, 이 환자는 족관절의 가성통풍 발작으로 관절액 저류가 있다. 족관절 전방의 검은 지방층이 앞으로 밀려나 있다. 이것을 **tear drop sign**이라고 한다. 진단에 자신이 없다면 초음파검사를 통해 관절액을 확인한다.

족관절의 가성통풍은 촉진을 통해 열감이 느껴지면 바로 의심할 수 있다. 변형성 관절증에서는 보통 열감이 없다. 손을 대보고, 양쪽 관절의 온도차를 느껴보자(➡ p111).

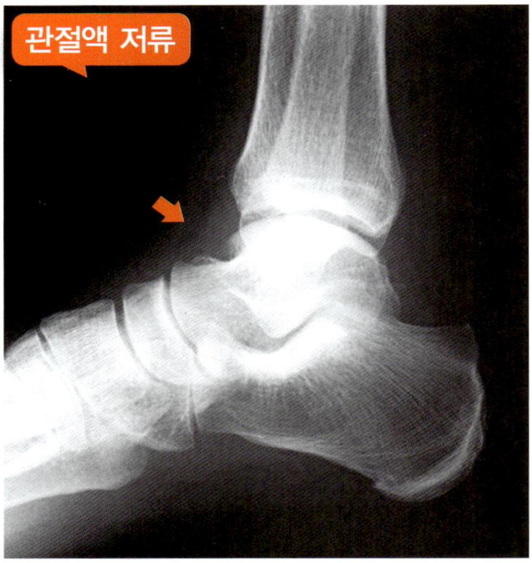

그림 11 Tear drop sign(족관절액 저류)
가성통풍 발작에 의한 족관절액 저류(하얀 수분 음영)로 검은 지방층이 앞으로 나와 있다.

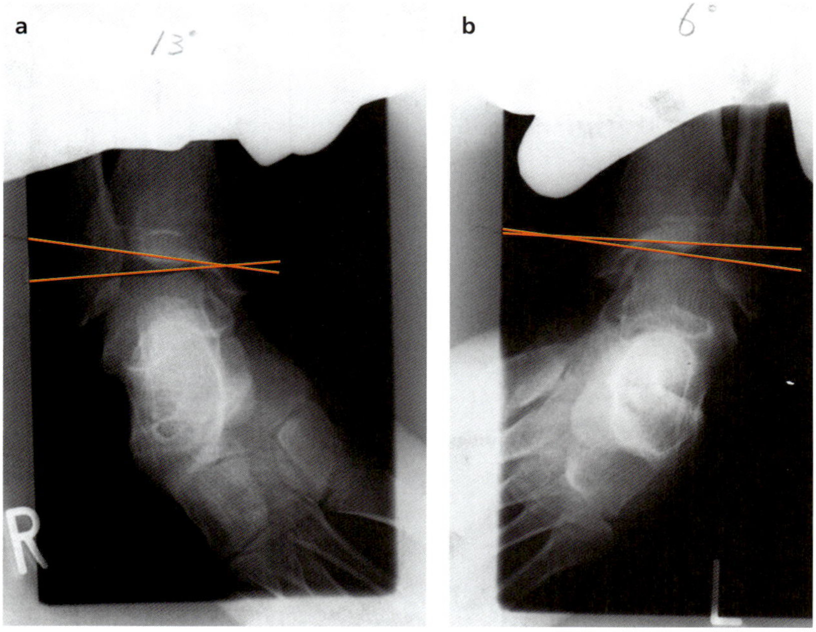

그림 12 족관절 염좌(stress view)
족관절 염좌는 족관절을 내반시키며 촬영(varus stress view)을 한다. 거골 경사각은 정상에 6° 이하이다. 이 증례에서는 우측 족관절(a)이 13°, 좌측 족관절(b)이 6°였다.

족관절 염좌

외래에 흔한 **족관절 염좌**는 대부분 발목이 내반되어 발생한다. 그러면 족관절 외측의 인대가 당겨지면서 파열이 일어난다.

스트레스 촬영 진단법

인대 파열 정도를 보기 위해 **스트레스 촬영**을 한다. 발목을 시술자가 내반시켜 스트레스를 주며 양쪽 족관절 정면 X-ray를 촬영한다.

그리고 거골 상면과 경골 하면이 이루는 각도(거골 경사각)를 측정한다(그림 12). 정상은 6° 이하이다. 그 이상이라면 전거비인대나 종비인대의 파열이 있다고 판단한다. 스트레스 촬영으로 6° 이상인 경우, cast로 고정하거나 수술하기도 한다.

반복 학습

❶ **신스프린트**는 경골 하방 내측 후방의 압통이 특징적이다.

❷ 육상선수의 발바닥 중족골 압통은 **피로 골절**을 의심하라. 2~3주 내에 X-ray에서 가골이 보인다.

❸ 무지의 발바닥 통증은 **이분 종자골**을 의심.

❹ 발의 내측 주상골 부근의 돌출 · 통증은 **부주상골**.

❺ **통풍**은 overhang lesion이 특징적. 골다공증은 없으며, 관절 간격은 말기까지 유지된다.

❻ 족관절 측면에서는 삼각형 지방 음영에 주의한다. 수분 음영으로 바뀌었다면 **염증**이 있다!

❼ **외반무지각**은 15° 이하(연필 끝 각도)가 정상이다.

❽ 족관절 전방의 수분 음영 돌출 tear drop sign으로 **관절액 저류**를 알 수 있다.

❾ 족관절에 내반 스트레스를 가하여 6° 이상은 **인대 파열**.

Q11 발에 강한 통증을 호소하며 내원. 진단은?

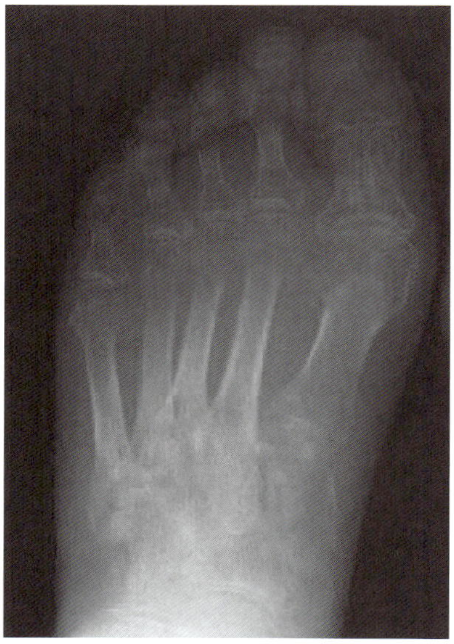

Q12 관절이 변형되었지만 통증은 없다. 진단은?

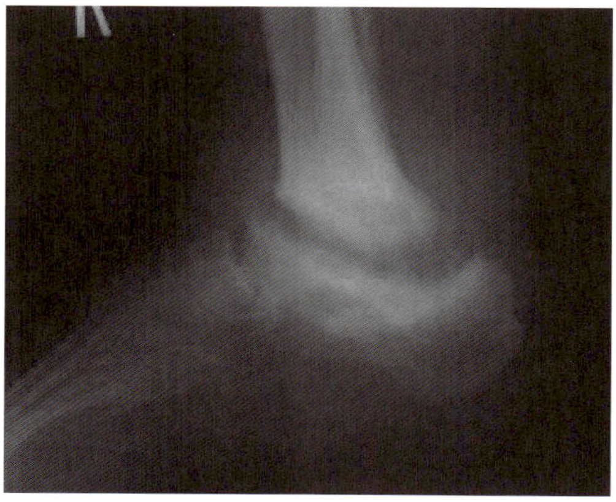

해답은 p144

Q13 발목 통증과 현저한 종창. 진단은?

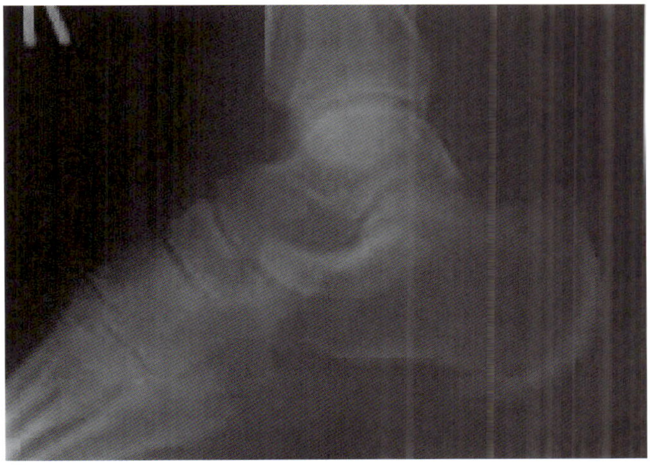

Q14 발목 염좌로 통증을 호소. 진단은?

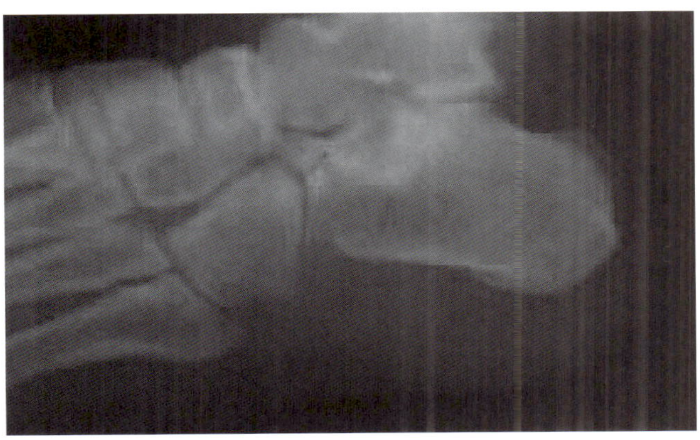

해답은 p145

소아

소아 뼈/관절의 X-ray 특징

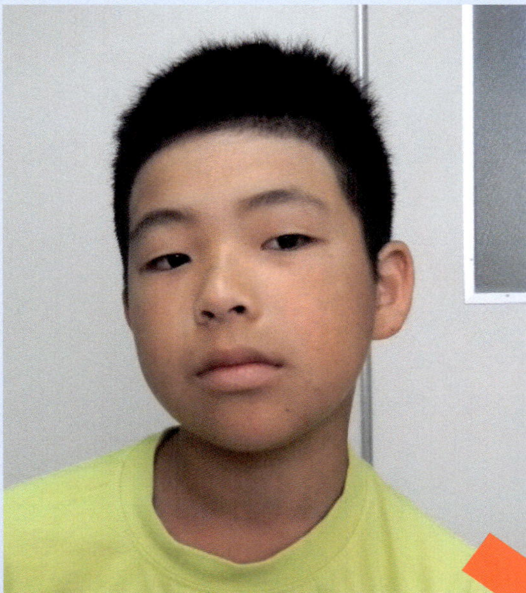

10세·남아. 내원 전날에 야구 배팅 연습. 평소보다 조금 일찍 눈이 떠졌고, 목에서 뚝 소리가 났다. 기상했을 때 좌측 경부 통증이 있어 내원하였다.

혈압 100/62mmHg, 맥박수 79회/분, 체온 36.7℃. 사시 없이 안구운동은 정상(활차신경 마비로 사경이 발생). 경부압통은 불확실. WBC 4,560/μL, CRP 0.06mg/dL. 아세트아미노펜을 처방하였다.

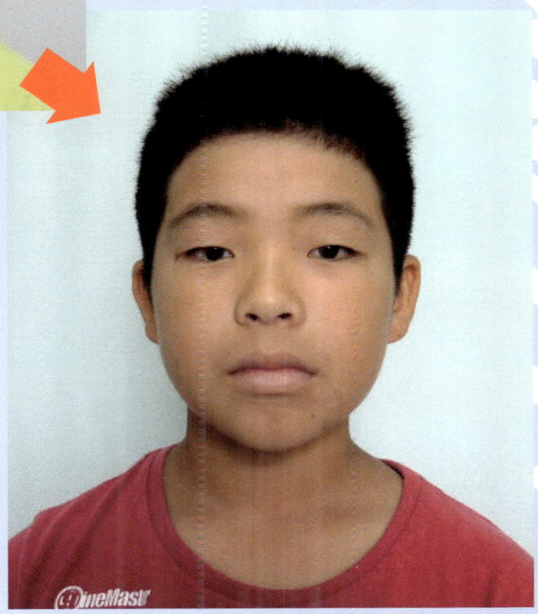

※가족의 동의를 받고 게재

Q

위 사진은 내원 시, 오른쪽 아래 사진은 7일 후 (호전 상태). 진단은?

지금까지는 내과를 방문하는 주로 성인, 그 중에서도 고령자에서 흔한 근골격 질환의 영상판독을 연습하였다. 마지막으로 뼈가 유연하고, 아직 성장 중인 소아 영상의 핵심을 알아보자.

Luschka 관절 병변(uncovertebral wedge)

앞 페이지 **급성 사경**(acute wry neck)의 진단은 왼쪽 C2/3의 **uncovertebral wedge**이다. 초진 시의 MRI 소견(T2 강조 영상)에서 이 부위의 **Luschka 관절**(uncovertebral joint, 구추관절)에 고신호강도 병변이 있었다(그림 1 위).

통증은 내원 4일 후 완화되었고, 7일 후 재진시에는 소실되어 경추 가동범위도 정상으로 회복되었다. 7일째에 MRI로 재검을 실시했지만 고신호강도 병변은 소실된 상태였다(그림 1 아래). 또한, 이 증례 발표는 일본 내에서는 첫 번째 일지도 모른다.

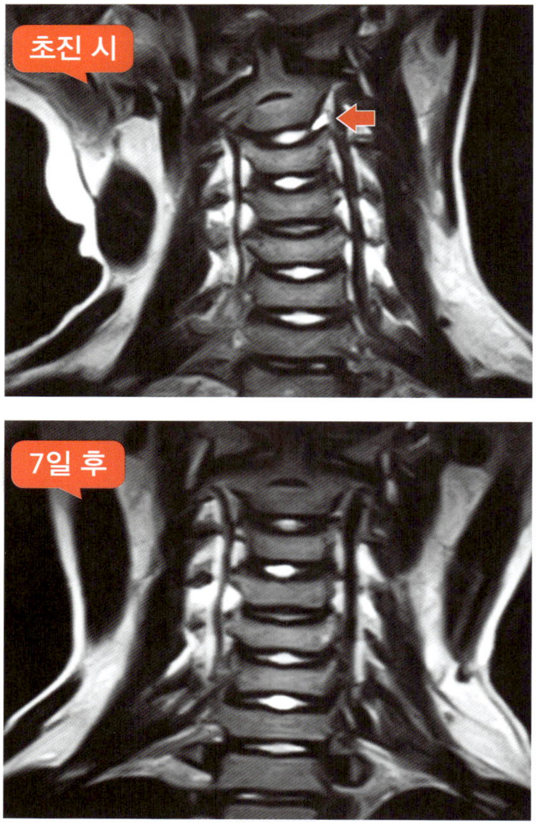

그림 1 Uncovertebral wedge의 MRI 영상 (T2 강조)

초진 시, 왼쪽 C2/3의 Luschka 관절에 고신호강도 병변이 관찰된다. 7일 후 재진 시 고신호강도 병변은 소실되었다.

급성 사경의 원인은 Luschka 관절의 염증 · 외상이었다!

이러한 급성 사경은 종종 외래에서 만나게 된다. 기존에는 환축추 회전성 고정(atlantoaxial rotatory fixation) 또는 환축추 회전성 아탈구(atlantoaxial rotatory subluxation) 등으로 불리며, 그 병태는 잘 알려져 있지 않았다. 경과는 대체로 양호하며 수시간에서 수일 내에 호전된다.

그런데, 2009년 큰 변화가 있었다. 러시아의 상트페테르부르크 소아병원 의사들이 우연히 발병 12시간 이내에 MRI 관상면(coronal view)을 촬영하였는데, C2/3 및 C3/4의 편측 Luschka 관절에서 삼각형의 고신호강도 병변을 발견한 것이다. 이것은 항상 통증 부위(환측)에 존재하였으며 그들은 이를 uncovertebral wedge라고 명명하였다[1, 2].

Luschka 관절은 경추 추체의 상방 외측에 있는 작은 관절이다(그림 2). 이 부위의 연부조직(periosteal-fascial tissue)이 머리의 회전이나 수면 시 경추 측굴 등으로 인해 Luschka 관절에 끼여 부종을 일으키는 것으로 추측된다.

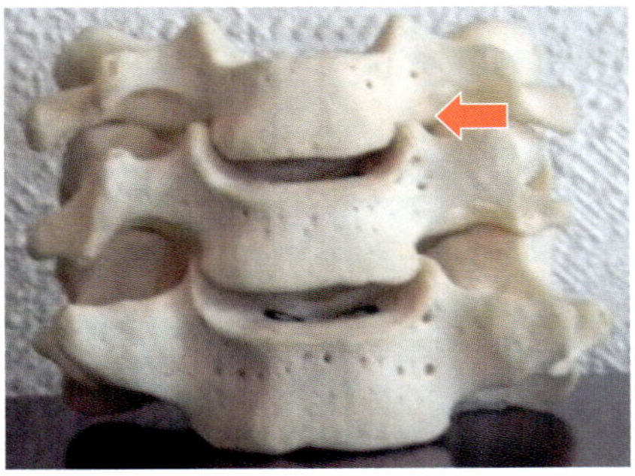

그림 2 Luschka 관절 (uncovertebral joint, 구추관절)
강아지의 귀처럼 그상돌기(uncinate process)가 추체 상면에서 그 위의 추체를 향해 돌출한다.

소아의 놓치기 쉬운 골절

소아 골절 중에 몇 가지 간과하기 쉬운 부분이 있다.

뼈의 윤곽은 보통 완만하다. 그림 3은 요골의 **녹색줄기골절**(greenstick fracture)인데 윤곽이 갑자기 변하면 골절을 의심해야 하는 중요 포인트이다. 그림 4도 녹색줄기골절이며, 압박력으로 인해 피질골에 융기가 발생한 것을 **융기골절**(torus fracture)이라고 한다.

그림 5는 **소성변형**(plastic deformity)이라고 한다. 소아의 뼈는 유연하기 때문에 이처럼 전체적으로 휘어진 골절이 일어날 수 있다. 알아두지 않으면 쉽게 놓칠 수 있다.

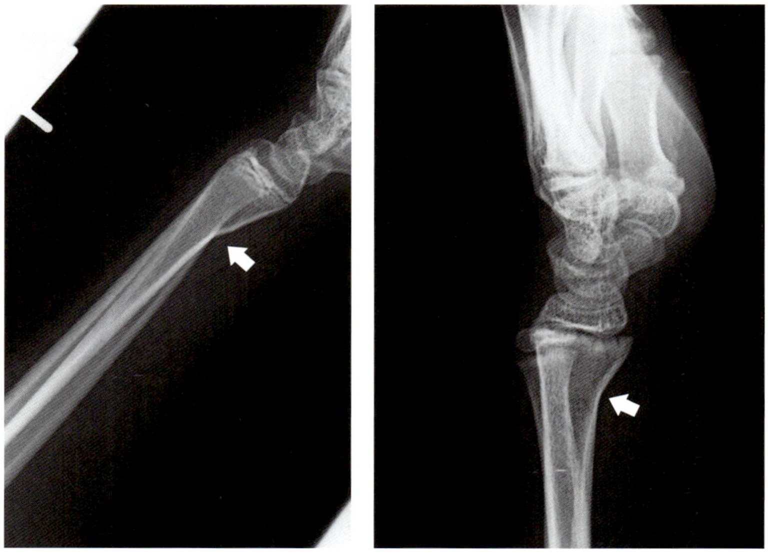

그림 3 요골의 greenstick fracture
뼈의 윤곽이 급하게 변하는 경우, 골절을 의심한다.

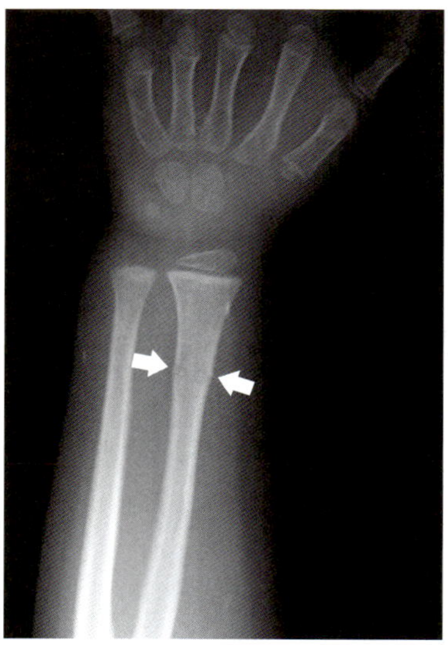

그림 4 torus fracture

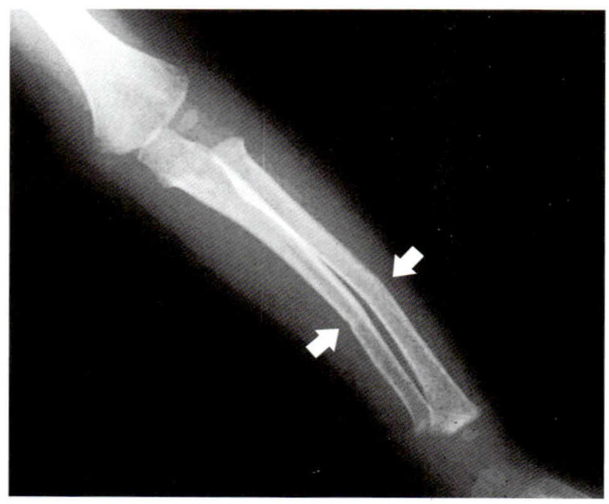

그림 5 plastic deformity
소아의 뼈는 무르고 유연해서 골절이 이와 같이 전체적으로 휘어진 변형을 일으키기도 한다.

골단선(epiphyseal line, 성장판) 골절

그림 6은 '오른쪽 어깨 통증'을 주소로 내원한 13세·남아의 상완 골두 부위이다. 오른쪽 어깨의 골단선이 왼쪽 어깨에 비해 벌어진(이개) 것을 알 수 있다(골단선 이개는 X-ray로 좌우를 비교하지 않으면 알기 어렵다).

이는 골단선 이개로 **little leaguer's shoulder**라고 한다. 이 환자도 소년 야구팀에서 투수로 활동하며, 투구 수는 하루 100개였다.

골단선 이개는 골단선 골절의 일종이다(Salter Harris I형).

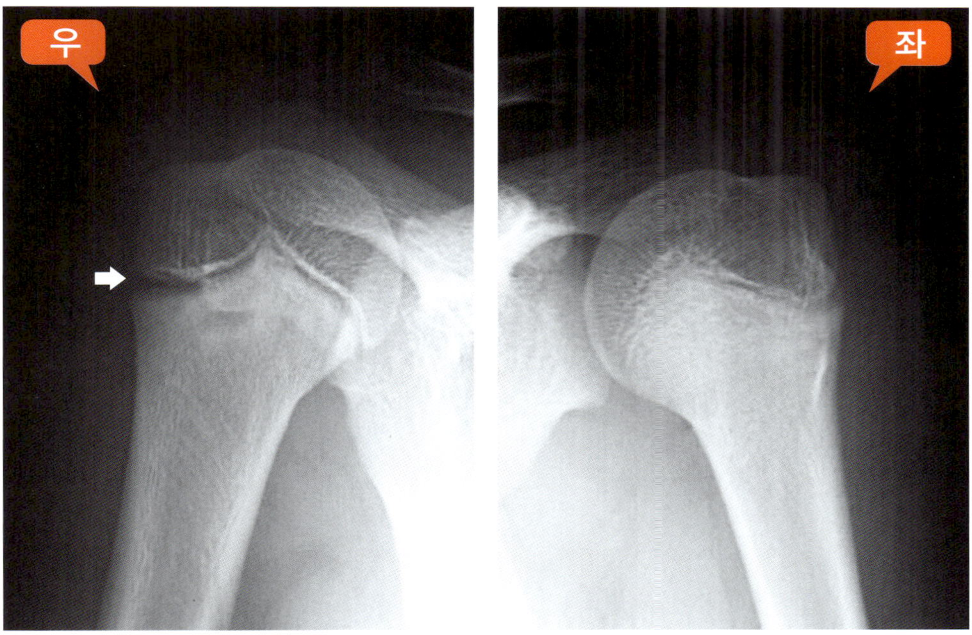

그림 6 Little leaguer's shoulder(상완골 골단선 이개)
13세·남아, 1일 투구 수는 100개. 왼쪽에 비해 오른쪽 골단선이 벌어져 있다.

골단선 골절의 예후가 일반적으로 좋은 이유 - 장관골 성장의 기전

이러한 골단선 골절은 일반적으로 예후가 좋으며, 그 이유는 골단선의 구조를 알면 이해할 수 있다(그림 7).

장관골의 성장은 ❶ 골단선에서 연골세포가 발생(증식층)하며, ❷ 세포 내에 글리코겐을 축적하면서 세포가 비대(비대층)해지고, ❸ 이어서 apoptosis(계획된 세포 죽음)를 일으켜 석회화된다(석회화층 : provisional zone of calcification. 이 부위는 X-ray로 확인 가능). ❹ 이 석회가 해면골로 치환되며 장관골이 성장하는 것이다.

골단선 골절은 글리코겐이 축적되어 역학적으로 약한 비대층에서 발생한다. 따라서, 연골세포가 발생하는 증식층은 남겨진다. 그러므로, 골단선에서 골절이 일어나도 다시 성장할 수 있다.

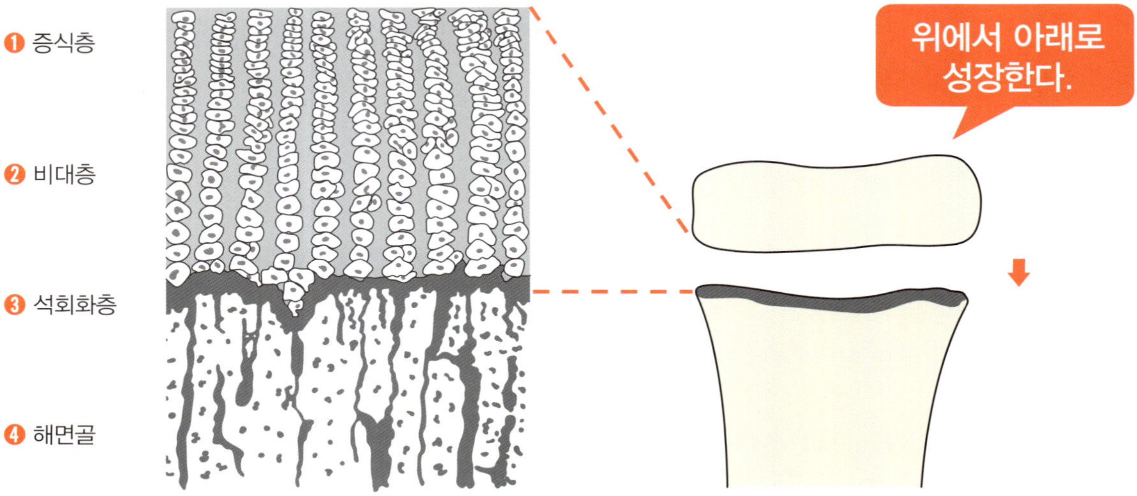

그림 7 골단선의 구조

연골세포의 ❶ 증식층 → ❷ 비대층(글리코겐 축적) → ❸ 석회화층(아포토시스를 일으킴. X-ray로 확인 가능) → ❹ 해면골(석회가 뼈로 치환). 비대층이 역학적으로 약하며, 골단선 골절은 여기에서 발생한다.

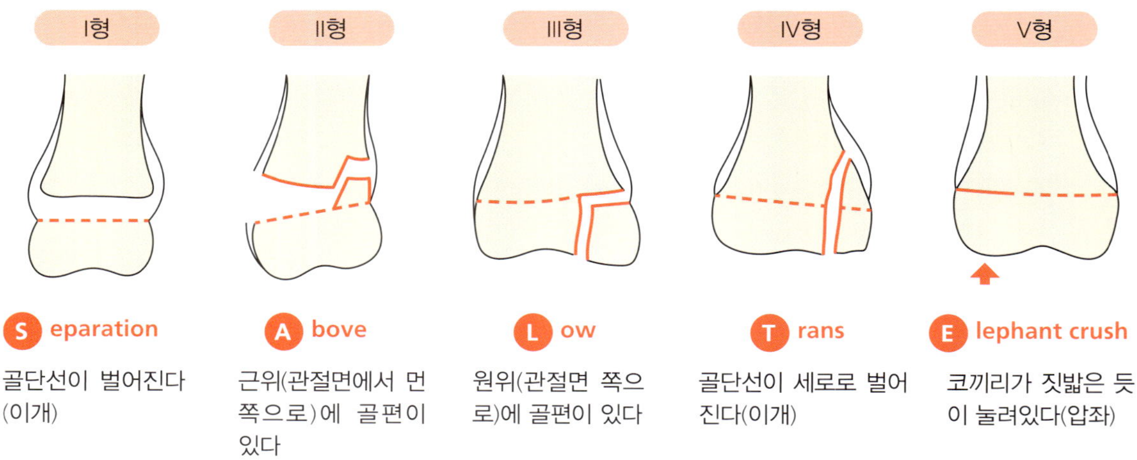

그림 8 Salter Harris 분류

골단선 골절의 분류. 암기법은 'SALTE(R)'.

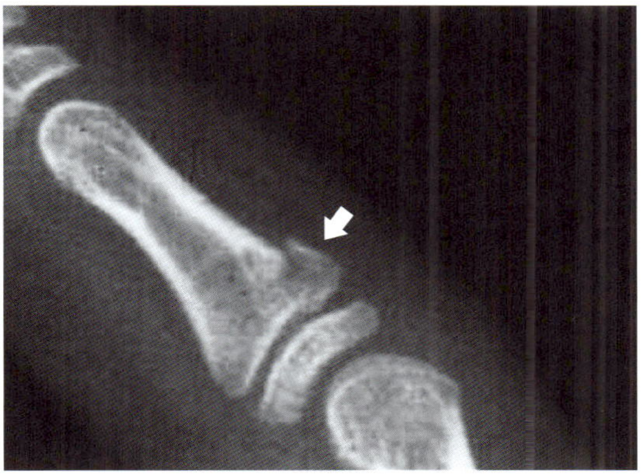

그림 9 Salter Harris II형
위와 같이 골단선 위에 작은 삼각 골편을 보았을 때는 Salter Harris II형의 골절로 볼 수 있다. 실제로는 골절이 골단선까지 침범하였다.

골단선 골절 분류 'SALTE(R)'를 기억한다.

골단선 골절에는 Salter Harris 분류(**그림 8**)가 있으며, 'SALTE(R)'라고 암기한다.

골단선에 평행으로 일어나는 골절〔I형, II형(**그림 9**)〕은 예후가 좋으나 골단선을 세로로 가로지르거나(IV형. 전위되면 골변형 유발), 골단선이 압좌되는 등의 경우(V형. 성장장애를 유발)는 예후가 좋지 않다.

팔꿈치의 골화핵 출현 순서 - CRITE 이웃친구 열하나

팔꿈치의 골화핵은 엄밀한 순서에 따라 출현하며(**그림 10**), 기억하고 있으면 유용하다. 암기하는

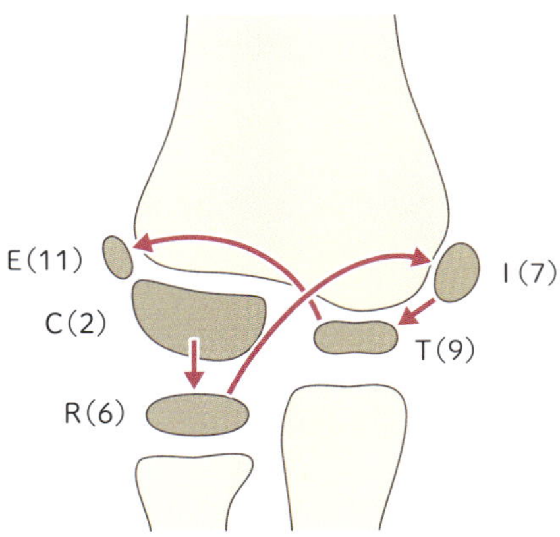

그림 10 오른쪽 팔꿈치의 골화핵 출현 순서
CRITE 이웃친구 11 (2, 6 7, 9, 11)을 손가락으로 따라 써 본다.
Capitulum(상완골 소두 2세) → **R**adial head(요골두, 6세) → **I**nternal(상완골 내측상과, 7세) → **T**rochlea(상완골 활차, 9세) → **E**xternal(상완골 외측상과, 11세).

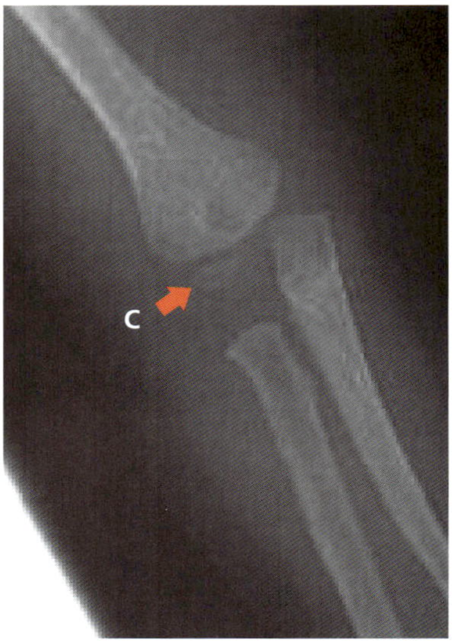

그림 11 **팔꿈치(2세)**
C(상완골 소두)만 출현하였다.

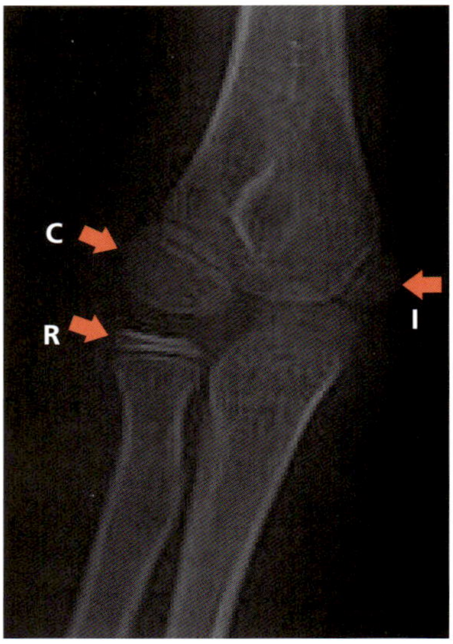

그림 12 **팔꿈치(7세)**
C(상완골 소두) → R(요골두) → I(상완골 내측상과)까지 출현하였다.

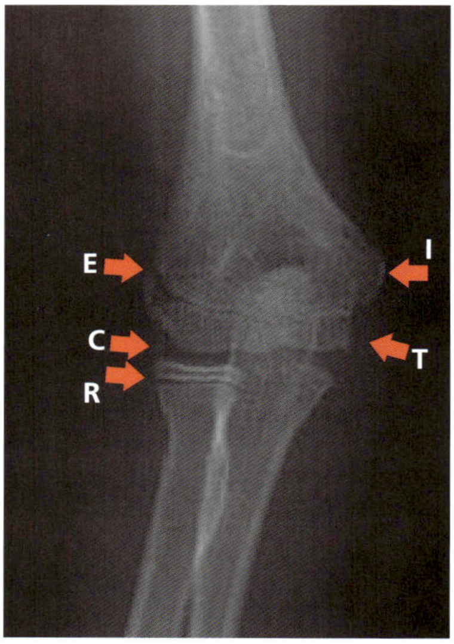

그림 13 **팔꿈치(11세)**
C(상완골 소두) → R(요골두) → I(상완골 내측상과) → T(상완골 활차) → E(상완골 외측상과), 골화핵이 모두 출현하였다.

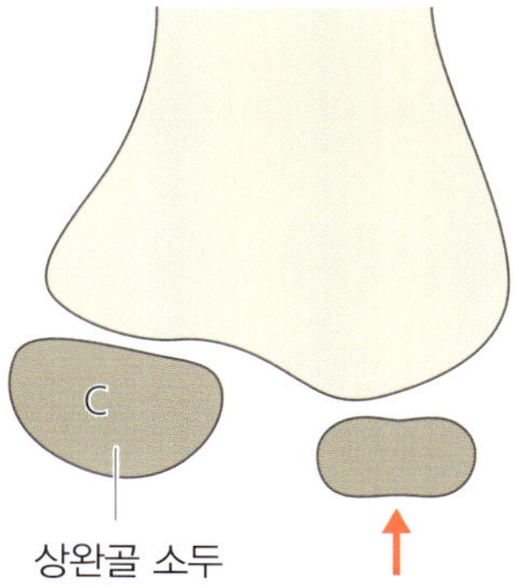

그림 14 **상완골 내측상과 골절**
상완골 내측상과가 보이지 않고, 상완골 소두(C) 내측에 상완골 활차가 보인다면(➡), 이는 상완골 내측상과가 골절되어 전위된 것으로 볼 수 있다.

방법은 'CRITE 이웃친구 열하나 (2, 6, 7, 9, 11)'이다. 순서는 다음과 같고, 연령은 대략적인 기준이다.

- Capitulum(상완골 소두) : 2세에 출현
- Radial head(요골두) : 6세에 출현
- Internal(상완골 내측상과) : 7세에 출현
- Trochlea(상완골 활차) : 9세에 출현
- External(상완골 외측상과) : 11세에 출현

그림 11 은 2세 팔꿈치로 C(상완골 소두)만 관찰된다.

그림 12 는 7세 팔꿈치로 C(상완골 소두) → R(요골두) → I(상완골 내측상과)까지 출현하였다.

그림 13 은 11세 팔꿈치로 C(상완골 소두) → R(요골두) → I(상완골 내측상과) → T(상완골 활차) → E(상완골 외측상과), 모든 골화핵이 출현하였다.

이 골화핵의 출현 순서를 기억하는 것이 유용한 이유는, 예를 들어 그림 14 와 같이 상완골 소두 내측에 상완골 활차의 골화핵이 보인다고 가정해보자. 상완골 내측상과가 나타나기 전에 상완골 활차가 먼저 출현하지 않으므로, 이는 상완골 내측상과가 골절되어 전위된 것으로 볼 수 있다.

반복 학습

❶ 소아의 급성 사경의 원인은 **Luschka 관절 병변**. MRI 관상면(coronal view)에서 확인 가능.

❷ 소아 뼈의 윤곽은 완만하다. 급격한 변화는 **골절**을 의심한다.

❸ 장관골(long bone)이 전체적으로 휘어지는 **소성변형**이 있다.

❹ **골단선 골절**은 「SALTE(R)」(separation, above, low, trans, elephant crush).

❺ **골단선 이개**는 양상지/양하지의 X-ray를 촬영해 비교하지 않으면 알 수 없다.

❻ 팔꿈치의 **골화핵** 출현 순위는 "CRITE 이웃친구 열하나".

참고문헌

1. Gubin AV, et al : Etiology of child acute stiff neck. Spine 34 (18) : 1906–1909, 2009. PMID 19680099
2. Gubin AV : General description of pediatric acute wryneck condition. Kook Jin Chung (ed) : Spine surgery. pp121–134, InTech, 2012.
https://cdn.intechopen.com/pdfs-wm/34188.pdf (2019年2月最終アクセス)

Q15 10세 남아가 하퇴 통증으로 내원. 진단은?

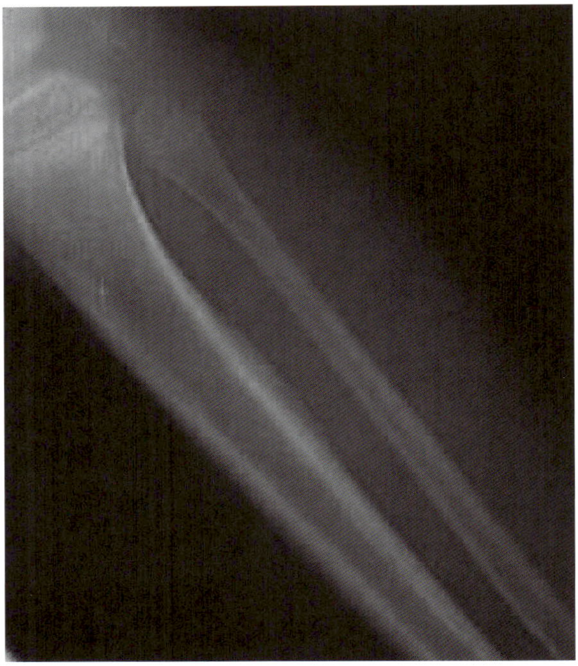

해답은 p145

Q16 8세 여아가 하지 통증으로 내원. 진단은?

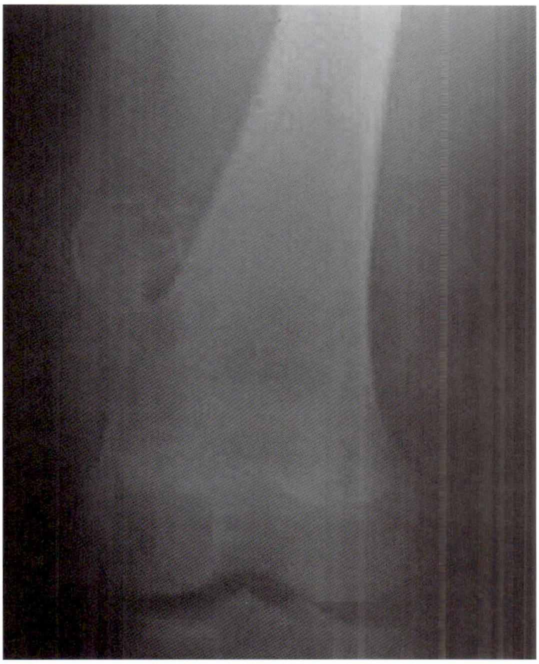

해답은 p145

LEVEL UP을 위한 연습문제 해답

Q1 (p28)

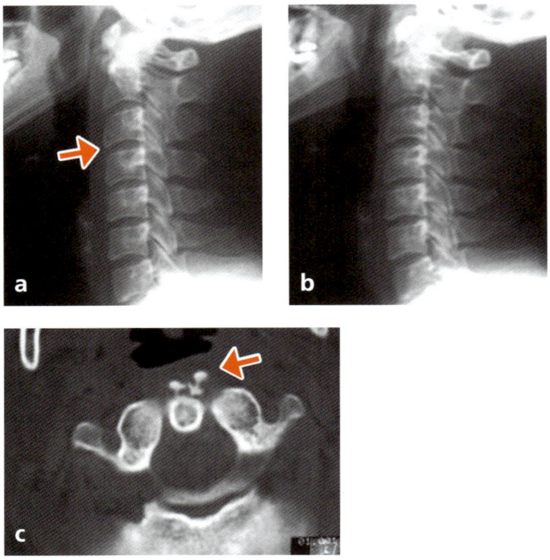

A1. 석회침착성 경장근건염 (calcific tendinitis of longus colli)

a는 경부 통증의 급성기, 경추 전방의 연부조직이 팽창해 있다. **b**는 일주일 후 조금 나아진 모습. **c**의 CT에서는 환축추 앞에 석회화가 확인된다. 아주 드문 질환은 아니다. 급성 경부 통증을 호소할 때는 이 질환도 염두에 둔다.

Q2 (p37)

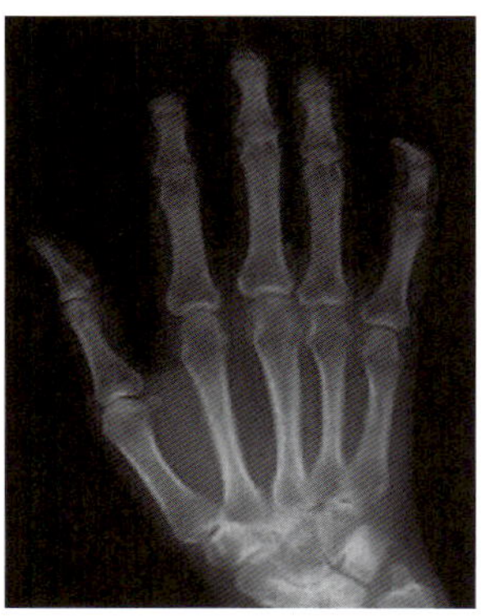

A2. 말단골용해증(acroosteolysis)

피부경화증으로 말절골 선단이 흡수되었다.

Q3 (p37)

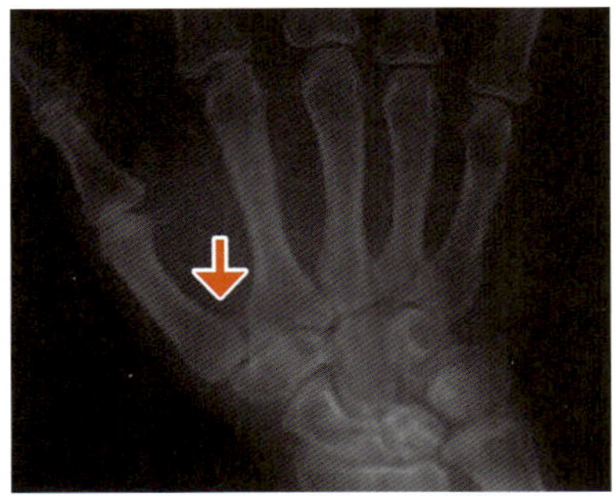

A3. Bennett 골절

무지 중수골 기저부에 부착하는 장무지외전근에 견인되어, Bennett 골절이 발생한다.

Q4 (p38)

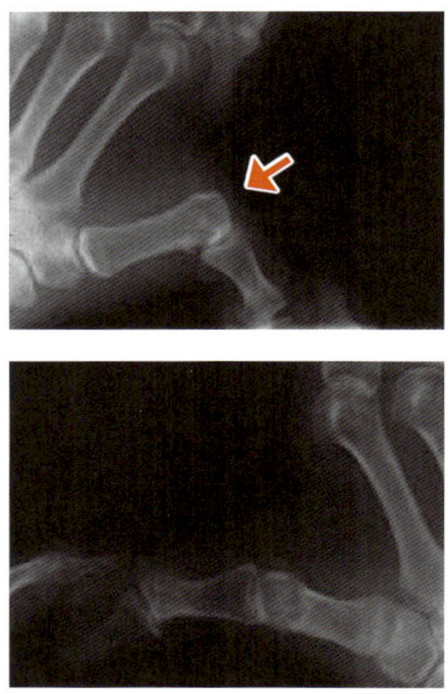

A4. Lt. Skier's thumb

스키 스틱을 쥔 채로 넘어져서 좌측 무지 MP관절의 척측측부인대가 파열되었다. 양측 무지에 부하를 가하고 있다(스트레스 촬영). 우측에 비해 좌측 MP관절이 더 크게 전위되었다.

Q5 (p55)

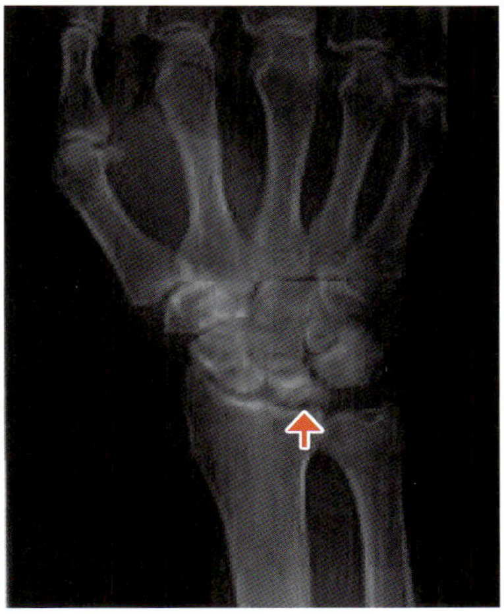

A5. 월상골 괴사(Kienbock's disease)

조선소에서 근무하는 동안 항상 망치 등을 사용하였다.

Q6 (p56)

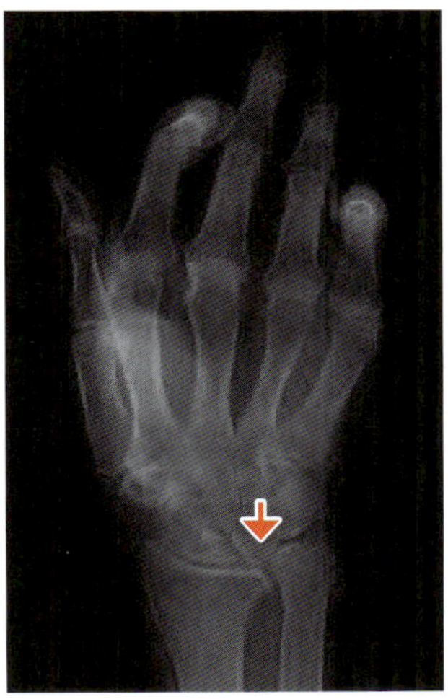

A6. 요척관절 변형 (caput ulnae syndrome, scallop sign)

요척관절 변형으로 척골두가 배측으로 돌출해 있으며, 이로 인해 제4, 5 신근건이 파열될 수 있다. 류마티스관절염에서 흔히 관찰된다.

Q7 (p98)

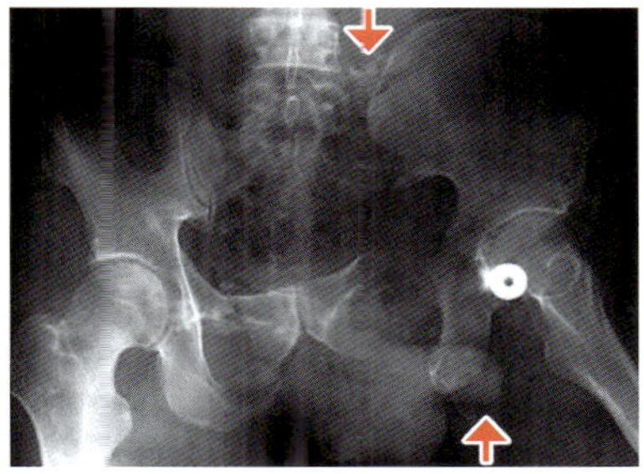

A7. Malgaigne 골절

골반환(pelvic ring)의 후방과 전방 모두 골절되었다. 오토바이를 타다 넘어져 교통표지판 기둥에 서혜부를 부딪혀 수상하였다. 매우 불안정한 골반 골절이다.

Q8 (p98)

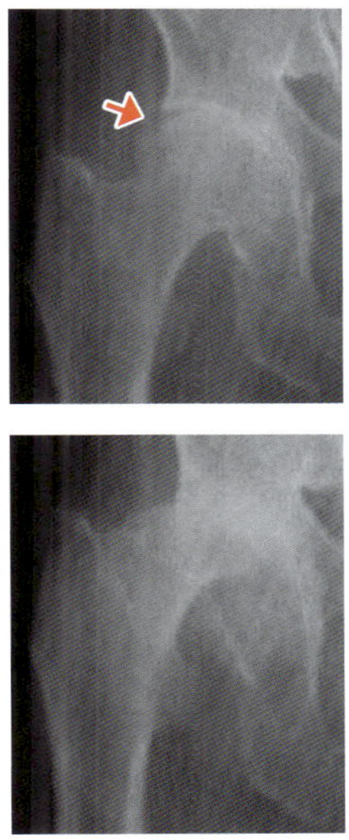

A8. 급속파괴형 고관절증 (rapidly destructive coxopathy)

초진 시(위 사진)에는 관절 간격이 좁은 정도였지만 3개월 후에는 아래 사진과 같이 편평 골두를 보였다. 결국 인공고관절치환술을 시행하였다. CPPD 등이 원인이 되기도 한다.

Q9 (p116)

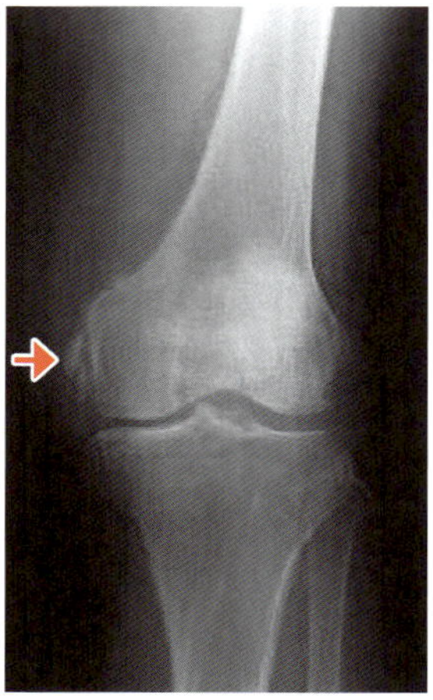

A9. 펠레그리니-스티다 병변 (Pellegrini-stieda lesion)

내측측부인대 손상 후 인대의 대퇴골 부착부에서 석회화가 발생한 것.

Q10 (p117)

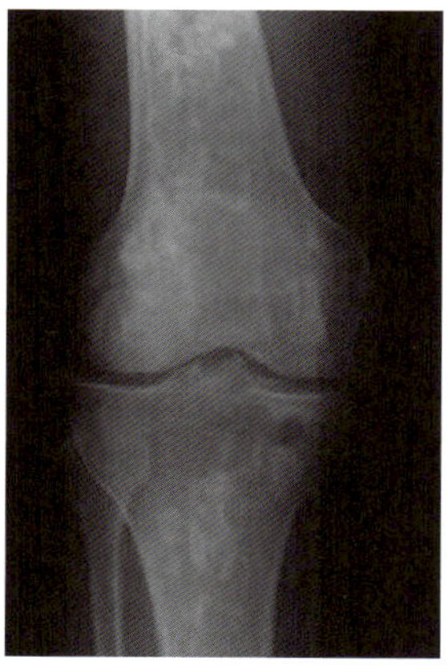

A10. 골경색(bone infarct)

골간단(metaphysis)이나 골간(diaphysis)에 발생하는 골괴사를 골경색이라고 한다. 골단(epiphysis)에 있는 경우에는 골괴사라고 한다. 경계가 선명하여 뱀모양의 석회화(serpiginous calcification)를 보인다.

Q11 (p128)

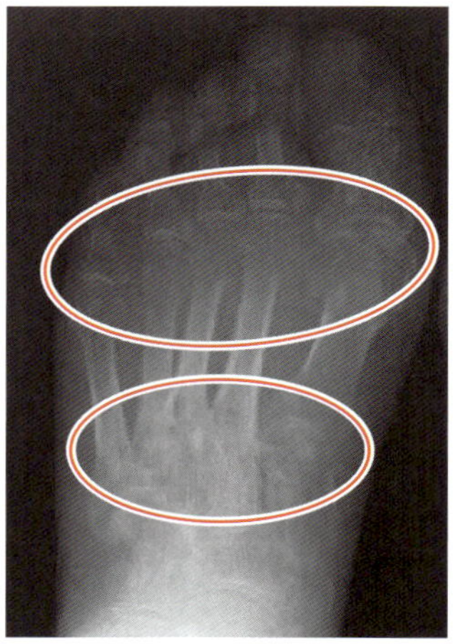

A11. 복합부위통증증후군 (complex regional pain syndrome : CRPS)

급속히 골다공증이 진행한다. 골간부보다는 혈행이 양호한 관절 주위(metaphysis)의 골흡수가 강한 것에 주목.

Q12 (p128)

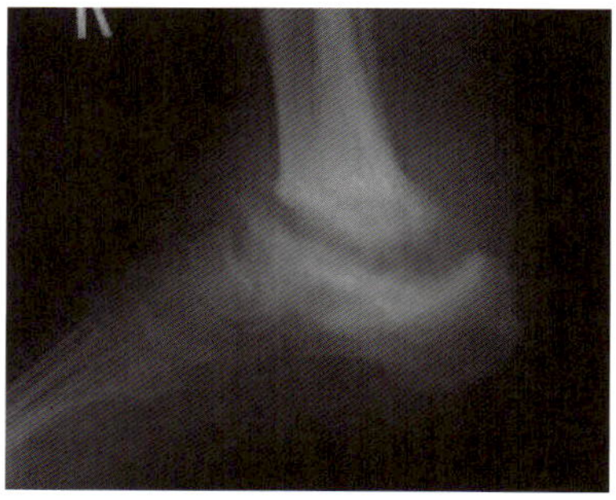

A12. 샤르코 관절(Charcot joint)

이 정도로 변화가 진행되어도 당뇨병에 의한 Charcot joint이므로, 통증을 느끼지 않고 보행이 가능하다.

Q13 (p129)

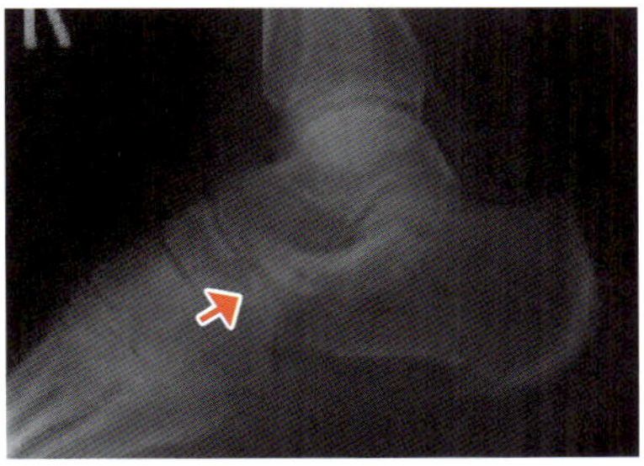

A13. 종골 전방돌기 골절 (anterior process of calcaneus fracture)

심한 염좌로 오인할 수 있다. 염좌로 붓기가 심할 경우 이 종골 전방돌기 골절과 입방골 골절을 확인한다.

Q14 (p129)

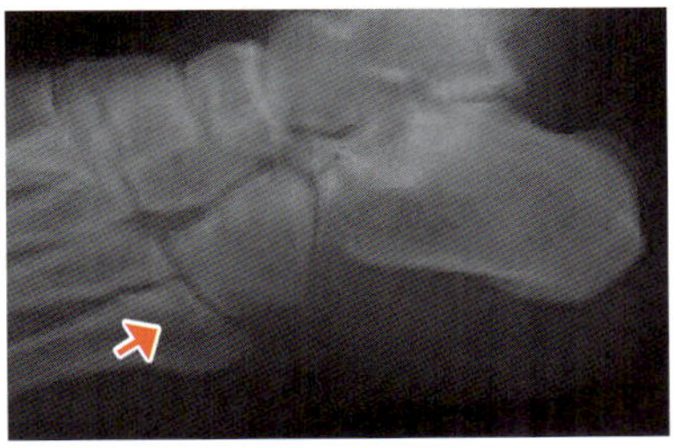

A14. 입방골 골절(cuboid fracture)

심한 염좌로 오진되는 골절. 제4, 5 중족골과 종골 사이에 호두까기처럼 끼여서 발생하기 때문에 호두까기 골절(nut cracker fracture)이라고도 한다.

Q15 (p140)

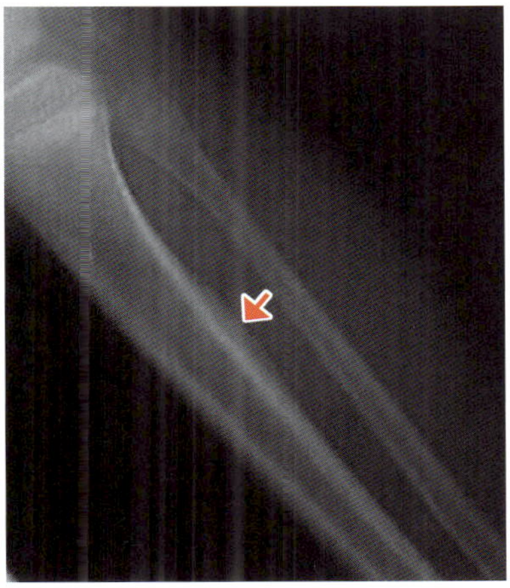

A15. 소아 경골 피로골절 (stress fracture of tibia)

달리기로 발생함. 경골 위쪽은 달리기로 인해, 아래쪽은 점프로 인해 피로골절이 발생한다. 골막반응이 있다.

Q16 (p141)

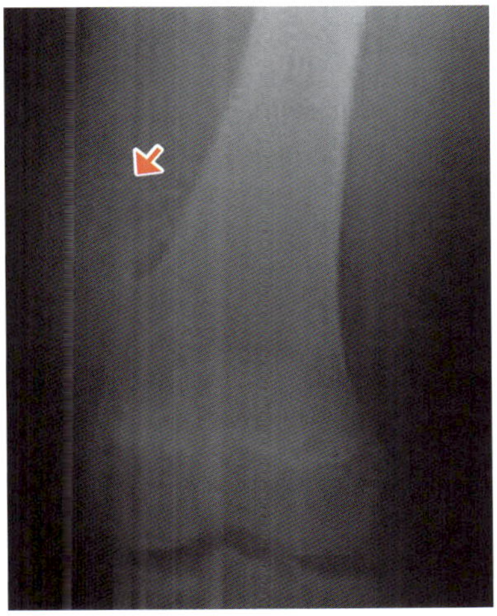

A16. 외골종(exostosis)

비교적 흔한 양성 골종양. 이소성 연골이 있으며 근육 부착부 근육의 견인 방향으로 성장과 함께 커진다.

찾아보기

한글

ㄱ

ㄴ·ㄷ·ㄹ·ㅁ

ㅂ·ㅅ

ㅇ·ㅈ

ㅊ·ㅌ·ㅍ·ㅎ

영문

A·B

C·D·E·F

G·H·I·K

M·O·P

R·S

T · U

기타